FROM NEW YORK'S TIMES SQUARE to Los Angeles' Sunset Boulevard, an ongoing scandal and outrage is continuing—the prostitution, sexual abuse, and ,sometimes the murder of children. For the sexual and monetary satisfaction of deviantly motivated people, thousands of children—often as young as age three—are forced to sell their bodies and/or appear in pornographic films. The effects of these sordid experiences on the victims are life-scarring: a lifetime of prostitution, becoming a chronic runaway, drug addiction, even suicide. And the cards are stacked against them. Often the perpetrators are respected members of their communities; current laws against the sexual abuse of children are either inadequate or not enforced; psychiatric treatment often proves ineffective because of both civil liberties controversy and the sheer will of the perpetrators to continue.

Investigative reporter Cliff Linedecker blasts the cover off this secret horror that continues in almost every large city or town across America. Working with extensive interviews with police, psychiatrists, rehabilitation officers, and, most importantly, the criminals—and victims—themselves, Mr. Linedecker creates a savage indictment of a society that often fails to protect its children.

You'll learn about the complex ways in which children are procured by wealthy men; how Boy Scout troops have sometimes been used as a cover for these illicit activities; how pimps steal runaways and turn them Rene Guyon So- paigns for sexual out the efforts of Frank Osanka and Dr. Judianne Densen-Gerber, active campaigners against the making and selling of child pornography; of Father Bruce Ritter, whose Covenant House works hard to save children who have been sexually abused; about reporters such as Marilyn Wright, whose intense investigative reporting pulled the cover back on a major child pornography/prostitution ring in Michigan.

The facts revealed in *Children in Chains* will shock, perhaps outrage, you, but you will never forget this shattering reading experience.

CLIFFORD L. LINEDECKER

Children in Chains

NEW YORK   Everest House   PUBLISHERS

Library of Congress Cataloging in Publication Data:
Linedecker, Clifford L
Children in chains.

Includes index.
1. Prostitution, Juvenille—United States. 2. Children in pornography—
United States. 3. Pornography—Social aspects—United States. I. Title.
HQ144.L56   1981   363.4'7'088054   80-28492
ISBN: 0-89696-088-9

CONTENTS

18. The Offenders 285

ACKNOWLEDGMENTS

During the past year I talked and corresponded with legislators, prosecutors, probation officers, corrections officers, police officers, journalists, behavioral scientists, medical professionals, social workers, prostitutes, pornographers, and child molesters. Their cooperation was vital to understanding the magnitude and gravity of the sexual abuse of children that is endemic in this country. I thank them all.

I owe special thanks to the following agencies and individuals: Dr. Judianne Densen-Gerber and the staff of the Odyssey Institute for interviews and advice; Margaret J. Hardy of the Odyssey Institute for compiling the state laws relating to criminal offenses that sexually exploit children; Dr. Franklin Mark Osanka of Lewis University for interviews, advice, and for opening his extensive files and correspondence to me; Jeanne King for conducting interviews; Mary Benninghoff for typing the manuscript; Blanton McBride of the *Orlando Sentinel* in Orlando, Florida; Fred Drewry of the *Herald-Chronicle* in Winchester, Tennessee; John Kinney, editor of the *Record-Eagle* in Traverse City, Michigan; Marilyn Wright, former *Record-Eagle* reporter; Bridget Guthrie; and Ricka and Rae.

INTRODUCTION

IT IS a privilege for me to write an introduction to this significant book. Child prostitution and child pornography are some of the more hideous forms of child abuse and neglect.

The public at large should be aware of the nature of this problem, be concerned about it, and actively seek, indeed demand, appropriate protective legislation and meaningful enforcement of existing laws. It is equally important that the public send a strong message to producers, distributors, and sellers of child pornography that we will not tolerate their behavior.

On the other hand, children co-opted into child prostitution and child pornography need our compassion, not our scorn. The boys and girls involved are children, and, as such, can be expected to make mistakes. We should not disregard them simply because they have sinned or broken the law. We should try to recover, counsel, and rehabilitate them.

Because of the subject matter, some people may want to avoid this book. During the campaign of 1977 and 1978 to educate the public about the social dangers of child pornography and prostitution our biggest roadblock was the reluctance of the average person to examine and confront the issue. Fortunately most people overcame their distaste for the subject matter in order to eliminate it.

The author has provided a meaningful service to us in exposing this most serious social problem. I expect this book to be widely read here and abroad.

DR. FRANK OSANKA
Professor of Sociology and Social Justice, Lewis University

CHILDREN IN CHAINS

"Your children are not your children.
They are the sons and daughters of Life's longing for itself.
They come through you but not from you.
And though they are with you yet they belong not to you."
                                                    —Kahlil Gibran

1.

"Tammy Is Ten"

EUGENE ABRAMS and his wife, Joyce, were living the American dream.

An aerospace engineer, Abrams was of near-genius intellect with an active, inquiring, imaginative mind so inventive that several devices he fabricated for the National Aeronautics and Space Administration were used in the first manned mission to the moon. He earned good money as an engineer, and his finances were bolstered by partnership with his father in several successful building and construction companies.

Abrams' genius and industry had helped him acquire a pleasant home in the tree-lined Long Island suburb of North Bellmore in Nassau County, New York. The house was far enough from the frenzied hubbub of Manhattan to provide a tranquil sanctuary, yet was close enough to the city to commute easily by train whenever it was desirable. The Abramses seemed to enjoy all the normal trappings of success and to be models of suburban respectability.

Abrams' home was also convenient for conducting a vigorous business in child pornography. It was so convenient that mothers and fathers came from the city, and from all over Long Island as well, leading their children by the hands and knocking on the Abramses' front door. They came in response to advertisements in *Screw* magazine, perhaps the country's most explicit and best-known sex tabloid and an unlikely publication to figure in the social or business affairs of North Bellmore or its sister communities on Long Island.

Nevertheless, not long after Abrams decided to use his skill as a photographer to supplement his earnings, advertisements in *Screw* helped him become the key figure in a nationwide ring doing an annual $250,000 tax-free business in child pornography.

The sordid enterprise came to official attention when Nassau County District Attorney William Cahn was tipped off by a United States

13

postal investigator about a Nassau County address in ads for eight-to-fourteen-year-old nude female models.

The district attorney's investigators found the ad in the classified section: "$200 FEE FOR GIRL MODEL, 8-14, 1 Day nude photographic session. Call Joyce Abrams (516-221-2041) or write me at 1033 Little Neck Ave., N. Bellmore, N.Y. 11710."

The next step was to determine what was happening to the photographs of the young girls whose services as models were worth $200 per day. Inspector Salvatore Fiola, head of the DA's vice squad, and two detectives scrutinized the tabloid only a few minutes before they picked out the connecting link. It was another ad: "TAMMY IS TEN . . . Unique photos are available of Tammy & other girls 8-14 years. $2 brings illustrated details. D & J Visual Services, Suite 504, 152 West 42nd St., New York, N.Y. 10036."

The age range, eight to fourteen, was significant enough to indicate a tie-in between the North Bellmore photographer and the Manhattan firm. Fiola moved quickly. He instructed a detective to write to D & J for a $2 set of introductory photographs; sent other policemen to the Greenwich Village offices of the magazine to obtain back issues and search for other ads with Nassau County addresses; ordered the house in North Bellmore put under surveillance; and directed a team of investigators to gather background information on Joyce Abrams.

Incredibly, investigators learned the name was not an alias. Joyce Abrams was the wife of Eugene Abrams. The couple was apparently happily married, the parents of two bright, healthy children, a three-year-old girl and a five-year-old boy. They hardly seemed the type to involve themselves in child pornography.

Yet the evidence was overwhelming. The Abramses were apparently deeply involved in a flourishing pornography operation that exploited young girls seduced or forced into posing for photographs during sexual relations with adult males. Some of the children were barely old enough to attend elementary school.

Perusing earlier issues of the sex tabloid, Cahn's investigators found other ads seeking little girls for nude photographs. Only an address was given in the earliest ads, but as time went on, the advertising grew bolder. The name "Ann Silner" began to appear, and a post office box number listed in East Meadow near North Bellmore. Detectives learned that "Ann Silner" was an alias and that the box was rented and maintained by Joyce Abrams.

When the investigation reached that stage, Cahn got a court order to search the house in North Bellmore. Early on St. Patrick's Day, March

17, shortly after many of the men in the quiet neighborhood had stepped out of their homes swinging briefcases and wearing green neckties or shamrocks, police cars began pulling up in front of the house on Little Neck Avenue. Puzzled housewives watched from the windows of nearby homes as grim-faced officers struggled back out of the house with huge cardboard cartons of material they loaded into a van.

At the DA's office in the county courthouse in Mineola, $70,000 worth of expensive cameras and sophisticated photographic equipment was unloaded along with some 4,000 nude and obscene photographs of juvenile girls, some younger than the "8-14" stipulated in the ads. Abrams himself had posed for photos showing him engaged in sexual activities with prepubescent girls and a few in their early teens. Some of the children were photographed having coitus and oral sex with other adults. One disarmingly innocent-appearing freckle-faced nine-year-old was shown having sex with her father. Cahn later disclosed that the Abramses' own daughter was photographed in some of the pornographic activities.

Investigators also confiscated mailing lists containing thousands of names from dozens of states. Addresses were especially prevalent from customers in New York, New Jersey, Pennsylvania, Connecticut, and Florida. But some orders were from foreign countries as distant as South Africa, Trinidad, and England.

One of the first couples linked to the ring with the Abramses was twenty-nine-year-old Louis D. Kahn and his thirty-year-old wife, Christina. The Kahns, who lived in Copiague on Long Island, were accused of bringing their seven-year-old daughter to North Bellmore for the photographic sessions. Thomas F. Byrnes, a father and unemployed steam fitter from New York City, was identified as another adult involved in the child smut operation. He was accused of bringing a nine-year-old girl to the Abramses for photographing. Then police learned that he had also procured a ten-year-old model and joined Abrams in having deviate sexual intercourse with the frightened child.

As the investigation broadened, nearly a dozen other men and women were eventually arrested on a variety of charges in connection with the activities. One was a registered nurse from New Hyde Park, L.I. Another was a Bronx man who headed a household with eleven children. Police learned that approximately 25 girls, some from as far away as Florida, modeled for Abrams before the ring was broken up.

Many of the children complained to their parents of being sexually molested during the photographic sessions, Cahn told the press. Yet "the mothers and the fathers forced their daughters to return and participate in orgies. It is beyond my comprehension how these parents could allow their daughters to pose nude and then leave the room," he added. "The parents knew those children were being molested, and yet they did nothing to stop it. They were more interested in money than in the welfare of their children."

One eleven-year-old girl ran crying from a bedroom after being told she would have to have sex with a man of forty. "Mommy, I can't do it. I won't do it," she sobbed. "You have to do it," her mother answered. "We need the money." The girl turned and walked back into the bedroom.

Investigators learned that Abrams arranged wih a photo studio in New York City to process and duplicate the film before it was passed on to a distributor who reportedly had crime syndicate connections. Only a few days after the frightened and bewildered children were photographed, their pictures were being sold by retailers across the country.

Named with the Abrams couple and others in an initial 75-count grand jury indictment and accused of permitting or forcing children to be used as models for pornography were Milky Way Productions, publishers of *Screw*, James Buckley, publisher, and Alvin Goldstein, executive editor. A few days later, a superseding indictment containing 78 counts and naming Milky Way Productions and 11 individuals was returned.

Abrams was charged with 75 counts of first-degree rape, incest, and various other offenses. His wife was named on 45 counts of endangering the welfare of minors and other charges.

Almost every parent accused of permitting his or her youngster to pose for pornographic photos had the child taken away and placed in a juvenile shelter or with relatives or foster parents.

Mrs. Abrams eventually pleaded guilty, in a plea-bargaining arrangement, to a reduced charge of attempted promotion of obscenity and was sentenced to five years probation. She divorced her husband.

Abrams was committed to the Mattawan State Hospital for the Criminally Insane, where he remained several months until he was determined to be sane and released to stand trial. Thirty prospective jurors were excused, after admitting they were so repelled by the charges that they could not maintain "total remorseless impartiality," before Abrams changed his plea to guilty to 77 sex and obscenity offenses.

The plea was accepted by Judge Raymond J. Wilkes in order to spare the children involved the ordeal of reliving their experiences on the witness stand. Abrams was sentenced to a 10-year prison term, a judgment under the New York State criminal codes that left him eligible for parole in 18 months. He surrendered to authorities and began his prison term only after exhausting all legal avenues for delaying execution of the sentence. He hadn't wanted to cut short a honeymoon with a new bride.

2.

Mobilization

Dr. FRANKLIN MARK OSANKA was teaching a course on child abuse and neglect prevention at Lewis University in suburban Chicago when he saw his first examples of chicken porn (child pornography). A policeman who was one of his students brought him several magazines and photographs of children engaged in sexual acts with other youngsters and with adults. The lawman wanted to know how the material was related to child abuse.

Dr. Judianne Densen-Gerber had been treating drug addicts and their children for 11 years when she saw her first example of child pornography. Someone sent her a kiddie porn magazine with an unsigned note asking for her reaction.

Both Drs. Osanka and Densen-Gerber were experienced researchers and workers in the field of child abuse. They had seen chilling examples: infants with broken arms and legs, and faces so swollen from beatings that the eyes were mere slits; stomachs extended with malnutrition; tiny bodies lacerated by rat bites; and skin blistered and peeling on pudgy fingers deliberately burned with cigarette lighters.

But they had never seen anything like the kiddie porn in the magazines and photographs with which they were now faced. Professionally produced on high-grade slick paper, the magazines were filled with color photographs of little girls and boys bent and twisted in the most explicit forms of sexual activities, performing with each other and with adults. Confused or frightened, the children sometimes stared off camera wide-eyed, as if looking for directions. It was an entirely new twist in child abuse. Even Osanka's own unhappy childhood hadn't prepared him for the filth featuring children, some barely old enough to toddle, which he found in magazines and later on in movie films. But long ago he had learned more than he wanted to know about other forms of physical and emotional abuse of children. The knowledge was absorbed first-hand as a victim.

18

Frank Osanka grew up as a ward of the child welfare system of Illinois. From the time he was orphaned when he was three years old until he was seventeen, he lived in 16 foster homes, three orphanages, and two juvenile institutions. He once shared quarters in a boys' school in Terre Haute, Indiana, with a gnomelike little boy who was first sodomized when he was ten years old. Like Osanka, the boy was also emotionally abused, beaten, and constantly shunted from foster homes to orphanages to boys' schools. He grew up unable to separate sex from violence. He has spent most of his adult life in prison, but he was free long enough in the late 1960s to mesmerize and lead a heterogeneous band of hippies to commit some of the most bloodthirsty and bizarre murders of the century. Charles Manson will probably spend the rest of his life in prison.

The foster care system in Indiana twisted the mind of Charles Manson. The system in Illinois almost killed Frank Osanka. He once had foster parents who referred to him not by name but as "You dumb Polack," and worse. Others beat him. One couple, respected churchgoers in their community and the parents of two healthy, happy children of their own, locked him in a coal cellar and allowed him upstairs only when he had work to do. He was fed scaps from the family meals and was expected to sleep curled up on the cellar stair landing. But the coal dust made him constantly thirsty, and when he would sneak a drink of water, he had to slip downstairs, being careful that the wooden steps didn't creak so that they gave him away. He mastered the steps, but inevitably he was betrayed by the water faucet. The pipes began shuddering and rattling the instant the faucet was turned on. Then he would cower and listen to the footsteps of his angry foster parents approaching the basement, and prepare to be beaten and kicked on his bloated stomach until he vomited.

He finally gave up. One day he could hardly stand the thirst, but he also couldn't stand another beating. So he curled up in a fetal position and waited to die. When he heard water dripping sometime later, he ignored it. As the dripping continued, however, his curiosity finally won out and he looked up. Just over his head, a beautiful golden faucet hung from a support beam. It was perspiring from the cold, with huge golden droplets of water swelling deliciously from its surface. He touched it, then drank until he was sated, and curled up to sleep.

The golden faucet awakened his survival instinct. He began retaliating for the beatings he endured by attacking the children of his foster parents. Every time he was hit, he rushed at the other children, biting, kicking, and clawing at them. The tactic worked. He was returned to the Illinois Department of Children and Family Services (DCFS) and placed in another home. It saved his life.

Shortly after he was seventeen, he ran away and joined the Marine Corps. The Marines were good for him. At last he had three meals a day, a clean, secure place to sleep, and a set of rules to live by that never changed.

Understandably, the entire issue of child abuse is especially close to Dr. Osanka. After he left the Marines and entered college, he began to study the phenomenon. It wasn't part of the curriculum, but it was a subject about which he had an insatiable curiosity. Initially, as with most people who have been abused as children, he had the vague feeling that he somehow had deserved the treatment he suffered, and that his experience was unique. As he continued his reading and studies, however, he realized that child abuse and neglect is widespread, both within the child welfare systems of the various states and within families. Eventually, as an instructor, he initiated the first college course on the subject in the country. His undergraduate students are taught how to identify, report, and intervene in areas of physical, emotional, and sexual abuse of children. Most of his graduate students are police officers, nurses, social workers, and other professionals who have already come into intimate contact with the problem. One of their most important projects is writing a research paper focusing on some aspect of their job that relates to the subject.

Dr. Densen-Gerber was never a victim of child abuse. When she was a psychiatric resident and pregnant for the sixth time in seven years of marriage, she asked for maternity leave but, instead, was assigned to work with drug addicts. Her superior considered the job easy and explained that all she had to do was punch in and out of work, then go home and take care of her children. He assured her that drug addicts couldn't be helped anyway.

She took the assignment but rejected the advice. Some addicts, she learned, could be helped. Equally important, the children of addicts and alcoholics could be helped. Dr. Densen-Gerber immersed herself in the work. A few years later she established Odyssey House, then incorporated the Odyssey Institute to treat drug and alcohol addiction and to provide health care for the socially disadvantaged.

Initially she focused on a therapy program to treat alcoholics and drug addicts by using former abusers, psychiatrists, and a team of other professionals. She was especially concerned with female addicts who were pregnant or already mothers.

Odyssey expanded rapidly. By the end of the decade, more than 40 shelters and programs were established in a half-dozen states in this country and in Australia, all supported by the private nonprofit charity.[1] Some acquired federal and state funding to pioneer treatment programs for adolescents and for parents addicted to alcohol or drugs who were abusing their children.

Dr. Densen-Gerber and the staff at Odyssey were looking into the root causes of drug and alcohol addiction and child abuse. One of the most disturbing revelations was evidence of a link between female addicts, incest, and the sexual abuse of the addicts' children. Most of the mothers treated at Odyssey were victims of incest, usually as children. As teenagers and adults they became addicted to drugs or alcohol, and as mothers they instigated or permitted the physical and sexual abuse of their children.

Further research disclosed the startling evidence that many male addicts treated and studied at Odyssey were also incest victims. Incest was at least as destructive to their emotional health as it had been for the females.

A full-figured, platinum blonde, capable of dropping the legal-medical jargon of her twin professions of law and medicine and talking street-fighter tough in a showdown, Dr. Densen-Gerber doesn't pull her punches or compromise when she is considering the welfare of addicts, alcoholics, or abused children. She once tangled with a lawyer and childrens' rights advocate over a program she established to care for pregnant addicts, even if they had to be held against their will. The lawyer complained that she couldn't legally or ethically justify holding an addict who wished to leave. "I have no problem with holding a pregnant addict for the sake of that addicted fetus," she retorted. "That woman's nine months with her unborn baby will affect that child's entire life. That child didn't ask to be born addicted."

The examples of kiddie porn had shaken and angered her and by late 1976 she was mailing samples of the smut to politicians and demanding action. One of them, a district attorney, suggested that she spend her time worrying about more important criminal activities—like mugging. Another blandly denied that the material was produced in his state.

Undaunted, she assembled a package of statistics, some grotesquely repellent kiddie porn, and a few ugly photos from the office of her husband, Michael Baden, New York City's chief medical examiner, and hit the road to spread the story of the widespread sexual abuse of children. On many of her cross-country jaunts she was accompanied by teenage runaways, junkies, and prostitutes who appeared with her at press conferences and on television talk shows.

Both she and Dr. Osanka had been aware that sexual exploitation of children is part of the overall phenomena of child abuse and neglect. (Incest, molestation by relatives, friends, or strangers, and prostitution are all factors in the sexual abuse of children.) But they were appalled to realize that kiddie porn and organized prostitution are other forms in the overall mosaic of abuse that had gone virtually unnoticed by the public.

Kiddie porn and prostitution had not gone unnoticed by certain sexual entrepreneurs, however, who saw big money to be made in the commercial exploitation of youngsters. Drs. Osanka and Densen-Gerber checked porn shops in a dozen cities and found material sold openly that featured children as young as three years old. Little boys and girls openly displaying their genitals and participating in coitus and oral and anal sex were pictured on the backs of playing cards, in magazines, and on movie film. The smut was available in almost every large city in the country and in many smaller towns as well. Dr. Densen-Gerber's seventeen-year-old daughter once purchased magazines featuring kiddie porn from a bookstore in a Department of Health, Education, and Welfare building.

As odious and bizarre as the sexual abuse of children seems to us, there is a long history of child pornography and child prostitution. For example, in the late nineteenth century, Charles L. Dodgson, the shy English mathematician and deacon of Christ Church in Oxford who wrote *Alice's Adventures in Wonderland* and *Through the Looking Glass* under the pen name Lewis Carroll, developed a reputation for taking tasteful nude photographs of little girls. As tasteful as they might be considered today, in those times the nudity was shocking. A stutterer who was ill at ease with adults, Dodgson actively sought out the company of little girls and became one of the earliest photographers of children.

André Gide, winner of the Nobel Prize for Literature and a dominant figure in European letters until his death in 1951, was an acknowledged homosexual who wrote frankly that he was a pederast—a lover of young boys.

In ancient Greece, most men of substance maintained boy lovers. It was part of the culture. But, contrary to popular belief, the youths had reached puberty and were sexually mature before becoming companions to an older male. Sexual relations with prepubescent children were frowned upon and punished severely. It was not until the days of the

Romans that boy prostitution is first known to have become a common occurrence. Boy brothels were stocked with slaves, some barely old enough to walk. The streets of old Rome teemed with child hustlers of both sexes. Roman soldiers were permitted to keep the young boys they captured during the wars; often, three or four legionnaires shared the upkeep and sexual services of a child.

According to Robin Lloyd in *For Money or Love: Boy Prostitution in America,* during the gold rush period in this country, runaway boys who had come to California seeking adventure were forced into prostitution and exhibited at "peg houses" where they were seated on greased wooden pegs. The pegs dilated their anuses, and clients merely examined the size of the pegs to select a boy with the desired dimensions.[2]

Pornography was confined to drawings and artistic renderings through most of history and ranged from crude to highly sophisticated, depending on the ability of the artist. But with the invention of the camera, exciting new frontiers were opened to aspiring smut merchants or collectors. In more recent years, technology has made it possible for amateurs as well as professionals to record pornography. It can now be produced by almost anyone with a few hundred dollars for equipment, less for models.

Cameras shoot and develop photos in seconds. Home movies permit amateurs to film and screen pornography in the privacy of their own living room. Portable video cameras and player recorders open still newer avenues for the amateur.

But use of still and movie cameras demanded models. Drawings rendered from memory or imagination were passé. Like the market for child prostitution, child pornography required young bodies. For a while most of the models in this country were adults, or at least young men and women in their late teens who were nearing adulthood. Small-busted, youthful-appearing women, dressed in little girl clothes and clutching props such as dolls and lollipops to give the impression that they were children, posed for pornographic movies and still pictures.

In the early 1970s, several factors combined to change all that. Collectors of child pornography no longer had to satisfy themselves with leering at photos of young adults masquerading as children. About midway into the decade, a deluge of kiddie porn featuring real children began to stream into the country, most of it from Scandinavia. Professionally produced six- and eight-picture sets of photos, both black and white and color, and magazines and films depicting girls and boys performing every imaginable sex act with each other or with adults were suddenly available. These could be ordered through the mail or picked up in so-called adult bookstores that specialized in salacious materials. Films and photos of naked children engaging in explicitly posed sex acts became the hottest-selling items on the market. The development didn't escape the attention of alert pornographers in this country. Aware of big money to be made in the sexual exploitation of children, they began producing their own films, magazines, and photo sets.

At first, some of the material was shipped to Europe and then returned to the United States so that it would appear to be of European origin. But before long even that pretense was dropped. Men and women in the sex industry began stocking the shelves of adult bookstores and filling mail orders with material moving directly from private apartments, storefront studios, and processing laboratories all over the United States.

The criminal justice system in the United States was caught unprepared by the sudden flood of child pornography. Legally, the filth wasn't considered child abuse, usually not even obscene. Supreme Court interpretations of the First Amendment had been pushed to extremes in dealing with pornography featuring adults. Existing state laws were challenged and defeated with the First Amendment arguments, and a mishmash of hastily fashioned new pornography and obscenity laws enacted to replace them often proved woefully ineffective. No one, apparently including the justices themselves, had any idea what the Supreme Court wanted or what new interpretations it was likely to announce next.

Society's ability to control the dissemination of smut was paralyzed, and the industry's spread to child pornography was inevitable. Broad changes in attitudes about relationships between men and women, between parents and their children, and about homosexuality contributed to the confusion, helping to create an atmosphere where panderers who dealt in young flesh could freely operate and prosper.

A series of United States Supreme Court decisions had opened the door for the free and easy production, distribution, and sale of pornography. Initially it was only a slight lifting of the lid. The Court ruled, maturely it seems, that First Amendment protections applied to literary works such as *Lady Chatterly's Lover* and *Ulysses*. In 1957, the Court determined that sexual content by itself was not sufficient to define what was obscene and what was not. The true test, the Court decided, was to determine whether or not the material "as a whole" appealed "to prurient interests." By 1966, the nation's highest Court went even further, declaring that, to be obscene, material must be "utterly without redeeming social value." The 1966 ruling was like a hit of adrenaline to pornographers. It was their green light, assuring even the most timid that anything goes.

Adult bookstores began to spring up openly in the larger cities. Their shelves were stocked with new lines of quickie books written in a week or less on contract for $500 to $1,000 each by an army of hacks. They were heavy on four-letter words and filled with one explicit sexual confrontation after another. Expensive slick magazines and home movie film showing everything in living color shared shelf space. Despite the high prices, the material had a fast turnover. The demand was heavy, and the delighted business people worked hard to keep new matter coming.

Penthouse entered the man's magazine market already occupied by *Playboy*. Others such as *Oui, Chic, Gallery,* and *Club* followed. Photographs of the gorgeous models who formerly lounged sinuously across the magazine pages became less graceful and more clinical.

Art theaters and neighborhood movie houses that found they couldn't make a profit showing cowboy shoot-em-ups and Walt Disney films began importing soft porn from Europe. Sweden's *I Am Curious-Yellow* drew crowds that lined up for blocks outside big city movie houses. It wasn't long before *Yellow* was forgotten, and couples were sitting through American-produced films that made the Swedish movie look almost Puritan by comparison. *Deep Throat, Behind the Green Door,* and *The Devil in Miss Jones* created a new movie market and new stars such as Linda Lovelace, Marilyn Chambers, Georgina Spelvin, Harry Reems, and Big John Holmes.

Deep Throat was the most successful of the new 35-millimeter porn movies and was produced for about $25,000. It grossed more than $50 million worldwide. And there were no million-dollar salaries paid to its stars. The profits were astronomical.

Crime professionals, especially in the distribution end of the business, were moving in. Adult bookstores were bombed by competitors in some cities, and some of the people who were producing, distributing, and selling smut were murdered. Politicians in state legislatures and in the United States Congress were belatedly addressing themselves to investigations of the phenomena, debating more laws to deal with the problem.

It was almost a decade after the 1966 Supreme Court ruling before American pornographers began to recognize the true moneymaking potential of children. There were always a few who were greedy and reckless enough to produce and distribute child pornography. People like the Abramses were in the vanguard. But it was the mid-1970s before America's smut industry was ready to move into child pornography in a big way. By 1979, the $250,000 annual earnings attributed to the North Bellmore scheme was being eclipsed many times over by professional operations grossing millions of dollars selling the sexual services of children.

There was no problem finding models. Many parents, such as those who delivered their frightened children to the Abramses, offered their youngsters as models for the most obnoxious kind of filmed filth in exchange for a few dollars. One assistant state's attorney in Chicago was so revolted by the evidence in a case involving parents who posed for pornography with their minor son and daughter that he asked to be transferred from child abuse cases. The evidence included more than 400 photographs of the mother sexually involved with the son, the father with the daughter, and all the family members participating in sexual activity with other adults.

Other models were easily recruited or forced into pornography and prostitution after being plucked from the more than one million runaway boys and girls in this country. Most are teenagers, but many are much younger, some under ten years old. Often the children have been forced to leave by alcoholic parents, incestuous fathers or other relatives, or merely because there is no money to support them and no love in the family. Social workers and others who are concerned with the welfare of youngsters call them "throwaway children."

Other prospective models and child hookers are available from among the nearly 2.5 million children of drug addicts and the nearly 3 million children of prostitutes. For example, a thirty-five-year-old prostitute and her twelve-year-old daughter were apprehended a few blocks from Chicago's Loop after a pimp offered the pair to a vice squad officer for $150. When the arrest was made the mother had disrobed and was preparing to perform oral sex to be followed by coitus while the daughter watched and spanked the bogus John.

There is, of course, considerable overlapping in the teeming reservoir of children available to the sex merchants. Some of the young victims can be counted in all categories: as runaways and as the offspring of prostitutes and drug addicts.

Whatever their background, many youngsters finding themselves on their own quickly learn that the sale of their bodies may offer their only means of survival. Pimps and pornographers or other seemingly friendly adults who take the children into their homes and feed and shelter them in exchange for sex become their new families. Ofte children are willing victims and trade themselves for what ...ey mistakenly perceive to be affection.

In Indianapolis, Marion County Juvenile Court Judge Valan S. Boring told a shocked state legislative committee probing the sexual abuse of children in the Hoosier state that "many of them [runaways] are selling their bodies to get enough to eat."

But hunger isn't the only way children can be seduced or forced into sex rackets. A sergeant with the Indianapolis Police Department's vice squad told a legislative panel about a fifteen-year-old girl from a well-to-do family who was talked into posing for some pornographic pictures. When she became frightened and decided she wanted the photos, she was forced into prostitution and narcotics abuse under the threat of having the pictures turned over to her parents.

Conditions in major cities like New York, Chicago, Los Angeles, Detroit, and San Francisco were horrendous. Girls and boys from five or six up through the teens were available for sex or pornography to anyone with a few dollars. And they were available in many smaller cities and towns as well. Many of the child victims who learned the ropes in prostitution and pornography in the city were runaways—or throwaways—from small towns.

Actor Robert De Niro teamed up with twelve-year-old Jodie Foster in a savage Hollywood movie that capitalized on illicit child sex and violence. *Taxi Driver* featured the girl as a young runaway and prostitute from Pittsburgh who is rescued from her brutal pimp by a New York cabbie. The movie was a box office smash and the lesson wasn't lost on hungry Hollywood producers. The combination of children and sex was a winning formula. Violence added to the appeal.

Years earlier, Vladimir Nabokov's book *Lolita* had focused attention on a child seductress, played by Sue Lyon in the movie made from it, and her affair with the quintessential dirty old man, Humbert Humbert, played in the movie by James Mason. The book and movie added a new word to the language, *nymphet*—a child seductress.

More recently, one of Hollywood's offerings to the newly discovered obsession with children as sex objects was *Pretty Baby*. Twelve-year-old Brooke Shields was cast as Violet in Louis Malle's treatment of the romance between photographer H. J. Bellocq and a charming little child prostitute in the Storyville, New Orleans, red-light district during World War I.

Hardcore, released in 1978 with George C. Scott as the star, focused on more current exploitation of the young. The actress was older than

Brooke Shields, Jodie Foster, and the youthful Sue Lyon of *Lolita,* but the film was a raw and brutal story of an angry father from the Midwest who learns while tracing his runaway teenage daughter that she has become a performer in pornographic movies.

Unfortunately, neither *Hardcore* nor *Taxi Driver* is overly fanciful. Hundreds of young girl runaways parade in boots and hotpants along the sidewalks of Times Square or Sunset Boulevard, prostituting themselves several times each night to provide thick bankrolls, gleaming new Cadillacs, and fine clothes for their pimps. The girls share the streets with fifteen- and sixteen-year-old boys in the same profession. Hundreds of other children have hitchhiked or traveled by bus to New York, Chicago, or Los Angeles with their heads full of dreams, only to find themselves in sleazy rented motel rooms and apartments performing as prostitutes or porn stars.

In Los Angeles alone, police have estimated the annual take on sales of pornography at about $125 million dollars. Few legitimate businesses in the United States can come close to matching that figure. Pornography generates so much money that in 1978 the California Department of Justice estimated that the nation's smut merchants were collecting approximately $4 billion a year. That about equals the amount of money turned over annually by the conventional motion pictures and record industries combined. And there are many close to the pornography business who believe that the $4 billion estimate should be doubled, perhaps tripled. It is impossible to estimate the take from prostitution, which is even less susceptible to control or auditing.

Surprisingly, perhaps, more boys than girls find themselves posing and performing for kiddie porn. As they reach their late teens and drop out of the business because they are no longer convincing as child performers, both boys and girls are replaced by a steady supply of newcomers. Many, perhaps most, of the young porn performers of both sexes continue on in the sex industry as prostitutes after their days as child stars of movies and magazines are over.

Dr. Densen-Gerber estimates that as many as one million youngsters may be victims of sexual exploitation in this country at any one given time.

Dr. Osanka believes that "it is not social or cultural need but individual greed that has given birth to the wholesale introduction of child pornography. It is not a First Amendment issue and has nothing to do with the freedom of the press or legislating the sexual fantasies of adults," he declares. "It is a matter of protecting the children."

By 1978, more than 260 different magazine titles featured juveniles engaged in sexual activities or otherwise posing lasciviously with other children or adults. Some of the better known titles were *Moppets,* a magazine featuring photos of wide-eyed little girls from three to eight years old; *Lollitots,* with child models from eleven to fourteen years old; and *Chicken Brats,* appealing to homosexuals, with young boys.

Others incorporate violence with the sexual abuse of children, or offer handy instructions for pedophiles. Magazines and books such as *Child Discipline,* which instructs its readers how to derive sexual pleasure from beating children, and *Lust for Children,* which among other things offers advice on how to avoid criminal convictions for molesting juveniles, are two. Other publications offer advice to child molesters on how youngsters can most easily and safely be lured from playgrounds, discuss the joys of incest, and instruct fathers how to clip locks on the labias of their little girls to keep them "all for you." An inestimable number of movie films, packs of playing cards, illustrated paperback books, and other materials in the nation's sex shops feature children.

Thousands of other children who do not pose for pornography and who are not sold as prostitutes nevertheless become victims of sexual abuse—usually at the hands of their fathers, stepfathers, or other members of their families, close friends, or neighbors. A series of federally funded studies by Children's Hospital National Medical Center in Washington, D.C., disclosed that sexual abuse may be a more common childhood affliction than broken arms or tonsillectomies.

Dr. Frederick Green, associate director of the hospital, said in 1977 that about 150 of every 100,000 children under age sixteen are victims of sexual abuse that is reported to authorities. But experts believe that for every case of childhood sexual abuse that comes to official attention there are two unreported cases, including everything from fondling and adult exhibitionism to sodomy and rape. Eleven percent of the victims are no more than five years old, and 35 percent are six to ten, he said. One of the studies indicated that boys are victimized nearly as often as girls, but abuse of boys is less likely to be reported to parents or police.

Child molesters have even begun using CB radios to lure children from their homes. An investigation by *The CBers News,* a national newspaper for CB radio buffs, disclosed that child molesters and young male prostitutes were using the radios to make sexual contacts. Publisher Michael J. McCormack reported that the scheme apparently began in California and then spread to other cities and towns throughout the country. The practice eventually became so widespread that some police departments assigned juvenile division officers to monitor CB channels, especially in neighborhoods near schools. One of the ploys used by child molesters was to tune into channels used by youngsters and sweet-talk them into meetings to swap CB gear.

Marijuana, alcohol, and other drugs are also valuable lures. And it is not uncommon for wealthy pedophiles to ply older children of either sex with expensive presents such as cars, motorcycles, jewelry, and vacation trips to exotic places. But some of the children are so young and innocent that they pose or participate in sexual relations in exchange for dolls, candy, soft drinks, or pizza.

An Elgin, Illinois, construction worker enticed nearly 40 teenage girls to pose naked for him in exchange for marijuana. As his apartment was being searched, three girls ranging in age from thirteen to sixteen years old appeared at his door and offered to pose before they noticed the policemen inside. Police confiscated 10 pounds of marijuana and about 50 amphetamines, in addition to 500 color photographs of naked children.

Nassau County police arrested a 450-pound Westbury, Long Island, man and accused him of luring at least 25 girls in their early teens to his apartment with promises of drugs, then photographing them participating in various sexual acts with him. Police accused him of drugging the girls, often with laughing gas, prior to the sex and photo sessions. They reported confiscating more than 500 pornographic photographs, various sexual devices, LSD, chloroform, mescaline, marijuana, and hypodermic needles from his apartment.

About a month earlier, two other men were arrested on Long Island's South Shore and charged with drugging 15 junior high and high school girls and photographing them during group sex.

Not all pornography or prostitution money can be traced to the exploitation of children, but this exploitation has kept the industries, especially pornography, healthy. And most older prostitutes began when they were teenagers or younger.

The traffic in pornography piled up such big dollars in the late 1970s that it drew significant attention from the legitimate business community. In 1978 it was the subject of a lengthy article in *Forbes,* one of the most prestigious business magazines in the country.[3] The article pointed out that some of the fastest and biggest money in pornography is in peep shows, the 16-minute, 8-millimeter "loops" shown in two-minute segments in machines placed in adult book-stores. Customers feed the machines with quarters.

Most of the films are also sold outright in the stores. Thousands of copies can be reproduced from a single negative, and reels sell for from

$20 to several hundred dollars each. One of the most popular loops ever shown was *First Communion*. The film opens with several little girls in crisp white dresses receiving their first communion. The ceremony is barely underway when a motorcycle gang barges into the church. Gang members beat the priest, chain him, and crucify him on the cross above the altar. Then they turn on the terrified children, rip off their clothes, and rape them. The film is silent, and the screams of the girls can't be heard, but their terror appears real. And their blood appears real. Other films show little girls orally servicing adults and animals, and wide-eyed boys of eight or nine being anally sodomized. One mother filmed her own eight-year-old daughter and ten-year-old son having sexual intercourse with each other.

Policeman Victor Rice, with partner John D'elia, once ran an adult bookstore as part of an undercover operation of the New York City Police Department to obtain evidence against distributors. He was quoted in *Forbes* as saying he would buy a film from a distributor for $3 and sell it for $20. "For children, you'd pay more, maybe $7, then you sell for $25," he said.[4] Rice observed that about 10 percent of his retail customers asked for "chicken stuff," child pornography. His customers were typical businessmen on their lunch hours or with a few minutes to spend after office hours before heading for their homes in the suburbs. Their shoes were shined, their nails manicured, and they characteristically dressed in suits and ties and carried briefcases. One Times Square pornography shop had a wealthy customer who regularly arrived in a chauffeur-driven car and sent his man inside to pick up pornographic magazines and films of young boys.

In Philadelphia, another attorney stopped in a porno shop a half block from the city hall and county courts building once a week and bought from $100 to $150 worth of pornography. The younger the girls in the films and magazines, the more he bought. Shortly before Christmas, he purchased nearly $500 worth of material on a single trip. He explained that he was buying gifts for special friends.

By the end of the decade, development of the video cassette recorder was making it more convenient than ever before to bring triple-X-rated films into the home. Retailers reported selling as many as 50 or 100 video tapes of films like *Deep Throat* and *Slaves of Love* for every movie like *Patton* or *Citizen Kane*.

The market is robust and it requires professional attention. Although members of organized crime have reputedly shouldered their way into at least the lucrative distribution end of the business, child pornography and child prostitution have also drawn from an extensive

range of legitimate professions including lawyers, clergymen, accountants, financiers, school bus drivers, disc jockeys, a former employee of
the Central Intelligence Agency, and, of course, professional photographers and members of the film industry.

Some child pornographers fit the stereotype of the nasty old man
prowling school playgrounds, parks, and candy stores seeking careless
youngsters he can lure back to his home. But they are in the minority.
The child pornographer or panderer of today is more likely to be sophisticated, mobile, educated, and wealthy. Often he is a pillar of his community and is respected for his involvement in youth-oriented activities
such as Scouting for boys or girls, church-sponsored programs, summer
camps, and other accepted activities known for building character in
the young. Several men connected to child pornography and child prostitution rings are millionaires.

The communities where organized rings have been discovered are as
diverse as the professions of the adults involved: New York, Los Angeles, Chicago, Houston, New Orleans, Boston, Providence, Indianapolis, Minneapolis-St. Paul, Las Vegas, and Denver. And they have been
uncovered in North Manchester, Indiana; New Rochelle and North
Bellwood, New York; Tampa and Coral Gables, Florida; Alto, Tennessee; and Elgin, Gurney, and Evanston, Illinois. Even tiny Shreve, Ohio,
drew national attention in 1979 when the village chief of police was
indicted on 34 sex-related charges accusing him of rape and other offenses involving four youngsters ranging in age from eleven to fourteen.

Some of the incidents, like the case in Shreve, involve only a single
individual or a few men accused of getting together to share their interest in sex with children. But sexual exploitation of children can be much
more sophisticated and more commercially rewarding.

Young boys are routinely transported from state to state for purposes
of prostitution. Their pictures and written descriptions are circulated
among wealthy pederasts in national newsletters. Some operations are
so sophisticated that names and descriptions of child prostitutes have
been programmed on computers so that the children can be delivered to
order from one state to another.

A boy prostitution ring in Boston trafficked in children as young as
nine years old. A convicted child molester was arrested in San Francisco
on charges of running a boy prostitution ring involving nearly 30 children. The policeman who made the arrest said the boys were taken to
prospective clients in various parts of the Bay Area and "exhibited like
livestock, naked."

Teenage girl runaways are picked up at bus terminals or other hangouts in big cities and seduced or forced into prostitution or pornography. The sexual merchandising of young Scandinavian types transported from Minneapolis to the sidewalks of New York's Eighth Avenue became so flagrant a few years ago that it precipitated a national outcry. The girls disappeared from the streets for a few days until media attention was diverted to other stories and then resumed their activities. New York police estimate that as many as 20,000 runaways under sixteen are wandering the city's streets, and pimps and pornographers feed on them like hungry sharks.

A probe by a Clark County grand jury in Las Vegas led to the breakup of a child prostitution ring involving girls as young as eleven and the arrest of five men including the sixty-year-old retired owner of a hotel gift shop. A sixth man, a prominent Las Vegas attorney, reportedly fled the country after his indictment.

Some children are sold by their parents or guardians. A couple in Security, Colorado, was arrested and charged with selling their twelve-year-old son for $3,000 to a wealthy Texas man for sexual purposes. In Los Angeles, a father began having incestuous relations with his son when the boy was six. By the time the child was eleven, he had appeared in dirty movies and pornographic magazines, had been involved in swap clubs, and was sold twice as a sex slave.

Chicago police arrested a fifty-four-year-old fortune-teller after she reputedly offered to sell her six-year-old grandson to an undercover investigator. Youth officers were probing child prostitution in New Town, Chicago's so-called gay ghetto, when they learned that a woman had been passing the word that she had a young boy to sell for $12,000. A detective said he contacted the woman and haggled with her until she agreed to reduce the price to $9,000. He then gave her $5,000 in cash, along with a handwritten note she dictated in which he promised to pay the additional $4,000.

After her arrest, police disclosed that the woman claimed to have had the boy since he was five years old. She reportedly never asked the buyer to identify himself or explain why he wanted the child. But Youth Division officers know the area as a neighborhood where young boys are highly prized for sexual purposes and a child's worth as a sex partner can be translated into dollars according to a formula directly related to his age.

In Los Angeles, police found a three-year-old girl and a five-year-old girl who were sold into the pornography trade by prostitute mothers.

One Los Angeles mother rented her child for $3,000 for nine months, and another gave written permission to a photographer to take her three sons on pornographic film expeditions.

The mother of the three-year-old was a performer in pornographic movies, and she and a photographer were charged with conspiracy to contribute to the delinquency of a minor after the man allegedly took lewd pictures of the little girl. (Specific intent to contribute to the delinquency of the child could not be proved against either the man or the woman, and both were acquitted.)

The mother of the five-year-old consented to sexual activities between the little girl and a wealthy man. The man, in his fifties, was arrested, and, after the prostitute testified against him, he pleaded guilty to contributing to the delinquency of the child. He was sentenced to undergo three months of psychiatric treatment.

By early 1977, Drs. Densen-Gerber and Osanka were recognized as two of the country's most zealous and outspoken opponents of the sexual exploitation of children. Inevitably, their paths crossed, and on February 4 they held a joint press conference in Chicago. The timing was unfortunate. That evening and the next day the newspaper headlines and television and radio specials focused on the crash of an elevated train that plunged off the tracks on the edge of Chicago's Loop killing 11 rush-hour commuters and injuring another 266.

Nevertheless, muted though the immediate results were, the press conference marked the opening salvo in the concerted public awareness campaign to mobilize the citizenry and urge strong new laws to combat the wave of child prostitution and pornography.

Drs. Densen-Gerber and Osanka stepped up their interviews and appearances with the print and electronic media and spoke before private and governmental bodies.

Protest marches were organized and led outside adult bookstores in cities as diverse as New York; Chicago; Portsmouth, New Hampshire; Shreveport, Louisiana; Highland Park, Michigan; and Salt Lake City, Utah. Marchers chanted slogans and carried signs reading "Odyssey Pickets Pee Wee Porno," "Child Porn, A Cause To Mourn," and "Leave Porno Where It Is—In The Dirt."

Counterpickets responded in some cities yelling abuse at the demonstrators and hoisting signs reading "Sex Is God," "Equal Rights In The Bedroom," and "My Ancestors Were Slaves, Let Me Read What I Please."

Some of the women pickets against pornography carried infants or pushed babies in strollers. Dr. Densen-Gerber referred to her crusaders as "hiccup pickets" because they changed days and locations at will. Pornographers in some cities, including Flint, Michigan, where Odyssey investigators purchased kiddie porn, cleared their shelves of the magazines before picketing could be organized.

Another individual, though not as well known nationally as Densen-Gerber and Osanka, played a prominent part in pulling the rug out from under some entrepreneurs feeding on the sexuality of children. Barely two months after the February press conference, Marilyn Wright, a reporter for a Traverse City, Michigan, newspaper, disclosed in a series of painstakingly researched and copyrighted articles that a chicken pornography and prostitution racket had been uncovered that extended into more than a half-dozen states.

Police were already closing in on and arresting pornographers and pedophiles in Michigan, Louisiana, Massachusetts, New York, New Jersey, and Illinois. Mrs. Wright's articles in the *Record-Eagle* detailed how members of the loosely federated ring had formed their own church and other tax-exempt fronts to get state revenues to carry out their sex-for-sale operations under the guise of foster home care for orphaned or troubled boys.

"This thing was utterly disgusting," remarked editor John Kinney. "But you talk about pursuit. . . . Marilyn pursued that story like a tight end. She has the instinct."

The campaign against the child sex merchants was in full swing. Radio, television, and other newspapers picked up the story, detailed in the carefully reported series of articles in the *Record-Eagle*. When the prestigious *Chicago Tribune* printed a series of front-page articles by a trio of investigative reporters who had probed the sexual exploitation of children, state and federal lawmakers began to take notice.

A group of radical homosexuals paraded angrily in front of the *Tribune* offices after the articles were published, screaming abuse at the publisher and reporters and hurling angry charges that the newspaper was picking on gays. The protesters missed the point. The articles, as did the efforts of Drs. Densen-Gerber and Osanka, represented a legitimate warning aimed not at gay or straight sexual life-styles, but at pedophiles—adults who sexually abuse children of either sex by prostituting them or using them for pornography.

The pedophiles understood. Several wealthy chicken hawks had already run to Europe or South America and were hiding out to avoid arrest on a variety of criminal charges related to the sexual exploitation of young boys. The sophisticated network of commercial Boy-Love operations was in a shambles, and the slick kiddie porn magazines were disappearing from the racks of adult bookstores.

Densen-Gerber, Osanka, and others who had joined the campaign kept the pressure on. There had been crackdowns before. This time, there would be no slacking off until there were strong new state and federal laws to control the sexual exploitation of children, tightened regulations for foster care programs, and new public awareness and attitudes.

[1] New Hampshire, Louisiana, New York, Utah, Arizona, and Michigan.
[2] Robin Lloyd, *For Money or Love: Boy Prostitution in America* (New York: Vanguard Press, 1976),
[3] *Forbes,* 18 September 1978,
[4] Ibid.,

3.

North Fox Island

THERE must be times when Gerald S. Richards looks back on the mid-1970s as the best years of his life.

He has told acquaintances about those years in Port Huron, Michigan. Married and a father, he was the scion of a respected family.

Richards was not the kind of citizen whose family or friends would expect him to be arrested on a morals charge. Nevertheless, the day came when he was charged with criminal sexual conduct in the first degree and was accused of inducing a ten-year-old boy to commit fellatio.

As Gerald Richards' snug little world began to crumble, there were other equally startling revelations. Investigators carried armloads of pornographic material, some in stamped envelopes ready for mailing, from his car and office. Files were crammed with nude photos of young boys in a variety of sexual poses. There were lists with names and addresses of customers and contacts in the boy pornography and prostitution trade.

Detectives could hardly have asked for a more cooperative or articulate suspect. A slender man with bony features, a thick, dark mustache, prominent ears that stick out from his head, and quick, nervous movements, he talked freely with police, court officers, Michigan state legislators, journalists—and finally testified before a U.S. Senate subcommittee.

By the time the loquacious pedophile stopped talking and investigators had finished sifting through his voluminous records, they had uncovered a loosely knit but widespread ring of men who were exploiting boys for pornography and prostitution. The network extended west across Michigan to an island near Traverse City, and reached into a half-dozen other states in the East, the Midwest, and the South.

Richards told a story, later confirmed by investigators, of Boy-Love, or B-L, operations that used foster care programs and churches as tax-exempt fronts for collectors of pornography and wealthy pederasts who paid hundreds of dollars for sexual soirees with young males. One group infiltrated and took over a Boy Scout troop, and other pederasts attempted—unsuccessfully—to worm their way into the Big Brothers and similar organizations.

Richards had not planned to become a flesh profiteer. He was married and a college student earning a degree in youth services and electronics, he said, when he began working part-time at one of the first pornography shops in Port Huron. The work was easy, he needed the money, and he was frankly curious about the operation.

As he recounted the story to news reporters and law-enforcement authorities, before long he was beginning to make money on the side, reselling porno prints he obtained at the store. He had also made contacts with distributors, publishers, and customers. He studied the operation carefully, learning everything he could about the trade. Eventually he left the store and went into the mail order business for himself.

Within a short time, he had put together a stable of some 30 boy models, none older than fifteen. Recruiting them was easy. He looked for boys without strong moral or religious backgrounds, or boys with absent fathers or fathers who spent little time with their sons. "They didn't have a chance. They are brainwashed and left sexually confused. They can end up like the men who entice them," he explained.[1] The boy he eventually got into trouble over was reportedly "tested" on a camping trip when he was eight years old to determine whether or not he would fit into the operation.

Richards was an amateur magician, and a twelve-year-old neighbor, who helped him in his magic act and babysat, became one of his first models and procured other youngsters for the pornography scheme. Richards presented his magic act before civic groups, in nightclubs, and at fund-raising events, as well as before various gatherings of children.

Richards claimed that, although he was aware of his homosexuality since his elementary school days, his affairs were always with males near his own age prior to his experience with the babysitter. He admitted to a two-and-a-half-year affair with the boy.

As the pornography operation expanded, it became routine procedure to keep a blackmail photo file of each boy who posed or participated in overt sexual activities. The picture of the young assistant was eventually thrown away, however, because the boy was so efficient and trustworthy that his mentor decided the photo was not necessary.

Although he used his home and a downtown office, Richards' family never suspected his activities. He was careful about how he spent the money he made. He bought more sophisticated photo equipment, and his only outward sign of wealth was his Cadillac.

In the meantime, he was moving more deeply into B-L and chicken porn activities, contacting publishers and building up a file of pederasts who used the publications and the mails.

In a California publication called *Better Life Monthly*, which described itself as "America's No. 1 boy love journal," Richards turned up an ad that helped him find a business partner. The men corresponded for four months before Richards was finally satisfied with the man's sincerity and felt assured that he was not a U.S. postal inspector or a policeman. The masthead on the magazine advised that it was the "news magazine of Better Life, an international service organization that is seeking liberation for boys and boy lovers."

Richards was knowledgeable in the pornography and Boy-Love business, but he became even more experienced with the help of his new partner. They made several trips together to Chicago where they talked with hotel clerks and porno shop operators, making new contacts for boy models.

It was also through *Better Life Monthly*, Richards told investigators, that he first heard of the Church of the New Revelation, which offered help to readers in establishing child care organizations and camps. As "The Reverend" Richards, he was later quoted as saying that after he replied to the ad in the newsletter an enterprising salesman named Dyer Grossman came to Port Huron to help form Brother Paul's Children's Mission. During that trip, it was later alleged, Grossman committed sexual acts with two Port Huron boys in a motel room.

With assistance from Grossman, Richards formed Brother Paul's as a tax-exempt front for his B-L activities. Richards was listed as president of the mission and director of the nature camp, both located on 835-acre North Fox Island across the state, northwest of Port Huron and just above Grand Traverse Bay in Lake Michigan. An alleged co-conspirator, Ann Arbor millionaire Francis D. Shelden, owned the island and was named on incorporation papers filed with the Michigan Secretary of State as a director of the mission.

Grossman was from Carmel, N. Y., and a member of a wealthy Long Island family. He taught science at two exclusive East Coast boys' schools and became vice-president of the childrens' mission on North Fox Island, as well as executive director of the Ocean Living Institute and youth director of the Church of the New Revelation, both headquartered in New Jersey.[2] Brother Paul's was registered as a Delaware corporation and operated under auspices of the church.

The former New York science teacher was later described by Kenneth Wooden, director of the National Coalition of Children's Justice, at U.S. Congressional hearings as "one of the worst chicken hawks in this country." Wooden testified that Grossman used the mails to instruct other chicken hawks how to get into the foster care business and how to obtain federal funding for their illicit activities.

Grossman's activities and the role of the church in the B-L operations were also alluded to in a letter to the U.S. Assistant Attorney General designate, Benjamin Civiletti, of the Department of Justice's Criminal Division, by Robert F. Leonard, president-elect of the National District Attorney's Association.[3]

Leonard, who was Genesee County, Michigan, prosecutor in Flint, pointed out the difficulties that local district attorneys often encounter dealing with organized sexual abuse of children because of jurisdictional problems involving multistate operations. He urged more assistance from federal authorities.

A national conspiracy existed, made up of an inter-relating network of foster homes, churches, nature camps, and similar programs ostensibly set up to handle wayward, incorrigible, homeless youngsters, he pointed out. Recommending an investigation of Grossman, Leonard said that the organizational wizard apparently went from state to state setting up child care tax fronts, sometimes affiliating with the New Jersey church under circumstances that avoided scrutiny by the IRS.

"These phony organizations are established in such a way as to be the conduit to accumulate youngsters to be used in making porno films and being available for sexual activities with adult perverts," he charged.

"These programs are being stocked with young children by overburdened courts, insensitive parents, and, in some cases, well-meaning officials," the prosecutor cautioned. "Once the youngster is placed in the program . . . he is trapped and becomes easy prey for the sexual deviates who in most cases are running the programs."

"These adult perverts appear to be aware of the network and travel between states attending these camps and sexually abusing these children for money, usually paid to the camp officials. Many of these people involved in this type of activity are very wealthy individuals and some are respectable community leaders in their home towns."

Authorities were just beginning to unravel the confusing web of interlocking corporations, foundations, churches, and missions registered in Michigan, Illinois, New Jersey, and Delaware when in 1977, the *Record-Eagle* broke the story based on a four-month investigation into the activities of the B-L ring. The exposé by the 24,000-circulation daily exploded in the public consciousness in Michigan and was quickly picked up by the national press.

Suddenly, what may have appeared to be a series of isolated incidents was perceived as an organized movement furthered by always imaginative, often wealthy, child molesters who had made a business out of the sexual exploitation of boys.

The Church of the New Revelation and various other front organizations established by the resourceful pederasts were granted tax-exempt status by the Internal Revenue Service. Both the church and the Ocean Living Institute were incorporated in Delaware, reputedly because of lenient incorporation laws, but listed principal places of business in Kearney, N. J. The incorporators of the church claimed it was formed to train ministers and other clerics and to ordain them to carry out its work. It was later disclosed, however, to be no more than a post office box number.

The Ocean Living Institute was ostensibly formed to promote education and research in oceanography. As Mrs. Wright, of the *Record-Eagle*, dug into the maze of 20 or 30 interlocking corporations and foundations, she turned up ties to a suspicious operation in the Caribbean. A nonprofit corporation had been established by members of the ring, supposedly to provide books and other literature to impoverished Third World countries. But the reporter said she believed the Caribbean front was actually set up to route American-made chicken porn so it would appear to have originated in foreign countries. The Church of the New Revelation was the parent company for almost all the front organizations.

Even though Grossman was pinpointed as the chief organizer traveling between states to tie the threads of the loosely knit organization together, there was an even more mysterious figure prominent in the chain of interlocking corporations—Adam Starchild.

Listed as one of the incorporators of Brother Paul's, Starchild was also named as president of the Church of the New Revelation and of the Ocean Living Institute, and as a trustee of the Educational Foundation for Youth, which was incorporated in Illinois. The Foundation was a nonprofit arm of a profitmaking corporation supposedly in the import-export business.

During a telephone conversation with a man who identified himself as Starchild, Mrs. Wright was told that "nothing ever came" of the

Foundation. He claimed it was one of Grossman's pet projects and that the former school teacher was scouting other states, including California, as possible locations for youth camps.

A probe by the New Jersey Commission for Investigation confirmed that "Adam Starchild" was an alias. And Richards later added personal confirmation, explaining that the name was coined from "Adam," the first naked man, and children who starred in the ring's photographic productions—thus "Adam Starchild."

The *Record-Eagle* investigation was sparked by a telephone call to the city room from a reporter for another Michigan newspaper who was tracking down rumors that a wealthy philanthropist was involved in a chicken porn and prostitution operation in the area.

Editors assembled their staff and assigned different aspects of the story to various reporters. Mrs. Wright had been with the daily for about six months as a police reporter, and she tackled her assignment with enthusiasm. After her stories were published exposing the shenanigans on North Fox Island, it became her permanent assignment. She dug through court records, swapped information with journalists in Delaware, New Jersey, and other states, and interviewed policemen and pornographers.

Before long she had identified Shelden as the "wealthy philanthropist." State police provided her with Richards' name and background. He became a regular correspondent, writing letters to her, detailing the chicken porn operation, and finally preparing a meticulously fashioned organizational chart pinpointing interlocking individuals and organizations in several states. The reporter also received a large amount of anonymous mail. One of her nameless correspondents mailed her a copy of what was purported to be a marriage certificate uniting Shelden with another man.

Mrs. Wright realized that an entire fraternity of sophisticated pederast entrepreneurs was at work, organizing the commercial exploitation of young boys for sexual purposes, not only in Michigan, but in several other states as well.

Delving into operations in her home state, she learned that Michigan law contained rigid licensing requirements for all summer camps and similar facilities for children. It is the job of the Department of Social Services to enforce the regulations, but the DSS was not aware that the camp existed because no one had applied for a license and there were no citizen inquiries about the facility. Observers speculated that the operators of the camp probably would have been granted a license, anyway, because of their education, wealth, and respectable backgrounds.

Soon after the North Fox Island story broke, however, Michigan lawmakers and other officials moved to tighten regulations and to beef up the DSS staff to provide closer investigation and supervision of foster homes, children's camps, and the like so they could no longer be exploited as recruiting grounds for victims of child sex.

Shelden's name repeatedly surfaced as Mrs. Wright dug into her research. A lifelong bachelor approaching fifty, he was a graduate geologist and part-time university professor whose pedigree could match that of anyone in Michigan for prestige. His ancestors included Russell A. Alger, a founder of the Edison Electric Light Company (now the Detroit Edison Company) who was a U.S. Army general, a governor of Michigan, a U.S. Senator, Secretary of War under President William McKinley, and a candidate for the presidency. Other ancestors prospered in the drygoods business, and his father and uncles formed the Shelden Land Company shortly after World War I and developed one of Detroit's finest subdivisions.

Born wealthy, Shelden was an amateur botanist who busied himself professionally as a land developer, oil consultant, and market investor. He was quoted in an interview for *Detroit*, the Sunday magazine of the *Detroit Free Press*, as saying that he was active in the Big Brothers, an organization through which volunteer adults spend time with young boys from homes without fathers. "Many weekends he takes young friends along to North Fox Island," the article advised.

Spokesmen for Big Brother organizations in Detroit, Port Huron, and Flint later denied that Shelden had ever been affiliated with their organizations. An official with the Young Men's Christian Association in Ann Arbor told the *Record-Eagle* that Shelden was a volunteer with a Big Brother group sponsored by the YMCA there. The group was not affiliated with Big Brother Inc., although it was patterned after its namesake. Shelden was reportedly active with the YMCA-sponsored Big Brothers for less than two years when he broke off contact. After his involvement in the North Fox Island affair was disclosed, state police questioned the boy for whom he had acted as Big Brother, but established no evidence of criminal conduct.

Richards reportedly tried to affiliate with the Big Brothers in Port Huron, and Grossman applied for Big Brother membership in Oakland, California. Neither was accepted. The organization has strict rules and thoroughly investigates applicants. Nevertheless, the wrong people sometimes slip through and are accepted for the program.

It would be impractical and unfair to expect that, under existing laws and conditions, all the pedophiles attracted to youth programs could be weeded out. Obviously, the most that can be expected is that their success be minimized through close scrutiny.

Shelden's investments were scrutinized closely by the tenacious journalist, and she learned that in 1960 he had purchased North Fox Island in Lake Michigan some 35 miles off the coast of Charlevoix, Michigan.

An annual report filed by Richards stated that the purposes of the mission and camp were to provide remedial tutoring, counseling, temporary lodging, boarding retreats, and emergency care for runaways. "Our mission is dedicated to the prevention and control of juvenile delinquency," it declared.

Literature distributed by Brother Paul's pointed out that, although the cost per boy for a six-day session at the camp was $85, no fees were charged. Donations were sought instead. Use of island and air transportation was "graciously donated by BPCM, Inc." (Brother Paul's Children's Mission).

The nature camp was described as "unlike other summer camps where a child spends most of his time at play. . . ." It was claimed instead that "our camp promotes an appreciation for nature lore, an appreciation for physical fitness, natural living and natural health care, safety, hygiene and a deeper appreciation of the natural gifts of God through the philosophy and practices of naturopathy and naturalism." Instructions in care of the body, elementary anatomy, and sex education were included in the curriculum.

Michigan state police investigators disclosed that the camp, instead, promoted altogether different activities for the runaways and troubled boys brought to the island. They were introduced to oral and anal sex with other boys and with adult males. There was no evidence or testimony that force or violence was used. Instead, the boys were seduced with bogus friendship and affection. According to police, alcohol and stag films were sometimes used to stimulate the boys before they participated in orgies. At least 10 photographs believed to have been taken on the island were reproduced in hard-core pornographic magazines. Unique sand dunes and a log cabin were identifying landmarks.

The summer of 1977 was bad for pedophiles in Michigan. For a time it seemed that hardly a week passed without someone prominent for wealth and social position, or for work as a clergyman, teacher, doctor, or public official, being accused of criminal sexual conduct involving children.

For a time, newspaper headlines were written about a social worker from Highland Park, near Detroit, who was popular with children in his neighborhood until he was charged with having sexual relations with a twelve-year-old boy. Police confiscated a list of more than 24 names of other children from his home. Other stories concerned the head of the English department of Detroit's Cody High School who was accused of sexually molesting a fourteen-year-old male student in his office. Or they described another Detroit school teacher who was initially accused of forcing several male pupils to perform oral sex on him, then was permitted to plead guilty on a single reduced charge in a plea-bargaining agreement.

Charges against a priest in Farmington Hills led to a legal brouhaha between a judge and the Michigan Association of Broadcasters over a court order to suppress details of the child sex case to protect the defendant's right to a fair trial.

In Pontiac, a thirty-three-year-old man was accused of operating a sex club thought to have possibly involved as many as 200 children. There was talk of a similar club in another community involving married couples and their teenagers, but no charges were filed. Some of the adult participants were community leaders.

Four Chicago area arrests at about the same time pointed to Michigan as a location of B-L operations. More than 60 rolls of undeveloped film, including three 50-foot reels labeled "Michigan Trip," were confiscated from a suburban Park Ridge apartment. One of the men arrested told investigators he had worked at a summer camp near Hastings, Michigan, where the film was shot.

Detectives also learned that Park Ridge children were sent to summer camps in the Hastings area and admitted concern over the possibility that one of the men arrested, who was active in youth group work in this suburban community, might have had a hand in selecting the camps.

A misstep helped the three-month investigation when two of the men reportedly gave four rolls of 8-millimeter film to an undercover officer who claimed he could process it and arrange national distribution through crime syndicate connections. They were quoted as saying that they planned to sell 2,000 copies of the film for $50 each. A new kiddie porn movie was about to be filmed in a far northside motel room when the initial arrests were made, police said.

There was no Illinois state law specifically dealing with pandering by boys, and police described Chicago as a national center for boy prostitution. Young actors are easily recruited for smut films, such as those produced in Chicago and elsewhere, from among runaways, state wards, or boys with little or no parental supervision. Procurers patrol bus stations, arcades, fast food restaurants, and other popular youth hangouts.

Two of the men were accused of filming a pornographic movie involving two fourteen-year-olds—the first child porn movie known to have been filmed in the city, police said. A third man was a foster parent and was accused of engaging in sexual activity with his foster son, one of the fourteen-year-olds. He had been arrested a couple of years earlier on charges of deviant sexual assault involving a sixteen-year-old boy and was placed on five years probation prior to receiving a temporary license from the Illinois Department of Children and Family Services (DCFS) to become a foster parent.

Charges against the quartet were reduced from felony offenses to misdemeanors after the state's star witness, one of the fourteen-year-olds, admitted he was a prostitute and then ran away. The boy later turned up and recounted a dismal history of neglect and abuse. He said his mother died of a drug overdose, his stepfather beat him with a baseball bat, and he left school after being raped by a friend of his stepfather's when he was ten. A social worker backed up his story. There was no way the boy could be presented as a credible witness.

In Charlevoix, the mainland community closest to North Fox Island, authorities had no shortage of credible witnesses. It was the defendant who was missing—the friendly millionaire and owner of the camp property, Frank Shelden.

Residents were shaken at the disclosures of his alleged boy-sex activities. He had once described himself as a semirecluse, but was known in the rugged country near Grand Traverse Bay as a good neighbor and generous man who had permitted various members of the community to visit the island for deer hunting in season.

People who live in upstate Michigan make judgments based on their personal observations, and they are hesitant to condemn others, whom they have known and respected for years, on rumors or unproven accusations. So they were not quick to believe the stories about Frank Shelden, the always pleasant, considerate, and hospitable man who granted educational scholarships to their children, clattered through the town's small business district at the wheel of an aging Oldsmobile to shop in their stores, and flew in and out of their airport in his private Piper Seneca II when he visited the attractive home he maintained on the island.

One resident who believed the charges was police chief Jack Mol. Although Mol had been a guest of Shelden's on deer hunting trips to the island and had an easy relationship with him, he had known of the suspicions and state police investigation for months. And he knew that police agencies are especially careful to make sure of their suspicions before charging anyone with sex crimes. The stigma attached to sex criminals usually remains, even when a suspect is declared innocent by a judge or jury.

Executives with Boy's Republic, Inc., a residential center in Farmington Hills for troubled adolescents, also expressed shock when they learned that Shelden, a member of their board of directors, was a suspect in the boy-love ring. But center director, Gordon K. Boring, also indicated that he was relieved when he was able to report that Shelden had no direct contact with any of the boys cared for there. Only professional therapists worked with the residents. Shelden had resigned a few months earlier from the board of governors of the Cranbrook Institute, a private boarding school for boys in another Michigan community.

Juvenile authorities in Grand Traverse and Leelanau counties, which were nearest to the island, also were quick to point out that no youths from their jurisdictions were referred to Brother Paul's. Most of the youngsters came from downstate communities or from other states.

Shelden was charged with two counts of criminal sexual conduct. One involved a fourteen-year-old boy in Port Huron. The other accused him of a sexual encounter with an eight-year-old Port Huron boy that occurred on North Fox Island. But Shelden never replied to the charges. When police went to his home in Ann Arbor, he was gone. He also failed to show up at his home on North Fox Island or at his business offices in downtown Detroit.

Grossman was also charged with criminal sexual conduct for an alleged affair with a ten-year-old-boy and a fourteen-year-old boy in the Port Huron area. And, like Shelden, he dropped out of sight before he could be arrested. Both men were named on federal fugitive warrants enabling the FBI to join in the investigation. Authorities later speculated that Grossman had headed for California, and, variously, that Shelden had headed for an island off Spain, the Caribbean, or the Netherlands. Investigators pointed out that the Netherlands has no extradition agreement with the United States and thus would provide a safe refuge for a fugitive.

Despite his prominence in the multistate **investi**gation, no charges were filed against the New Jersey man unnamed by police who was the alter ego of Adam Starchild. Richards was arrested months before the activities of Shelden and others named in the ring were brought to light, and he alone had been left to face the music.

Richards was contrite. He talked of having wanted to sever his ties forever with other pornographers and with boy prostitution long before the scheme collapsed, but admitted that he was making so much money he had not been able to force himself to quit. When he was arrested by Michigan State Police, he had built up his mail order business to some 600 customers.

He pleaded guilty in St. Clair County Circuit Court in Port Huron and on September 13, 1976, was sentenced to serve from two to 20 years in prison. Prosecutor Peter E. Deegan later explained that additional charges were not filed or were not pressed because of Richards' cooperation.

Richards' probation officer wrote the superintendent of the prison urging that the new inmate be immediately given a thorough psychiatric examination and that special care be taken for his safety. The young pederast was described as a suicide risk because he had overdosed after hoarding medication in the St. Clair County Jail. Both the probation officer and Richards' attorney advised that the frail convict had already been assaulted by other prisoners in the county jail. His attorney, a former schoolmate, said that the approximately 110-pound, five-foot-nine man was "totally defenseless" physically. It was pointed out that the nature of Richards' offense would quickly become known to other prisoners and it was urged that he be segregated for his own protection. Child molesters are traditionally scorned by other inmates, and they are often raped or beaten. In fact, Richards was burned on the genitals with cigarettes for refusing to commit homosexual acts.

In prison, Richards became an enthusiastic letter writer and jailhouse lawyer, filing motions, threatening civil rights suits, criticizing his therapists, and composing long rambling tirades to court authorities complaining of mistreatment.

In a motion to vacate sentence, he complained that he was denied proper psychiatric treatment in prison, which he had been promised by detectives in return for his cooperation in their investigation of the child pornography ring and for his guilty plea. He complained that he was instead assigned to group counseling that jeopardized his safety, health, and personal relationships by further exposure.

As "The Rev. Gerald Richards," he wrote to St. Clair County Circuit Judge Ernest F. Oppliger:

Dear Judge Oppliger:
You are working for the *Lord*— we live in a sick society and it's getting sicker every day. I am the first American Martyr to the "Boy Love Movement." Someday our philosophy and beliefs will be legalized. We

are now treated as criminals, and are compared, unfortunately, with child molestors (sic), homosexuals who go for young boys, those who would assault children and so on! We will continue to be persecuted by society until "Existential" psychiatry and the law moves in our favor. "B.L." is a 1,500-year-old virtue with *high moral standards*. I am glad now that the Appeal Process has passed because my imprisonment *proves* how sick this society really is. It takes *martyrs* like me who must be persecuted like the Lord Jesus to shed light on the discrimination of those who love boys as *Mentors, tutors,* and *Guides* according to the mystical and devine (ancient) practices of the *Dorian Culture,* (also parts of ancient JAPAN.)

I found *one* (1) man in Port Huron who *could* understand and appreciate my belief—that was Hiro Ota—a Counselor and psychologist at Port Huron Counseling Center. He knew I was sincere and he knows how I have had to *suffer* because of this *insane society*. I've *done nothing wrong* except to acknowledge that I've had some religious experiences—and some personal problems, the appearance of the *Boy Jesus* and the *messages* telling me to have Faith. By telling about these—it's a testimony to my sincere intentions. I will *not* associate with those who are not true B.L.'s. I have helped numerous boys keep out of juvenile trouble—and always preached about the poisons of drugs. Then, they trap me into giving information against myself—by having the "victim" call me for the name and address of a "witness" *against* me! *That's supposed to be justice?*

If I *had* gone to a mental hospital, it would have been bad for the B.L. Movement as people would have thought of B.L. as craziness—Now, I am convinced, even though my mind gets hazy at times due to some personal marital problems, that I must have been right all along. Jesus appeared at 3:40 a.m. and said plead *"guilty"*—Dr. Katz said to also—because our sick society does not yet accept B.L. Also, I would get help for some marital problems.—They lied to me there alright. It gets real confusing to me at times, but I've been a licensed clergyman for years and know I must suffer so much in this inhumane, barbaric, and insanely depressing squallor for the sins of the world. I refuse to give them any information or they'll try to keep me as a psycho here for *EVER* (20 yrs.) Keep up the Good Work—I pray for you, Judge, everyday. God has given me the *Mission*.

P.S. GOD WILL Forgive our Enemies—.

Sincerely Yours,
The Rev. G.S. Richards, N.D. God Bless *You*+ P.S. I don't *Associate with Anyone Here*—It's contaminating for sure!

More than a year after Richards was transported from St. Clair County to the Southern Michigan State Prison in Jackson, where he remained until his release on parole, Governor William G. Millikin signed a new felony law providing heavy penalties for persons using children under 18 in pornographic films or sound recordings. Support for the law was admittedly prompted in great part by the North Fox Island scandal. The law was signed on Marilyn Wright's desk in the city room of the *Record-Eagle* on New Year's Eve, 1977.

Richards was correct on at least one count; there are aspects of our society that are "sick." But police, prosecutors, and other elements of the criminal justice system were working on that.

[1] *Chicago Tribune*, May 15, 1977

[2] *Record-Eagle*, Traverse City, Michigan, April 4, 1977

[3] Dated March 4, 1977, in Chicago. Civiletti was later appointed U.S. Attorney General.

4.

Mission Work

RUSTY corn stalks loomed like shabby sentinels in the fields around the crossroads community of Alto, Tennessee. Most of the harvesting of the corn, wheat, and soybeans grown in Franklin County was complete, but an occasional pickup truck or flatbed bumped along the dusty paths girding the fields.

One of Alto's leading citizens, the Reverend Claudius I. "Bud" Vermilye, farmed a different crop. His cash crop was boys. And he was secure in his position as founder and director of Boys' Farm, Inc., which he established in 1971—ostensibly as a home and refuge for troubled youths.

Despite domestic problems that included separation from his wife and the presumed death of his missing eldest son, the Episcopal minister's professional life was satisfying. He was well liked and respected in the community. It appeared that the friendly, ambitious preacher was doing a good job shaping the lives of the teenagers placed in his care.

The approximately 1,000 residents of Alto were friendly, as the people of Tifton, Georgia, had been a few years earlier when Vermilye moved to that community to assume his first ministry as pastor of St. Anne's Episcopal Church. A clergyman assuming a pastorate has ready-made friends among his congregation, and it was easy for the Vermilyes to fit themselves into the activities of their new home. A native of Long Island, New York, Vermilye completed a four-year stint in the Air Force prior to graduating from Tusculum College in Tennessee with a B.A. degree. He then moved to the University of the South's School of Theology in Sewanee, where he earned his master's of divinity. Although he was older than most fledgling clergymen when he was ordained in Georgia, some of his ideas were a bit too liberal for some members of his congregation. But he was new, energetic, and easily liked, and the problems were worked out.

He was pastor of the church barely a year when he established St.

Anne's Home for Boys to care for disadvantaged and homeless youths. From all appearances the new pastor was making positive and necessary contributions to the community.

Trouble struck in 1966. He was accused of trying to seduce one of the boys in the home. One of the young men in the congregation complained that he also was subjected to sexual overtures by the minister. Vermilye resigned from his pastorate and avoided an investigation by the church.

Out of a job, he moved his family to Augusta and found work as chaplain of the State Youth Development Center. There he counseled troubled boys and provided advice and comfort to parents. He was there only a few months, but the job held up long enough for him to develop an easy familiarity with aspects of state government—especially facets of the welfare and juvenile justice systems relating to the care of homeless, troubled, or delinquent boys.

In 1971, he requested and was granted reinstatement as a clergyman by the church's Georgia diocese. He moved to Alto as vicar of Christ Church. Although relocated in the Diocese of Tennessee and licensed to officiate there, he continued to be responsible to the Bishop of the Diocese of Georgia.

In Alto, Vermilye was back in territory he knew well and among people with whom he was at ease. The hamlet is only 12 miles from Sewanee where he had studied for the ministry. It didn't matter to him that at Alto his responsibilities and congregation were substantially less imposing than they had been in Tifton. When the people of Franklin County worship, most of them go to churches associated with the Baptists, Church of Christ, or Methodists. Nevertheless, there are respectable numbers of Episcopalians.

As he had done in Georgia, Vermilye organized a home for troubled boys. Boys' Farm, Inc., was chartered in 1971 "to solicit funds for the purpose of operating a home for teenage boys and to acquire real estate. . . ." It was more than five years before authorities learned that there was another, darker purpose.

Vermilye had learned his lesson well in Augusta. He established an easy familiarity with the state bureaucracy and he understood child care and other social service agencies. Before long the first young residents of Boys' Farm were carrying their belongings in suitcases and brown paper bags into the $70,000 A-frame structure they were to share with the minister and his family. Child care agencies and parents from as far away as the state capital in Nashville, some 100 miles northwest, and as near as the Franklin County seat in Winchester were providing student-residents.

Some of the boys had experienced minor brushes with the law. Others were emotionally troubled or merely came from families unable or unwilling to care for them properly

Years later, Fred Drewry, the soft-spoken, white-haired editor of the Winchester *Herald-Chronicle,* remembered that the minister was "very personable . . . a good public relations man," and that he would sometimes stop in the newspaper offices to chat about Boys' Farm and the church or community-related activities. Occasional features were written about Vermilye's work, and the newspaper company even did a bit of commercial printing for Boys' Farm, Inc.

By 1975 and 1976, however, some agencies were beginning to take a closer and suspicious look at Boys' Farm. The state correctional department tangled with Vermilye when the pastor attempted to retain custody of a repeat juvenile offender who had been ordered to stay away from the institution and return to his mother. Vermilye lost.

Drewry, too, had begun hearing unsettling rumors. But they concerned the possibility of drug abuse, such as marijuana smoking. Nothing was said about illicit sex. Nevertheless, the minister's free and easy relationship with his neighbors was beginning to show signs of wear.

Perhaps his reputation showed the first signs of damage when his wife left and filed for divorce. Or perhaps it was as early as July, 1974, when his twenty-two-year-old son, William Mark Vermilye, disappeared. It was a mystery. One night young Bill Vermilye was seen at an off-campus apartment near the university in Sewanee, and the next day his car was found abandoned on the winding road leading to his father's home. The young man's empty wallet, which the elder Vermilye said should have held several hundred dollars, was found in the car. Sheriff's police and others searched nearby Monteagle mountain and dragged the beds of lakes and ponds, but Bill Vermilye was never seen again.

His father's thoughts were on other things, however, when he authored an article in *The Living Church,* a magazine about the Episcopal Church. In the article "The Farm That Works," he wrote about Boys' Farm and his own responsibilities and role as "a father figure." Vermilye declared it his belief that the wayward boys in his charge must relinquish their independence—a quality some of them were previously forced to nurture to survive, and "revert, in some respects, to a childlike dependence on someone and relive their adolescence."

He also referred to some authorities or individuals who disagreed with his concepts, and sniped at Tennessee State Juvenile officials whom he blamed for creating adult criminals. Criminality could be nipped, he observed, with a combination of "patience, forgiving love and continuous trust."

The article appeared on November 7, 1976. On November 4, sheriff's policemen and officers from the Tennessee Bureau of Investigation had swooped down on Boys' Farm.

The amiable Mr. Vermilye was absent, but two young adults and two fifteen-year-olds were present. The juveniles were later released to the custody of their parents. The older youths were not held but were advised to prepare for grand jury appearances.

Armed with a search warrant, the raiding party carried away more than 1,000 photographs of nude boys and adults engaging in a variety of homosexual acts. Vermilye appeared in some of the photos, as well as adult patrons of Boys' Farm who were eventually identified and traced to a dozen states.

Other pornography included three 8-millimeter movies titled *Kinky Kids, Wet Dreams,* and *She Loves It.* More important, a brown metal box containing names, addresses, and telephone numbers of 270 active and 87 inactive sponsors, other records, and letters with photos of nude boys were also confiscated.

Churches, civic groups, and individuals who apparently had no inkling of the true nature of the Boys' Farm activities were listed as sponsors. Other sponsors were obviously very much aware of the traffic in pornography and young boys that originated at the home. They had purchased pornography featuring the youths, and, in several instances, traveled to Alto to take their own photographs and to engage in sexual relations with Vermilye's young charges. Some correspondents were from locales as far removed as Australia and several provinces in Canada.

Several hours after the raid, Vermilye surrendered to a TBI agent at the home of a friend in nearby Tullahoma. The usually affable minister was grim and unsmiling when he encountered newsmen at the Franklin County Jail in Winchester. After he was booked and released on $10,000 bail, however, he emerged, grinning broadly, posed for photographs, and quipped: "I guess we've put Alto on the map."

He was initially charged with a single count of committing a crime against nature with a fifteen-year-old boy in 1974. A few days later, a Franklin County Grand Jury indicted Vermilye on eleven additional charges of crimes against nature, aiding and abetting crimes against nature (by photographing the activity), and contributing to the delinquency of a minor, offenses that investigators claimed were tied to a nationwide ring distributing pornography and the sexual services of teenagers to adults.

Investigator J.T. "Pete" Bouldin, of the District Attorney General's Office, and TBI agent Jim Parrott disclosed that Vermilye's activities at the Farm had been under suspicion for several months. The first evidence turned up when a roll of film confiscated in the Michigan investigation was developed, and pornographic photos of Boys' Farm residents were recognized. Materials confiscated at about the same time from members of a boy sex ring in New Orleans, as well as letters and photographs accumulated in vice investigations in Washington state and Connecticut, also pointed to the Farm as the center of a major vice operation.

Bouldin was quoted by Marilyn Wright as telling her that Frank Shelden's name was among the list of Boys' Farm sponsors. The investigator added that his probe also turned up a link with the Church of the New Revelation. "There is no church," he said. "It's just a referral agency which distributes the pornography around the country."[1]

The fate of Vermilye's home for wayward boys was sealed when anonymous letters were mailed to Bouldin's boss, District Attorney William Pope, followed by the arrest in nearby Winchester of a fifteen-year-old former student-resident.

The letter writer, who signed himself "Jilted," accused the priest of using his boys for prostitution and pornography in return for sponsorship fees for the Farm. The fifteen-year-old was a Chattanooga boy accused of a marijuana offense, and he admitted during questioning that he performed homosexual acts with other student-residents and with Vermilye at the Farm. He added that Vermilye regularly performed sexual acts with other boys there and encouraged the youngsters to have sex with each other while he took photographs. Beer and whiskey were sometimes provided to break down inhibitions before the orgies, he said.

Church authorities in Tennessee moved quickly to disassociate themselves from the troubled priest. It was pointed out that the Episcopal Church had no association with Boys' Farm and that Vermilye was not affiliated with the Tennessee Diocese. The Right Reverend John VanderHorst, Episcopal Bishop of Tennessee, said he had revoked Vermilye's courtesy license to officiate at services in the state, and the priest had already relinquished his duties as vicar of Christ Church in Alto prior to the vice investigation and his arrest.

State authorities with the Tennessee Department of Welfare denied that they sent boys to the Farm at Alto. A spokesman pointed out that state law required that anyone caring for two or more foster children under seventeen must be licensed. Vermilye once picked up application forms but never returned them, so it was assumed that he had dropped his plans to operate a foster care home. "We had no reason to believe he wasn't on the up and up," said one official. "After all, he was an Episcopal priest with letters of recommendation from all sorts of good people."

The State Corrections Department conceded, however, that at least four boys were transferred to the Farm from the Spencer Youth Center at Nashville. The youngsters were removed as soon as corrections officials learned of the investigation.

Paul Humphries, chief of the department's foster home program, disclosed that, although the Farm was never officially disapproved, it was given a low priority as a single-parent home. Nevertheless, he said, Vermilye visited the Youth Center often and had established a good relationship with some staff workers who considered him well qualified as a foster parent. They permitted him to take some of the boys home with him on weekends.

The Youth Center in Nashville was having troubles of its own. Barely two months before the scandal at Boys' Farm broke, officials launched an investigation of reports that homosexual rapes were occurring at Spencer. One of the residents reported that he witnessed one rape and barely avoided being victimized himself. Homosexuality was a constant problem at institutions like the Center, the director said. But he promised closer supervision in dormitories and shower rooms.

No one seemed certain of the exact number of youths who were either long-term or short-term residents of Boys' Farm. Estimates ranged from 10 to 30, but it appeared that no more than six were housed there at any one time. Officials finally determined that many of the boys were placed with Vermilye through private agreements between the clergyman and parents.

Six months after his arrest, Vermilye went on trial before Circuit Judge Thomas A. Greer in Winchester. The courtroom was packed when Pope began his opening statement. The attorney general promised to show a "continuing course of action" using juvenile males to commit "unnatural sex acts" with the defendant, sponsors, and among themselves.

"This was staged by a ringmaster, the Reverend Mr. Vermilye, with the motive of profiteering for Boys' Farm, which was allegedly a rehabilitative home for young boys," Pope declared. "Instead, the state submits, it was a house of horrors.

"When it all unfolds, you are going to see acute perversion by a mastermind trying to bilk the public, who were sick enough to buy his product and bilk these boys. I submit that this has been the greatest case of perversion in the annals of our state."

Dressed neatly in a brown suit and tie, the defendant watched impassively from a few feet away, seemingly unaffected by his characterization as a Fagin of sex offenses. He was prepared for a grueling trial. The prosecution had lined up some 50 witnesses for the prosecution, including several of the Farm's sponsors and some of the former student-residents. Vermilye pleaded innocent, contending that some of the Farm's sponsors conspired with certain boys to stage orgies and film pornography without his knowledge.

Thirty-five-year-old Bruce Dunlap of Wilmington, Delaware, was one of the first witnesses. He told the jury of 10 men and two women that he had been donating money to Boys' Farm for four years after spotting an advertisement in a sexually oriented adult magazine that read: "Priest needs help raising boys. Send donations." Dunlap said he visited the Farm three times. During his last visit, two weeks before the raid, both he and the minister participated in sex acts with a pair of tenth-graders.

A full-color magazine entitled *Big Boys*, which featured one of the student-residents on the inside front cover, as well as several hundred photographs of naked boys performing homosexual acts, were introduced into evidence. They were shown to the jury despite defense objections that they would "inflame" the panel against the defendant. Many of the pictures were obtained from Dunlap, and several featured sex acts between two brothers. Other pictures were confiscated from Vermilye's bedroom during the raid and showed two boys involved in sex acts on his bed. Some photos showed the use of artificial sex devices.

Several other men, including a paraplegic from Panama City, Florida, who had been crippled during the conflict in Korea, and who donated $360 to sponsor one of the boys for a year, testified about receiving letters from Vermilye with photos of naked boys involved in sex acts. He said he visited the Farm once and slept with one of the boys, performing unnatural sex acts.

He said he told Vermilye of the acts the next morning, and the priest replied that anything the youth wanted to do was "all right with him." A Nebraska man said he first learned of Boys' Farm through an advertisement in *Love Times*, a publication originating in Honolulu.

Some of the most dramatic testimony of the trial came from two former residents of the home. One sheepish fifteen-year-old who appeared in court with uncombed hair and floppy blue jeans said the priest first asked him to pose naked for "artists' pictures" and later urged him to pose with other student-residents for pornographic photographs. The youngster said he committed acts of sodomy and fellatio with Vermilye on numerous occasions and that the clergyman had urged him to engage in sexual acts with visiting sponsors. "He told me to do the things they wanted to do," he mumbled, slouching in the witness chair, "the things gay people want to do."

The disappearance of the defendant's son emerged during the testimony of Paul Cross, a twenty-four-year-old resident of Sewanee, former friend of the missing man, and former member of the board of directors of Boys' Farm, Inc. Cross testified that he and Bill Vermilye had sexual relations with two women at the Farm while the defendant took pictures. Cross was the last person known to see young Vermilye alive.

Seats in the courtroom were at a premium when Vermilye appeared as a witness for his own defense. He denied being a homosexual, denied engaging in sexual activity with any of the boys, and denied photographing the youngsters in homosexual activities. He conceded that he had taken photographs of naked boys, including his own son, and mailed them to sponsors throughout the country. During his college years he had once majored in psychology, and he insisted that he applied his knowledge by using the nude photos in counseling homosexuals to help them "sublimate" their sexual desires and "rejoin the straight world." He admitted, however, "I'm a little disappointed in the way things worked out."

Twenty-one-year-old James Puckett and fifteen-year-old Danny Smith, both former residents of the home, testified in Vermilye's defense, insisting he was innocent. Puckett's testimony caught the prosecution by surprise. It was in direct contrast to information he had given the grand jury earlier. At that time, he swore that Vermilye had sexual relations with him and photographed him performing sexually with other youths. At the trial, he claimed the pornographic pictures he posed for, which an angry assistant attorney general was waving in his face, were arranged and photographed by sponsors, unknown to Vermilye.

The younger boy said he was not getting along with his family and that Vermilye practically raised him. He also contended that the priest had no knowledge of the pornography-prostitution operation.

Sponsors came to the Farm while Vermilye was away and staged and filmed homosexual orgies, the youngster claimed. They then paid the boys and left the film to be developed in the darkroom and mailed to them later. Smith conceded at one point that when he was eleven or twelve years old the Boys' Farm director took a series of nude pictures of him.

The testimony of Vermilye and the two youths was unconvincing to the jury. It took the panel slightly more than an hour of deliberation to return a verdict of guilty to three counts of committing homosexual acts with young boys and of five counts of aiding and abetting crimes against nature by filming them. Judge Greer had directed a verdict of not guilty to one charge of committing unnatural sex acts with Smith following the startling testimony by the boy and by Puckett. Additional charges were dismissed at the request of the prosecutor just prior to the beginning of the trial.

Vermilye was sentenced to 25 to 40 years in the Tennessee State Penitentiary. Continuing to maintain his innocence, but peering ahead to the prospect of long-term imprisonment, the clergyman remarked that he looked upon his coming ordeal as a minor inconvenience for someone who has faith in eternal life. Anyway, he quipped, he needed some time to write and for quiet reflection.

Trouble continued to haunt Boys' Farm and participants in the case. The priest was barely pronounced guilty when perjury charges were filed against Puckett. The young man was subsequently convicted and sentenced to three to six years in prison.

A petition to have Vermilye declared a pauper so that taxpayers could defray his legal expenses during the appeals process was suddenly and mysteriously withdrawn. "I don't know why they dropped it," Pope observed. "All I know is we're ready for them and it probably would have been quite an embarrassment for certain people." There was speculation that some local residents had contributed to Vermilye's defense, and Vermilye did not wish to identify his financial backers.

While Vermilye was free on bail during appeals, four months after his conviction, he was arrested in East Ridge, Tennessee, on charges of reckless driving and of possessing a tape player without a serial number. The charges were later dismissed.

A class-action federal court suit asking more than $1 million in damages was filed by a Chattanooga youth against state corrections officials, Boys' Farm, Inc., and sponsors of the home. The plaintiff claimed that while he was a juvenile he was sent to the Farm by corrections department authorities, and when he arrived there, he discovered that it was "an operation for male prostitution and pornography. . . ."

He complained that boys like himself, who refused to participate in the activities, were beaten, harassed, and pressured to conform. "Others who gave in and did participate were filmed, and the films were distributed to the various participating sponsors, who then used the films to pick out a boy," it was alleged. "After sufficient payment to defendants Vermilye and Boys' Farm, Inc., the boy of the sponsor's choice was delivered to him for the requested activity and then returned to the defendant's custody."

A few weeks after the conviction, the five-bedroom home that had housed Boys' Farm, Inc. burned to the ground. Investigators said someone had drenched it with gasoline and lit it.

In June, 1978, more than a year after Vermilye was convicted, spokesmen for the Georgia Diocese of the Episcopal Church announced that he had renounced the priesthood and was officially defrocked. "Unquestionably, I could have pushed harder," the Bishop of Georgia conceded. "I would have to plead guilty to being busy and to a natural human tendency to procrastinate."[2]

There were other lessons to be learned from the case that were germane to the welfare, foster care, and juvenile justice systems of every state.

Church leaders as well as agency officials may have learned that they do no service to their fellow humans when, merely to avoid scandal or embarrassment, they refuse to take prompt action against an individual who abuses his or her position. When that occurs, the miscreant is free to move on, wiser and better prepared to profit by mistakes.

Some parents may have learned not to place blind trust in an individual or an institution merely because of its outward respectability.

State agencies need to tighten licensing requirements for shelters and individuals involved in the care of orphaned or institutionalized juveniles, including a better system of discovering those operating without licenses. Obviously, greater care must be taken to prevent sexual exploitation or abuse of children confined to foster homes.

Writers have traditionally used the plight of homeless children and their mistreatment as the basis for novels and plays. Classics such as *Jane Eyre* and *Oliver Twist* and, more recently, more lightly written gothic novels feature the abuse of children.

The orphanage was frequently painted as the villain, and, unfortunately, too often lived up to its shoddy reputation. Some years ago, reformers turned to foster homes as a promising alternative. It appeared that foster homes might indeed provide a more untroubled, family-like atmosphere for orphaned or socially maladjusted children. Regrettably, this has not always worked in the best interests of the child or the state.

Some foster children have been emotionally abused, beaten, mutilated, raped, and murdered. Girls have given birth to babies fathered by foster parents. Girls and boys have been enticed or forced into prostitution and pornography.

A seventeen-year-old boy in Chicago was permanently disfigured, losing an eye and an ear, after he resisted the sexual advances of his foster father. The man retaliated for his rejection by hurling lye in the boy's face and beating him with a hammer. A subsequent investigation disclosed that the foster father had been twice convicted in Detroit and imprisoned for assaults on boys placed in his care. The first conviction was for sodomy. The second, for dousing his victim's face with acid. A year after the man received clearance in Chicago to become a foster parent, a boy accused him of a homosexual act and was removed from the home. But by that time the unfortunate seventeen-year-old had already been placed in the home by other social workers.

Another foster father in Detroit, who was a supervisor for the judicial data system of the Michigan Supreme Court, was arrested after a fifteen-year-old boy in his care testified that the man forced him to perform homosexual acts. Prosecutors said they had been investigating the foster parent for some time but could not convince his suspected victims to testify. At that time, the Michigan Department of Social Services was already under fire because of the death of a seventeen-year-old girl runaway who was fatally beaten as she slept in her foster home. The operator of the state-licensed foster home was diagnosed as having homicidal tendencies and formerly committed to a mental hospital after assaulting a woman.

A convicted bank robber and federal prison escapee on the FBI's Most Wanted List was selected and licensed as a foster parent in California. His criminal background came to light when he was arrested for the execution-style murder of three people in Los Angeles. Another foster father in California had the habit of circumcising eight- and nine-year-old boys with a stone. One of the boys bled to death.

Placement agencies are not always solely at fault. The DCFS in Illinois, like child welfare agencies in many states, complained of being hampered by a federal privacy law that prohibits criminal background checks of persons who apply for foster parent licensing. States can enact superseding laws that permit background checks, and several have acted.

The same excuse was initially cited by Illinois DCFS spokesmen when it was learned that seven youths from sixteen to twenty years old had been placed in the home of a reputed bisexual who worked in a bar frequented by a gay clientele and had a record of 10 arrests for offenses including possession of stolen property, possession of marijuana, and theft. Records later showed, however, that Paul Musselman's initial application to serve as a foster parent was rejected partly on the basis of his criminal background. But Musselman appealed and, after an investigation by a private child welfare official hired as a consultant by the DCFS, he was approved for a license. He subsequently signed a contract with the department to care for as many as six youngsters at a time.

Although foster care children do not easily confide in police, Musselman was arrested on drug charges after one of the sixteen-year-old boys in his care complained to them of narcotics abuse and drinking in the house. He claimed conditions were intolerable, and then led investigators to a safe in the house which police later claimed held more than two pounds of marijuana. Several pornographic books were also reportedly confiscated.

Even though it would appear that Musselman's career as a foster father would have ended with his arrest, it didn't. The agency hired a supervisor, housekeeper, and tutor to care for the children at the home and ordered Musselman to stay away. Astonishingly, he continued to receive a monthly check for more than $2,500, and reporters and others learned that he also continued to frequent the home.

Four of the boys defended their foster father and refused to leave. The director of the Illinois DCFS subsequently determined that they could remain temporarily in his home despite the controversy. One social worker pointed out that Musselman was uniquely qualified to work with state wards with certain sexual identification and behavioral problems because of his street knowledge and unorthodox background.

He foster parented streetwise boys who could not function well in more conventional homes. Boys living with Musselman at various times included a homosexual, a transvestite, a boy involved in a homicide, a youngster who had been an alcoholic since he was eight, and a boy who was confined to a mental institution for 10 years.

One of them was also among a group of youths previously placed at a northside YMCA with a reputation as a hangout for homosexuals. Their rent was paid and they were given spending money. But the experiment at the YMCA was cut short after the boy overdosed on drugs, nearly dying, and newspaper columnist Mike Royko told the story. Royko also pointed out that some of the boys were supplementing their income from DCFS with prostitution at a notorious chicken corner on Chicago's north side.[3]

The Musselman case generated other criticism of the DCFS from police and a children's home director who complained that, as a matter of policy, the agency did not report runaways. As an example, the critics cited a young girl found by narcotics detectives hiding in the bathroom of a hotel room during an investigation. Checking her background, they learned that she was a runaway from a school for girls in a Chicago suburb. Administrators of the home had not reported her missing and refused to take her back.

Joe Monday, director of another foster home in Chicago, said the DCFS "just don't want any reports, missing or otherwise, of a ward of the department. Employees of the department told me they would be fired if they reported a runaway case or anything else to the police."[4]

Runaways are nevertheless easier to place than children like those living in the Musselman home. Children with sexual identity problems do not do well in conventional foster homes, and there is growing sentiment in some areas for special care in the placing of homosexual children so that they live with adults who understand their unique needs.

As gay rights have become a cause celebré, courts, welfare departments, and other child care agencies have begun in certain cases to permit adoption of children or foster care licensing by homosexual men and women.

One of the most notable instances occurred when Family Court Judge James Battista in Catskill, N.Y., confirmed the adoption of a thirteen-year-old boy by John Kuiper, a minister of the Reformed Church of America and a part-time writer. Kuiper, divorced from a wife he said was so much into the so-called feminist movement that she did not want children, adopted a son, Alden, prior to "coming out" and disclosing his homosexuality. When the judge learned that Kuiper had announced his homosexuality and was living with a male research engineer, he reopened the case. After extensive studies of the boy, his adopted father, the father's lover, and the home, the judge made the adoption permanent.

Earlier, another openly homosexual man, also a minister, the Reverend Robert David Dykes, was permitted to legally adopt a child in California. Gay rights activists looked on both decisions as precedent-setting for gay-parent adoptions.

Not long after the Kuiper case made national headlines, a row erupted in New Jersey when it was leaned that, since 1975, the state's Department of Human Services had placed several homosexual teenagers in the foster care of known lesbians in two homes.

A department spokesman said the practice began when officials realized they were dealing with a growing number of homosexual children, and that the youngsters were placed with lesbians only after approval of the natural parents. "Some heterosexual foster parents just can't deal with the kinds of problems these kids have," she said, "and some of these kids don't function well with other kids in the foster families." A clinical psychologist with a sexual counseling service added support, observing that the placements made sense and had the potential of enhancing the teenagers' self-esteem and self-worth.

Other sources were sharply critical. The Catholic Archdiocese of New York was one, and a spokesman denounced the state of New Jersey for apparently giving up on "any rehabilitation of homosexual teenagers. From a moral position, it's just fostering and perpetuating an unhealthy immoral situation," the church leader complained.

A couple of adoptions in California and New York and a handful of placements in South Jersey do not mean that the controversy over the appropriateness of homosexuals as foster or adoptive parents has been laid permanently to rest.

But Judge Battista may have been close to the solution when he commented about criticism he anticipated for his ruling in the Kuiper adoption. "Look at it this way," he said, "the man doesn't beat his son, and when you look at all the cases of child abuse you get from so-called straights, you grasp for words . . . You do the best you can and hope it works out."[5]

Los Angeles has group homes for adolescent homosexuals. Most of the boys and girls were street children picked up in Hollywood. Group and individual therapy is provided, and efforts are made to teach the teenagers that they can lead happy productive lives, regardless of their sexual orientation. Activities tailored especially to gay children are scheduled for them, but they are also encouraged to mix with straight youngsters so they do not isolate themselves.

Whatever the final answer for placing heterosexual and homosexual children who are public wards, seeking the solution has not been simple. A half-million children, representing a $1.5 billion chunk of the country's total welfare investment, are involved.

Most states compound the problem by failing to designate any one agency as the primary authority for dealing with homeless or wayward children. Cities, counties, states, even townships—and, of course, the courts—all take a hand in child care placement. Even states such as

Illinois, which has a centralized agency, the DCFS, attract regular criticism, including charges of losing track of their wards.

One of the major problems is that the system does not police itself. In most states, getting into the child care business is simple for anyone with even a minimum knowledge of how a city, state, or federal bureaucracy works. In some homes, children are worse off than if they were on the street. Although the majority of children in foster families, group homes, and child-care institutions are not abused, enough are to make foster care one of the most inefficient and saddest of all government services.

Osanka believes that foster care can be an acceptable alternative to parents who endanger their children. But too often the system is used as "a way-station," he complains. "Instead of terminating parental rights, they (child welfare agencies) keep the child in foster care, bouncing from one home to another."

There is never a lot of time in which to help wayward or homeless adolescents. They need love, roots, and a set of rules that are fair and unchanging. A child shifted to a dozen or more foster homes and institutions finds it almost impossible to develop feelings of security or trust. The trauma clings during his or her entire life. Some do not survive.

A young woman, who for a time was a resident patient at Utah Odyssey House in Salt Lake City, is one who might have survived with more timely help. Dr. Densen-Gerber told "Linda's" tragic story in a booklet, "Child Abuse and Neglect as Related to Parental Drug Abuse and Other Antisocial Behavior."

Linda was born to a Mormon mother who was a patient at the Utah state mental hospital. Her father was believed to be one of the attendants. She was a month old when she was adopted by her maternal aunt and uncle.

The uncle was alcoholic and violent. He beat his wife frequently in the child's presence and, when the girl was five, he sexually molested her. He raped her before she was seven, and continued the sexual activity three or four times a month until she was thirteen and ran away.

While she was living with her adoptive parents, her aunt frequently beat her, once so severely that she could not go to school for two weeks. Her home life was so miserable that she ran away several times, and by the time she was nine she was using drugs. After each flight she was picked up by police, placed in a juvenile detention center, and returned home. When she quit school at the end of the sixth grade, authorities did not bother to ask why.

Between the ages of nine and thirteen, she attempted suicide several times and would always be returned home after a period of hospitalization. She saw several psychiatrists, but missed many of her appointments because of the beatings from her adoptive mother.

Her marriage at fourteen was no happier than her tragic abbreviated childhood. Her husband was an alcoholic and beat her. She was married barely a year when her father-in-law, a Mormon bishop, raped her. She gave birth to three children, but again attempted to commit suicide and was abandoned by her husband after he told her she belonged in Salt Lake City's red-light district on Second South.

Linda underwent nearly two years of commitment in a mental hospital where was diagnosed as a schizophrenic, but was finally released and resumed care of her children. She moved more heavily into heroin use, however, and was again hospitalized. The last time she was released from the hospital, she went to work on Second South, and, at her own request, gave up custody of her children.

At last she found her way to Odyssey House where she spent the only two-and-a-half untroubled years of her life. She was twenty-nine when she committed suicide in a hotel, one week after receiving a letter from her uncle. A single tear had been tattooed below her right eye.

Ironically, Utah has one of the better systems for dealing with child abuse. But it didn't work for Linda. It failed her completely because none of the many adults who had official contacts with her and witnessed ample evidence to suspect that she was abused filed a report of their suspicions. Neither the school system, the hospitals, the psychiatrists, the youth detention center, nor the police apparently made any attempt to pinpoint her as an abused child, Dr. Densen-Gerber pointed out.

"Utah had a fairly sophisticated matrix of services for children and a mandatory child abuse and neglect reporting system. The repeated failures of persons in that system to take the initial step of reporting completely prevented the engagement of the resources designed to intervene in this extreme case," she said.

Early placement in a group home or some other shelter for juveniles may or may not have been better for Linda.

A reform movement that began in the late 1960s and early 1970s disclosed that many juvenile correctional institutions brutalized and dehumanized the youngsters in their care. Children were marched in formation, had their heads shaved, were beaten by staff members, and were sexually assaulted by the staff and by their fellow residents. Conditions were equally as bad in institutions for children, whose only crime was being an orphan, or for others who are throwaways, truants, emotionally disturbed, or mentally retarded.

Staff members of a camp in Florida for emotionally disturbed children were accused by a former house parent of beating or choking their young charges. State investigators determined that the accusations of physical abuse were unfounded, but confirmed that the children were "emotionally abused" by workers who cursed them and, in one instance, poured ketchup on a boy.

At least equally as disturbing, however, was the revelation that the former house parent himself had been previously accused of sexual assault charges involving two boy patients when he worked as a psychiatric aide in the children's ward at South Florida State Hospital. One charge was not prosecuted, and adjudication of guilt was withheld on the other after the man was placed on two years probation with the requirement that he receive psychiatric care.

In 1979, child abuse investigators in Chicago found that boys and girls were being sexually and physically abused in Chapin Hall, an institution with a capacity of 74 children. The previous year, more than $1 million was paid by Illinois for care of the state wards there who ranged from two to nineteen years. The same week, other investigators were probing reports that a foster father was forcing sexual relations on some of the six boys in his care. Investigators reported locating an album of nude photos of the boys and their foster father, a truck driver.

Authorities in New Orleans were appalled at the condition of the Louisiana Academy, a home for juvenile boys, when they arrested two administrators on charges of contributing to the delinquency of a minor and of falsifying public documents. One was also charged with indecent behavior involving a fourteen-year-old resident. The home, where boys were sent through juvenile court or private placement, was "a pigsty" in the words of one policeman. The arrests were reportedly an outgrowth of another investigation of a group of tightly organized pederasts operating in the city.

Selection of an obscure religious sect as sponsor of a group home in Chicago was no less appalling. When the DCFS placed children with the Dominican Fathers of the Old Roman Catholic Church, which has no relationship to the Roman Catholic Church or its Dominican Order, it was an experiment with an organization that was to be crippled by contract killing, reports of beatings and tortures of youngsters, homosexual solicitation or attacks, and housing of the state wards with ex-convicts, alcoholics, and mental patients.

The state withdrew its wards early in 1978 after widespread allegations that the administrators were performing or permitting sexual abuse and permitting improper supervision. But even after the children were ordered removed, one girl was found to be still living there when police picked her up for soliciting for prostitution at a nearby hotel.

Earlier, a fourteen-year-old girl was raped by a thirteen-year-old boy resident. Investigators were asked to probe other complaints of serious mistreatment, including a charge that one girl was forced to pull down her pants for a beating, many children were whipped, and some were made to kneel on stones for long periods of time.

The center director, the Reverend Richard Bernoski, was accused of inviting adults and teenagers to the shelter for orgies and homosexual activities. A probation officer said Father Bernoski, who was also bishop of the church, admitted that boys and girls were beaten and forced to kneel on rocks. It was accepted church discipline, he said.

Less than a year later, after state funding for his children's home had been permanently withdrawn, the Reverend Bernoski was dead. He was gunned to death by a woman in front of his home as a man stood across the street shouting, "Shoot him again." Eight months later, police arrested a twenty-three-year-old prostitute and a twenty-nine-year-old armed robber for the slaying. Another man was picked up later and accused of paying the first two to kill Bernoski because the priest had swindled the third man's grandmother in a phony real estate scheme. Still later, a fourth man was charged as a go-between in the slaying, and a new motive was announced. Prosecutors said Bernoski was murdered because of an internal power struggle within the church.

The church's notoriety and troubles did not end with Bernoski's death. In late 1979, another "archbishop" was placed on probation after pleading guilty to charges of contributing to the sexual delinquency of a child and of unlawful use of a credit card. Howard Fris was accused of an offense involving a fifteen-year-old youth. Fris and his two partners in the nonprofit corporation all had police records, authorities said.

The most outrageous instance of unscrupulous entrepreneurs, sexual deviants, and madmen hiding behind religion to qualify for state and federal funds to care for foster children is the late Reverend Jim Jones of the People's Temple. More than 50 children placed in the Temple's care by California social workers or under legal guardianships approved by the state's courts were among the nearly 1,000 victims of the massacre at Jonestown, Guyana. There may have been more. It was known that at least 150 children from Mendocino County, north of San Francisco, were in foster homes connected with the Temple. California prefers to place children with individuals rather than in institutions, but Jones solved that problem handily. He had Temple members listed as foster parents.

It was also known, although too late to do any good, that the children in the care of the Reverend Jim Jones were subjected to psychological, physical, and sexual abuse. Yet, until Congressman Leo J. Ryan's fateful journey to Guyana, no one among all the politicians and celebrities so anxious to be photographed or identified with Jones—the wife of the President of the United States, the governor of California, and activist/actress Jane Fonda, among others—ever questioned the cavalier foster care placements and legal guardianship bestowed on Jones's Temple by social workers and the courts. No one questioned the obvious illegal removal of some of the foster children from this country, or heeded the pleas of relatives of Jonestown captives who told of the torture and cruelty. And no one was anxious to talk of Jones's use of children as prostitutes to curry favor with politicians.

Senator Alan Cranston of California later estimated that hundreds of thousands of dollars in government child support may have been funneled into the cult's coffers. Cranston was chairing subcommittee hearings into the use of federal funds to finance child care facilities where youngsters are abused. When the hearings opened the committee on child and human development already had evidence that various institutions for abandoned, delinquent, or handicapped children were receiving millions of dollars in federal support but "providing abysmal living conditions."

"We have heard reports of children being strung up by the arms and legs in iron cages, held in solitary confinement in leg irons and handcuffs, tear gassed and placed, as punishment, in dormitories with older inmates who sexually abuse them," the senator said. Cranston added that millions of federal dollars were "financing virtual hellholes where children are beaten, starved and sexually abused."

Jones and priests of the Old Roman Catholic Church were not the only cult leaders to join in ill-starred partnerships with government agencies. Kenneth Wooden, founder of the National Coalition for Children's Justice and author of *Weeping in the Playtime of Others,* says hundreds of children were placed with the operators of Synanon in California.

Some reports indicated that the narcotics and alcohol rehabilitation center turned multi-million-dollar cult, which describes itself as a "religious movement and alternate lifestyle," was obtaining more than $2 million annually in public funds for the care of 200 children in Marin County. Children and others who claimed inside knowledge talked about frequent beatings and discipline that could take such violent forms as repeatedly slamming a runaway against a metal building. Some older members have told of compulsory marriages, divorces, sterilizations, vasectomies, and abortions.

Synanon still supports centers in various cities throughout the United States, even though it fell on hard times when two of its members—one a former Marine veteran of Vietnam, the other the son of bandleader Stan Kenton—were accused and later convicted of placing a rattlesnake in the mailbox of an attorney who had been tilting with the group. Paul Morantz was bitten, but lived. He insisted the murder attempt could be traced to Synanon. Only three weeks earlier, a couple he represented had won a $300,000 default judgment against the cult after charging false imprisonment, brainwashing, and kidnapping.

As Jones, Vermilye, and others were aware, churches and the ministry provide excellent cover for pedophiles who are either sufficiently business-oriented to acquire government funding for child care programs or who merely wish to use the umbrella of religion to meet and sexually exploit young people.

There are few communities of any size which have not at one time or another had a clergyman exposed for sexual involvement with boys or girls in his congregation or in some youth group. In Greenwood, Indiana, at the south edge of Indianapolis, it was the Reverend Clarence Barnett, a young minister of youth and music at the Calvary Baptist Church. His arrest in Indianapolis two weeks before Christmas resulted from a child pornography probe by the Illinois Legislative Investigating Commission. Two other arrests, both in Illinois, had previously resulted from the inquiry.

A Commission agent who placed an advertisement in a pornographic magazine said Barnett responded and offered him five obscene photographs of young boys for 50 cents each. Investigators were quoted as saying that Barnett was suspected of selling photographs in Indiana, Illinois, Texas, and Georgia. The minister had lived in Indianapolis less than six months, after moving from Warner Robbins, Georgia, where he was an assistant pastor of a church. Police said more than 200 obscene photographs of juveniles, a camera, business cards, and pornographic magazines and books were confiscated from his home.

Barnett eventually pleaded guilty to selling the obscene photos and was placed on probation and ordered to undergo psychiatric counseling. The prosecutor's office reportedly agreed, as part of a plea-bargaining agreement, not to press charges of his molesting three young boys.

The Reverend Richard Ginder once was a leading crusader against obscenity. He was a former associate editor of the nationally circulated Catholic weekly *Our Sunday Visitor,* and later, associate editor of *The Priest,* another magazine. Then the clergyman, who had campaigned so extensively against the "tide of filth" and "glut of sex stimulus," was arrested in his Pittsburgh, Pennsylvania, apartment. Detectives reported confiscating narcotics, pornographic magazines, and 2,000 color photographs of teenage boys and girls—and Father Ginder—all naked and engaging in a variety of sex acts.

Persistent, or lucky, pedophiles have no need to hide behind either church or government, however, to acquire custody of an unlucky child. Parents can be as carelessly culpable as placement agencies. Many parents are so anxious to ease the burden of care or to reduce financial demands on the family that they take the first opportunity to ease, or shove, the youngsters from the nest.

A fourteen-year-old Brooklyn girl jumped at the opportunity when she was asked to babysit for the four children next door. She had brothers and sisters, and the extra money would be appreciated by her mother who was having a difficult time raising her brood.

Consequently, when the two women and a man next door announced that they were moving to Ohio and would like the teenager to accompany them as a full-time babysitter, both the girl and her mother agreed. The neighbors said they would feed, clothe, and educate her. Five months later the mother heard from her daughter again, a telephone call from a booth in a service station in Waukegan, Illinois. The frightened girl sobbed that she had just escaped from the trio after being held naked in a locked bedroom closet for weeks, where she was forced to crouch in her own body wastes. She was released only when she was wanted to sexually service the man or the women.

After talking with the mother, the service station attendant notified the police. Less than an hour later, Karen Dalton and Barbara Filipski were arrested on charges of kidnapping and sexual abuse of a minor, when they walked into the police station to file a missing person report on the girl. William Dalton was arrested several days later in Cleveland where he had fled with his children.

Questioning of the suspects disclosed that investigators were dealing with a crime even more serious than the abduction and sexual abuse of a child. Dalton was charged with, and convicted of, the murder of a young Wisconsin woman in Kenosha, Blanchie Penna, whom he had beaten and strangled to death during a sexual attack. Miss Penna's sister was the mother of one of his children. Dalton's wife and Miss Filipski were the mothers of the others.

Dalton, who admitted to raping and forcing sex with women for more than 15 years, told detectives he might have murdered as many as 12 people. He confessed to slaying a sixteen-year-old Chicago girl he once worked with at a day labor center, and was named as a suspect in the sex slaying of a twelve-year-old girl near Waukegan.

The clan lived primarily off welfare, credit card scams, bad checks, and the earnings of Dalton's women who worked periodically as topless go-go dancers, strippers, massage girls, and street walkers. They collected substantial welfare payments, sometimes simultaneously from two or three states after the women used the children to sign up for aid to dependent children under a variety of names.

The girl, a petite seventh-grader whose mother insisted was a virgin before leaving to live with the Dalton clan, told authorities that she was not sexually molested when the group first moved to Milwaukee, then to Zion, Illinois, near the Wisconsin state line. "Then," she said, "everything went berserk."

One day Barbara Filipski instructed her to take a bath. When she stepped out of the tub, the woman took off her own clothes and, a moment later, Dalton walked into the bathroom naked. She said she was forced to perform oral sex with the woman and was then raped by Dalton. After that she was sexually abused almost every day. When she tried to escape, she made it as far as a telephone booth before she was caught and forced back to the house. After that she was stripped, her body hair was shaved off, and she was locked in the closet. Dalton also took pornographic photos of her and threatened to give them to police so she would be sent to "a home for bad girls" if she tried to escape or telephone her mother again.

Wherever children are, adults anxious to exploit them for money, power, or sex will find them. Some of the oldest and most respected organizations in the nation have tremendous problems protecting the very children whose lives they have set out to enrich.

[1] *Record-Eagle,* Traverse City, Michigan, April 5, 1977.
[2] *Chattanooga Times,* June 13, 1978.
[3] *Chicago Daily News,* May 17, 1977.
[4] *Chicago Tribune,* May 19, 1977.
[5] *Us,* July 24, 1979.

5.
Scout Troop 137

NEW Orleans is one of the most cosmopolitan, yet picturesque, cities of the South. Sprawling along a crescent of the Mississippi River, a mere 110 miles northwest of the Gulf of Mexico, it is an important port and a major center of commerce, with a busy petrochemical industry, a NASA Space Flight facility, and flourishing tourism.

Tourism annually contributes nearly $2 billion to the city's economy. People from around the world flock to the French Quarter with its colorful courtyards, unique ironwork, overhanging balconies, and an architectural blend of French, Spanish, neo-classic, and Victorian houses built flush with the street.

Historians talk proudly of the Battle of New Orleans when Andrew Jackson led a ragtag band of Louisiana militia, Kentucky and Tennessee long riflemen, and Barataria pirates to a victory over the British in the War of 1812.

But there is another, more sinister, side to the history of New Orleans. There are the fires, hurricanes, and annual plagues of yellow fever of the early years.

Curiosity persists about Storyville, the notorious red-light district where prostitution was legal for two decades around the turn of the century and where many of the early jazz artists first worked professionally in whorehouses as musicians.

The history of prostitution in New Orleans is as old as the city itself, hopelessly entertwined with the community's early affairs. Many of the first white women in the community were prostitutes, thieves, or other so-called fallen women rounded up in Europe and shipped to the New World. Long before the heyday of Storyville, which served sailors, fishermen, riverboat crews, and all sorts of womenless men from 1897 until 1917, New Orleans supported a series of red-light districts such as Basin Street and The Swamp, as well as thousands of freelancing bawds who lurked in the murky light of gas lamps.

Hordes of prostitutes from across the country flocked to New Orleans following Jackson's troops. Most of them stayed. When missionaries urged an early governor, Antoine de la Mothe Cadillac, to expel "loose women" from Louisiana during the early eighteenth century, he refused. "There would be no females left, . . ." he responded.[1]

Not everyone in New Orleans is proud of the lustier aspects of the city's early history. The desire to repress information about that facet of New Orleans was so overpowering at one time that newspapers and periodicals in the public library were vandalized. Stories someone apparently considered bad for the city's image were clipped and destroyed. The city's oldest newspaper, the *Times-Picayune*, discarded files of photographs in 1938 and in the 1940s, and the city council changed the names of some of Storyville's streets.

But censoring old newspaper reports of New Orleans' licentious history of prostitution did nothing to prevent a new sex scandal from erupting in the late 1970s. The scandal broke when police learned that a band of pederasts had wormed its way into leadership of a Boy Scout troop. The plotters exploited their position of trust to launch and operate a sophisticated scheme to seduce and use Scouts and other young boys in a wide-ranging child prostitution and pornography operation.

Boy prostitution was not new to the city. In the brawling, robust days of turn-of-the-century New Orleans, boys were easily procured for men with a lust for children of their own sex. At least one bawdyhouse was staffed with young boys in drag. But authorities were more tolerant then, and the operators were content to serve strictly a local clientele. The men who ran Troop 137 in the 1970s provided boys to wealthy pederasts and maintained connections with procurers and pornographers in other parts of Louisiana and in other states.

Police smashed the operation after an employee of a photo-processing studio noticed that some of the snapshots being developed were of men and a young boy locked in naked embraces and engaging in lurid sexual activities. One photograph showed a young boy performing fellatio on a man. In another, the features of the teenager were contorted in fear and pain as a man bent over him and performed anal intercourse. The studio owner telephoned police.

Investigators quickly pinpointed Richard Halvorsen as the owner of the film. Obtaining a warrant to search the home of the fifty-year-old New Orleans man, a volunteer probation officer and Scoutmaster of Troop 137, they impounded a file cabinet full of names, addresses, and pornographic photos of nude men and boys engaged in sex acts. Some of the material implicated other pederasts, some from as far away as Saudi Arabia.

It was apparent to the veteran police team that the New Orleans based operation had tentacles that spread to more than a half-dozen other major American cities, among them, Coral Gables, Florida.

A handsome, bustling city of clean, palm-lined streets and some 45,000–50,000 citizens, Coral Gables is a residential community, popular winter resort, and the home of the University of Miami. It is not the sort of city that usually figures prominently in Federal Bureau of Investigation Uniform Crime Reports, or that draws national attention for its violence or sex scandals.

Yet events there had provided the first hints of an operation involving interstate pornography and prostitution of boys. It was mid-summer of 1976 when a woman reported to officers in the New Orleans Police Department's Juvenile Division that she was suspicious of the Adelphi Academy in Coral Gables, which her son had attended on a scholarship. She had no proof but provided officers with a list of names of adults her son said took sexual advantage of him.

Peter Bradford, the school principal, was one. Bradford's friend, Robert Lang, was another. Lang had recently moved to New Orleans where another friend lived. That friend was Richard Halvorsen. New Orleans police immediately checked Halvorsen's background. His credentials were impeccable. He appeared to be a man dedicated to helping young people, a shaper of character, and an understanding father-figure who worked earnestly with Boy Scouts and parolees who looked to him as a role model. State authorities also ran a check on Halvorsen, and again he came up clean. Then the photo studio reported the obscene pictures.

Ironically, while police initially believed Halvorsen to be a bedrock citizen, suspicions of Florida authorities had earlier led them to official contact with him. Gathering information about a foster parent named John Douglas who was suspected of having abused his wards, state investigators turned up Halvorsen's name. They wrote to him, asking about Douglas' character.

Halvorsen responded with a glowing tribute, describing Douglas as a highly regarded, upstanding individual who was a pillar of the community. Much later it was learned that "John Douglas" was an alias used by Halvorsen.

Shortly after Halvorsen was taken into custody, two other local Scout leaders were arrested: Harold Woodall and Harry O. Cramer, both assistant scoutmasters. Cardboard boxes full of vile examples of chicken porn were confiscated. Some were so unbelievably filthy that hardened policemen shook their heads in disgust. There were photographs of men and boys engaging in sex with each other and with animals, and of men manacled with handcuffs and leather straps, or with rings piercing their nipples and penises. Some of the photos were of teenage residents of Boys' Farm in Tennessee. But the most jarring of all was a set of pictures of a man crouched on all fours as a companion jammed a fist into his rectum nearly up to the elbow.

Stacked with the photos were magazines listing young boys who were available as prostitutes in various cities. One publication from Titusville, located about midway along Florida's Atlantic coast, advertised 200 boys. Other Florida cities were pinpointed, including Coral Gables and Miami, but clearly the tentacles also extended to Boston, Los Angeles, Chicago, and to smaller communities in Michigan and Tennessee.

Investigators began identifying the men and boys in the photos. New arrests were made. The son of the woman who had originally approached New Orleans police about the school in Coral Gables was questioned. Soon police had two boys, eleven and thirteen, who told of being sexually abused by Scout leaders in New Orleans, and later at the private school they were transported to in Coral Gables.

Lieutenant Charles Rodriguez telephoned the Coral Gables Police Department to ask about the Adelphi Academy, explaining that, after returning home to New Orleans, two former students had reported that they were anally raped and forced by the principal and other adults to perform fellatio.

Sergeant S. T. Spooner took the call and was momentarily taken aback. He knew the school. It was less than a block from Police Department headquarters. It had both state and county approval and focused its services on boys with learning disabilities or other problems that resulted in poor performance in public schools. The Academy had other facilities in Dade County, as well as one in Tampa. The school had been experiencing some financial difficulties, but there had been no hint of anything improper occurring there. Spooner asked for more information.

Within 48 hours, he and his partner, Sergeant Anthony E. Raimondo, were looking over statements from the two former Adelphi students and their parents, and sifting through a handful of mug shots of men arrested in the probe by New Orleans police.

Before nightfall, Spooner and Raimondo were disembarking from an airplane in New Orleans. Detective Frank Weicks met them and drove them to headquarters. If the two Coral Gables policemen still had lingering doubts about the gravity of the case, those doubts were dispelled when Weicks showed them the photographs and other confiscated material at the station. The host detectives gave Spooner and Raimondo some time to look over the pictures and printed matter, then turned to the information about activities of the gang in Coral Gables. The sworn statement of the thirteen-year-old was incriminating.

The youngster had not needed any prompting. He was old enough to realize that he had been exploited and he was angry. He wanted revenge and he talked freely.

The child said that Cramer was the first person who sexually abused him. As Cramer was giving him a ride one night, they drove to the Scout leader's apartment. When they were inside, the Scout leader made him take off his pants and perform a homosexual act. Several days later, the thirteen-year-old was introduced at a Scout meeting to Halvorsen and Woodall. He said that after the meeting he was driven to Halvorsen's home and forced to perform oral sex on both men. Later, still another Scout leader took him to a motel and forced him to submit to anal intercourse.

With permission of the parents, the officers from the Coral Gables Youth Resource Unit talked with both boys. They learned that Halvorsen had approached the parents and suggested that their sons begin attending Scout meetings. In his capacity as a volunteer probation officer, Halvorsen had apparently learned that the boys were both from extremely poor families and were having difficulties in school. Involvement in Scouting would presumably improve their behavior. It sounded good to the parents. They were flattered and relieved that a busy, important man like Halvorsen would show such interest in their sons. It seemed reasonable to expect that membership in Scouts would benefit the boys and they were enrolled in Troop 137 with full parental blessings.

Halvorsen seemed to develop a genuine fondness for the pair. When he approached the parents some time later to suggest that the boys enter a private school in Florida, he had no trouble obtaining approval. He promised to arrange for full scholarships and provide transportation. There would be no cost whatsoever to the families. Raimondo later concluded that Halvorsen recruited at least four other boys from New Orleans for Adelphi the same way. Halvorsen and a friend, Richard A. Pass, were eventually accused of affiliating themselves with community volunteer agencies working with troubled boys to recruit prostitutes and models for pornography. They sometimes gave the boys presents, including guitars and motorcycles.

The older boys subsequently told the Coral Gables detectives that Bradford paid for their plane fare to Florida. He also supplied high school certification documents costing $150 a set for the boys. Once the youths arrived in Coral Gables, the boy said, he, his friend, and several youths lived with Bradford and attended school at Adelphi. All the boys were forced at different times to perform oral sex on their host and were anally sodomized. If they objected, they were beaten, sometimes with a belt.

The horror stories mounted. Boys told of having telephone calls between them and their relatives monitored at the Academy. If the boys appeared ready to complain of sexual or other abuse, a member of the staff would break in or cut off the call. One boy reported that he was once driven to a gay beach in the Florida keys, tied naked facing a cocoanut palm, and repeatedly raped.

The older of the two New Orleans boys filled more than two pages of testimony with single-spaced accounts of beatings and sexual abuse suffered at the hands of the school principal. He also provided the names of two other victims and the nickname, "Scotty," of an older boy whom he saw sodomized.

Spooner and Raimondo were disgusted but determined as they returned home. Both men were already feeling the thrill of the hunt. It was obvious now that a far-reaching, sophisticated operation had been uncovered with Coral Gables at the center.

Raimondo was appalled. Despite his experience in the police department, he had never before been exposed to such vile examples of sexual perversion. Evidence that the perversions were being forced on hapless children infuriated him. The father of a young man in a seminary and of an eight-year-old son, he was so upset that one of the first things he did when he returned home was to run background checks on the adult leaders of all activities his youngest son was participating in. No one would object if they had nothing to hide, he reasoned.

The police sergeant need not have worried about his son. But the experience enabled him to develop tips that he continues to offer to other parents for protecting their children. They are:

• Always be suspicious if youth leaders pay excessive attention to one child, especially if he asks if the child may go first to a public event, and later to a private affair, such as an overnight camping trip.

• Beware if children of one sex frequent an adult's house and children of the opposite sex are never seen there.

• Looks are deceiving, and it is impossible to detect a child molester on sight. But there are certain types of boys who attract pederasts. They are usually light-complexioned, fair-haired, slender youths. Boys like "Scotty."

Raimondo was puzzling over the identity of the boy, Scotty, whom the New Orleans youth had remembered. And he was certain that somewhere he had also heard of Robert Lang, one of the men his brother officers in New Orleans had implicated in the child sex ring.

Scrutinizing records in the Youth Resource Unit, Raimondo came up with the full name, Scott Edward Baker. The boy had been involved in the department's juvenile rehabilitation system for about eight years, from the time he was nine years old. He was from a poor but hardworking and honest family. Perhaps they were too hardworking, because his parents were unable to keep him from drifting into a series of minor scrapes with authorities over truancy and curfew violations. He was never accused of an actual crime.

Nevertheless, social workers had decided that he could be better cared for in foster homes than with his natural parents. He was placed for a time in a foster home, then transferred to Boys Town, a Catholic home in southern Dade County for wayward boys. At Boys Town he was listed for adoption, but he rebelled and was moved to another foster home. The history of his treatment while he was a ward of the state from that point on illustrates incredible carelessness on the part of authorities, according to the account of his experiences which he eventually related to Sergeant Raimondo.

When he was fourteen, he was sent to stay with a bachelor who lived by himself on a yacht. The foster father seduced him. Three months later, his sex education already begun, Scotty was returned to the Parkway Childrens Home. After two days, he was sent to another foster home where he lived for a month before being returned to the wealthy yacht owner. The boy was ashamed of submitting to his foster parent earlier and resisted his advances. But after several weeks of living in such close quarters with the man, he gave in again. After forced sex, Scotty cried.

Finally he was once more returned to the Parkway and his sex education took a new turn. When he was raped by a Black counselor, Scotty reached his breaking point. After the initial rape, he gave up and meekly submitted. The sexual assaults became a regular part of his life at Parkway. The counselor eventually began taking Scotty home to spend the night, and other employees talked admiringly of their colleague's dedication and the personal interest he was taking in the boy's rehabilitation.

Scotty was finally placed with another foster parent, a man already known to police as a habitual sex offender. Somehow the boy survived, and after several months convinced a social worker that he was old enough to take care of himself. He was finally permitted to return to his natural parents. A few weeks later, he had found himself a girlfriend and obtained a job with a company engaged in research with tropical fish.

As soon as Raimondo located Scotty, he gave instructions to have the boy brought into the police department for a talk. Then he stepped up his search for Lang and put out a pick-up order for Bradford, the former principal of Adelphi. Bradford had left his job and Coral Gables inches ahead of police. The Academy was sold to new, legitimate owners, who assumed management just in time to reap the hurricane of bad publicity that blew up with the demise of Scout Troop 137 and the search for Bradford, Lang, and their co-conspirators.

A few hours after the pick-up orders were issued for Bradford, Raimondo was informed by fellow investigators that neither Bradford nor Lang could be found. Speaking with Lang's former neighbors, police learned that he was well thought of. He had a good job with the U.S. Postal Service and appeared to be honest and a steady worker. No one could understand why he had left his home so abruptly. One woman pointed out that his reputation was so spotless that he had been certified by the State of Florida as a foster parent. There was every reason to believe that he was exactly what he appeared to be: a good neighbor and a kind, community-spirited man who took troubled boys into his home. Raimondo hit the ceiling when he learned that Lang was a foster parent. The information was confirmed at the Division of Family Services in the Florida Department of Health and Rehabilitation Services. Lang complied with the standards established by city, county, and state authorities. He had good credentials. Before moving to Florida, he was a policeman in Oregon.

Seeking Bradford, Raimondo and his partner learned that he had worked briefly for a steamship line catering service in Miami, but was fired after smuggling a young boy aboard a cruise ship. After that he dropped completely out of sight.

But Scotty Baker was located at the fish research firm where he worked, and willingly came to police headquarters for the talk with Youth Resource Unit officers. He was neatly dressed and courteous, and he impressed his listeners with his behavior as he told his story to Raimondo and Spooner. The youngster allowed his voice to drop only a few times while recounting some of the most embarrassing incidents. By the time he was finished, Raimondo and his partner were staring at each other in amazement, shaken at the abuse inflicted on the slender, good-looking youth and at the casual manner in which foster parents were selected. It seemed that everywhere the investigation turned, another foster father was found who sexually abused the young boys put in his charge.

Talking with the youth, Raimondo learned that Scotty's first foster father had been an intelligence officer in the U.S. Army, a former employee of the Central Intelligence Agency, had authored a half-dozen books, and was a successful businessman in Coral Gables. He was obviously a man who could be a formidable enemy.

Raimondo was not intimidated. He proceeded to build a case against the aberrant foster parent and against the other man Scotty had named. The boy submitted to examination by polygraph and his story was verified. Information was prepared for a grand jury.

The grand jury never considered the evidence. A telephone call from the Dade County morgue brought Raimondo and Spooner the most shocking and depressing news of their investigation. Scotty Baker was dead. He had stripped the insulation from an extension cord, taped the exposed wire over his heart, and plugged it into a wall socket. The sensitive young man had not been able to shake off the trauma of years of homosexual rape and abuse, after all.

Without the star witness, it was useless to prosecute the two foster fathers and the Parkway Home employee. However, although they were not criminally prosecuted, the foster parent licenses of the two foster fathers were removed, and the Parkway employee was fired. It was a small price to pay for a boy's life.

Scotty's death was evidence to Raimondo of the dangers to young people from homosexuals. He is convinced that a nationwide crime network exists to feed the demands of chicken hawks for young boys Sometimes the youngsters are sent half-way around the world to pro- vide sex for a wealthy pederast. Probing Bradford's background, Rai- mondo said, he turned up information about a boy who was about to be flown to the Philippines for a weekend of sex. Travel, hotel accommo- dations, and the fee for the boy were computed at between $3,500 to $4,000.

"Most people don't want to talk about things like this, not even police officers," Raimondo says, shaking his head in anger. "But it comes down to the fact that these guys are ruining kids. They're turning them into homosexuals and thieves, ruining them for the rest of their lives. It's a crime against nature. To me, it's even worse than murder."

According to Raimondo, young male hookers often steal credit cards from their customers. Boy prostitution, as does female prostitution, breeds other crimes.

In New Orleans, meanwhile, the investigation was expanding. Near-

ly twenty men were either in police custody or charged and being sought
in connection with boy prostitution and pornography. Boys had been
located who posed for lewd movies and still photos.

"It has been like dropping a pebble into water," observed Orleans
Parish District Attorney Harry Connick. "You think you've got it all
but the ripple ring keeps spreading." The DA noted that some of the
defendants had been previously prosecuted in England and in the Philippines for sexually abusing children.

In Chicago, where she was attending a convention, Dr. Densen-Gerber called a news conference and named New Orleans as part of the
multicity network of pimps and pornographers who were annually
exploiting as many as 300,000 boys, some as young as eight years old.
She charged that the youngsters were constantly shuttled among New
York City, Los Angeles, Houston, New Orleans, and Chicago.

Authorities in New Orleans pointed out that although much of the
activity centered around the discredited Scout troop that not all the
boys in the organization were involved. It was becoming increasingly
apparent also that many boys with no connection with the troop had
been lured into the ring's web of unsavory affairs.

By that time, Woodall had been charged with 13 counts of unnatural
carnal knowledge and was awaiting trial. He was committed for a while
to a state mental hospital suffering from severe mental depression and
suspected suicidal tendencies.

Fifteen charges were lodged against Richard C. Jacobs, a millionaire
from the exclusive Boston suburb of Arlington, Massachusetts, and
part owner of the New England Patriots. He was accompanied by two
lawyers when he surrendered himself to face accusations of engaging in
oral and anal sex with Scouts from Troop 137. He was officially charged
with aggravated crimes against nature, offenses that carried penalties
up to 15 years imprisonment on each count. He posted bond, then failed
to appear for his scheduled trial. Newspapers reported at that time that
he was also being sought in Britain on similar charges. At one time,
police believed him to be hiding out in South America and living on a $3
million nest egg.

Before the probe was exhausted, it had extended into 34 states. One
of the most disturbing aspects of the investigation was the high economic and social standing of many of the adults involved.

It was obvious that pedophilia was not a phenomenon related solely
to a few dirty old men who hung around parks and bus stations dressed
in semen-stained raincoats. The wealth and respectability of the new
breed of panderers helped them to deceive lackadaisical social workers

and agencies. Government funding and employees were frequently put at their disposal to promote and carry out their schemes. When the New Orleans Scout leaders were arrested, they had already prepared applications for state and federal funding to operate homes for troubled or abandoned boys.

As Halvorsen, Woodall, and Pass had demonstrated, the men who deal in boys and sex know how to worm their way into positions of authority in organizations that work with youngsters. One detective with the Juvenile Division in the New Orleans Police Department pointed out that Troop 137 was taken over by homosexuals who accepted minor positions in the organization and gradually worked their way up to scoutmaster or assistant scoutmaster. He explained that for a while they organized so many camping trips and outings that the fathers of the boys could not keep up with the schedule. When the parents were no longer there to keep an eye on their youngsters, the time was right for the chicken hawks to move in.

The situation in New Orleans was not unique in Scouting, although it appeared to be better organized than most similar operations. The Boy Scouts of America deal with more than a million volunteer leaders and it is almost impossible to keep a few bad apples from slipping by. The national organization has a file of some 4,000 sex offenders and other undesirables who are blacklisted from Scouting programs. But selection of leaders is made by local officials, and it is relatively easy for a determined individual to change locations and identities. Many others who might choose to abuse their positions of trust in an establishment that works with young people may never before have indicated that they were not completely trustworthy.

Woodall was never in trouble with the law prior to his arrest in the Troop 137 scandal. His family was respected, and he had a better than average education, reasonable earning capacity, and financial status. There was not the slightest blot on his reputation and no reason to believe that he might not make an excellent scoutmaster.

The shockwaves from disclosures that the troop had been infiltrated and taken over by chicken hawks were being felt nationally, however. The Scouts were already experiencing a declining membership, and the organization was moving as quickly and efficiently as it could to meet the changing needs of the young people of today. The trouble in New Orleans led a spokesman to concede that some 3,000 boys who would normally have been expected to enroll from the area had not joined. He attributed the slowdown in interest to the sex scandal.

Horrified Scout leaders quickly cautioned against overreacting and indiscriminately identifying the Scouts with abuses like those that occurred with Troop 137. They cited their organization's long record of service with boys. Spokesmen, however, awkwardly conceded that there was already some discomfort in regard to programs for both boys and girls because of sex scandals across the country and the brutal murders of three children during a Girl Scout campout in Oklahoma.

David Buerklin, director of field services for the Chicago Area Boy Scout Council, talked frankly to *Chicago Tribune* reporter Michael Sneed about the troubles with adult leaders. "Child molestation is an age-old problem, and we have tried our best to keep it from our organization. But bank robbers are attracted to banks like child molesters are attracted to youth agencies," he said.[2]

About the time that the activities in Troop 137 came to the attention of authorities, it was learned that a man wanted in New York for child molesting had changed his name and become a leader of different troops in Santa Monica, California. By the time he was arrested in California, he admitted molesting 300 children. He was eventually prosecuted for sexually abusing one of the young Scouts under his care in a back room during a troop meeting.

In Chicago and in suburban McHenry County, Illinois, some Scout leaders were arrested a few days apart and charged with molesting boys. Although they did not display the organizational abilities of the New Orleans group, they were accused of using their positions to seduce Scouts in their troops.

Twenty-six-year-old Patrick A. Weglarz, scoutmaster of Troop 294 in Chicago, and his assistant scoutmaster, twenty-two-year-old Charles Fugate, were charged with taking indecent liberties with an eleven-year-old boy during a camping trip. Several other Scouts told police they witnessed the sexual encounters. The troop was sponsored by a southside church.

During their investigation, police learned that Fugate had been convicted previously of contributing to the sexual delinquency of a minor and had been placed under court supervision for a year. Ironically, the troop charter expired prior to the arrest of the pair, and renewal was delayed pending the investigation of drinking and card playing by adult leaders during an earlier outing. Police entered the case when they were called to Fugate's home to break up a fight between him and the father of the victim. The day he returned home, the child had told his father of the incident.

The suburban Scout leader who got into trouble was Robert C. Sample, a thirty-five-year-old officer of the Wood Dale Police Department. A leader of Troop 65, he pleaded guilty to contributing to the sexual delinquency of a child after an incident that occurred in a motel during a weekend he spent with the boys at a ski resort.

Two Scout leaders in Worcester, Massachusetts, were arrested on charges of rape and other sex offenses after being accused of attacking several boys ranging from eleven to fourteen years old. Both men, who lived together, had been Scout leaders for two years, and one was director of a scheduled show called *The Wonderful World of Scouting*.

A few years earlier a homosexual ring preying on boys eight to sixteen years old was uncovered in Waukesha, Wisconsin, after the president of the Waukesha Memorial Hospital committed suicide. Two Scout leaders were accused of being members of the gang, and the dead man was publicly identified as a ring leader.

Back in Coral Gables, Raimondo was intensifying his efforts to locate Bradford and Lang and to follow up new leads. The tenacious policeman obtained old attendance records from the Adelphi School. He found several former students who admitted having sexual relations with Lang. The information, including sworn depositions from the boys, was referred to the state's attorney's office.

Equally as promising was information identifying a youngster from the Daytona Beach area who was a favorite of Bradford's. The man and the boy were said to be devoted companions. Raimondo and Spooner talked to the boy and his grandmother.

He gave police a sworn statement, 37 typewritten pages of lurid testimony detailing his relationship and sexual dallying with Bradford. He told of orgies, beatings of other boys, nude bathing, experiments with valium and marijuana, and of submitting to anal intercourse with the former principal. The youth said he first met the man when he was sent to Adelphi. When his adult admirer moved to a new city the boy was taken along. In fact, the boy related, Bradford was so enamored of him that he continued to telephone every few days.

It was an exciting development. It meant that Bradford might yet stumble into their net if he made the mistake of continuing to telephone his young paramour. But if he called, Raimondo and Spooner did not hear about it.

They learned from other officers, however, that the name "Bradford" was an alias for Peter Mueller, a naturalized citizen from Europe. Officers were prevented from gathering other helpful information from various governmental agencies and private companies because of restrictions spelled out by the Federal Disclosure Act.

A few months later, the Coral Gables policemen learned that Bradford was in Holly Hill, Florida, near Daytona Beach. They notified Volusia County sheriff's officers and the suspect was quickly arrested. He was carrying nearly $10,000 in cash and travelers checks. Bradford waived extradition and was returned to New Orleans to face charges. Bail of $50,000 was established. Bradford posted bail—and disappeared. A federal fugitive warrant was issued for his arrest, and authorities in Dade County, Florida, added an indictment on three counts of sexual battery to the charges already pending against him in New Orleans.

Raimondo and his partner were disappointed, but they were not the type to brood over lost opportunities. Raimondo was especially incensed and anxious to bring all the members of the boy pornography and prostitution cabal to justice.

One of his targets was Richard C. Thompson, Jr., publisher of a weekly tabloid, *This Week,* in Titusville, Florida. When Raimondo first told police there of his suspicions that Thompson was involved in chicken porn, they were dubious. Although Thompson was controversial and no special friend of the police department, he was a respected official in the local Democratic party and a leader in the community. Officers knew Thompson as the individual who sparked a state investigation of their police chief by mailing copies of newspaper articles to the Florida governor accusing the law enforcement official of fixing traffic tickets. The police chief was subsequently cleared.

From almost the first day Thompson arrived in the bustling little community across the Indian River from Cape Kennedy, he had drawn attention to himself. Energetic and gregarious, Thompson was soon appointed chairman of the Titusville Drug Abuse Commission. His tenure ended after six weeks when he tangled with the City Council over his efforts to expand the Commisson membership by adding three teenagers to the body. He also campaigned spiritedly for the eighteen-year-old vote.

If he sometimes immodestly bragged about his position as the scion of a wealthy family in the East who had added to his inherited fortune with wise investments, and talked proudly of a Ph.D. in psychology he earned at Georgetown University, it was excusable. He obviously enjoyed the recognition of his scholastic achievement, which most of his acquaintances acknowledged when they addressed him as "Doc" or "Dr. Thompson." And he obviously enjoyed his role as crusading newspaper editor, criticizing and picking fights in the columns of *This Week* with some of the most respected and influential members of the community. True, he was pugnacious and sometimes appeared to be overly anxious to quarrel, but there was no reason to believe that he would take indecent liberties with young boys or deal in pornography.

So it was a surprise when Titusville Police Sergeant Ron Clark learned from a background check that Thompson had served more than two years in the Florida state prison for showing obscene movies to minors and three months in a federal prison for distributing child pornography through the mails. Other blots on his character and background were also uncovered. His name was not Thompson, but Allen Andrew Parsons. He apparently changed names almost as often as he changed socks. There was no Ph.D. in psychology and no record of his attendance at Georgetown.

He was quickly ousted from his seat on the Brevard County Democratic Executive Committee. And as a convicted felon who had not had his civil rights restored he was charged with illegally registering to vote.

Once aware of his true background, Titusville police began probing Thompson's activities with young boys. Drawing on information from Raimondo and Spooner in Coral Gables, and the results of their own investigation, police arrested him on several charges of morals violations, including lewd and lascivious assault on a thirteen-year-old boy.

A search of his home unearthed a stockpile of pornography and paraphernalia. Among the ropes, vibrators, and panties, and obscene photographs, movies, magazines, and books, were diaries that recorded sexual encounters with young boys with nude photographs and notations listing specific acts, dates, and payment, according to police.

Authorities announced that Thompson was suspected of taking nude photographs of young boys who came to his home and then sexually assaulting them; receiving stolen property; falsifying circulation claims of his newspaper to fraudulently obtain legal advertising from the municipality of Titusville; parole violation; and failure to file income tax returns. Internal Revenue Service spoksmen were quoted as linking him to the publication of B-L magazines that featured nude shots of youthful males. One of Thompson's favorite tricks, police said, was paying boys to tie his naked body with ropes and then leave him helpless on the floor, as if he were the victim of a robber, until a roommate returned home and freed him.

The loquacious Thompson, who was once a champion high school debater from Fort Lauderdale and the first teenager to address the Florida state legislature, fought back. After more than two years of trials and other legal maneuvering, he finally was returned to federal prison for violating a special conditon of his probation that stipulated that he should not again become involved with pornography. A guilty plea to failure to file income tax returns brought an 18-day sentence, and he drew 60 days in the county jail on a misdemeanor charge of receiving stolen property.

He won acquittal on the lewd and lascivious assault charges but drew a seven-month jail term for tampering with a witness after admitting that he had offered $1,000 to a man to prevent a youth from testifying against him in the trial. There were no other convictions. Circuit Court Judge David U. Strawn ordered all the confiscated pornography, except that showing juveniles, returned to him. The former publisher was "entitled to the possession of pornography in his home—it's an American right," the jurist explained. He ordered the child porn destroyed, however, because of its "blackmail potential."

Thompson did not return to Brevard County to serve his time in the county jail after release from federal prison. Officer Clark was neither surprised nor disappointed. "I'm satisfied as long as he stays away from here," the young detective observed. "I don't care if I ever see him again."

Investigations and court actions were being wrapped up in Coral Gables and New Orleans as well. Raimondo was nauseated by Scotty Baker's death, and he pressed his campaign against chicken hawks more determinedly than ever. He provided information that led to morals charges against a prominent attorney, a former judge, and another Dade County official. And though it was outside his jurisdiction, he gathered evidence that helped expose a gay Catholic priest acting as a youth counselor in the Miami area.

Twenty-two men rounded up in the wide-ranging investigation were eventually convicted and sentenced for sex offenses involving children. Seventeen were involved in offenses directly linked to New Orleans and Coral Gables conspiracies. Woodall was the first to be sentenced, drawing prison terms totalling 75 years after conviction on 11 counts of crimes against nature involving Scouts from Troop 137. One of the boys was nine years old.

District Attorney Connick remarked that the sentence was "most appropriate" and "realistic." He added that harsh sentences, such as Woodall's, could "drive people like this out of the community." Orleans Parish Criminal District Court Judge Oliver P. Schulingkamp remarked in a five-page statement that "The facts . . . show that the defendant, Raymond Thomas Woodall, cunningly . . . exploited the naiveté, ignorance and/or situational status of the respective parents of the victims. He took advantage of and used—for his own unlawful lustful and contorted purposes—a great, useful and wholesome American institution, namely the Boy Scouts of America."

The former scoutmaster was denounced for damaging the reputation of the Scouts and for being responsible for "an undeserved blotch on the record of a fine organization which serves high human purposes." The judge said that, in returning the harsh sentence, he was considering the repulsive nature of the crime and the potential damage done to the young victims. "Indeed, it is likely . . . a trauma and a stigma which will haunt the young victims throughout the course of their lives and probably to their graves." The angry jurist pointed out that families shared the psychic trauma with the boys.

Halvorsen, Cramer, Lang, and Pass were also convicted, along with about a dozen other defendants. The men were sentenced to 2,640 years of penitentiary time. Other convictions were returned in cities across the country. The work of the detectives from Coral Gables, Titusville, and New Orleans had been done well.

Even Scotty Baker's death was not without meaning. His suicide, and the hideous burning of a sixteen-year-old foster child drenched with gasoline and set afire outside his Opa-locka home at about the same time, sparked a sweeping investigation in Dade County of the sexual and other abuse of children in state-licensed homes. Vernon Swain survived the burns inflicted by two other boys who claimed their foster father had instructed them to set the victim on fire for misbehavior. The boys' guardian was acquitted of a charge of attempted murder, but lost his license as a foster parent after an investigation disclosed that he had a long arrest record.

---

[1] Al Rose, *Storyville, New Orleans,* The University of Alabama Press, 1974.

[2] *Chicago Tribune,* July 10, 1977.

6.

A Secret With Daddy

TRADITIONALLY, home and school are the two most strengthening and protective influences in the life of a child. In the home the first steps are taken to mold character and personality. Learning begins there, then continues at the school which becomes the surrogate parent, caring for and nurturing the child while protecting him or her from harm.

Both home and school are designed and expected to generate absolute trust in children—and both sometimes violate that trust in the worst possible manner. There are an estimated 25 million incest victims in the United States, who have been sexually violated as children by a parent, step-parent, sibling, uncle, aunt, grandparent, or other close relative. Thousands more naive girls and boys are seduced or coerced into sexual activity with trusted instructors or non-teaching employees of schools, including janitors and school bus drivers. Pedophiles whom children love, respect, or fear, including incestuous relatives, know how to manipulate the sexual and emotional feelings of the innocent and malleable.

According to Douglas Besharove, former director of the U.S. Department of Health, Education and Welfare's National Center on Child Abuse and Neglect, an estimated 60,000 to 100,000 children in this country are sexually maltreated every year by family members or close family friends. Authorities with federally sponsored centers for runaways report that from 20 to 40 percent of the children they shelter or otherwise assist were sexually abused by a family member or someone close to the family.

Using a research grant from the National Institute of Drug Abuse to study drug-related child abuse, Odyssey House learned that 44 percent of the women treated for narcotic problems were cross-generational incest victims—meaning that they had been raped or otherwise sexually molested by someone not of their own generation, such as a parent, step-parent, or grandparent. Seventy-five percent of the victims were abused before they were twelve, and 45 percent before they were nine. About one-fourth of the victims were molested with the knowledge of their mothers.

Many of the children are first molested before they are old enough to have any comprehension of the act, and are too helpless to resist the assault. A study of Philadelphia incest victims indicated that one-third of the subject children were five or younger when first approached. The majority of the remaining children, 48 percent of the entire sample, ranged from six through twelve years old.

Dr. Densen-Gerber tells of a young Massachusetts woman who was rehabilitated at Odyssey House after she turned to heroin and other drugs following a childhood made miserable by an alcoholic father who forced her to have sexual intercourse with him, and a mother who violently beat her. She was nine when her mother actively consented to the girl taking her place in the marriage bed. The mother had more pregnancies and children than she could cope with and felt that as a Catholic she preferred this alternative to using birth control or sterilization.

The girl was forced to submit to her father two or three times each week until her menstrual periods started and she was replaced by a younger sister who was considered unlikely to become pregnant. The older girl left home at fifteen, was married at seventeen, and divorced her husband a few months later when she learned he had made sexual advances to her sister.

Shortly after that, her heroin-addicted brother moved in with her and turned her on to the narcotic before her first child was born. Her drug abuse continued until the time she was pregnant with her third child and entered Odyssey House for treatment. She was rehabilitated after many months of care.

There is a definite relationship between incest in the young female and subsequent antisocial behavior, Dr. Densen-Gerber observed. An estimated one in four women in prison has a history of incest—and social scientists have learned more recently that a large number of male prisoners had similar experiences during their childhood.[1]

Cross-generational incest mutilates self-image and feelings of self-worth. The results can be especially damaging to the later relationships of female victims with husbands, lovers, or other men toward whom they should logically have a strong emotional attachment. Women who have been child incest victims frequently have difficulty demonstrating affection in a non-sexual manner. No one knows exactly how destructive early sexual abuse may be, but children are especially vulnerable at an age when they are striving to cope with psychological and physiological changes within their bodies and to define differences between sex and love. Although it is much less common than father-daughter incest, mother-son incest also occurs, and the psychological trauma that results can be devastating.

Brother-sister incest also occurs, of course. It is one of the most common forms of interfamilial sex and is thought to be the least harmful. Every imaginable combination of incest occurs, even mother-daughter.

Antisocial acts appear to be one common response of children to the frustrations and guilt they develop from incestuous relations. The father, step-father, or other sexual partner of their mother, or other perpetrator, usually cautions or theatens the victim not to tell anyone about the incident. Guilt is commonly associated by the child with keeping the secret and with the deceit that must often be practiced on the other parent.

The guilt feelings can be increased if a child informs another adult about the activity and it results in the father or other breadwinner being taken away to jail or to a hospital. The child is then cast as being responsible for the family's subsequent financial, emotional, legal, and other troubles. Very often, she, or he, misses the parent or other authority figure, who is still loved.

Research has proved that many children never fully recover from the psychological trauma and the belief that they were somehow responsible. The burden of proof in incest cases also usually rests with the victim, who has already been betrayed by one of the most imposing authority figures in his or her life. It is a burden that three-, four-, or five-year-olds, as well as most older children, cannot handle.

The reactions of mothers vary, but quite often they blame the child for lying, for initiating the sexual activity, or for being responsible for having "Daddy sent away." One young girl in a treatment program told of being slapped and called a liar when she mustered up the courage to tell her mother that she was forced almost nightly to have coitus with her father. Another girl was thrown out of the house. Still another became the family pariah after informing on her father. She was branded as a liar, then ignored by other members of the family. If she was in a room when her father walked in, he would curse and stalk out. One young woman said that, despite more than five years of psychotherapy, she was never able to relieve herself of guilt feelings over the knowledge that her testimony caused her father to be sent to jail.

A young woman counseled by Dr. Osanka was sexually abused by her father from the time she was three, physically abused by her mother, and emotionally abused by both until she became pregnant at a party of high school classmates and married. Her pregnancy ended 12 years of sexual abuse. Her father did not want her any more, she learned, because she had shared her sexual favors with someone else. And the pregnancy had brought disrespect to the family.

The patient remembered that her father was considered "an angel" for living with his wife who was known for her irrational explosions of temper and violent acts. The woman was known by neighbors to chase her daughter with a butcher knife, sometimes slashing the girl's hands and feet. Neighbors never intervened or reported the abuse.

Almost all child abuse laws make it mandatory for persons in positions of authority, such as teachers, social workers, doctors, and others, to report suspected cases of child abuse. They need have only reasonable suspicion that abuse is occurring to justify filing reports. The same laws provide immunity from criminal and civil charges.

A study by a research team at the University of Washington School of Medicine in Seattle, however, indicated that as many as nine out of ten instances of sexual abuse of children in this country are unreported to authorities, even though most of the cases brought to the attention of doctors involve serious injuries. Laws mandating reports are routinely ignored. Of 96 doctors who replied to an anonymous letter survey of general practitioners and pediatricians, fewer than one-half said they generally reported child molestation to authorities. Two-thirds of the physicians indicated that they believed it would be harmful to the families if the incidents were reported because the legal justice system is not set up to deal with the sexual abuse of children without inflicting additional harm on everyone involved.

The injuries inflicted on Dr. Osanka's patient from the knife and from other physical and sexual assaults were never reported to authorities by anyone who came in contact with her. She was aware that no one in the family got along well together. But she was an adult before she realized that her father was using her as a sexual surrogate for his wife.

She remembers vividly one time when she was sixteen and ran away. She was picked up a few days later and placed in a juvenile detention home. It was one of the happiest periods of her childhood. She knew, sitting in the room looking at the bars on the doors and windows, that she could go to bed at night and not be sexually molested by her father, or threatened, beaten, or cut with a knife by her mother. The safe period was short and she was returned home after a few days. No one had asked her why she ran away. She recalls that when she was being sexually used by her father, she had never heard of incest and had no concept of what it was. She assumed that the same sort of behavior occurred in every family.

When pregnancy finally enabled her to escape from the intolerable life at home, she did not stop being an incest victim. The marriage did not last long. Nor did three others. In each of her marriages, she unconsciously selected men who abused her emotionally and physically. She could not stand a man who adored her, and instead sought out men who were abusive.

During her third marriage, she became so agitated at the thought that her husband might be involved in an incestuous relationship with her little girl that she became physically ill. It was much later before she realized that they were simply engaged in normal father-daughter cuddling. She is one of those people, whom Dr. Osanka calls "the walking wounded," who will remain incest victims for the rest of their lives.

Divorce is common among incest victims. Many women who have been sexually molested in the home as children cannot hold marriages together because of distrust, according to Dr. Osanka. "So you see four and five and six marriages." Others, he said, avoid marriage because they fear becoming pregnant and bearing female children who may be abused as they were.

Studies have shown that female incest victims often choose mates who sexually abuse their own children. "It's not likely that a female victim will abuse her own child, except that in some circumstances she selects a man who is very similar to her own father in personality structure," Dr. Osanka says. "So she sometimes adds her own confusion as to what is right and wrong, and she may set up her own child to be sexually molested. It's subconscious, we think. But it's clear that there is some setting up of the child." Males who have been sexually abused by a father or another man may grow up to molest other youngsters, many times selecting children of the approximate age they were when they were abused.

There is a popular myth that most incest occurs among the lower income, ghetto, or minority families. That may not be true. Most students of the phenomena believe it is not so. It is found in the homes of doctors, lawyers, accountants, farmers, policemen, factory workers, and welfare recipients. It occurs among all religions and races. There appears to be especially high occurrence in families with strong religious taboos. Despite his wife's obvious behavior problems, the father of Dr. Osanka's patient was a respected member of his community. Most men who sexually molest children in their families are respected by outsiders.

Incest is often depicted in modern plays and cinema. One of the most recent examples occurred in the movie *Chinatown*, which dealt with a father who seduced his daughter. Incest is spoken of in the Bible. It occurs in the creation mythology of many great religions, between mother and son, father and daughter, brother and sister. Institutionalized incest has occurred among the nobility of various cultures and civilizations, often in order to protect the throne and the royal bloodline. Ancient Egypt and Hawaii, where coitus between brothers and sisters was encouraged, are two of the best-known examples.

Delving into ancient Greek mythology for the story of a young man who murdered his father and became his mother's lover, Sigmund Freud coined the psychoanalytical term "Oedipus complex," which he used to describe jealousy of a son for his father and a subconscious or conscious sexual longing for his mother.

Signs that a child is being sexually abused are usually less obvious than with a battered child. A black eye or a broken arm is easily discernible. A battered ego, even physical damage to genitals which are covered with clothing, is less obvious. Nevertheless, there are signals that teachers, social workers, health care and other professionals, or parents who are aware and caring can recognize as indicators of father-daughter incest. Overpossessiveness or jealousy by the father of boyfriends, or school chums, is one indication. A mother who appears to be jealous of her husband's attention to her daughter is another.

Victims themselves may react to incest by bedwetting, depression, sudden changes in behavior, emotional disturbances, excessive nervousness, trouble in school, excessive bathing, or secretiveness. Some young girls may become particularly flirtatious around their father or other men, behaving as seductive Lolitas because they have been "taught" that it is the way to get attention and obtain love.

Another common reaction, especially among older children, is running away. They are the brave ones. Many children who have become prostitutes or models for pornography are runaways who have fled incestuous homes during early adolescence. By that time, they have already been taught that their bodies are commodities of value to others, and that they are salable.

Investigation of the runaway of three sisters in Red Bank, Tennessee, led to the arrest of their father, a Marine gunnery sergeant, for sexually molesting them. The girls were ten, twelve, and fourteen when authorities with the Tennessee State Human Services Department and other agencies learned of the problem. He had begun enticing and coercing them into sexual behavior when he was stationed in Hawaii and continued after he was reassigned to duty near Chattanooga.

Police were notified after the sisters crawled through a bedroom window and ran to the home of a friend for help. Police said a search of their home turned up some 400 pornographic books or magazines and nude photographs of the girls. It is generally difficult to convict suspects of engaging in interfamilial sex. The victims are often too young, too frightened, and too confused to complain—or they are not believed. They make poor witnesses. Faced with the accusations of three daughters, however, the Marine admitted photographing the girls nude, fondling them, and performing other sex acts short of coitus, and was sentenced to prison on four morals charges.

Incest damages the entire family, and therapeutic programs that are beginning to become available generally recognize that. If the perpetrator is the husband and father, and he has not been sent to jail, he is treated with other family members.

Studies indicate that father-daughter incest occurs many times when there have been marital problems relating to sex; when loss of a job causes feelings of impotence by the family breadwinner and fathers reach out to their child for emotional support through sexualization; and after various other traumas. The incestuous parent has been described as a victim of temporary regression in his sexuality who seeks love or affection he may have missed as a child. The motives are varied and occult.

The basic relationship between a child who has been abused by his or her parent and that parent has been altered forever. Neither the parent nor the child can ever again interact on the same level. Interactions in communication, discipline, play, and other relationships are all changed.

The principal victims are sometimes kept in foster homes, with relatives, or in juvenile institutions, while the parents, and sometimes the siblings, undergo initial treatment. Peer group sessions and psychodrama are becoming increasingly popular treatment.

The best-known and most highly respected treatment program in the country may be the one in San Jose, California, developed by Dr. Henry Giaretto who serves as director of the Child Sexual Abuse Treatment Program of the Juvenile Probation Department of Santa Clara County. A humanistic psychologist, Dr. Giaretto approaches interfamilial sex as a symptom of the overall ailment—the troubled family. Most families can be saved, he says, if a proper vehicle is provided to help the family re-enter society as a strong cohesive entity.

Testifying before a Congressional study panel, he described the program as "a resocialization process. . . . We borrow from the winner family to teach the loser family," he said. "This is really what it amounts to. Traditional therapy . . . would be insufficient in the treatment of sexually abusive families. Certainly punishment doesn't work. The self-help concept is useful, but it is not sufficient." The therapist claimed that 90 percent of the families entered in the program were salvaged and that 95 percent of the children were able to return home.

A key element in the teatment is the requirement that the father have a face-to-face confrontation with the wronged child and accept full responsibility for whatever occurred. Mothers, too, must face the child and admit a share of the responsibility for faults in the marriage and family that contributed to the abuse. Some women, perhaps exhausted from child-bearing or for other reasons, consciously or subconsciously push their husbands and daughters into incestuous relations. Almost invariably they then react with jealousy toward the child. The mother's attitude can be among the most traumatic aspects of the total incest experience for the victim. Mothers are expected to be protective and loving, and for them to act otherwise is a betrayal that children are aware of.

Children who have been sexually traumatized at a very young age tend to sexualize the world. They cannot relate to anything except in sexual terms. "One of the reasons it's so difficult to treat a sexually traumatized child is because you can't touch them," according to Dr. Densen-Gerber. "You can't hold, you can't do any of the normal things. You might do something as innocent as putting your arm around a child in a normal comforting way and that child will misinterpret it. It's nothing more than normal touching, and it's perceived as a threat."

Treatment of the principal victim can be lengthy and demanding. Physical damage in the case of very young children, or in instances where sexual assaults have been particularly brutal and rough, can usually be repaired in much less time than the psychological and emotional destruction. Broken spirits are not quickly restored. But even examination of child victims of incest or sexual molestation by others not necessarily family members presents unique problems.

A paper titled "Emergency Management of Sexually Abused Children: The Role of the Pediatric Resident," cites a study of the cases of 100 sexually abused youngsters seen by pediatric residents at the University of California at Irvine Medical Center and provides insight into the special difficulties of working with young victims of sexual abuse.

Prepared by Donald P. Orr, M.D., and Susan V. Prietto, M.S.W., the paper deals with emergency treatment of child victims of sexual abuse, and includes such functions as collection of evidence samples and pelvic and other physical examinations, as well as protocol for dealing with patients and families.

During the approximate two-year period, 86 girls and 14 boys ranging from one through fifteen were examined. The mean age was just over nine years old, and 27 percent of the children were six or younger. Most of the cases involved allegations of genital contact, usually vaginal or rectal penetration. The suspected perpetrator was known by the victim in 74 percent of the cases, and half of them were relatives, most often a father, step-father, grandfather, or the mother's boyfriend.

Orr and Prietto reported that 12 of the 14 boys were allegedly assaulted by their fathers or step-fathers. "This incidence is surprising, as homosexual incest is rarely reported," they wrote. It was added that "at an unconscious level, the mother allowed and subtly encouraged her sons to substitute sexually for her."

Also of special interest was an initial reluctance by senior pediatric residents to become involved in the examination and treatment. Most expressed concern about inexperience in performing pelvic examinations. As their confidence and experience increased, however, they began to acknowledge that their reluctance had in reality been tied to "their strong revulsion in regard to child sexual abuse."[2]

There are other ways in which the trust and helplessness of children are betrayed by parents and other family members. Police in Detroit arrested a laborer on charges of persuading his fourteen-year-old daughter to prostitute herself for pocket money. They said he drove her to the red-light district and waited to collect from her customers. In suburban Pittsburgh, thirteen- and fourteen-year-old sisters were forced into prostitution by their mother. They were forced to have sexual relations with four to six clients almost daily for nearly a year before one of the sisters telephoned police and reported being raped. Investigators said the woman was collecting $5 to $20 for each act. One of the girls had not attended school for weeks. She had no shoes.

In Rockingham County, New Hampshire, members of the sheriff's department arrested a man who was paying his daughters for every inch they permitted a bottle to be inserted into their vaginas. A spokesman said there was a high incidence of incest in both the county and state, and one deputy said he knew of at least 27 cases where pornography was present as an instigating factor in intrafamilial sex involving children.

An Elkhart, Indiana, man admitted that child relatives were among his models after police arrested him and a woman companion and confiscated one of the largest caches of kiddie porn ever found in the state. During the trial of Earl A. Beach, witnesses testified that he blackmailed the children into committing sexual acts with each other and with adults. Most of the children were from eight to eleven years old.

Police carried two truckloads of child pornography from Beach's attic apartment, along with 19 cameras and photo-processing equipment. Beach was sentenced to prison for distributing obscene material involving children under sixteen. Charges against his alleged companion were dismissed after she agreed to testify against him.

Case histories at Odyssey House, and at other social agencies servicing sexually abused children, read like a chronicle of horrors. A California teenager's mother murdered the girl's father, then sold her to a pimp. A six-year-old California girl was sold by her father to men for $1,000 a night for approximately a year before she was rescued by police. A boy developed tremendous emotional and behavioral problems after he was sexually violated by his mother. Another boy was sexually abused by a succession of babysitters. Files are bulging with similar recitations, each one worse than the other.

"The most important thing to remember," Dr. Densen-Gerber says, "is that these are children to whom something has been done, not children who were born a bad seed, an evil seed, or sinful. And that's what is so terrible."

According to Stephen F. Hutchinson, vice-president and legal counsel of Odyssey, many children three through seventeen are recruited as models for pornography by organized narcotics rings through their addicted parents. The money earned by the children, perhaps $50 to $300 for films retailing for $30 to $90 each, is used to feed the narcotics habits of the mothers and fathers.

Children of mothers who are narcotics-addicted prostitutes grow up without options. Some are born addicted, and grow up, as did Louis Malle's Violet in *Pretty Baby*, assuming that prostitution and pandering are an acceptable way of life. Children learn or are socialized by mimicking and by imitation. Dr. Densen-Gerber tells of an unusually pretty five-year-old girl who "set up boy after boy who was fourteen, fifteen and sixteen. She definitely was an aggressor. But she lived with her mother who was prostituting. She was imitating the behavior of her mother." The Odyssey House chief estimated that there are some 2 million American children living with parents who are involved in some phase of the sex industry.

Under the age of about twelve or thirteen, Dr. Densen-Gerber says, children "are what we call polymorphous perverse. It means that . . . they really don't have a sense of sexual guilt. They do not have a sense of appropriate sexuality."

For decades, taboos and revulsion concerning incest and child molestation restricted research, but new work in the field shows that most sexual abuse of children occurs in the home, the neighborhood, or the school. "There's no way you can tell if your children will be safe with someone; teachers, Scout leaders, or whatever," Dr. Densen-Gerber says.

Police in Providence, Rhode Island, broke up a sex club composed of neighborhood children nine to thirteen years old who were awarded points based on the quality of their sexual performance and were rewarded with BB guns and bicycles for high totals. Investigators expressed amazement that the children's parents never questioned where the items came from. Two men were charged with sodomy in the case.

In Denver, a young hospital nurse and a male companion were arrested and accused of luring girls from eleven to seventeen into a makeshift photo studio set up inside a former ambulance parked at a shopping center. Police said the victims were enticed with offers of $20 to $50 to model for catalogs and forced to pose for pornography.

If there is anywhere that a child should be as safe as in the home or neighborhood, it is the school. Yet children have been sexually molested in schools or recruited from their classrooms into pornography and prostitution. One of the most controversial matters dealing with the protection of children from sexual exploitation in the schools centers on the question of homosexual teachers. Challenges to the right of homosexuals to teach have been especially strong in areas of the country such as south Florida and among movements such as the "Save Our Children" campaign headed by Anita Bryant. It is an emotional issue that has been muddied by faulty statistics, twisted facts, and deliberate misstatements.

Most, if not all, anti-gay forces who oppose homosexual teachers are missing the point. Some teachers and other school employees sexually exploit or abuse children. But heterosexual or homosexual preferences do not appear to be a determining factor except in relation to the sex of the victim. Heterosexuals are apparently just as likely to molest a student as a homosexual. Indeed, gay rights activists point out that most children molested in school are abused by heterosexuals. A facetious correspondent once wrote to syndicated columnist "Dear Abby" and suggested a crusade to prohibit heterosexuals from teaching children of the opposite sex because statistics reputedly indicated that more than 90 percent of child molesters were heterosexual.

It is, of course, easy to juggle statistics and cite "proof" of a favored thesis. Presumably, there are more heterosexual citizens, so it stands to reason that there would be more heterosexuals involved in child molestations in classrooms or out.

California State Senator John Briggs sponsored a measure known as Proposition 6 that would have permitted local school boards not only to fire teachers who practiced homosexuality, but those perceived to be defenders of homosexuality, as well. Senator Briggs linked his campaign to "Christian morality," as did the "Save Our Children" forces. Proposition 6 was promoted as a means of keeping gay teachers out of the classrooms and reducing incidents of sexual molestation of students, but the measure lost at the ballot box.

By the late '70s, there were an estimated 2.4 million school teachers in the United States. Using that figure and the estimated percentage of homosexuals among the general population, there may be anywhere from 120,000 to 240,000 homosexual teachers. No one really knows how many there are, however, because most gay teachers are convinced, sometimes correctly, that they can only come out of the closet at the expense of their jobs.

Some parents and educators worry that children may become confused about establishing sexual and other aspects of their emotional identity if they have homosexual teachers. The most emotion-charged issue, however, continues to revolve around a widespread concept of the gay teacher as a child molester. The attitude is unfair and uninformed.

"My opinion is that it depends on a person's sense of responsibility, not whether one is a homosexual or a heterosexual," according to Katie Bond, director of the Children's Division of the American Humane Association based in Denver. "Some heterosexual males molest little girls. Are we going to say that we aren't going to allow any heterosexual males to teach in our schools because of this?"[3]

Maria Piers, of the Erikson Institute for Early Education, a psychologist knowledgeable in the field, believes there are more important concerns than a teacher's sexual preference. "The main thing is for teachers to respect the developmental needs of children and not act in any way that could be destructive," she says.[4]

Stephen Hutchinson observes that, "There are certain gay people

I've known who would have no problem teaching in public school. There are others that are inappropriate. It would be extremely difficult to legislate this and have a blanket rule that no homosexuals can do that. I think it would be more logical to say that any individual from whatever sexual persuasion who inappropriately acts out or inflicts morally sensitive sexual positions in the classroom is out of order. . . . If they step out of bounds in a number of behavioral ways, respond to that. And I would respond quickly."

When charges of child molesting are leveled, the emotion focused on gay teachers carries over to any individual associated with the educational system. Law enforcement authorities, school officials, the press, and the public sometimes react with near hysteria.

One of the most celebrated instances of a teacher being accused of sexual involvement with students occurred in tiny Gurnee, Illinois, a few miles from the Wisconsin state line. Headline stories on the front pages of area newspapers advised that a junior high school science and sex education teacher had been accused of being the head of a secret sex club that may have included as many as 200 boys and girls. Stories and rumors spread through Lake County about "animalistic sex orgies." The national television networks, radio, and the print media picked up the story and spread it around the country.

About a week later, Sheriff Orville S. Clavey announced that the size of the ring and the descriptions of the activities had been based on the word of a fifteen-year-old girl who reported she was kidnapped at gunpoint and raped. After further investigation, it appeared that a handful of boys and girls, not one or two hundred, had been involved in the club, and burglaries and vandalism were as prominent in their activities as was sex.

Richard Bretzlauf, a teacher in the school system for 10 years, was arrested on several charges including rape, kidnapping, taking indecent liberties with a child, and theft. He was accused of conspiring with a group of boys, former students of his, in area burglaries and of taking nude photos of a seventeen-year-old girl. She told investigators that he forced her to accompany him to the Viking Junior High School, made her disrobe, and then took the photos. She said he told her he was going to block out her face and use the photos in his sex education classes.

The charges were shocking enough. Bretzlauf was known as a community leader who had been active in the Boy Scouts, 4-H, and entertained church groups. Parents and other residents of the village were shaken. People began looking suspiciously at or questioning children who had been students of Bretzlauf's, or who had been in youth groups he was involved with.

In an 80-page statement, and later in court, Bretzlauf was identified as a closet homosexual who had fantasized about his problem and formed a small group of youngsters which he dubbed "The Family." All told, The Family consisted of the teacher and no more than 25 boys and two girls. They had no criminal or sexual purposes initially, but then, eventually, The Family drifted into burglary, vandalism, and related crimes. Some rapes did occur at gunpoint, and nude photos were taken, it was added.

Bretzlauf was eventually sentenced to four to 20 years in prison on burglary charges after a plea was negotiated. Charges detailing kidnapping, sex crimes, and other offenses were dismissed. Some of the boys involved in the burglaries and thefts were placed on probation.

Gurnee's notorious sex-ring had been forever shattered, and tranquility returned to the peaceful community. But it didn't return to the nation's schools. Since Bretzlauf's arrest and sentencing, hundreds of school employees have run afoul of the law for sexually molesting students.

In Warren, Michigan, near Detroit, an educator who was twice cited as "Teacher of the Year," once by a Parent-Teacher's Association group and another time by the Jaycees, was arrested on charges of sexually assaulting two teenage boys. He was already on probation for a similar incident involving an eight-year-old boy four years previously when he was an elementary school principal.

A New Jersey man who had taught at a Staten Island, New York, school for 10 years was arrested on federal charges of selling child pornography and mailing obscene material, after local police, FBI agents, and U.S. Postal Inspectors raided his home and confiscated a small truckload of kiddie porn. Nude photos of boys and girls as young as eight, and letters from all parts of the country containing money for child pornography, were among the material seized from the suspect. Authorities said that he held a second job as a psychology instructor at a local college and was pursuing a doctorate at Rutgers.

Several months later, in nearby Flushing, a junior high school teacher who had taught history for 19 years was arrested and charged with promoting the sexual performance of a child. Police said they confiscated photos of 15 to 20 different children and three adults posing in various homosexual acts, as well as photographic and film-processing equipment.

In the Chicago area during a period of more than two years, arrests of school employees charged with sexual offenses involving children included a basketball coach, a janitor, a shop teacher, a school bus driver, and a popular suburban science teacher and athletic trainer. The bus driver was acquitted by a jury after a judge refused to permit a key prosecution witness to testify that tests he conducted showed semen stains on the cap of the alleged ten-year-old girl victim. The bus driver also worked in a school lunch program and did volunteer coaching.

Students and staff were shaken when a bearded science teacher, one of the best-liked instructors at Glenbrook North High School, and a former state-approved foster parent, was arrested on a series of charges including kidnap, murder, and deviate sexual assault. Among other crimes, he was accused of abducting the seventeen-year-old son of a policeman, and binding, gagging, and sexually assaulting him before the boy died. Authorities said that fear and shock caused by the ordeal apparently aggravated an existing ailment and caused the boy's death. Other teenage boys later told of being abducted by the teacher while hitchhiking, and raped.

One of the most chilling aspects of the case was its similarity and proximity to the 33 murders attributed to suburban Chicago contractor John Gacy. Gacy lived only a few miles away and confessed that he preyed on teenage boys and young men whom he bound and sexually assaulted. Unlike the gregarious Gacy, however, the science teacher was not accused of torturing victims, and he was described as "a loner." There is a clear sadomasochistic streak in pederasts who are exclusively interested in boys, according to Dr. Osanka. Binding, manacling, and torturing victims is common.

On the West Coast, federal funds paid the salary of a young convicted felon with a three-page-long criminal record who was employed as a security guard in the San Francisco public schools. Hired under the Comprehensive Employment and Training Act, he distributed narcotics and canvassed girls at the first school he was assigned to, seeking prospective prostitutes, according to authorities. When his actions were uncovered, he was assigned to another school. By the time he arrived at a third school, the principal had learned of his reputation and refused to accept him. He was assigned to the offices of the Board of Education and was finally fired for missing work. Sometime later he was arrested on a variety of charges, permitted to plead guilty to three counts of pandering, and sentenced to prison.

Investigator Barbara Pruitt, a thirteen-year veteran of the Los Angeles Police Department, testifying before a U.S. Congressional subcommittee, provided as much insight as anyone into the vulnerability of children to abuse and exploitation. "All children must be protected against abuse stemming from within the home or outside of the home," she said. They "must be secure from exploitation by those who profit financially or otherwise at the expense of children."

1 Dr. Judianne Densen-Gerber, J.D., M.D., F.C.L.M., "Child Abuse and Neglect as Related to Parental Drug Abuse and Other Abnormal Behavior," Odyssey Institute, Inc., New York, 1978.
2 Donald P. Orr, M.D., and Susan V. Prietto, M.S.W., "Emergency Management of Sexually Abused Children. The Role of the Pediatric Resident," *American Journal of Diseases of Children.* 122 (6): 628-31, June, 1979.
3 *Chicago Tribune,* July 4, 1977.
4 *Chicago Sun-Times,* January 4, 1979.

7.

Sex By Age Eight

"Sex before age eight, or else it's too late."
—*Rene Guyon Society*

THE use of children for the sexual gratification of adults was accepted by almost every major civilization until Western nations began to denounce the practice about a century ago.

Some of the earliest records of organized sexual exploitation of children tell of six- and seven-year-old girls used as temple prostitutes in Near Eastern countries about 300 B.C. In some societies, girls were taken to the temple where they remained until they were chosen by a man willing to pay for sexually initiating them. In certain countries, the girl returned home after surrendering her maidenhead. In others, the girls were required to remain and service many customers until a large amount of money was earned for the temple treasury.

In still other civilizations, including those of Babylon, Egypt, India, and Greece, girls at about the age of puberty were dedicated to temples as sacred harlots and became priestesses for life. Well-born youngsters, including some from royalty, were among the children and young women who staffed the temple brothels.

Competition inevitably developed outside the temple, and for hundreds of years young boys and girls were freely available throughout the Middle East, Asia, North Africa, and the Orient. Girls as young as ten were sold by poor families to become courtesans in ancient Egypt. Children were treated no better in many of the civilizations of Europe. Ancient Greece is still notorious for its boy lovers. It is less well known that the hardy Norsemen also took young boys under their wings to nurture and train in the warrior arts — and to use as bed partners. Some of the most respected Roman soldiers and solons took advantage of the natural instincts of suckling infants to satisfy their sexual desires. The Kiwai of New Guinea, until a few years ago, were known to sodomize young males during puberty rites.

Early in this century, wealthy gentlemen in China could still purchase prepubescent girls from poor families as concubines who provided sexual services and handled household chores, as well. And in Japan,
young girls were funneled into the notorious Yoshiwara, the fenced-in
red-light district of Tokyo, where they toiled as prostitutes until their
youth and beauty were gone. As recently as World War II, Japanese
girls were purchased or kidnapped by procurers and shipped overseas
to staff brothels and sexually service their country's men in uniform.
During Japan's feudal period, monks and temple priests, as well as
Samurai, the respected warrior class, sexually used young boys.

In England, during the reign of Queen Victoria, the trade in white
slaves was so brisk that girls not only filled the brothels and streets of
their home country, but were also shipped to the continent to be auc-
tioned off like so many cattle. Some of the skittish or very young children
were sedated with opium or sealed in coffins with small airholes for the
miserable trip across the channel. A group of crusading women, dismayed at the destruction of young lives, eventually managed to have the
ages of children who could legally staff their nation's brothels raised
from nine to thirteen.

London police complained then of some of the same problems that
their brother officers in the United States complain about today. No
matter how brazen the soliciting by child and adult prostitutes, the men
they approached refused to testify in court.

By the mid-nineteenth century, all kinds of vice, including child
prostitution, were rampant in the United States. Girls as young as ten
were working in New York, Boston, Philadelphia, and many smaller
communities. By the time of the Civil War, girls as young as eight were
being held prisoner in kiddie prostitute houses where they serviced
wealthy, well-spoken clients old enough to be their grandfathers. Later
in the century, boys and girls were still available in specialty brothels in
New Orleans.

While people in this country and elsewhere were clandestinely toler-
ating child prostitution, anthropologists like Bronislaw Malinowski
and Dr. Margaret Mead were studying contemporary societies in such
varied locations as East Africa, India, Malaysia, the Amazon, and the
Trobriand Islands where it was considered as important for children to
develop sexual expertise as to develop other social skills.

Malinowski reported as early as 1929 that children in the Trobriand
Islands were playing sexual games at four and that girls as young as six
and boys as young as ten were beginning to participate in regular
sexual intercourse. In Australia, the aborigines considered it impossible

for a girl to achieve sexual maturity unless she had regular sexual intercourse with an adult male.

The Rene Guyon Society, the Childhood Sensuality Circle, the North American Man-Boy Love Association (NAMBLA), and the Paedophile Information Exchange (PIE) are related to neither Trobriand Islanders nor Australian aborigines, but each espouses sexual relations between children at an early age, or between children and adults.

Named after Dr. Rene Guyon, a judge on the Supreme Court of Thailand for 30 years and the author of books and papers relating to human sexuality, including that of children, the Society has lobbied on state and federal levels for changes in laws relating to children and sex; circulated newsletters and provided a speakers bureau; and promoted its own summer camping program for the daughters of members.

An aerospace engineer and former Sunday school teacher from Beverly Hills, California, used the pseudonym "Tim O'Hara" when he testified in Los Angeles before the Congressional Subcommittee on Select Education of the Committee on Education and Labor during a federal probe of child pornography and prostitution. O'Hara urged that laws be altered so that children are encouraged to have sexual relations with each other and with adults as early as possible. The Society's motto is "Sex before eight, or else it's too late."

"Sociologists feel that a child's moral attitudes are pretty well set by the age of eight, and after that it's pretty hard to change them," he testified. The spokesman cited Sigmund Freud, Baron von Krafft-Ebing, and several contemporary psychiatrists and authorities in the field of sexuality to support the Society's claim that early sexual activity by children is beneficial.

He claimed that Freud recommended in 1897 that "children should have heterosexual experiences at the very early ages of four, five and six. . . . Freud said that this body guilt makes young people either suicidal, and that includes alcoholism and dope abuse, or antisocial, which goes up to murder, as a crime," he continued.

After the hearings, O'Hara later directed letters to the Congressional Select Committee on Ethics complaining that the Guyon Society was permitted only 10 minutes to testify. Supporters of legislation opposed by the Society were permitted some 80 hours of testimony, he added.

Claiming to represent an organization with "5,000 supporters, psychiatrists and parents," and established for 16 years, he charged that testimony was rigged, warned that more children would become prostitutes, contract venereal disease, and commit suicide because of restrictive laws, and urged an investigation of how the committees gathered evidence and testimony. Finally, he asked that "remedial" legislation be introduced.

Guyon Society literature, initially mailed from Alhambra, and later from Beverly Hills, California, called for even stronger measures by lawmakers. It asked that statutory rape laws be changed to permit parents and guardians to give consent for their children to engage in sexual activities, and that they be required to allow sexual activity by their youngsters by the age of eight. It also advocated the use of male rubber contraceptives or finger stalls by little boys, and contraceptive vaginal foam by girls of about twelve or so, to prevent venereal disease and pregnancy.

The society is family oriented, and counseling is offered to reluctant wives and mothers who have doubts about their young children becoming sexually active. Membership estimates of the society, which is centered in but not restricted to Southern California, have ranged from 670 to the "5,000 supporters, psychiatrists and parents" claimed by O'Hara.

The society teaches that most of the problems of American children and adolescents are caused by repressive sexual attitudes, and that children should be sexually liberated at as early an age as possible. Puberty is the time at which it becomes possible for children to reproduce, not the age at which sexual pleasure begins.

Society newsletters are often rambling and filled with slogans such as "Children *keep* family sex secrets." Books by authors as diverse as Philip Wylie, Dr. Wilhelm Reich, former San Quentin Warden Clinton Duffy, and, of course, the Society's namesake, Dr. Rene Guyon, are recommended. Testimonials, sex hints, and attacks on St. Augustine for his condemnation of premarital sex, and pleas for modest financial contributions, also appear. One newsletter suggested that contributions be remitted by money order signed "John Doe" so that funds could be accounted for to the IRS while protecting the anonymity of supporters.

The Childhood Sensuality Circle, CSC, which at times refers to itself as a lay research organization, is equally as protective of its anonymity and has operated out of a San Diego post office box. Perhaps the CSC's most impressive accomplishment is fashioning "A Child's Sexual Bill of Rights." The nine-point statement of purpose stipulates that children should be extended: legal protection of their sexual rights no matter what their age; the right to privacy for his or her personal thoughts, ideas, dreams, and exploration of his or her own body without any kind of adult interference either direct or indirect; accurate sex information and protection from misinformation about sex; the right to develop mentally, physically, emotionally, and spiritually while developing tolerance and appreciation of other individuals and of their sexuality; the right to experience sensual pleasures without shame or guilt; the right to learn lovemaking as soon as he or she is able to understand; the right to loving relationships, including sexual relationships, with parents, siblings, or other adults and children while being protected with contraceptives to prevent venereal disease; the right to live a sex life based on natural desires without regard for tradition; and the opportunity to acknowledge what they know and feel about sexuality.

In a later position paper, the CSC pointed out that "sexual relationships that span wide age differences" are ". . . neither good nor bad; it depends upon the enjoyment of those involved. Affection often overlooks age differences, and so children should select sexual partners by their own standards. . . ."

Correspondence is handled by the editor of the newsletter, and guiding spirit of the CSC, who calls herself Valida Davila. The CSC offers a long list of pamphlets and other printed material ranging from *Polynesian Sex and Birth Practices* to *Children's Sexual Freedom in Family Life—in New Zealand, Giving Birth in the Home, Porno For Children,* and *Letters from Sucky Lucy, Age 11.*

For a time, a Chicago based group that called itself PAN, for Pedophiliacs Anonymous, distributed pamphlets advising that "sensitive, loving adults are the only reasonable agents for the furtherance of childhood sexuality."

Then in 1978 the North American Man-Boy Love Association was formed in Boston to promote pedophilia as a lifestyle, to defend men accused of sex crimes involving boys, and to lobby against age of consent laws for sexual activity. NAMBLA took a special interest in the indictments and arrests of 17 New England men accused of participating in a boy prostitution ring involving youths who were wards of the Massachusetts Department of Public Welfare and had been placed in foster homes. NAMBLA proclaimed that adults involved in the ring were motivated by love instead of money, presumably legitimizing the sexual activities. Seventy boys from eight to thirteen years old were among youngsters police said were seduced into performing sexual acts by their pederast-procurers who used beer, drugs, heterosexual stag films, and cash as inducements. The boys were paid $5 for each act of oral sex and $25 for anal intercourse, investigators said.

Seven other men were indicted at the same time the boy-sex ring was exposed, but were accused of morals offenses involving other children. There was apparently no link between the two groups.

Although the first cabal operated from a modest three-story apartment house in Revere, a working class suburb north of Boston, the roundup netted men representing a wide cross-section of American society. Dr. Donald M. Allen, a child psychiatrist from the exclusive Back Bay area of Boston, was probably the most prominent of those arrested and convicted. The divorced father of five children, who was placed on probation and ordered to obtain treatment, claimed he met the teenage boy he was accused of having sex with as part of a research project on male hustlers. Others arrested included a teacher and a retired assistant headmaster of the prestigious Fessenden School; the president of an investment firm; the operator of a judo and karate school; and a mechanic. Most of the men knew each other.

Charges included rape, sodomy, committing an unnatural act, and indecent assault and battery. Police disclosed that clients traveled from as far away as Miami and Michigan and paid fees from $30 to $50. "This is a bunch of guys who liked to get together and party with little boys," said Thomas E. Peisch, assistant Suffolk County District Attorney. "This is sex for hire. People patronizing it come from all over the country."

Authorities first learned of the presence of the ring when a school bus driver was convicted of raping young boys. One hundred photos of naked boys were confiscated during the investigation.

Shortly after the arrests, NAMBLA held its first annual national conference in Boston. A year later, in 1979, the second annual conference was conducted at the Church of the Beloved Disciple on West 14th Street in New York City. Panel discussions and workshops were presented at the church, and the conference wound up with a party and Sunday brunch at other locations. Much of the focus of the second conference was aimed at enlisting the support and sympathy of other segments of the gay community. Success was negligible, and the pederast movement remained as controversial among homosexuals as among heterosexuals.

Like other groups espousing sex between adults and children, NAMBLA produced a newsletter to keep in touch with members and to inform others. One copy of the *NAMBLA News* sought cash donations for a New England hair stylist who fled the country after being convicted of assault with intent to rape a child under sixteen, following an encounter with a fifteen-year-old high school football player in a sauna.

The man fled to Holland where he was met and helped by representatives of the Werkgrupp Pedophilie, which is an arm of the Netherlands Association for Sexual Reform. The Werkgrupp provided food, housing, and legal aid.

Similar organizations have formed in other parts of Europe. The Norwegian Pedophile Group, NAFP, and an international organization, Amnesty for Child Sexuality, are based in Oslo, and the Studizgroep Pedofilie in Antwerp, Belgium.

The best known of any of the child-sex organizations, however, is probably the Paedophile Information Exchange (PIE) which grew out of the campaign for homosexual equality in England and was formed by members of the Scottish Minorities Group in October, 1974. Many responsible homosexuals, shocked and troubled by the linking of pedophiles to gay lifestyles in general, quickly adopted a hands-off policy toward the organization or publicly condemned it. In retaliation, members of Britain's Campaign for Homosexual Equality, which refused to line up in support of PIE, were accused by the organization of treating pedophiles no better "than gays were treated in straight society."

PIE relies heavily on a study from Holland, "The Speijer Report," prepared for the Dutch Council of Health and the Ministers of Justice and Social Affairs. The pedophiles point to the study as indicating that sexual activities between children and adults are harmless and beneficial.

The report was also quoted to buttress a contention that a homosexual affair with an adult could be a positive experience for a youngster with homosexual tendencies "insofar as they might reduce or even eliminate the sensations of stress and frustration. . . . For the most constructive way of adapting to his sexuality, it is necessary that the homosexual minor is admitted to environments with equals, where he or she will be able to meet persons of their own age group as well as older people . . . to find and accept one's own identity and eliminate all feelings of guilt, fear and loneliness."

The organization claims that it seeks to build a sense of community for pedophiles, providing a forum for public debate of pedophilia and child sexuality, and to "relieve through public education and law reform the very real suffering of many adults and children."

Claiming that there is no justification for assuming that overt sexual experience is in itself harmful to children, PIE paradoxically states that any damage to the child is inflicted by society and the law. Unfair laws and societal attitudes, the pedophiles indicate, cause children to suffer humiliation, ostracism, separation from loved ones, feelings of sexual guilt, and, in most extreme instances, suicide. "It is not the paedophile (sic) who corrupts the child," they say, "but the puritans."

The organization, which claims many school teachers among its supporters, is also dedicated to campaigning for legal and social acceptance of pedophilia, while attempting to show that "most pedophiles desire gentle, loving and mutually stable relationships."

PIE maintains a speakers' bureau, publishes a magazine called *Magpie,* provides a contact service for pedophiles, and serves as a lobbying agency. Another newsletter, *Childhood Rights,* is published periodically by PIE's Children's Rights Group.

In a paper prepared for England's Home Office Criminal Law Revision Committee, PIE proposed abolition of ages of consent, and removal of references to consensual sexual activity among all ages from British criminal law. Those problems should be dealt with in a new non-criminal framework, the authors said. Lowering or abolishing the age of consent would reduce child prostitution because people would be allowed to express themselves together naturally, PIE contended. Spokesmen, however, conceded that tight legal sanctions against child prostitution might be needed to prevent exploitation. A series of age groupings was proposed, the youngest dealing with children up to three years old, whom it considered too young to communicate verbally or otherwise indicate consent to sexual activity. In instances where children in that age group were found to be sexually involved with an older person, the pedophile group suggested that local authorities be notified and an injunction obtained to prevent continued activity. The action could include removal of the child from the home, if necessary, and fines or imprisonment for violators.

Some doubt about the ability to communicate consent can also exist for certain youngsters in the next age group (four to nine) PIE conceded. There should be legal sanctions when parents, guardians, or others have reason to believe that sexual activity was not fully consented to, or when sexual activity results in mental or physical harm, or follows intimidation or the use of drugs or alcohol. Restrictions on sexual relations between children in the ten to seventeen age group should be minimal, according to the recommendations.

Rules covering sexual acts between children call for no restrictions on sexual acts between youngsters in three overlapping age groups: zero to nine, seven to thirteen, and ten to seventeen.

By 1979, authorities in England had filed action against PIE on grounds of conspiring to corrupt public morals, and criticism was leveled at public funding of other groups that supported the child sex movement. The charges were based on an invitation to members of PIE to exchange letters "round-robin" style, detailing their sexual fantasies. A jury determined that writing such letters was against post office regulations, and early in 1980 PIE Chairman Tom O'Carroll was sentenced to two years in prison.

The case had rapidly developed into a national scandal, and began attracting international attention when it was disclosed during the trial that a "senior British diplomat" left pornographic material on a bus, that was later found and turned over to police. A search of the home of the diplomat, said one of ten men at the trial who was warned by police to discontinue sending obscene material through the mails, produced more pornography, including material tied to PIE. A member of Parliament later publicly identified the diplomat as Sir Peter Hayman, 66. Hayman's diplomatic posts included the position of British Ambassador to Canada from 1970 to 1974. He served other assignments in Baghdad, Iraq; Belgrade, Yugoslavia; Berlin; with the North Atlantic Treaty Organization; and, from 1961 to 1964, as Director General of British Information Services in New York.

PAL, Paedophile Action For Liberation, is still another London based rights group seeking to liberalize treatment of child sexuality. PAL also publishes a bimonthly paper.

The Guyon Society and other organized pedophiles might appear to be flirting with illegality, but, in the absence of proof that members are converting their philosophy into reality, there can be no prosecution. Apparently children do keep family secrets.

In attempting to justify their own desires to engage in sexual relations with children, the pedophiles are trying to equate childhood sexuality with adult sexuality. Some argue that children, like adults, are sexual beings and therefore cannot be harmed by a full sex life. One American group is said to require its adult males to have deflowered a male or female child eight years old or younger as part of their membership requirements.

A magazine purchased by Dr. Densen-Gerber at a porno bookstore in Philadelphia carried an illustrated article contending that it is the responsibility of adult males to initiate preteen females into sexuality. Another magazine went even further, charging fathers with the responsibility of initiating coitus with their daughters before the children reach the age of puberty.

No matter how articulately pedophiles and the sexual avant-garde may argue that children must be allowed to grow at their own pace and develop loving, sexual relationships with others—including older people, as well as their peers—premature sexual activity can be emotionally and physically devastating.

Six-month-old, nine-year-old, or fourteen-year-old girls and boys have neither the "right" nor the emotional and intellectual maturity to consent to sexual activities or to weigh the consequences. Furthermore, there must always be an element of duress in sexual relationships between children and adults. The disparity in strength and social status cannot be ignored.

The question of children's rights, nevertheless, has presented the professionals in sociology and medicine and in the criminal justice system with difficult decisions. Where indeed are the lines to be drawn between laws and policies formulated to protect children and those that unjustly inhibit their emotional, intellectual, and sexual growth?

Throughout history, most cultures have considered children to be the property of their parents. Aristotle wrote that "the justice of a master or a father is a different thing from that of a citizen, for a son or slave is property, and there can be no injustice to one's own property." Ancient Romans could kill their children, or, if they preferred, sell or abandon them. Infanticide is a part of the history of most cultures, and only a few hundred years ago some children in Europe, Asia, and Africa were deliberately crippled or otherwise mutilated to enhance their value as beggars or freaks.

Disobedience to a parent was punishable by death in early Connecticut and Massachusetts. A Stubborn Child Law, adopted in Massachusetts in 1654, was reaffirmed by the state's highest court in 1971 in a ruling that children have no right of dissent against the reasonable and lawful commands of their parents or legal guardians. It was repealed in 1973.

Certainly, perceptions of the rights of parents or guardians have altered since 1654, but seldom, if ever, with the unanimous agreement of institutions and the individuals elected or appointed to make the decisions. In 1979 the U.S. Supreme Court ruled 6-3 that children have no constitutional right to challenge formal attempts by their parents or guardians to commit them for psychiatric care. Yet lawyers safeguarding children's rights argue that mental institutions are used by parents as "dumping grounds" for some youngsters. According to statistics from the National Institute for Mental Health, more than 80,000 children are admitted annually to state, county, and private mental institutions and to the psychiatric units of general hospitals.

The big problem deals with the age of consent. English lawmakers

experienced difficulties a few years ago when a study by a royal commission recommended that the age of consent should be abolished. Public
reaction was so violently opposed to the report that the recommendation was ignored. Nevertheless, there has been a trend in Western
European countries, and considerable interest in the United States,
toward lowering the age of consent.

There is no consensus among the states about the magical age when
children are legally acknowledged as having the intelligence and emotional maturity to willingly consent to sexual activity. In California, the
age is eighteen. Alabama statutes, at the other end of the spectrum,
permit consentual sex at twelve for girls. Statutes in other states are
equally arbitrary. In New Jersey, sixteen was the age of consent for
both boys and girls when the legislature voted in 1979 to reduce the age
to thirteen.

Many young boys are accused of rape, simply because they are
caught in sexual relations with a peer. It is easier for the girl, or for her
parents, to cry rape than to admit that she consented. Yet lowering the
age of consent for girls leaves them vulnerable to the sexual attention of
older men, and could prevent prosecution for a wide range of offenses.
In this age of permissiveness, the problem has become increasingly
difficult for lawmakers to cope with.

But the intent of the revised law in New Jersey was widely misunder-
stood. Public reaction was so violently opposed that the age was restored to sixteen before the new law went into effect. Unfortunately, the
state penal code dealing with statutory rape was left so crudely written
that a child sixteen years and one day old could be prosecuted for
engaging in consentual sex with a partner only two days younger.
Clearly, a law taking age differential into account would have been
more practical.

Although Dr. Densen-Gerber decries outdated statutory rape laws
that unfairly punish boys for sexual activity with girls in the same age
grouping, she firmly supports retaining an age of consent. "And we
have to have severe penalties for adults who destroy children," she
insists.

The difference between protection and oppression can be finely
drawn, and even those in legitimate children's rights movements set
goals that vary widely over how to safely extend the rights of youngsters
while preserving the protected status of minors.

The Youth Liberation Press, formerly of Ann Arbor, Michigan, and
later of Brooklyn, New York, was begun in 1971 by a group of twelve-
to fifteen-year-olds and has campaigned for a decade for an end of what

they believe to be discrimination in American society against the young. The group prepares and distributes material dealing with the right to privacy and corporal punishment, children and sex, the "experience of being young and gay," and other issues. Legal actions, such as the late 1979 rulings of the California and U.S. Supreme Courts stipulating that parents do not have the authority to consent to police searches of their teenage children's living quarters, are of special interest to the Press.

Children, however, can have too many rights, especially if exercise of their "rights" presents a danger to their physical safety. Former Commander Harold Thomas of the Chicago Police Department's Youth Division has strong feelings about some of the dangers of equating childhood rights and responsibilities with those of adults: "Children are NOT adults, and they need help," he says. In one two-year period, he was faced with four runaway girls who were murdered in separate incidents after police in Chicago were prevented from holding them in custody while psychological or other help was sought. "They were killed out on the street," he said. "One child dead is a tragedy, just one."

Curiously, delinquents or street children who are veteran criminals are rarely the victims of serious violence. Delinquents commit criminal acts and are either caught or go home. The victims are status offenders, runaways, curfew violators, and truants, children who do not know how to take care of themselves. If they are not murdered, or seriously beaten, they are sexually exploited. "They're fourteen- and fifteen-year-old girls and they're into prostitution, sleeping with people, doing a lot of things," said Thomas.

Right or wrong, children obviously indulge in sex in greater numbers and at younger ages than during the more conservative 1940s and 1950s. Supreme Court decisions since then have upheld the right of children to obtain abortions or birth control information and aids without the cooperation of their parents. Approximately 184,000 abortions were performed on girls seventeen and younger in 1978, and about one-third occurred without parental involvement. A New York state law forbidding sale of nonprescription contraceptives to youngsters under sixteen was struck down in 1977, despite attorneys' arguments that the code demonstrated the state's disapproval of sexual activity among children. "It is as though the state decided to dramatize its disapproval of motorcycles by forbidding the use of safety helmets," Justice John Paul Stevens wrote in the decision. A 1978 survey of 1,000 teenagers of various ethnic and income groups in New York City determined that 76 percent of the boys and 64 percent of the girls had engaged in coitus as least once, most of them by the time they were sixteen.

Far-reaching changes in sexual mores and adult sexual practices have occurred, and it was inevitable that child sexuality also would be affected. It would be impractical to believe that children could be insulated to any significant degree from the modern sexual revolution.

During the last two decades, there has been a decline of the double standard as women have achieved increasing sexual freedom in or out of marriage; wife swapping, or swinging, has almost become a middle-class cult; deviant or alternative sexual lifestyles have met with increased tolerance; and men and women have become more willing to experiment with variety in sexual activity.

New stresses have developed along with increased freedom, however. A parent confused over what is sexually appropriate is hardly able to provide helpful sexual guidance for a child. Influenced by various movements that stress doing your own thing so long as it is pleasurable, and, aware that the carefully structured society they grew up with is rapidly being chipped away, parents often feel helpless and cannot instill sexual values in their young because they themselves are so unsure of the boundaries.

Children are not born with instinctual morality or the ability to make discriminative decisions about harmful or non-harmful sexual activities. According to *Personality of a Child Molester*, children will automatically do anything that is pleasurable until they are conditioned otherwise by their parents or other authority figures.[1]

A few years ago, police in Toronto shattered a prostitution ring organized by girls eleven to fourteen years old who performed for $5 fees. The only adults involved in the operation were the clients.

In Indianapolis, police picked up two sisters, eleven and twelve years old, whom investigators said performed oral sex with a succession of men to raise money for candy. Detective Thomas R. Rodgers of the police department's vice division said he was seated in his car when the girls approached him and offered to perform sexual acts for $1 if he would meet them in an alley. Then they hiked the price to $20.

Rodgers, who is a child pornography investigator, said he observed the sisters for about two months and believed that someone else was instructing them to raise their rates and how to avoid police detection. The girls admitted that they had been charging fifty cents to $1 for candy money and had acquired at least ten regular customers.

A man was charged with engaging in sodomy with the sisters a few months before their apprehension by Rodgers, but the case was dismissed when the girl's mother said she would handle the problem herself. Neighbors in the peaceful middle-class residential neighborhood said the sisters seldom played with other children, but instead strolled along the street. "They were just two little fat girls," Rodgers said.[2]

Children need to be taught to differentiate between situations where love and affection are properly demonstrated by attention and nonsexual cuddling, and ter-life experiences where coitus and other overt sexual practices fit into different kinds of loving relationships. They must be taught that sex is more complex and rewarding than a commercial transaction or a means of experiencing tactile pleasure.

Children who are used sexually by adults or who are seduced, enticed, or forced to pose for pornography are left almost inevitably with severe psychological scarring that can never be erased. Child prostitutes and other youngsters sacrificed to the sex and smut network share common experiences that leave them scarred with feelings of worthlessness, guilt, betrayal, and rage. According to Dr. Densen-Gerber, psychological damage is especially severe when "highly sexualized behavior" is imposed on children in the latency stage between the ages of approximately eight and thirteen. In addition to the permanent association between sex and personal powerlessness, of being "suffocated or overwhelmed," these children typically grow up with feelings of personal worthlessness, taking upon themselves the guilt for what they accurately perceive as a distorted and socially unacceptable form of behavior. "Children are destroyed by these experiences," she declares. "They are emotionally and spiritually murdered."

The emotions can be acted out inwardly. As Scotty Baker tragically demonstrated, suicide is not uncommon among young people with a history of sexual exploitation. Self-destructive behavior can take other paths as well. Some victims withdraw into isolation, unable to cope with the emotional trauma generated by their experiences. Some turn to drugs or alcohol to desensitize themselves during the years they are being sexually exploited, or, later, to deaden memories.

Children who become sexually active during their normally sexual latent years are likely to vent their frustrations and guilt more directly with lifelong entrapment in perversion, prostitution, and other more violent forms of antisocial behavior.

According to Dr. Densen-Gerber, penetrating sexuality—within the mouth, anus, or vagina—is especially damaging and can make children feel that they have no control over their bodies or their destiny.

"At this stage of life, the child is getting work gratification, learning to study, to feel good about himself or herself," she said. "And if you interfere with that, telling them the way to feel good about themselves is

by using sex, they're developing attitudes that this is the way to cope."
The children are learning that the way to obtain candy, toys, bicycles,
new dresses, drugs, or merely the esteem of their adult role models is to
trade their bodies. Emotional development can be stunted, and the child
can grow up distrusting all authority figures whom he or she understandably equates with the adults who have exploited him or her, Dr.
Densen-Gerber said.

A sexual experience with an adult can terrify a small child. "The
physical difference between a 200-pound man and a little girl of 40 to 60
pounds is frightening in regard to physical weight alone," Dr. Densen-
Gerber observes. "What we are talking about is the inappropriate use
of a child for someone's sexual needs. I'm not talking about the 'Let's
play doctor' between a couple of five-year-olds, but about an adult
transgressing against a little boy or girl and making that child act as if it
were an adult. You just do not have sexual intercourse or other sexual
activities with a child long before that child can handle it, understand it,
integrate it, or use it in a positive way."

Severe injury can occur to small children who cannot physically
accommodate an adult sex partner, and some have died from internal
bleeding or asphyxiation. "Girls at nine were not designed by nature to
satisfy the perverted needs of adult males," says Dr. Densen-Gerber.
The Guyon Society advises that a girl cannot accommodate an adult
penis in her vagina until she is ten or eleven years old. Little girls suffer
lacerations of the genitals, and both boys and girls have incurred severe
damage to their rectums after anal intercourse with adults. Some older
boys have been victimized by pederasts who force their entire fist and
part of the arm into the rectum. Other children are abused by perverts
and pornographers who use soft drink bottles, light bulbs, fruit, and
professionally made plastic or hard rubber dildoes to penetrate vaginas
or rectums. There is no limit to the perverse imagination.

Arguments by promoters of early sex for children who insist that the
physical well-being of boys and girls can be safeguarded merely by
"gentle loving care" and the use of contraceptives disregard evidence to
the contrary. A study by Dr. Malcolm Coppileson, a gynecologist and
Odyssey board member in Australia, focused on 100 promiscuous adolescent girls who had gotten into trouble with authorities for moral
offenses. They were examined and compared with 40 adolescent girls
who were virgins. The presence of cellular abnormalities in the cervixes
of the promiscuous girls was five times greater than that among the
other group. This study and others establish the link between early
sexual intercourse and the premature incidence of cervical cancer

among females in their twenties and thirties. Hysterectomies, or death, are almost always the ultimate result. Also, prepubescent girls do not have the vaginal pH that older women have to protect against infection and they commonly contract vaginitis and other local genital infections.

Adolescent girls face the additional dangers of pregnancy, and both girls and boys can be exposed to severe physical damage from venereal disease. A fourteen-year-old boy placed with a foster father in Chicago who was a pederast was found to have gonorrhea of the throat after he went to police for protection and begged to be removed to another home. Young girls have become permanently sterile as a result of damage caused by gonorrhea that went undetected for too long.

More than one million girls under nineteen become pregnant each year, many of them not yet in their teens. Some studies have shown that 50,000 babies are born annually to girls under fourteen, including 9,000 to girls under eleven. Dr. Densen-Gerber was still in medical training when she delivered a son for a girl who was nine years and eight months old. The young mother had been forced into prostitution by her own mother when she was three, and she rejoiced that her baby was not a daughter who could be abused as she had been.[3]

Most of the pregnancies are the result of coitus between peers, and today most are aborted. Nevertheless, the statistics say something about the dangers of pregnancy among girls victimized by incestuous relatives or other adults. The average age today of menarche, or the beginning of menstruation, is 12.5 for American girls, and many have reached puberty by the time they enter the fifth or sixth grade. The lower the age of the girl, the greater are the medical risks of pregnancy for both mother and baby. The incidence of birth defects increases for infants born to younger mothers. And researchers claim that the risk of pregnancy is highest for girls who begin sexual activity before they are fifteen because they are less likely to use contraceptives than their older sisters.

Pre-teen and most teenage mothers have no resources to care for themselves or their babies. Ripped prematurely out of the maturational system and thrust into adult womanhood, the young mothers have no salable work skills and are unable to develop themselves educationally. This leaves them and their children at a tremendous social and economic disadvantage in today's increasingly sophisticated and technological society.

Child exploiters who masquerade as advocates of children's rights to further their opportunities to sexually abuse the young are spouting the worst kind of self-serving propaganda.

Dick Drost, operator of Naked City, a nudist camp at Roselawn, Indiana, some 50 miles southeast of Chicago, is good at propaganda, although he would undoubtedly call his skill public relations. About the time Drs. Osanka and Densen-Gerber were launching their campaign to curb the sexual exploitation of children, Drost was operating the Adam and Eve Restaurant, a nude truck stop just outside the camp. Among other employees were an eleven-year-old girl and her fourteen-year-old female cousin who cleaned tables. The girls worked nude.

The younger child was a seasoned veteran of Drost's promotions, and once placed second in the female portion of a "Mr. and Miss Nude Teenybopper Universe Pageant," which was conducted annually at Naked City. Drost is an enterprising individual who was chosen by Chicago's Junior Chamber of Commerce (Jaycees) as one of the city's Ten Outstanding Young Men of 1965 when he was president of a corporation there.

Indiana State Police and Newton County Sheriff's Deputies had raided the Adam and Eve Restaurant in 1975 and found a room full of truck drivers munching on hamburgers and sipping coffee while two nude women, and another wearing only a studded belt, waited on tables. About 30 truckers, Drost, and a woman who called herself "Miss Nude America" were among those arrested.

State troopers claimed that on a previous trip to the restaurant undercover officers had photographed unnatural sex acts between a man and a woman. Drost was eventually fined $100 and costs after pleading guilty to keeping a house of ill fame. A six-month jail term was suspended on condition that no further illegal activities take place at the nudist camp.

Two years later, the eleven-year-old and her cousin were discovered working nude in the restaurant. The younger girl was looking forward to competing in the approaching nude teenybopper pageant. Dr. Densen-Gerber was speaking at a convention in Chicago when she heard of the pageant and immediately called a press conference to denounce the contest. She threatened to lead picketing of the camp if it was necessary.

"I am objecting to the idea that children eight to sixteen will be asked to parade nude, and will be photographed by dressed people who pay $15 to take pictures of them," she stated. "I am also objecting to the fact that their parents will be paid $10 to exhibit their children." She pointed out that she had no quarrel with nudists, but was bitterly opposed to any abuse of children, including sexual exploitation.

The publicity worked. Indiana Governor Otis Bowen and State's Attorney General Theodore Sendak filed an injunction suit, contending that the contest amounted to "abuse, neglect, or cruelty to children and was against the public policy of the state." It was further contended that the contest, which was to have naked children parading before a panel of other youngsters acting as judges, and a paying audience, most of whom would be wearing clothes, would constitute an obscene performance before minors and violate child labor laws.

A judge issued a restraining order to block the pageant, then converted the order into a temporary injunction. Drost did not attend the hearing on the injunction, but reportedly buzzed the county seat town of Kentland in a helicopter as spectators jammed the courthouse below. Final judgment was announced almost a year later, permanently enjoining Drost from conducting nude contests for children from six to sixteen years old. It was stipulated that state police should be permitted onto the camp grounds to verify compliance with the order.

In the meantime, Indiana Senator Birch Bayh had attached an amendment to pending federal legislation to restrict child pornography that also blocked further nude contests with children. Throughout the controversy, an infuriated Drost vociferously denied that the nude child pageants were pornographic or harmful. He charged, furthermore, that Bayh previously knew about the pageants and said nothing after being asked four years earlier to serve as a judge and declining the invitation. Drost threatened to run for office against the senator.

The lawmaker was unimpressed by the threat. Bayh branded the pageant as sordid and characterized it as pandering to people "interested in child pornography and sex, while at the same time it is exploitive to children and potentially damaging to their mental health."

Regardless of the sexual practices of Trobriand Islanders or the promotions of people who deal in commercial sex, premature introduction to overt sexual activity, whether with their peers or with adults, can be injurious to children. And descriptions by articulate pedophiles of the reputed psychological and emotional benefits of kiddie sex, no matter how glowing, are specious and self-serving.

"It's a full threat," Dr. Densen-Gerber warns. "There is a worldwide movement, particularly in the English-speaking world, to permit the sexual use of children. And it's done under the guise of civil rights and civil libertarianism. Citizens should organize against this."

---

[1] Calvin Hall and Alan Bell, *Personality of a Child Molester*. Chicago: Aldine Publishing Company, 1971.

[2] *Indianapolis Star*, April 5, 1979.

[3] Judianne Densen-Gerber, J.D., M.D., F.C.L.M., "Child Abuse and Neglect as Related to Parental Drug and Other Antisocial Behavior," Odyssey Institute, Inc., New York, 1978.

8.

Runaways

Luz Valentin could have been almost any one of the little girls she grew up with in the predominantly Hispanic neighborhood of Humboldt Park on Chicago's northwest side. She was pretty and petite with inquisitive dark eyes and a clear hazelnut complexion. She was a month old when she was brought to the city and adopted into a family of four boys and another girl. She was six when her oldest brother raped her. He was twenty-nine.

Two other brothers began abusing her sexually after the initial rape. They warned her that if she said anything to their mother they would kill her. She did not say anything, and for four years her brothers took turns using her. Sometimes they gave her money or candy.

She was ten years old when she snorted her first cocaine. A favorite cousin who was four years older gave it to her. The cousin was a prostitute and had already been working the streets for a year. It was easy for her to talk Luz into running away.

The girls had been spending more and more time together. Luz progressed from snorting the spirit-lifting drug to shooting it into her veins. But the older girl had plenty of money, enough for clothes, for sweets, and for cocaine. She had a pimp who took good care of her. And when Luz ran away, she was given to the pimp by her cousin as a present.

The pimp claimed to be a Chicago policeman and had a stable of twenty girls, most of them in their early teens, but none was as young as Luz. She was soon promenading along State Street and strolling in and out of Rush Street bars and strip joints where conventioneers, businessmen, and salesmen from Chicago's near northside hotels congregate and play.

She was traveling in fast company for an eleven-year-old. She met doctors, lawyers, and executives, men who had sons and daughters older than Luz, but could not resist the perverse lure of sex with a prepubescent hooker. Luz never had any formal schooling. There was

124

no time for that, and she could not read or write. But her pimp and her sisters on the street taught her how to count, something every whore needed to know.

Sometimes she counted $100 bills, or $50, hardly ever anything smaller than $20 for a quick trick. And she lived more extravagantly than she had ever imagined. Her man saw to it that she was put up in a comfortable hotel near Rush Street. Some of her tricks took her to even more luxurious hotels and to fancy restaurants. There was always plenty of booze, and coke to snort or shoot.

But even an eleven-year-old can become tired, and sometimes she was too exhausted to continue. It seemed that entire platoons of men were marching in and out of her door. "One goes in the door, one goes out," she recalled years later. She became so tired sometimes that she cried. Then she would be beaten. Pimps beat their whores on the stomach and on the breasts, on the arms and legs. They use their fists and their feet. Sometimes they use wire coathangers heated over flames from a kitchen stove or a cigarette lighter. Usually they are careful not to break bones or cut the flesh. They try not to leave too many marks, because a whore is valuable property and men do not spend their money for a body that has been made ugly by cuts and bruises. Sometimes, of course, they may make an example of a girl to keep the rest of their stable in line. The victim does not always survive.

But Luz survived her beatings and returned to the street. Occasionally, she was delivered to a customer's door. And, occasionally, she was arrested. But she was a juvenile and could not be charged under the same laws as older prostitutes. Police asked her if she had an adult to take care of her and when she replied that she did they released her to her pimp.

She was on the street three years before she went home. It was two miles, perhaps three, from the glittering sidewalks of Rush Street to her mother's home at the edge of Humboldt Park. Luz was not afraid of her brothers anymore, and she told her mother, finally, why she had run away. Her mother screamed at her, calling her a "puta" (whore) and a liar. Luz left and never went back.

At fifteen she was in South Florida making dirty movies, posing for pornographic magazines, and performing with other girls in live sex shows. The sex shows paid well, $600 a performance. The other activities apparently paid well also, but she was never certain. Her pimp collected the money and doled out only enough for her to live on. The nightly rounds of sex and the lack of freedom were exhausting and suffocating. She began secretly building a nest egg, surreptitiously putting away spending money and even risking beatings by turning an occasional trick on the sly. Eventually she collected enough cash to run away again, this time to New York City.

The streets were no different in New York except that this time she was working on her own. Unfortunately, she did not know much about birth control and became pregnant. There was no pimp to arrange for an abortion, and, as she lost her shape, she lost her ability to support herself. Pregnant hookers are not in heavy demand, not even in New York.

When she became hungry enough, she applied for welfare. Good fortune and a concerned counselor directed her to Odyssey House. She was fed well at Odyssey, her diet was efficiently controlled, she received good prenatal care, and drugs were abruptly stopped.

Her son was born with a brain infection. She was certain that it was punishment from God, and she vowed to change her life. She began by learning to read and write. She also began to travel with staff members of the shelter to tell her story. She told it to newspapers, on radio, and on television.

Sometimes journalists treated the story of her experiences as if it was too lurid and bizarre to believe. They could not understand why, even at the tender age of eleven, she would so willingly submit to the exploitation and mistreatment by her pimp. She would explain then that he was the only man who had ever shown her any love. And sometimes she would ask if they would try to get in touch with her friend Maria. Her friend was fourteen and a whore in Chicago. Luz was afraid her friend would die there. Perhaps she did.

Luz Valentin had a hideous childhood. But she may be one of the lucky ones. She found help and the new direction she needed to rebuild a life as a productive human being with a new sense of self-worth. Thousands of runaway children are not that fortunate.

The FBI estimates that one million boys and girls under eighteen run away from home every year, most of them between thirteen and fifteen. (One survey found that a slight majority are girls, but another survey pinpointed boys as the most likely to run away.) Many of the youngsters stay in their own neighborhood or go no more than 20 or 30 miles and return home within a few days. Others hitchhike or board buses that take them across the country. Police and social agencies who collect statistics dealing with such things estimate that about six of every 100 never return home.

Social scientists, police, and the people who operate shelters for footloose juveniles say there are as many reasons for running away as there are problems. "A kid's life is divided into three categories. Family, school, and social life," said John Collins, a one-time runaway who became a volunteer with the Runaway Hotline in Houston, Texas. "If one area is out of kilter, a kid can usually handle that, but if two are— that's two-thirds of the child's life and often they just want to get away from it."[1]

Children flee when they have problems they feel they cannot talk to their parents about. A bad report card can precipitate a major crisis in a child's life. Or there may be trouble within the family, jealousy over a sibling, a drug problem, or merely a desire for independence and freedom. A girl may be pregnant, or run away with a boyfriend because her family disapproves of him or believes she is too young to go steady. Boys and girls also run away because they are tortured, beaten, or sexually abused.

Frequently children run away from home because they have not been able to establish communication with other family members. It is a means of getting attention. Most of those children return home, but occasionally they insist on coming back only on their own terms and that is not always possible.

They run from families that are rich and those that are poor. They run from pleasant suburban ranchers with new bicycles in the front yard and swimming pools in back; and they run from dilapidated tenement homes in cities where rats prowl the kitchens and bedrooms at night and the dimly lighted hallways are stained with graffiti and urine.

Most children who do not return home in a few days head for the big cities. Any money they may have slipped from their mother's purse or saved mowing lawns and babysitting is quickly exhausted, and they become wanderers, sleeping in vacant lots, abandoned buildings, and junk cars, or temporarily bunking down with friends. The lucky ones find their way to shelters operated by one of the 166 federally funded runaway programs in this country or one of those operated by church or other private organizations. Those who do not find their way to shelters, and there are thousands, quickly discover that they have extremely limited survival options.

According to William Katz, executive director of the American Society for the Prevention of Cruelty to Children, the laws of New York state permit a child of sixteen to leave home and attempt to deal with society as an adult. But the same laws also prevent the child from obtaining a job without working papers, and working papers cannot be obtained without the signatures of a parent and school principal and without acquiring a physical from the Board of Health.

"What we're saying to that kid is: 'Okay, you can run away at sixteen, but you can't work until you're eighteen unless you get papers or work illegally. And by the way, you'll probably only be able to earn $3.18 an hour, and you can't live on that,' "Katz asserted. " 'But if you go out and deal drugs, that's cool. Or if you go out and become a prostitute or make $600 or $700 a week doing porn, that's cool, too. You'd have to be stupid not to.' "

Laws work similarly in most other states. They prohibit children under certain ages from borrowing money, renting apartments, or obtaining even the most menial, low-paying jobs. So children beg. Or steal. Or, as Katz observed, become prostitutes and models for pornography. They have no skills, and their bodies are often their only salable product.

Runaways usually identify with the people they meet who are anti-establishment. Once they leave home, they themselves are living outside the law, or, at the very least, are in conflict with it. And they identify with others who, like themselves, fear or dislike authority. Crime, drugs, and the most atrocious forms of sexual exploitation are waiting for them.

One of the most tragic aspects of the "freedom flotilla," which brought more than 100,000 Cuban refugees to this country in 1980, involved the children. At least 1,400 were unaccompanied by adults, and many of them were street children who had already become runaways or throwaways before leaving Cuba. Resettlement camps were barely established before horror stories began circulating about widespread gang rapes and other sexual assaults on children of both sexes. An investigation of conditions at Camp McCoy, Wisconsin, disclosed the rape of one girl by 54 men, and the rape of another by nine men. An eleven-year-old boy at a camp at Indiantown Gap, Pennsylvania, was also raped by nine men, and none of his attackers was arrested. Other reports told of people who sponsored young female refugees, then attempted to work them as topless waitresses and prostitutes.

Perhaps the most pathetic of all the children who become homeless wanderers are those who are called "throwaways," "trashed kids," and "pushouts" by police and social workers. It is believed that their ranks grow by as many as a quarter of a million every year. They are children whose families no longer have the ability or the desire to care for them. The problems can be an inability on the part of the parents to deal with sexual promiscuity, disagreement over family rules, trouble in school, or adolescent drug abuse. Sometimes the problem is money. There may be too many children and simply too little money or food to go around, so someone has to leave. At other times the trouble may be precipitated by parents who subconsciously blame a child for their personal problems, and the boy or girl is cast out. Whatever the reason, when a child who is a throwaway begins hitchhiking to the nearest city, it is a good bet that he or she will find it more difficult to survive than would a chronic runaway or juvenile delinquent.

A certain number of homeless children are streetwise and have learned to take care of themselves while sidestepping most of the pitfalls that await their more naive brothers and sisters. Usually the chronic runaway has been thinking of leaving for some time and has made plans, put some money aside, selected a town or city, and perhaps contacted friends who can help when he or she makes the break.

The separation is usually more unexpected and sudden for throwaways. Usually the child leaves with only the clothes he is wearing, and possibly a few dollars in his pocket. A Philadelphia boy was booted out of his middle-class home three times between the time he was sixteen and seventeen. The first time occurred after the youth was in an accident with the family car and lied about it. His father beat him and threw him out. The boy was not even permitted to come back inside to retrieve one of his shoes that had slipped off. He was luckier than some. He had friends and relatives to stay with, and they sheltered him each time he was thrown out until his father cooled off and permitted the boy to return home.

After a seventeen-year-old girl was picked up in New York City by the police department's runaway unit, her mother was located in the South. When notified by telephone that her daughter was in New York, the mother launched into a tirade about all the embarrassment and hurt she had suffered since the girl left. She avoided mentioning the girl's return until asked directly if she would take her back. She finally agreed that the girl could return but only if she sincerely wanted to. She said she doubted, however, that the girl wanted to return. The mother refused to cooperate with travel or financial arrangements. It was obvious the girl was not wanted.

A girl from Oklahoma whose mother had been a runaway was equally unfortunate. The older woman was determined that her daughter would not do as she had done. Consequently, the mother continuously scolded the girl, and beat her so badly when the girl was nine that she had to be hospitalized with a head injury. For a time after the mother's marriage broke up the girl stayed with friends and in foster homes. But when she was twelve her mother brought her home, and the beatings began again.

There were more trips to state juvenile institutions and mental hospitals until the girl was thirteen and escaped from a reformatory. She hitchhiked to the East Village in New York. For a while she panhandled and lived with a succession of men who took care of her until they tired of her sexual services. She finally became a hanger-on with a motorcycle gang. She paid for the modicum of security she obtained from the relationship by becoming the victim of frequent rape and a drug abuser.

In some ways, her late teens paralleled the life of a young Texas woman who testified in Washington before a House Republican task force on welfare reform in the fall of 1979. Identifying herself only as "Mary" from Houston, the twenty-eight-year-old witness said that during her twelve years with the Banditos, a motorcycle gang, she saw girls and women raped, beaten, and swapped for motorcycles.

While she belonged to various members of the gang, she said, "I witnessed and was victim of their beatings and sexual molesting. Women are not human beings to these gangs; rather they are property to be bought, sold, and abused like a cycle, or a gun or drugs."

Women carry drugs and guns for the gang so that if anyone is caught with the contraband it is the female who goes to jail, not the biker. Mary was sixteen when she first became involved with the Banditos. Many of the biker's women are sixteen or younger and are often put to work as topless dancers, drug dealers, or prostitutes. At other times they are used in welfare schemes, the subject of the Congressional hearing.

The witness said the first ride a girl takes with a biker often signals her introduction into sexual servitude. "A biker will take the girl to a club meeting where she will be sexually abused by each club member. That night, for her, the drugs and booze are free. After that, she is expected to earn her keep.

"I want to stop it from happening to some other girl," Mary declared. "They're afraid to leave, but there's somebody out there to help them. I want the public to know, to be aware of what these people are doing. They can brainwash little kids. That's what they are, fourteen- or fifteen-year-old little girls."

Mary Bell Vincent never crossed paths with the Banditos, but she was a chronic runaway who paid dearly for the freedom she sought. Few people in Sausalito, California, knew the real name of the fifteen-year-old from Las Vegas who adopted the last name of her twenty-six-year-old boyfriend and called herself Maria Vargas. They knew only that she roamed the streets of the artist's community near San Francisco dressed like a flower child, which was a bit odd since it was 1978 and the last of the original flower children had turned in their denims and mini-skirts years earlier.

The teenager had run away several times before, so often in fact, authorities later said, that her parents did not bother reporting her missing the last time she fled. In Sausalito she lived in the back seat of a car with her boyfriend. It was parked next to the restaurant where he washed dishes while she hustled quarters and half dollars selling roach clips she had decorated with scraps of wire, feathers, and beads.

The police arrested her boyfriend on a rape charge involving another fifteen-year-old girl from Sausalito. His car was impounded and Maria no longer had a place to sleep. The next time anyone in Sausalito heard of Maria it was after she was found wandering dazed and bleeding along the side of a highway east of San Francisco. She was naked, and her arms had been hacked off with an ax just below the elbows.

She had been hitchhiking when a tall, fat man with a scarred face, glasses, and a dwindling hairline pulled his late model van to a stop and motioned for her to climb in. He told her his name was Larry. She fell asleep, and when she awoke she was being tied with rope.

The van driver raped her twice and forced other sexual abuse on her. The sun had set when the van stopped and he pushed her outside. Disregarding her cries and frightened pleas to be released, he led her bound and naked along a desolate stretch of back country road. When he stopped, he lifted an ax and severed both her arms.

Police later theorized that he expected her to bleed to death and intended to prevent identification of her body through fingerprints by cutting off her arms and disposing of them elsewhere. Instead, the force of the ax blows closed her arteries, saving her life. The next morning she was discovered stumbling along the highway more than two miles from where she was mutilated.

Police arrested Lawrence Singleton, a fifty-one-year-old merchant seaman at his home in Sparks, Nevada, nine days later. A neighbor said Singleton had carefully washed his van inside and out within an hour after he arrived home on the morning the girl was found. The sailor was subsequently convicted of attempted murder, kidnapping, mayhem, rape, and other sex charges.

The girl watched quietly from the front row as her attacker was sentenced to 14 years and four months in prison. Singleton's attorney asked that special security arrangements be made in prison for his client because placing him in the general population would be "tantamount to a death penalty. There have been specific threats against his life," the lawyer said. "People have said they want to kill him."

A fourteen-year-old Georgia girl is another runaway who learned the hard way how difficult life could be on her own. She left home because she did not like her stepfather. She got as far as Houston before she met her first close friend, a twenty-five-year-old carnival worker. They traveled together until they got to Los Angeles where they ran out of money.

Her boyfriend told her that she was too beautiful to be broke. He was certain he could get her a job as a model. Not long after that, she was introduced to a photographer and began her first modeling job. The photo session started innocently enough, but before it was over she had posed for a wide range of heterosexual and lesbian pornography. Other photo sessions followed, some with her boyfriend and some with him and another woman.

The photographer gave her a handful of photographs and $500. It was not enough to live on in Los Angeles for more than a couple of weeks, so she turned to a new trade—burglary. She was not very good as a burglar and she was caught. Police found the photos and a cache of pornographic magazines with her pictures in them when they searched her home looking for additional evidence of burglaries.

She refused to swear out a complaint against her boyfriend and the photographer, and police could not force her to do so. She was a minor and could not be prosecuted as an adult, so her parents were notified. They flew to Los Angeles and returned her to Georgia.

The Georgia girl was a willing victim. A thirteen-year-old from Baltimore was not. And when her parents came to New York to pick up their daughter, it was only hours after she had escaped from a pimp who held her in a hotel room and raped and beat her trying to turn her into a prostitute.

She and two fifteen-year-old girlfriends had been picked up minutes after they walked out of the Port Authority bus terminal in New York. The thirty-seven-year-old man who struck up a conversation with them lured them to his room in a nearby hotel with promises of work. He reputedly talked the two older girls into becoming prostitutes, and raped and beat the younger girl when she refused. He left the hotel to deliver the older girls to another pimp, she told police.

Transportation terminals are notorious hunting grounds for pimps. Commander Thomas of Chicago says that bus stations are prime for picking up young girls or boys to be inducted into prostitution. Trains no longer carry the great number of passengers from small towns and farms that they did once, and runaways generally cannot afford air travel. Consequently, they hitchhike or ride buses.

Thomas knows what he is talking about. A veteran police officer who gained most of his experience working with juveniles, he knows why children run away, where they go, and the type of people who are likely to shelter or exploit them. He has also seen dozens of pimps in action.

His men and women officers regularly patrolled the Trailways and Greyhound bus terminals in the Loop hoping to thwart the perfumed men in the flashy suits, wide-brimmed Superfly hats, and expensive gold jewelry who lurked inside waiting for naive, frightened children. When the police lost and the pimps won, it meant some child would be turned onto the streets as a hapless, spiritless prostitute within a few hours after arriving in Chicago.

A delicate little fifteen-year-old blonde runaway who had just gotten off a bus from Tennessee when she met one of the pimps was one of the unlucky ones. She was tired, dirty, and almost broke. She knew that her divorced parents and their respective lovers in a Chicago suburb probably would not be overjoyed when they learned she was home.

There was a two-hour layover before she could get another bus for home, and she was not unfriendly when a middle-aged man introduced himself. She was agreeable when he offered to show her the town. And it sounded perfectly reasonable when he suggested that she walk out of the terminal first and he would follow because he did not want police to see them together.

He stopped at a shoe store where he bought her a pair of shoes and then drove her in his Cadillac to his apartment in a highrise along Lake Michigan. They drank, smoked marijuana, and spent the night. When they awoke the next morning, her older friend explained that he was a pimp and that she was going to work for him. She began working that day, picking up her first tricks in a bar. When her pimp moved her to a couple of hotels a few days later, she learned that she was never to go near the desk, but was to walk directly to the elevator and talk to the bellboy. The bellboy would show her to a room, and was to be given a $5 tip. She charged $25 to $100 a trick.

After a few months at the hotels, she was shifted to a couple of the suburbs and eventually began working at migrant camps and truck stops. She and three other girls would make the nightly trips to the camps and accommodate 20 to 25 men for $20 each. She was allowed to keep 40 percent of the take and had Wednesdays off.

The truck stops just south of Chicago and across the state line in East Gary, Indiana, were more of the same. The trucks were parked with the drivers waiting inside, and she would knock on the door and ask if they wanted company. The system was old-fashioned. Less than a year later, truck stop hookers were using CB radios.

Seven prostitutes were rounded up in one raid at a truck stop in Calumet City, Illinois, after vice squad police borrowed a rig with a CB band and contacted the women via radio. The women were charging

$25 to $50, with an occasional $100 trick for specialties or a motel room. One prostitute monitored on the CB said she was tired and going home because she had handled more than 100 tricks that night.

The fifteen-year-old was not among those picked up in the truck stop raid. She had already run away from her pimp. She had been with him in his luxury apartment when he began beating her with his fists and feet. Then he straightened out a pair of wire coathangers, taped them together, and whipped her. He said he was angry because he had heard she was going to leave him. When he pushed her out and told her to go back to work, she went to the police.

Police files are bulging with stories like that. Police know all about the pimps who use bus terminals as hunting grounds, but find it difficult to arrest them. They are cunning and sly, and they know how to make the laws work in their favor.

One of the procurers is a tall slender native of Texas who is a few years over forty and has a two-page arrest record. As a career criminal, he has spent more than one-third of his life in various penitentiaries, including 11 years for armed robbery. At some point in his life, he apparently realized that pimping paid better than holdups and was safer.

In approximately six years as a panderer he has only two vice arrests, neither of them resulting in a conviction. During that time he has recruited dozens of teenage girls and regularly maintains a stable of nine to 16 prostitutes. Each one was personally handpicked as she struggled uncertainly through the loading dock doors of a bus terminal, dragging a suitcase or precariously balancing paper bags full of possessions.

He is careful how he approaches a girl. He never openly addresses her the first time, but will stand next to her and make a comment to no one in particular. If she responds and is agreeable, he buys her a cup of coffee and begins the sweet-talk. He has estimated that of 100 girls he approaches, only 10 will talk to him. Only one of those will leave with him. But that girl is certain to be prostituting herself for him the next day.

Management of the terminal knows what is going on, and private guards and uniformed policemen are on duty at all times. In 1977, Greyhound was reported to be spending $85,000 for private security guards in efforts to intimidate and frustrate panderers.

Thousands of dollars expended for support of Chicago police officers assigned there can be added to the overall cost of the effort. Youthful appearing policewomen in plain clothes lug suitcases through the terminal doing their best to look wistful and lost. Sometimes a panderer makes the mistake of approaching one of them and is arrested. But pimps maintain high-priced stables of lawyers as well as streetwalkers and are usually back on station the same day, as hungry as ever for new flesh—although possibly a bit more cautious. Coaching from attorneys apparently led to the practice of some pimps of purchasing bus tickets so they have an excuse to loiter in the terminal. The tickets are cashed in after they have served their purpose.

Police know the pimps by sight, but it is difficult to make an arrest for loitering if the panderers show a ticket or say they are waiting for someone. One man ejected from the vicinity of a special seating section for women responded to the insult by filing a discrimination complaint against the operators of the terminal. Pimps complain of violation of their civil rights and threaten law suits if private security officers or city police attempt to run them off or arrest them. Even those few who are arrested and successfully prosecuted look forward to no more than a few months probation or a fine of a few hundred dollars.

As costly and sincere as efforts are to discourage the pimps, they have not stopped the recruitment of young girls for prostitution. More than 200 buses carrying some 5,000 passengers arrive or depart from the busy terminal every day. Almost every bus carries one or more girls who are on their own for the first time and looking for excitement, adventure, or escape.

Occasionally pimps use one of their women to help lure a girl into the trade. A nineteen-year-old Moline, Illinois, woman on her way to visit relatives in Indiana accompanied two women and a man from the bus terminal in Chicago to a west side apartment where she was told a party was in progress. She said she was beaten and repeatedly raped in efforts to coerce her into becoming a prostitute. She escaped by leaping through a first-floor window.

Transportation terminals are not the only source of new girls for procurers who use promises, abduction, and violence to acquire new flesh. Taxi drivers have been arrested for trying to sweet-talk young undercover policewomen into permitting themselves to be set up in business as whores.

The experience of a fifteen-year-old student at a south side Chicago high school was even more frightful. She spent seven terrifying weeks as the prisoner of a young couple who beat and tortured her, forcing her to commit as many as 150 acts of prostitution in apartments, hotels, and in parked cars near the Great Lakes Naval Station.

The girl said she was walking from school when a woman leaned out of the window of a parked Cadillac and yelled, "Hey, I know you, don't I? Come here, I want to talk to you." The teenager approached the car and a man seated beside the woman pulled a gun, ordering her to climb inside.

The couple, whom she came to know as "Don Juan" and "Pinky," drove her to their home and informed her that she was going to become a prostitute. The man placed the gun to her head, the woman flashed two long knives, and they warned her that she had better cooperate. Then the man raped her.

That night, the couple drove her some 40 miles north to a town near the naval station where Pinky roamed the bars and lined up clients whom she brought outside to the car where they had sex with the girl. Pinky collected $50 from each of the men. After a trip to Milwaukee, where she was forced to entertain several of Don Juan's reputed friends, she tried to escape. Don Juan caught up with her a few blocks away. He took her to a north side apartment and forced her to strip in front of four other men, then thrashed her with three coat hangers he had bent into whips and heated over a flame.

She escaped for good after Pinky drove her to Chicago's Rush Street area of bars, go-go joints, and restaurants and instructed her to pick up some tricks. She asked the first man she approached for help and he took her inside a hotel where employees telephoned police. The girl identified Pinky and Don Juan from mug shots, and they were charged with pandering and contributing to the sexual delinquency of a minor. Don Juan had a three-page arrest sheet for prostitution and narcotics violations.

A fifteen-year-old Miami girl survived a similar ordeal. The junior high school student was on her way to church when she was tricked into accompanying a woman and then held prisoner. She was tied up in a closet for a time and beaten and tortured with a heated metal comb to force her into sex acts with at least 15 men who visited the apartment during the two weeks she was held.

The girl finally slipped the bonds with which she had been tied to a bed, pulled a dress over her naked body, and jumped out a window. She ran to a police call box and telephoned for help. Police took her to a hospital where she was treated for severe burns on her breasts, buttocks, and sex organs. When police officers went to the house to question the couple, the man attacked them. As they fought him off, his wife escaped out the window.

The fifteen-year-olds from Chicago's south side and from Miami were spunky and fighters. Despite repeated death threats, beatings, and sexual abuse, they fled from their captors at the first opportunity. Yet other girls willingly ride off with men so obviously in the sex business that even the most naive farm girl should recognize the danger. Many of them stay for months or years, despite repeated opportunities to escape, putting their faith instead in brutal men who see them only in terms of dollar signs. Why?

Many runaways view their pimps as substitute fathers, according to Samuel S. Janus and Dorothy H. Bracey, psychologists who interviewed 79 runaways, ranging from fourteen to seventeen years old, who were involved full time in prostitution or pornography. "The pimp builds upon the family model, with himself as the exploiting father," the psychologists wrote in the January 1, 1980, issue of *The Odyssey Journal*.

Once within the group, the new girls become "wives-in-law," (freelancers or girls in other stables are "outlaws.") There is a strict hierarchy. The Number One lady is at the top. It is she who rides in the gleaming pimpmobile, wears expensive clothing and jewelry, and handles the other girls like a tough master sergeant.

The meticulously structured family functions on discipline and strict adherence to more regulations than most people can find in *Roberts Rules of Order*. After experiencing the uneasy freedom of a runaway, many girls welcome the structured security of their new situation and may develop ferocious loyalty to their pimp. Other, more experienced members of the stable reinforce the pimp's appeal, assuring doubtful newcomers that he is banking the money they earn and building a nest egg for the day they retire so they can live in style.

The pimp shamelessly exploits his women. Nevertheless, he is the respected father-figure and the fulcrum of the family unit. As a member of the stable, the prostitute knows she plays a vital part in his family and business. A successful pimp must be everything to his women— father, baby, analyst. They look to him for authority, they pamper him, and—paradoxically—they look to him for comfort.

"This strong male who begins by offering structure and nurturance and then demanding help and obedience evokes tremendous loyalty from the girls," according to Janus and Bracey. They point out the close parallel with religious cults, the other major magnet for runaways. Both offer the supportive yet remote male figure who is the source of strict discipline. And the fact that one demands sexual activity, while the other usually forbids it, is irrelevant to a "girl who is emotionally neutral as far as sex is concerned."

The fact that most big city pimps are Black is a phenomenon that is intriguing to law enforcement officers and sociologists alike. Many of them believe they know why the combination of Black pimp and white teenage prostitute works so effectively.

James Greenlay, a sergeant with the New York Police Department, who specializes in runaways, believes one of the reasons to be that many white parents would not permit their daughter to date a Black person. Black men have become, so to speak, forbidden fruit. Runaways are estranged from their parents, and when the girl arrives in the city she is probably anxious to flout their authority. "Now, most of our pimps in this city are Black, and when a young girl meets a pimp on the street, she's determined to prove she's not prejudiced," Greenlay said. "She won't say no when he asks her to go for coffee."[2]

Judy Dietl was not a runaway, but the tragedy of her life gives some credence to Greenlay's theory. Judy was voted the prettiest girl in the senior class at Colchester High School in Colchester, Vermont, before she packed her bags and set off with a girlfriend for Boston, her heart set on becoming an airline stewardess. In Boston, the girls enrolled at Bay State Junior College and found themselves rooms at a YWCA.

Unsophisticated and somewhat intimidated by the city and the sinister neighborhood, they spent their early weeks close to school and their rooms at the Y. One night, however, they met three Black men at a nearby grocery store where they stopped to buy cupcakes to celebrate the friend's eighteenth birthday. Two of the men, Damon and Louis, asked the girls out. Judy reportedly hesitated because she and her girlfriend were white and the men were Black. Her mother was later quoted as saying she remembered a paper written by Judy at about that time commenting, "I knew I wasn't raised this way, and I didn't want to go." But her girlfriend urged her to go and she relented.[3]

Judy's date was older than her father. According to later statements by her girlfriend, he was also a pimp and had been for more than 20 years. Boston police said they had no record of morals arrests for the man, but Judy's roommate said it was because he used frequent aliases.

After the first date, Judy began writing to her sister, Debbie, about the "two guys." "We figured that they must have spent at least $100 on us," she wrote. She talked of fine dinners in a Polynesian restaurant, rides in limousines, gifts of nice clothing and jewelry. "This is not like Vermont at all," she added.

Debbie kept her sister's secret for a while, then she telephoned her mother and told her that Judy was dating a Black man. Debbie was afraid he was a pimp. The girl's roommate later swore in an affidavit that Judy had worked as a prostitute. The roommate was also once quoted as saying, "We were sitting around the Green Room at the Y and she asked him, 'Damon, when do you want me to start working?' I think he was surprised," Judy's friend said. She added that Judy was ordered not to date any Blacks or any white men under thirty because Damon "didn't want to lose her to a straight guy."[4]

Mrs. Dietl went to Boston and surprised Judy in her room. She found an identification card with her daughter's photo and the name "Sherry D'Amico." The card carried instructions to notify Damon in case of emergencies. It was later learned that the Beacon Street address on the card was that of a house that vice squad detectives had raided several times as a result of prostitution investigations. The distressed mother found other evidence that she believed pointed to an illicit involvement with Damon. Judy returned with her mother to the family's home near Lake Champlain.

But Colchester and the ice cream store her parents operated no longer held much interest for the young girl who had turned eighteen several months earlier. Damon was telephoning her, but her mother advised her that if she returned to Boston it would be the end of her family ties. Nevertheless, Judy went to nearby Burlington and was apparently waiting for a bus to return to Boston when her seventeen-year-old brother caught up with her. He called home and Judy's mother arrived a few minutes before the bus was to leave. Judy was returned home again, and for the next few days she had to accompany her mother any time either of them left the house.

After eavesdropping on a disturbing telephone call one day from Judy's girlfriend in Boston, Mrs. Dietl asked her daughter outright if she was returning to the city. Judy said she was.

According to a chronology of events later related in court by attorney Charles Tetzlaff, Mrs. Dietl went to church a few hours later and prayed. She worked at the store all day the next day, and that night Judy reiterated that she was going to leave. Mrs. Dietl did not sleep that night.

"In the early morning hours, as the children were leaving for school and her husband was preparing for work, she heard a voice say, 'Today is the day she dies,' " Tetzlaff continued. The woman loaded two of her husband's handguns, the attorney said. During the afternoon, she learned from her youngest daughter that Judy planned to leave the next day.

Mrs. Dietl asked Judy to take a ride with her to a quiet synagogue in Burlington, mentioning something about a rummage sale. In the parking lot, Mrs. Dietl pulled a .38-caliber revolver from her purse and pointed it at her daughter. She squeezed the trigger.

"No, Mama! No, Mama!" her daughter cried.

The distraught mother continued firing, then turned and screamed, "Judy, I can't let you go." Later she walked to a nearby house and asked the people there to telephone the police.

Marilyn Dietl was charged with second-degree murder, although the prosecution admitted that it appeared to be a classic instance of first-degree murder. But a conviction of first-degree murder could mean a life term in prison, the state's attorney pointed out, and he did not think she deserved such harsh punishment. In her mind, she considered the shooting a mercy killing, he said. Mrs. Dietl pleaded guilty and was sentenced to five to 15 years in prison.

Sometime later Judy's friend told a newspaper reporter that she knew why Judy was apparently willing to become a prostitute. "She told me, 'He treats me the way I've always wanted to be treated. He's kind to me.' " Judy was anxious to please her boyfriend and prove she could earn money for him, the girl said.[5]

Prosecuting pimps can be frustrating and unrewarding. Prostitutes, like very young children, make poor witnesses. Their credibility is almost nil. Their stories are often filled with contradictions. Even when they have become angry and gone to the police they are undependable. Fear or a revival of misplaced notions of love may make them suddenly deny previous statements or to take all the blame for their prostitution on themselves. In New York and in most other states, the law requires corroboration of the testimony of a prostitute in order to prosecute her pimp. This could mean another witness, or getting the prostitute to visit her pimp while wearing a concealed tape recorder to obtain a taped admission from him. Either is highly unlikely.

Law enforcement authorities cite these difficulties when they are accused of laxity in prosecuting pimps. A sergeant with New York's pimp squad—the first in the country—once noted that he could identify 1,000 pimps by name but could not arrest a single one of them.

It's not like you have a housewife who says, 'This guy knocked on my door saying he was the exterminator and then he raped me.' When you take a prostitute and put her before a jury of twelve straight people, they think that she's as bad as he is," the policeman explained.[6]

No matter what police try to do to curb the problem of teenagers recruited into prostitution, it will never go away, according to Commander Thomas of the Chicago Police Department. "Pimps like to grow their own, find them themselves, educate and raise them. Their influence over them is greater that way," Thomas says. "In contrast, an experienced prostitute will only go with a pimp if she desires."

Ironically, just as laws make it difficult to successfully prosecute pimps, laws also make it difficult for police and private agencies to protect runaways.

Thomas points out that, first of all, runaways are missing persons. And being a missing person is not a crime. If police are looking for a burglar, a rapist, or a bank robber and they locate him, they can take him into custody and hold him—at least until he makes bail. The suspect is accused of a crime. "But if I find a sixteen-year-old or a fifteen-year-old, or a thirteen-year-old that's been away from home nine months, I can't put him in an institution. I can't, even though he's run away from home and violated what we call the Status Offense Act of the Minor in Need of Supervision," the police officer explained.

The child cannot be placed in a secure detention facility while other arrangements are made to get help for him, even if police know—but perhaps cannot prove—that he or she has been involved in prostitution. Instead, they must refer him or her to the courts and surrender custody to the Illinois Status Offenders Services Agency. The child is picked up by an agency representative and usually placed in a foster home.

"Well, as you can imagine, a lot of them just run from the foster home. That's why I think society is spinning its wheels," Thomas sighed. "All children are not able to make rational decisions about what is in their best interest. Some adults can't.

"The most negative thing going for children under seventeen is the ruling that we cannot hold them, even if it is an attempt to provide services for them," Thomas said. "Even if we know they're going to leave two minutes after we release them. There is some mistaken belief that we're violating their civil rights and that, unless we have a criminal charge to place on them, we can't hold them.

"I'll admit that we certainly don't want to violate the rights of any youngsters, but dealing in the field of youth for 27 years, I know that a lot of youngsters need help. And those we help by holding them for some mental, psychological, or psychiatric help they may need will far outweigh those we might harm by violating their so-called civil rights."

William Katz of the ASPCC agrees with many of the things Thomas says. A burly, bearded, plainspoken man, Katz studied at the John Jay College of Criminal Justice in New York, planning to become a policeman. But he became aware of so many problems and inconsistencies in the criminal justice system that he decided upon another line of work.

"I don't think it's particularly significant why kids run," he says. "The answers are as varied as the kids who choose to go. Some run because life is very bad at home; and others because life at home is very good. The most important problem that we face with runaways today is what society does when kids run."

Not so long ago there were stories about bus drivers who stopped their vehicles at the first rest stop and quietly called the sheriff's department after spotting a runaway aboard. Today, that same driver unconcernedly pushes on. He does not want to become involved in a lengthy and probably futile brouhaha over children's rights.

Civil libertarians have functional authority figures in this society in a state of fear, Katz complains. The same gray area in the law that once permitted law enforcement officers to abuse an individual citizen's rights also allowed them to protect that citizen's child. Police expected answers when they asked a suspected runaway, "Who are you?" and "Where did you come from?" They continued asking the questions until they extracted satisfactory answers.

Today, people have become so conscious of and concerned with human rights that they are almost forced to treat children as little adults instead of individuals who have not yet reached emotional, intellectual, and physical maturity. Katz believes that the most important rights children have are the rights to be nurtured, protected, loved, educated, and directed until they reach their majority. Only then should they be afforded the rights and privileges of adults.

"Unfortunately, civil libertarians would have you believe that children have the same ability to exercise rights as grownups do," he says. "That's one source of the problem. Adults have formed certain perspectives on life and have taken responsibilities on themselves out of necessity. But you can't convince me that a twelve-year-old kid should be expected to exercise the same degree of judgment. Therefore, we set standards for children. We don't give them carte blanche."

Laws have changed as the courts found it increasingly difficult to deal with problem children. For some time in New York state, the law provided special treatment for runaway girls under the age of eighteen, but permitted boys to be dealt with as runaways only until they were sixteen. Then someone decided that the different age groupings constituted sex discrimination. They sued and won. Instead of boosting the age group cutoff for boys to eighteen authorities lowered the age for girls to sixteen. Thus, no additional protection was extended to boys, and the previous protection and services available for girls between the ages of sixteen and eighteen were eliminated.

"What's happening," Katz declared, "is that people are saying to children: 'Well, you're unmanageable, so we're not going to try to manage you.' . . . This is the age of deregulating. They're not going to regulate the airlines, they're not going to regulate the oil companies, and they're not going to regulate the kids."

There has been a pattern during the past 30 years of lower age limits, lesser penalties, and lowered standards of due diligence in state and federal laws. The tendency, says Katz, is "to reduce, rather than to deal with."

The new attitudes probably make it easier for a child to run away. But they do not make it any easier or safer for him or her to survive on the street. In the late 1960s, runaways sometimes were fortunate enough to fall in with people who treated them fairly. Runaways were a part of the scenario in Haight-Asbury of San Francisco, Greenwich Village and the East Village in New York, Powellton Village in West Philadelphia, Quincy Marketplace on the south end in Boston, and other communities where so-called hippies or flower children congregated. Runaways peddled flowers, crafts, and underground newspapers on streetcorners alongside their peers and were fed and allowed to sleep in crash pads supported by various free communes and groups like the Diggers. One of the best known and earliest of the self-help communalist groups associated with the flower children of the late 1960s, The Diggers established free stores, giving away food, medical care, shelter, clothing, and money they acquired by scavenging or begging. Those communities were products of their time and, for the most part, no longer exist.

Today, when a child arrives in a major city, he or she falls in with a different type of street person, one who deals with a runaway in a commercial manner. If the child knows no one in this new city, the relationship he or she formulates may be from the need to have a friend. Consequently, he or she becomes a potential victim of ripoffs or robbery. When the money is gone, one of three alternatives remains: to return home, to become involved in an organized program for runaways, or to find a sponsor.

Many return to their homes. Others filter into public and private agencies that provide shelter and counseling. But a number of children are not ready to accept either alternative. Most of these children eventually find someone who is supportive, but almost invariably the new-found friend and protector plans to exploit the child, either commercially, criminally, or sexually.

People actively looking for a child to exploit do not have to look very hard. Runaways loiter in the same places that other children do—in arcades, movies, record stores—and, in rural or suburban areas, in shopping centers. If a chicken hawk or pimp frequents an area that attracts transients or tourists and sees the same child there five or six days consecutively, the youngster is probably a runaway.

People who make a business of picking up children can spot a runaway as handily as a poker player can win with a straight flush. From that point on, it is simple for an experienced procurer to approach the child, begin a conversation, buy a sandwich or soft drink, and take the victim home.

Katz estimates that from 10,000 to 20,000 boys and girls are engaged in sex for pay in New York City. Only a handful are ever apprehended. When they are arrested, they lie about their age, posing as adults so that they can quickly return to the streets. The ASPCC official cited, as an example, a girl who was fourteen when she ran away to New York and was turned out as a prostitute. She was arrested and prosecuted 10 times in two years but each time she reported she was over sixteen and was always back at work within 24 hours.

Sometimes, despite the involvement of several government agencies working with a single runaway, bureaucratic bungling and indolence can combine to destroy the child. Six public and private agencies in New York had some contact with Veronica Brunson during the year she walked the streets of the city's midtown area and served short sentences in its jails as a prostitute.

None of the agencies intervened or acted firmly enough to redirect her life or to save it, before she was pushed, or fell, from the tenth-story window of a seedy Manhattan hotel frequented by pimps and prostitutes. Veronica was about five-feet-one, weighed 110 pounds, and was twelve years old when she died. She had become a prostitute when she was eleven.

Communication breakdowns and bureaucratic barriers added to the failure to help the child before it was too late, according to a spokesman for agencies which had contact with her. People who have studied the case and who work with sexually exploited children in New York consider it to be a classic example of how easily a child can be passed back and forth through the system without getting any help.

Veronica was the only girl in a family of four children, and was two years old when she moved with her mother and older brothers from North Carolina to Brooklyn. The fatherless family soon went on welfare.

With public assistance Mrs. Brunson provided her family with a neatly kept three-bedroom apartment in a building operated by the public housing authority. Although each of Veronica's brothers became involved in scrapes with police and came to know their way around the juvenile courts, she was well-behaved and got along well with her mother, teachers, and other children in the project.

She listened to soul or rock music with other children, talked and giggled with other little girls, or wheeled past clusters of youngsters and adults as she rode her bicycle back and forth along the sidewalks near her home. Her mother gave her pocket money and sewed most of her clothes, but Veronica typically dressed in blue jeans. She was bright and cheerful and did not appear to be sensitive about her slight lisp or about difficulties in school. She was not a good student and she was held back one year in elementary school. Then she was transferred to a program for slow learners.

The first serious trouble occurred when Veronica brought home an older girl, Diana, whom she had met at Coney Island. When the girl asked if Veronica could visit with her in Manhattan for a few days, Mrs. Brunson refused. Her daughter was too young, and the other girl was uncomfortably worldly. It seemed strange that an eighteen-year-old would be attracted to a girl as young as Veronica as a best friend.

A short time after Mrs. Brunson met Diana, Veronica disappeared. She returned home three days later, blithely explaining that she had been staying with her new friend. After that, the absences continued, initially for two or three days at a time. Veronica periodically telephoned her mother to assure her that she was safe. Mrs. Brunson never reported the absences to police.

When school opened that fall, Veronica did not attend. Several weeks later, her counselor telephoned her home to ask why she was not in school. Mrs. Brunson admitted then that she had not seen her daughter in six weeks. Responding to the urging of the counselor, Mrs. Brunson filed a police report.

The next day, Veronica was arrested on a prostitution charge. She told the truth when she was asked her name and age. She was released to the custody of her mother and her case was referred to Family Court, which deals with criminal matters involving children under the age of sixteen.

Veronica eventually returned to school. But although they did not know of her prostitution arrest, her teachers were aware she had undergone an incredible change. Her faithful blue jeans had been replaced by fashionable, color-coordinated clothes, nylon stockings, and high heel shoes. She was using makeup. Veronica had changed from a naive, playful child to a girl who was precociously streetwise and obviously trying her best to grow up overnight. She told at least two of her teachers that pimps were attempting to recruit her for their stables.

She missed 121 of 180 days of class that year, and when teachers or counselors inquired about her absences they were usually told she was ill. One of the few days she attended school was on December 5, her twelfth birthday. She knew one of her teachers was planning a party for her. Veronica was not as sophisticated as she wished to believe.

An officer with the Manhattan Family Court Probation Department meanwhile had interviewed the girl and her mother as a result of the arrest and determined that the matter would not be referred to the courts. He preferred keeping her record clean and recommended outpatient counseling at the Brooklyn Center for Psychotherapy. A few months later, apparently unaware of her truancy and continued contacts with pimps, prostitutes, and other habitués of the criminal subculture, the Probation Department closed her case.

It is unclear if the girl kept her appointments at the Brooklyn Center for Psychotherapy because the institution sealed her records after her death, citing confidentiality. One thing is known for certain: she continued to skip classes at school and continued to haunt the red-light districts along Eighth Avenue and Forty-Second Street in Manhattan. She was known to other prostitutes by her childhood nickname, "Bay-Bay," or, because of her size, as "Shortie."

In one three-month period she was picked up 11 times by police, usually on misdemeanor charges of loitering for prostitution. She was sufficiently streetwise by then to carry no identification and to use a false name and address. Vanessa Brown and Paula Brunson were two of her favorite aliases. She always said she was eighteen, and was usually released after spending the night in the police station. At least twice, however, she was convicted and spent a total of 12 days in the Women's House of Detention with adult prisoners.

She revealed her true age and identity only once during the string of arrests and told police she wanted to call her mother. Again, she was released to the custody of her mother and referred to Family Court. When a Probation Department officer suggested that Veronica be institutionalized or placed in a foster home, her mother was unsure whether or not she favored a placement plan. Another interview was scheduled for a few weeks later.

A few hours after the initial interview, Veronica, using one of her aliases, was picked up again by police for allegedly soliciting. She remained on the street, enduring occasional arrests. She missed her next appointment with the Probation Department officer. Various agencies still involved with her case knew she was missing, but bounced responsibility for dealing with her back and forth.

Her last known prostitution arrest occurred on July 18. A Criminal Court judge, assuming that she was eighteen as she claimed, ordered a 15-day jail sentence for her. She jumped bail.

Eleven days later, some of the guests at the Markwell Hotel on Forty-Ninth Street, just west of Broadway, heard a scream and the dull thump of a body smacking into the pavement. Nearly naked, Veronica Brunson was unconscious on the sidewalk. She did not regain consciousness and died four days later.

Investigators never learned exactly how the girl came to take the fatal plunge. Other whores and street people said that she was sitting on a window sill quarreling with her pimp when she accidentally tumbled over backwards. According to other stories, the tiny girl was quarreling with a pimp who hurled her out of the window.

There was one thing only that vice squad detectives knew for sure: Veronica Brunson, one of the youngest streetwalkers in the city, was dead.

[1] *Indianapolis News*, August 24, 1979.
[2] *Viva*, November, 1978.
[3] *Chicago Tribune*, July 19, 1978.
[4] *Provident Sunday Journal*, November 19, 1978.
[5] *Ibid.*
[6] *New York Times*, March 12, 1978.

9.

The Minnesota Pipeline

THE girl was a honey blonde, petite, with tired blue eyes whose glitter had been stolen by drugs and the life she led. The strong light of a late afternoon sun softly illuminated her carelessly groomed hair and the beauty of her classic Scandinavian features.

A year earlier her smile may have been warm and captivating, but it had turned plastic and artificial. It was closer to a grimace, a forlorn caricature of a smile that better fitted the business she engaged in as she slowly promenaded along New York's seedy Eighth Avenue between 40th and 50th Streets near Times Square.

There on the infamous Minnesota Strip she walked and tarried 14 to 16 hours every afternoon and night until she earned her "nut," the amount of money a girl must accumulate before her pimp permits her to go home. If she returned with less, she could expect a severe beating before being pushed outside again to work until she made up the shortage.

In the late 70s, a hard-working streetwalker could earn $100 to $150 a night. By 1980, inflation pushed the nut for some girls to $150 to $200, accumulated from a succession of men at $20 or $25 a trick. For that amount a man could tarry for roughly 20 minutes in a shabby hotel room with a teenager or slightly older woman.

Some girls are no more than thirteen or fourteen, occasionally as young as Veronica Brunson. Even experienced vice squad detectives sometimes find it difficult to assess a girl's true age. Hot pants or miniskirts and boots or platform shoes make them look as alike as clones. Heavy cosmetics, generously, if carelessly, applied, mask the juvenile acne and other imperfections on their pale skins. And the business quickly adds age lines.

Scores of teenagers like the blue-eyed, blond, once naive girls from farms and small towns have been funneled through a cruel pipeline that spills directly into the heart of Manhattan. A disproportionate number

148

of them are fair haired and of Scandinavian ancestry, and most of them grew up in the Northern Plains states—especially in Minnesota.

The Minnesota Strip extends only a few short, tawdry neon-illuminated blocks, but it is an open cesspool of sex and crime. Almost any thrill can be bought there. Men loitering on the streets snort white powders as openly as others pass around bottles of cheap muscatel and white port. The sweet, cloying odor of marijuana hangs around the X-rated movie houses, peep shows, topless bars, and pornographic bookstores on the Strip. It is a virtual Disneyland of sexual perversity.

A man can mince self-consciously, wearing silver hotpants, a lowcut blouse, fishnet stockings, platform shoes, and a blond wig without attracting so much as a snicker. A shopper can purchase *Slaves For A Nazi Stud*, and *Sisterhood of Torture* easier than he can locate a Bible, a dictionary, or a restaurant guide.

Times Square and the surrounding cross streets always have been wide open. During World War I, soldiers and sailors in the New York City area headed for the erotic playground as soon as they were off duty. Officers and civil authorities looked the other way when the doughboys lined up flashy dates. A war was going on and the young soldiers needed recreation.

By the time World War II began, nothing much had changed. "Victory Girls" were available to GIs and civilians alike for a price. (Morale was also important on the home front.)

There have been clean-up campaigns, of course, but they have been uniformly unsuccessful. A few years ago, tenants in the neighboring theater district complained that streetwalkers were ruining their businesses and petitioned the police for help. Scores of hookers were swept off the streets in the ensuing crackdown. But the girls had posted bond and returned to their old haunts before the arresting officers could complete their paperwork. That night they worked harder than ever so they could return safely to their pimps.

Crime is so blatant in Times Square and along the Minnesota Strip that police in patrol cars rarely pay more than the most casual attention to the prostitutes who hug the doorways of the hotels and sex arcades. There is simply too much violent crime and too little concern about the young whores to justify wholesale prostitution arrests.

The streets are at least as dangerous for the youthful hustlers as for anyone else. Police were almost certain that the two young victims of twin mutilation killings in 42nd street hotel room in 1979 were prostitutes or runaways. Investigators could not be sure, however, because the girls were so horribly butchered. The psychopathic killer had severed their heads and hands with surgical precision, then doused their bodies with gasoline and ignited them.

The gruesome crime had disturbing similarities to the dismemberment murder nearly a year earlier of a teenage prostitute from California. Helen Sikes was a runaway known to girlfriends on the Minnesota Strip as "Bouncy." Bouncy's body with the head nearly severed was found dumped in Queens, her legs about a block away.

Two months after the Sikes slaying, two reputed prostitutes were shot to death as they slept on the floor of the F. Yoo Massage Parlor in Midtown Manhattan. A twenty-year-old bartender-bouncer, said to be enraged because he had not been paid, was charged with the killings. Another woman testified in court that the accused killer also put a gun to her head and pulled the trigger, but it misfired.

Girls from Minnesota and other Plains states have fed the New York flesh markets for decades. But the most noticeable jump in the numbers of blond, fair-skinned Midwesterners occurred in 1975 about the time the state of Minnesota adopted legislation establishing a mandatory 90-day jail sentence for a second prostitution conviction. This could mean lost earnings of $10,000 or more for one girl. Pimps along Nicollet Avenue from 14th to 26th Streets in Minneapolis' Sixth Police District, one of the busiest and most infamous red-light areas between Chicago and the Pacific Northwest, began scurrying about, looking for safer, more lucrative territory. They found it in New York, and Eighth Avenue near Times Square acquired its nickname as the Minnesota Strip.

Legislators and the courts in New York were less hardnosed about the prostitution business than those in Minneapolis. Clients were available in greater numbers and were often more generous. And if a working girl happened to be unlucky enough to get arrested, she could usually count on returning to the street after posting nominal bail, paying a small fine, or spending no more than a night or two in jail. Simple geography provided added appeal. The 1,000 miles or more to New York from Minnesota was one more important factor in the pimps' efforts to isolate the young girls they called "packages" or "flatbacks" from their families.

The year after the get-tough legislation was adopted in Minnesota, Minneapolis police estimated that some 400 girls and young women, many of them barely into their teens, were filtered through the pipeline to New York. Three years later, authorities were talking about 1,000 girls moving through the Twin Cities (Minneapolis-St. Paul) to New York.

Actually, police say, the pipeline is geographically triangular, involving a loose federation of pimps with some ties to Memphis, Tennessee, who recruit and often train their girls in the Twin Cities area before moving them to New York. Stopovers are occasionally made in Chicago and other cities where the girls toil briefly and are sometimes traded or sold.

One Minneapolis policeman close to the street scene remarked that he personally knows of at least 200 pimps who recruit in the city or work their girls there. He estimated that there must be at least another 100 he did not know.

As in Chicago and other cities, pimps patrol the bus terminals of Minneapolis, watching for new talent arriving from the small towns and rural areas of Minnesota, the Dakotas, Nebraska, and Iowa. Minneapolis is a magnet for runaways from states throughout the Upper Midwest. Some pimps offer $25 bounties to high school girls to pinpoint classmates who are having boy friend problems or troubles at home. Still others prowl the IDS Crystal Court, a towering office building with a wide plaza where runaways congregate.

Three teenagers who were picked up by pimps on Minneapolis streets and turned into prostitutes in Manhattan testified before a New York State select legislative committee on crime, which was investigating the possible role of the mob or syndicate in juvenile prostitution. The girls, all blondes, were flown to New York for the hearings and were masked as they told legislators how they had traveled through the pipeline from the Midwest to the East Coast.

One fourteen-year-old girl said she was lured into prostitution after a smooth-talking pimp approached her one morning as she was walking in the downtown business area and offered to buy her breakfast. She accepted. He was charming, attentive, generous with his money, and she was flattered at the attention from an older man. And she felt more than a tiny sense of excitement and adventure, with some pride in her own daring, because she was white and he was Black. She slept with him that night.

There was no trouble when she left the apartment in the early hours of the next morning. The trouble occurred when her parents demanded to know where she had been and why she thought she could get away with staying out until all hours of the night. She ran away after the quarrel.

Her new friend took her in, but he explained that she would have to earn her keep and her bus fare to Chicago by hustling and stealing money from her tricks. She paid their fare to Chicago and three weeks after they arrived there added another $800 to their nest egg. New York was their next stop, and her pimp taught her to work an area near the luxury midtown hotels. She continued to steal from her tricks when she had the chance.

Somehow the good times and the luxurious life she was promised did not materialize, and the teenager began to complain. Selling herself to five to ten men a night, $20 at a time, six and seven days a week, was a chore, and there was nothing glamorous about it. She did not want to work anymore and she said so to her pimp. He beat her so brutally that he broke her jaw. When she left the hospital, the bones were still wired shut. But there was no reason she couldn't work with a broken jaw, and he pushed her back on the street with instructions not to return until she had earned her old quota.

She tried suicide once but failed. The suicide attempt was a desperate cry for help. The next time she cried out to her family for help. She telephoned her parents and told them where she was and what had happened to her. Police were notified and the girl was returned home. Her pimp drifted off somewhere. In less than three months, the gullible teenager had earned more than $4,000 for him.

The $4,000, however, did not begin to compare with the earnings of a sixteen-year-old witness who estimated that she took in an incredible $100,000 on the Minnesota Strip before she was able to free herself from her pimp. She was a runaway in Minneapolis when the man who was to become her pimp offered to allow her to move in with him. He turned her onto the streets the next night, with a warning not to return until she had earned $150. She worked so hard that she was arrested for prostitution.

Obviously concerned with the 90-day jail sentence mandated for a second prostitution conviction, her pimp flew her to New York as soon as she was released from custody in Minneapolis. During 16 months as a streetwalker in Manhattan, she was arrested 42 times for prostitution and once for grand larceny. She did not serve a day in jail. Like the fourteen-year-old, when she tried to leave her pimp beat her so viciously she had to be hospitalized. Of all the money she had earned by that time, when she finally broke away she had saved only $800.

The oldest of the girls was eighteen when she testified to the panel that she hustled in Times Square for nearly a year and a half before escaping from her pimp only four weeks before the hearing. She said she took her tricks to midtown hotels and massage parlors that charged $5 for a few minutes in one of their rooms.

Her pimp broke her nose and burst one of the eardrums during a beating, and when she broke away she dashed into the street. Fortunately, a police squad car happened to be cruising by as the pimp chased after her, and he was arrested. The girl said she had met him at a bus stop in Minneapolis and he sweet-talked her into going to New York by telling her it was a "dream city" and she could "make a lot of money in prostitution."

Despite the hearings, it was not New York state legislators who finally focused national attention on the Minnesota Strip, but a pair of Minneapolis policemen, one of them a "born-again Christian" who sprinkles his talk with references to Jesus and thinly veiled threats to break a few bones.

Al Palmquist was a minister in the Independent Lutheran Church and a community relations officer with the Minneapolis Police Department when his attention was first drawn to the problem of child prostitution one night in 1977 as he was watching television. An episode of "Police Story" traced the activities of a pimp who picked up a runaway girl at a bus station. Using seduction and kidnapping, he eventually tied her to a bed and injected drugs into her arm. Soon after that, she was walking the streets for him.

The husky, red-headed cop found the story hard to believe. He talked to his partner, Lieutenant Gary McGaughey. McGaughey had been working in vice control and he showed his friend photographs of several young Minneapolis area girls who were murdered after trying to escape from their pimps. Some were shot, some burned, one had her head split open with an ax, and another had been dumped into an acid bath.

Palmquist was appalled. But he realized that the television story was very close to the truth. Palmquist learned that pimps will somtimes get a girl high on dope or booze and take movies or still photos of her engaged in sex with several men at one time, or with animals. The activity itself is traumatic enough, but when the photographs are shown to a girl the effect is devastating.

The breaking-in process can also involve a man having forced sex with a girl, then leaving money on the bed. She is accused of already being a whore and told that the money is the "proof." This is all part of a program that has worked thousands of times before, eliminating resistance by breaking a girl's spirit and destroying her sense of self-worth.

Palmquist vowed to do his best to help curb teenage prostitution in Minneapolis, to cut off the Minnesota pipeline, and to help girls who had already been ensnared.

A man who claimed to have "met Christ" at a Billy Graham rally in 1961, Palmquist began preaching after three years of theological training at Bethany Fellowship in Minneapolis. Accompanied by his wife, he moved to Manhattan seven weeks later to begin working with problem children as a director of Teen Challenge, a fundamentalist Christian-oriented drug rehabilitation center.

He organized a similar drug treatment program called Midwest Challenge several years later after returning to Minneapolis and joining the police department. On his father's side, Palmquist is a Lutheran Swede with a family tree full of clergymen. His mother is Irish Catholic, and many of the men in her family were policemen. It appeared that the burly Minnesota native had been true to both sides of his family.

When he talked with his superiors about opening a shelter for young prostitutes, and about forming a small task force to stem the flow of runaways through the Minnesota pipeline, he received a go-ahead on both fronts. Getting the girls to cooperate and take advantage of Safe House, which would be operated in conjunction with the Midwest Challenge program, was more difficult. If they had learned anything on the streets, the unhappy teenagers hustling along Minneapolis' Nicollet Avenue knew to distrust men who promised to do nice things for them. Eventually, however, Palmquist recruited his first prostitute for Safe House. Others slowly began to trickle in.

Some of the teenagers ran away after only a few days. At the Safe House, the former runaways, thieves, and girls (facetiously called "chili-dog hookers" because they wandered the streets munching chili-dogs and popping bubble gum) were awakened early. They had strict discipline and fully scheduled days, studying the Bible, praying, working, attending group therapy sessions, and "testifying" about their former wasted lives and of their turnabouts and conversions to Christ. The program at Safe House was not an easy way out of their old lifestyle. But some of the girls stayed. A few of them contacted friends who were still on the street, urging them to break from their pimps and accept the protection and redirection of their lives offered by Palmquist's program.

People were beginning to notice his work with young prostitutes and drug addicts, and the clergyman-cop was becoming a local celebrity. He was more concerned, however, that hundreds of teenagers had already passed through the pipeline and were working the streets, hotels, and massage parlors of New York, Chicago, and other cities. He and McGaughey flew to Manhattan in November 1977 to round up and return home as many Midwestern girls as possible.

Palmquist knew the value, if not all the pitfalls, of publicity, and he had talked freely to local newsmen of the upcoming trip. The trip was turned into a circus sideshow. The story captured the interest of journalists across the nation, and when the policemen stepped off their airplane in New York, six television camera crews and a horde of newspaper and radio journalists and photographers were waiting to interview them. Three reporters had followed from the Twin Cities.

Newsmen and women dogged the trail of the Minneapolis policemen during their frustrating three-day stay in the Big Apple. The first day was windy and rainy, and the temperature was a bone-rattling 40°. When Palmquist and McGaughey got to the sidewalks of Eighth Avenue, there was not a blue-eyed, blond hooker in sight.

Palmquist and McGaughey retreated from the wind-driven rain and moved inside. In the offices of the New York Senate Select Committee on Crime, they swapped and compared photographs of missing Minnesota girls with videotapes of Manhattan prostitutes. The out-of-town guests also visited Covenant House, a store-front shelter on 44th street near Eighth Avenue run by a Roman Catholic priest, Father Bruce Ritter, who takes in boy and girl hookers and other children in need of help.

The next two days were no more productive than the first, at least as far as locating and rescuing Minnesota's lost daughters. There had been too much publicity. The two policemen returned empty-handed to Minneapolis.

Their safari to the Manhattan jungle was not completely in vain, however. They had drawn nationwide publicity from the print and electronic media. Palmquist and McGaughey were interviewed by newspaper and radio reporters and appeared on television talk shows. Their quest had focused nationwide attention on the Minnesota Strip and on the worn out child-women trapped there.

Some six months later, Palmquist slipped back into Manhattan. The second time, his arrival was more furtive, unannounced. He was met by several former prostitutes and drug addicts who were participating in the Teen Challenge program, and who drove to New York in a van to help convince their sisters to leave their pimps and return with them to Minneapolis. The Lamb's Ministry, a religious group from New York, joined the Minneapolis fundamentalists in the street corner campaign, talking to habitués of the Strip and handing out cards listing telephone numbers that prostitutes could call for help. Most of the hookers were frightened or hostile. They walked away, usually after ridiculing the young men and women from Minneapolis.

Ironically, the one person who did listen was a thirty-one-year-old

Black man and former musician. He was a pimp, and he was lounging a
block or two off Times Square keeping his eye on the four girls he had
working the street for him. (The girls had worked hard enough and long
enough to keep him in cocaine and booze, to pay for an expensive sports
car, and to purchase one house and part of another.)

He was living in luxury in the most expensive city in America when
the Midwest Challenge van rolled up to the curb and the former drug
addicts and hookers climbed out. His curiosity was piqued, and he
walked up to one of the crusaders to ask what was going on. A member
of the Lamb's Ministry recognized him. The urban missionary had
played with the pimp in a jazz group years earlier.

The two men talked, and more than an hour later the pimp approached his women and told them he was leaving. They were
dumbfounded. When he insisted that he was leaving to find himself in
Minneapolis, they turned and walked away.

The pimp's defection from the Minnesota Strip provided a needed
boost for the crusaders from Midwest Challenge. But it did not do much
to help offset some problems developing for Palmquist on the home-
front.

Weeks before his second trip to New York, the clergyman-cop had
lead a small band of plainclothesmen and Midwest Challenge workers
in a sweep of the Crystal Court, Mineapolis' downtown shopping mall
in the IDS building, to search out juvenile prostitutes. The Court was a
popular hangout for young prostitutes and runaways and consequently
was a favorite hunting ground for procurers.

IDS guards pointed out several juveniles and said they had watched
them solicit customers. About a dozen girls were detained, checked for
identification, and questioned. Some were escorted into a Midwest
Challenge van, which was parked nearby, for "deprogramming" and
talks with former prostitutes and counselors. A seventeen-year-old admitted she was a prostitute and agreed to leave her pimp and move into
the Safe House. A thirteen-year-old, who was being wooed by a pimp
and was on her way to his apartment when she was stopped, agreed to
stay away from the man and to keep in close contact with Midwest
Challenge counselors.

The others were released, most because they were eighteen or older
or because their parents, who were telephoned, said their daughters
were not runaways. Some of the girls and their parents were angered at
the tactics used by Palmquist and his mixed Midwest Challenge and
police team, however.

Less than 48 hours later, Palmquist and the police department were being blamed by the Chief of the County Public Defender's Office for violating the civil rights of the girls who had been detained in the mall. Critics also argued that the use of the Midwest Challenge van for interrogation and its presence at the scene potentially violated the concept of separation of church and state.

Public Defender Bill Kennedy had been a frequent critic of what were called the city's Gestapo tactics in fighting pimps and prostitution. Meeting with the mayor's prostitution task force, he warned that if Palmquist and his team did not have sufficient evidence to make arrests at the Court, they had no right to detain the young women.

Palmquist heatedly replied that he was more concerned with the activities of the pimps who lurked in the mall violating the rights of the unworldly young girls who congregated there. Teenagers were being picked up in the shopping center, beaten, raped, and turned into prostitutes, he pointed out. The policeman suggested to Kennedy that he might feel differently about civil rights if he had a daughter trapped into prostitution. The lawyer responded that he would have filed a federal civil rights suit if his own teenage daughter had been in Crystal Court and detained by Palmquists' raiders on the day of the sweep.

Publicity surrounding Palmquist and, to some extent, McGaughey, had peaked, however. Both policemen became less conspicuous in Minneapolis' subsequent efforts to control prostitution and to discourage the pimps.

Police Chief Elmer Nordlund expanded the vice squad from six to nine members and announced that it would be supplemented by members of the Organized Crime and Narcotics Division when appropriate. After Nordlund advised that McGaughey was not a member of the new strike force because he was "a loner and not a team player," McGaughey responded that he was dumped because of politics. It was political retaliation, he said, for political investigations that led to sanctions against two city councilmen.[1]

Police estimated that there were about 1,500 prostitutes in the Twin City Minneapolis-St. Paul area and that about one-quarter of them were no older than seventeen. The population of the metropolitan area is about 1.5 million. In one six-year period in the early 70s, the number of prostitution arrests rose from 60, with no juveniles, to 389 involving 73 juveniles. The average age of the women charged with prostitution at the beginning of the period surveyed was twenty-five, but it had dropped to 19.5 six years later.

At about the time the campaign to rid Minneapolis of prostitution was at its peak, the parents of a fourteen-year-old runaway from a rural hamlet some 150 miles from the city informed police that their daughter was allegedly lured into a call-girl operation by a gang of procurers who used a photo studio near the Sixth District Police Station as a front.

The studio was raided on Christmas Eve, 1977, and police confiscated a card file which they said contained 8,300 names of customers of the "Dial-a-Blonde Modeling Service." The file reputedly listed names, addresses, occupations, favorite girls, and sexual preferences of about 7,000 out-of-town businessmen and some 1,300 local residents. Investigators said the photography studio was a front for one of the most extensive call-girl operations in the history of the city.

James M. O'Meara, a deputy chief of investigations for the police department, was quoted as saying that the call-girl service on Nicollet Avenue had been operating about two years and was one of many new commercial sex establishments. Only a few years earlier, there had been no porno movie houses and only a handful of adult bookstores. Barely a half-dozen years later, there were some 15 adult movie houses and porno bookstores spread throughout the city.

Minneapolis carried on with its anti-prostitution campaign, despite charges of overzealousness and use of Gestapo tactics. Police in Minneapolis knew, however, that they must work carefully to avoid violating the civil rights of fellow citizens.

During one two-week period in November, 1979, in New York, two women were awarded more than $18,000 in damages after being falsely detained by plainclothesmen rounding up suspected prostitutes under the city's anti-loitering laws.

A civil court jury awarded $10,000 to freelance writer Susan Heeger, an attractive twenty-six-year-old Manhattan woman, after her Civil Liberties Union lawyer convinced the panel that she had been arrested without probable cause and unnecessarily roughed up nearly a year earlier. The pretty blonde said she was walking to her apartment after attending a movie when a car pulled up next to her and a man jumped out and grabbed her by the hair, pulling her down. He was unshaven and wearing a soiled T-shirt and scruffy jeans. She began screaming for the police.

Later she learned that her assailant was a vice squad officer, and that a prostitute who had already been picked up had pointed her out as another hooker. The prostitute claimed the writer had robbed her. Much later the prostitute changed her story.

An attorney for the city vainly argued that policemen were entrapped by the other woman, forty-three-year-old Arlene Carmen, who was awarded $8,500 by a federal court jury. Miss Carmen said she was arrested early in 1978 as she talked to a prostitute on the Minnesota Strip. Although Carmen was administrator of the Justin Memorial Church in Greenwich Village, and counseled prostitutes as part of her job, the defense attorney charged that she did not make that known to police when she was stopped and did not protest her arrest. The woman, represented in court by the New York ACLU, said she would use the cash settlement to continue helping prostitutes, and she also vowed to continue efforts to have the controversial anti-loitering law declared unconstitutional.

New York has tried other approaches to discourage rampant prostitution. Mayor Edward Koch's "John Hour," which he initiated in 1979, was one of the most controversial of the new campaigns. The feisty mayor instructed management of the city-owned radio stations, WNYC-AM and FM, to broadcast names of men arrested and convicted for patronizing or soliciting prostitutes.

Recent state legislative action upgrading the charge of patronizing a prostitute from a mere "violation" to a more serious Class B misdemeanor was closely tied to the crackdown. The new classification boosted maximum penalties on conviction from 15 to 90 days in jail and increased fines from $250 to $500. Manhattan District Attorney Robert Morgenthau further added sharp new teeth to the law. He announced that there would be no plea bargaining and reduction of charges in "John cases." Almost immediately the men who patronized prostitutes in New York could no longer count on exercising their ancient near immunity from prosecution and publicity.

"I believe that it is unfair that we assess criminal penalties for prostitutes, but that we don't assess criminal penalties against the Johns, the men who use prostitutes," Koch observed. He said he came up with the idea after surveying "John cases" handled in Manhattan Criminal Court during a 90-day period and learning that 311 of 384 charges were dismissed.

Some of the first cries of dissent were sounded by the New York Civil Liberties Union. Executive Director Dorothy Samuels was quoted as saying that although she admired Koch's attempt to treat men and women equally, "judges should not be trying cases under political pressure from the mayor. That's the real civil liberties issue here."

The Reverend Harold Moody, pastor of the Judson Memorial Church, also chimed in, calling the move atrocious. The clergyman, who had counseled prostitutes, complained that the government should not be involved in efforts to regulate sex between consenting adults.[2]

The courts in Manhattan responded to the "get tough" and "no deals" policies of Koch and Morgenthau with wholesale dismissals of charges against Johns accused of patronizing prostitutes. During one three-month period, approximately two-thirds of the John cases referred to the courts were dismissed. Judges were clearly annoyed with the mayor and the prosecutor for interfering with their discretionary powers.

The Prostitutes of New York, PONY, which claims membership of 2,000 hookers and campaigns for decriminalization of their trade, responded differently. They mailed a letter to the mayor, thanking him for creating publicity and reputedly attracting additional out-of-town customers. A spokesman for PONY conceded that the crackdown in the Times Square area led to an increase in fines and paranoia, but insisted that it had not hurt the business.

Mayor Koch's approach to fighting prostitution in New York may be unique, but the problem itself is not. Every large city in the nation has a red-light area or problems with prostitution. And, increasingly, law enforcement and social service agencies are finding that a rising number of the females who inhabit the bordellos and massage parlors, walk the streets, or work out of apartments as call girls are juveniles.

Not all the blondes and other teenagers who travel through the Minnesota pipeline wind up in New York or Chicago. Some go to cities such as Boston, Atlanta, Los Angeles, Miami, and Detroit.

Prostitution probably is the worst kept secret in Detroit. Although most of the prostitutes are Black and natives of the area, a disproportionate number of the Johns are white and live in the suburbs. At one time, authorities and the news media in Detroit estimated that 32 hotels in the city catered solely to hot-pillow trade, renting filthy, barren rooms for as little as $5 "plus tax" for a half-hour.

The decayed and dingy Cass Corridor, from downtown to near the campus of Wayne State University, is the most notorious red-light district in the city. But children as young as thirteen have been found working another notorious hooker hangout, Woodward from West McNichols to Eight-Mile at the city limits. The teenagers usually pose as hitchhikers. If there are fewer teenage prostitutes on the streets of the downtown vice areas of Detroit, it is probably because they are afraid. Even police officers concede that the city's tough reputation has helped divert teenage runaways to less menacing cities. Most of the child prostitutes who join their older sisters in the city and suburbs are native to the area. An investigative team of journalists for the *Detroit News* in 1979 estimated that hookers working the city's bars and hotels handle some "$6.7 million in a year of weekends."[3]

A huge, muscular Black man with hamlike hands and a twisted penchant for sex and sadism was one of the more dangerous of the criminals attracted to Cass Corridor in Detroit's inner city. During a four-month period he strangled five prostitutes and seriously injured four others after sexually abusing them. His first known victim was a sixteen-year-old who was brutally beaten and strangled before her lifeless body was abandoned in a shabby hotel.

Detroit's whores were terrified. Their fears were magnified by the brutality of the murders and by reports of the killer's size. Hookers who survived his attacks, or saw him talking with their girlfriends, swore that he was at least six-foot-six and had immense feet. Some frightened women insisted that he had to be at least seven feet tall.

The fear that Bigfoot spread through Detroit's seamy vice subculture was so great that usually suspicious and hostile prostitutes and pimps were cooperative when police distributed composite drawings of his face. They responded with hundreds of tips. Pimps also talked ominously of their plans for Bigfoot if they caught up with him first. However, the slayings did not diminish the availability of commercial sex. The women had their nuts to make.

As the 1970s were drawing to a close, Atlanta, Georgia, acquired the unenviable title of "Murder City, U.S.A" with a gory record of the most murders per capita of any major urban center in the nation. Atlanta was already known as one of the most crime-ridden and wide-open towns in the nation. Plagued by political shenanigans, police department scandals, and civil rights anti-discrimination suits that blocked police hirings and promotions for six years, the law enforcement apparatus in the city was reeling. Overworked police officers had more than they could handle trying to keep the lid on the murders, rapes, and stickups that were keeping the midtown streets dark and empty of shoppers at night. The crime rate was spiraling upward so rapidly that 50 state policemen and 10 officers from the Georgia Bureau of Investigation were assigned to the city for three months late in 1979.

It was not surprising, considering all its other troubles, that Atlanta developed a reputation for lax enforcement of prostitution laws. Prostitutes began streaming into the city. The Minnesota pipeline undoubtedly contributed some. But there were other pipelines from Texas, California, Kentucky, Ohio, Florida, Alabama, and other states.

A core city area along Peachtree Street between Ponce de Leon Avenue and 14th street is known locally as "The Strip" and is Atlanta's major red-light district. But hookers work areas throughout the city, and, if they are young enough and pretty enough, they hang around Atlanta's nicer hotels and motels to catch the convention trade.

Faced with the huge influx of prostitutes augmented by increasingly violent activities of hundreds of home-grown hustlers, Atlanta was forced to initiate a campaign against vice. A task force was established under the direction of Major W. W. Clark of the Police Department.

The ages of prostitutes swept up in the anti-vice campaigns varied from about fifteen to the mid-forties. Most of the Johns who were arrested were residents of the metropolitan area, married men with blue-collar jobs.

A thirteen-year-old girl identified by her former professional name, "Tina," was white, with blond hair, brown eyes, and a fully developed 36-33-36 figure. She was from an upper middle-class family in the Miami area, but she became a whore.

Tina's story was told in a series of articles in the *Miami News* after she helped police arrest the man who had lured her into the trade. It was summer, just before she was to begin high school, and she and a girlfriend were sunning at a Dade County beach when a middle-aged man approached them and began to chat. He told the girls he was an optometrist, complimented Tina on her appearance and her name, and, after a while, wandered away.

There were other meetings after that, and the eye doctor insinuated his way into her confidence by continuing to compliment her on her poise and grammar and treating her as if she were an adult. When he turned the subject to sex, it was done so easily that she felt complimented instead of insulted or uncomfortable. And when he reputedly suggested that she could earn big money by pleasing men, she agreed to think about it. She had visions of exciting times with wild parties and wealthy men who owned luxurious yachts and big cars. Two weeks later, she told the optometrist that she had decided to accept his proposal.

She dated dozens of men, almost always well-dressed, well-mannered, and most of them married, she told police. Her friend arranged the $50 fee. Sometimes she was given tips after a tryst on a boat, the back seat of a luxury car, or in a motel room. One man who took her to dinner, dancing, and to a lounge for drinks before she accompanied him to a motel, tipped her $500.

The money was a problem. She had to be careful how she spent it so her parents would not become suspicious of her late night babysitting assignments and overnight slumber parties with nebulous girlfriends. The first $50 she earned was spent on a bag of marijuana, which she hid in her closet. With the rest she purchased expensive presents for her girlfriends, or treated her boyfriend to new mag wheels and a muffler for his Camero. The optometrist did not want any of the money. He was satisfied, the girl said, to have free sexual relations with her any time he wished.

After about a year of dates with men three times her age, the glamour began to wear off. She estimated that she had earned about $1,900, but she could spend hardly any of the money on herself. One day she told her friend that she was quitting. He objected. When he continued to insist, she told her mother of her past activities and the older woman notified police.[4]

FBI agents joined with local police in 1974 to break up an international vice ring centered in Boston that offered prostitutes as young as sixteen. Among those arrested by FBI agents and local police were a twenty-eight-year-old man, his wife, and his mother. All three were identified by authorities as leading figures in a loose federation of panderers who rotated prostitutes between more than a dozen cities to meet the demand for fresh, new bodies.

Most of the women were in their early twenties, but several were teenagers, including a sixteen-year-old said to have been transported from Warren, Ohio, to Buffalo, to Albany, to work in houses of prostitution. Other cities linked to the vice cartel included Atlanta, Chicago, Cincinnati, Denver, Detroit, Miami, Newark, New York, Philadelphia, Pittsburgh, Providence, Toledo, Springfield, Massachusetts, and Toronto.

Authorities estimated that the operation was a $4.5 million-a-year business involving individual transactions costing from $25 to $100. More than 1,500 file cards were confiscated, and each one listed a customer's name in code, date of birth, financial background, and sexual tastes.

The nation's capital has not escaped the problem of teenage prostitutes. The favorite turf for the prostitutes who inhabit the lowest rung of Washington's sex-for-sale industry is a malevolent and tacky section of 14th Street, N. W., stretching roughly from Florida Avenue to L Street and west of K and L Streets to 15th. The streets are filled with the sullen, aging faces of girls who have been homegrown in Washington's ghettos and suburbs—and with frightened teenagers imported by a ring of pimps based in the capital and in California.

A Superior Court special grand jury called in 1978 to investigate the unusual alliance of pimps, in what is usually a competitive business peopled by loners, estimated after hearing testimony from several of the young victims that at least 10 procurers, among some 500 believed to be active in the Washington, D. C., area, were involved in the scheme. The girls were found the same way they always are. Pimps combed California high schools, learning from students which of their female schoolmates were unhappy at home, were having boyfriend troubles, or were saddled with other problems. Then they would make their approach. Some girls were picked up after escaping from foster homes or institutions, and still others were found in shopping malls, arcades, and other locations that attract runaways. Once ensnared, the teenagers would be put to work briefly in or near their home city for a brief breaking-in period and then moved across country to Washington, all home ties broken.

When the grand jury investigation was launched, the Washington, D. C., police department already had a small but dedicated three-man juvenile prostitution unit. The unit had begun three years earlier when an officer in the morals division and another in the missing persons division compared notes and found a connection between missing juveniles and prostitution. The police chief gave them 90 days to experiment with the special unit they proposed, and, in the three months, more than 50 child prostitutes were removed, at least temporarily, from the streets. Only half that many had been apprehended during the entire previous year.

In 1978, the District police applied for a $343,000 grant from the Law Enforcement Assistance Administration to begin a nationwide research project focusing on child prostitution. The officers pointed out in their application that there was "increasing evidence that the recruitment and transport of youth for prostitution purposes is a highly organized interstate crime." More than half the juveniles involved in prostitution in the District were described as runaways from other areas or children specifically abducted and shipped to the capital to work as prostitutes.

While law enforcement in the capital was seeking to break up the network of pimps introducing teenage prostitutes from California to Washington's red-light district, authorities in Evanston, Illinois, were announcing the breakup of an eight-state vice ring that had been feeding off runaway high school girls. The three men indicted in 1979 on federal charges of transporting females across state lines for purposes of prostitution were not much older than most of their prostitutes. Two of the men were twenty-one, and the other twenty-two.

FBI agents and local police said ten young women, five of them between fifteen and seventeen years old, had been shipped back and forth to major cities in a seven-state area. The prostitutes worked in hotels and motels in Atlanta, Detroit, Minneapolis, St. Louis, New Orleans, Louisville, Miami, and Daytona Beach. A grand jury was told that the pimps also stopped at truck stops and motels while traveling between cities and sent the girls out to earn expense money.

The investigation began as a routine probe of the activities of five juveniles who were chronic runaways. Juvenile division officers with the Evanston Police Department noticed a disconcerting pattern in the comings and goings of the teenagers. Sometimes they would be gone several days, at other times, only for a day or two. Perhaps even more suspicious, the runaways returned home exceptionally well dressed. Blue jeans and a shirt or a sweater are the usual uniform for a runaway teenager.

Midway through the investigation, some six months after their suspicions were first aroused, Evanston police called in the FBI. The federal agency had the manpower and authority to follow up on the predetermined multistate investigation, and a few months later indictments were returned.

Barely a year before the Evanston arrests, an ex-convict accused of staffing a house of prostitution with teenage runaways from Illinois, Indiana, and Wisconsin was cleared of most of the charges against him after the state's fourteen-year-old witness disappeared. One of the charges previously filed against the ex-convict, who was on federal parole from a counterfeiting conviction, was based on his alleged soliciting of a fellow county jail inmate to murder the girl. The mother of the runaway reported that her daughter had telephoned from Arizona and California, but said she did not know her exact whereabouts. The accused procurer was eventually convicted of intimidating another teenager.

Police opened their investigation after a seventeen-year-old Hammond, Indiana, high school girl told them she was held against her will in a house several miles west of Chicago and forced to commit numerous acts of prostitution. She reported that she escaped after wrapping clothing in a newspaper and saying she was going outside to throw away garbage.

She and a fifteen-year-old girlfriend were running away when they were picked up by a recruiter for the alleged procurer, the teenager testified. The runaway said she was initially driven to Chicago and then to the house in the suburbs, where she was forced to commit her first act of prostitution. Authorities estimated that about 10 juveniles were involved in the operation. Investigators claimed that the juveniles were beaten, drugged, and sometimes chained to beds. One of the girls said they were told to wear their shoes at all times so they could run away if there was a police raid.

Stories are told, though difficult to trace, of a more sophisticated operator in the Midwest who staffed her whorehouse with teenagers. The madam was a woman of strong ethics and was dismayed at the lack of professionalism on the part of youngsters just breaking into the trade. Consequently, she established a school for prostitutes, teaching everything from pelvic movements and fellatio to hygiene and parlor talk. Pimps were said to occasionally bring their girls to her for training.

Across the country in California, child and adult prostitution has moved close to Disneyland. The sex-for-sale industry has invaded Orange County in force, and fathers who have taken their children to see Mickey Mouse and the Three Little Pigs can be treated to totally different fantasies along Harbor Boulevard. There are gaudy rows of massage parlors, adult bookstores, dance or modeling studios, and head shops. As the 1970s drew to a close, police in Anaheim disclosed that their prostitution arrests had more than doubled over the previous year. During a single week in 1979, 282 tourists and 36 accused hookers were apprehended and charged with violating the city's anti-prostitution laws. Some of the prostitutes drawn to the strip of sex-oriented businesses outside the family entertainment mecca are as young as sixteen.

Prostitutes much younger than sixteen can be found only a few miles northwest of Disneyland in Los Angeles. Teenage runaways of both sexes, and naive youngsters who have bid family and friends goodbye for the glamour and excitement of Los Angeles and Hollywood, fill the massage parlors, live sex shows, photo studios, motels, hotels, and streets.

[1] *The New York Times*, February 7, 1978.
[2] *Birmingham News*/Associated Press, October 10, 1979.
[3] *Detroit News*, February 7, 1979.
[4] *Miami News*, March 1975.

10.

The Meat Rack

SOME of the social scientists, journalists, cops, and kids who know it best call it the Meat Rack. It is an open air sewer, a square-block-long delicatessen of child sex whose busiest corner is on famed Hollywood Boulevard in the heart of Twinkle City.

There, a man who cares to can buy an eleven- or twelve-year-old boy or girl by the hour or by the night. The only stars discovered there appear in peep-show loops or longer films that will never be screened in neighborhood theaters.

It is the most notorious corner for child prostitution and other forms of commercialized kiddie sex in Greater Los Angeles, a city known as the pornography capital of the country. It is also the chicken capital. The chances are that any boy who stands still there for five minutes is either waiting for a bus or hooking, usually the latter. There are thought to be more boy prostitutes per capita in Hollywood and Los Angeles than in any other metropolitan area in the United States. If not, at the very least they are more visible.

Ever since the 1920s, when the men who established the motion picture industry in Chicago packed up their cameras and lights and hopped on trains for the more inviting climate of southern California, Hollywood has been the Emerald City of the starstruck, the adventurous, and the runaway. Fantasies grew there. A midwesterner with the milktoast name of Marion Michael Morrison became the plain-talking, two-fisted all-American hero, John Wayne. Hometown girl Betty Grable was said to have been discovered there before becoming the long-legged darling of girl-starved World War II GIs from Guadalcanal to Tripoli.

They were the lucky ones. Less fortunate adventurers arrived in Hollywood with no money, no talent, or no luck and were lured or forced into a different fantasy world. They catered to other people's fantasies as call girls, street-walkers, massage parlor hostesses, and porn queens.

Boys who were runaways, throwaways, or merely neglected joined their sisters as prostitutes and as models for pornography. As those who had made successful careers for themselves in the legitimate movie and entertainment industries moved out, pimps, pushers, thieves, con men, and pedophiles moved in to feed off the young.

By the late 70s, the center of the action often revolved around the Gold Cup restaurant at the corner of Hollywood and Las Palmas Avenue. It was a magnet for losers. Young male and female hookers, transvestites, sullen Black pimps in three-piece suits and Superfly hats—and white middle-aged pederasts and lesbians drawn to the Meat Rack seeking out little boys and girls for sex—cruised there, sipped gray coffee, and eyed the trade. A short distance away in West Hollywood, another strip along Santa Monica Boulevard between Deheny Drive and LaCienaga Boulevard attracted so many boy prostitutes it became known as Boys' Farm.

"Hollywood Boulevard is for (drag) queens, Sunset Boulevard is for girls, and Santa Monica is for us," a slender-hipped youth in the Gold Cup quipped, as he brushed a mop of blond hair from his forehead with the tattooed fingers of one hand. "But nobody has their name on a corner," he said, turning back to the pinball machine he was playing before being interrupted. He was about fifteen.

During a hearing before a U.S. Congressional committee, Detective Sergeant Lloyd Martin, Chief Investigator for the Los Angeles Police Department's sexually abused child unit, estimated that as many as 30,000 boys and girls in his jurisdiction were victims of sexual exploitation every year. His estimates were based on interviews with sexually abused children, chicken hawks, pimps, and people in the pornography trade. Martin told the grim panel that a hard-working twelve-year-old boy could earn as much as $1,000 a day by dividing his time between prostitution and posing for pornographic movies and stills.

"The young victims we are concerned with are usually runaways, reasonably streetwise, emotionally troubled children who trade themselves for money or for what they interpret as affection," the policeman observed. "Sometimes for the price of an ice cream cone, a kid of eight will pose for a producer. He usually trusts the guy because he's getting from him what he can't get from his parents—love.

"The child who has been sexually abused frequently turns to prostitution, pornography, narcotics, or other criminality, or will be encouraged to engage in this activity by an abusing adult after having outlived his novelty as a sexual partner," Martin testified.

One of the most difficult concepts for most people to understand and accept, he said, is that often the children are consenting partners. They learn quickly, he said, "that one way they can survive on the street in an adult world is by pulling up their skirts or by pulling down their pants." Even though the child may be the one who initiates the behavior, he or she is still the victim in the truest sense, the witness stressed.

California Congressman and anti-smut crusader Robert K. Dornan also testified at the hearing and charged that "The County of Los Angeles" was "perverting the country." He pointed out that Los Angeles led the nation in the production of pornographic films, as well as being "the leading rape county in the world." Films featuring hard and soft core, bestiality, sadism and masochism, bondage and discipline, and child pornography were all being produced in the city and county, he added.

Martin was the guiding force behind formation of the first sexually abused child unit in an American police department. The groundwork was laid in his spare time, out of frustration. A grizzled career cop who spent much of his childhood on his grandmother's sun-baked Arkansas cotton farm, he was a member of the vice squad when be became involved in a succession of investigations involving children. Each time he was pulled off the case, in line with department guidelines that called for juvenile matters to be referred to city youth agencies for further investigation and possible legal action. But followups were slow or nonexistent. Too many cases of criminal sexual abuse of children went unpunished.

The policeman set up an office in the garage of his home which he shared with his wife, two teenage sons, and a daughter, and began collecting case histories. After two years, he had assembled an impressive casebook of child-related sex crimes. His superior was impressed and gave him a month to follow up on some of the cases. Martin rounded up 300 suspects.

He had made his point. The city council approved funding of nearly $300,000. Martin became head of a new seven-member unit charged with protecting Los Angeles children from sexual exploitation and with tracking and arresting the people who fed on them. It was like turning Portuguese fishermen loose in an aquarium. The unit marked up some phenomenal successes.

One of the investigations that is especially vivid in Martin's memory dealt with a nine-year-old boy from Colorado who was leased by his parents for weekends with a middle-aged pederast. The business arrangement continued for two years until the chicken hawk moved to make it permanent and gave the parents a motel in Texas in exchange for the child. The parents experimented with operating the motel for two weeks before returning to Colorado and asking for money instead. The sum of $3,000 was finally agreed on, and the man left for Los Angeles with the boy.

Another even younger child worked as a prostitute on the beach at Venice, a popular California artists' colony routinely patrolled by chicken hawks looking for available youngsters. An eight-year-old, whose healthy, tanned body still showed traces of baby fat under his tiny swimsuit, also patrolled the beach. He looked much like any other grimy faced boy his age who might have been playing on the beach during a family outing.

But he was working. He was a professional whose bright blue eyes darted from side to side, scanning the beach until he made contact with just the right adult. When that happened, he walked up to the man and asked, "Say, mister, can you tell me where the bathroom is?" He could sense if the man was interested in sex. If the response was affirmative, after receiving directions the boy would ask, "Would you take me, mister?" Then he would grab hold of the adult's hand and together they walked away.

Once he was inside the restroom, the mask of innocence disappeared, and the towhead was all business. He would look up at his companion and advise, "It's $10, and you've got ten minutes."

Martin told the congressional panel of the widespread use of pornography by chicken hawks and child molesters to lure youngsters into sexual activities. It can be used to turn a normal conversation with a juvenile onto a sexual theme. The policeman cited an example of a pedophile leaving a pornographic magazine on a car seat when he picks up a hitchhiking child to purposely stimulate a conversation about sex.

Pornography is frequently used to sexually arouse both the molester and the victim, and the nature of the material often corresponds to the specific sexual predilections of the pedophile. However, if the boy is not responsive to homosexual pornography, an experienced chicken hawk may provide him with pornography involving young girls to arouse sexual feeling.

It is a useful tool for breaking down inhibitions. If a prospective victim is reluctant to engage in a specific sexual act, the pornography can be used as persuasion. The argument goes that if the young boy in the magazine is willing to remove his clothes and perform fellatio, what would be wrong with doing the same? To an adult, the reasoning is obviously full of holes. But to a child it can be extremely persuasive.

Formation of the sexually exploited child unit did not halt the traffic at the corner of Hollywood and Las Palmas. Boys and girls still loitered on the boulevard, thumbing through gay magazines—perhaps occasionally coming across the photo of someone they knew; sitting quietly before cold coffee and staring blankly at a wall with filmy Quaalude eyes; passing a joint on steps of the First Baptist Church on nearby Selma Avenue; or slouching against a street sign and squinting invitingly at the feral-eyed men slowly patrolling in big cars.

Every large city has a Meat Rack, and many smaller towns as well. Some cities have several. The three-way corner of Clark, Broadway, and Diversey is one of the most notorious pickup spots for boy prostitutes in Chicago. So many young hookers work the egregious corner that hardened street cops, using their best black humor, have come to refer to it as "Clark and Perversity."

Another hangout for boy prostitutes is several blocks south on Clark, nearer to the Loop, at Bughouse Square, a one-time preserve for soapbox oratory. First the orators were replaced by winos, then by young boys of fourteen, fifteen, and sixteen who languidly roam the shadowed sidewalks. Runaways and throwaways, or just kids whose parents do not care where they go, what they do, or if they ever come home, the boys stroll along the sidewalks, suggestively rubbing their crotches until they make eye contact and strike a deal with the driver of one of the cars that endlessly circle the block-long park from dusk until about midnight.

A teenager who testified anonymously at a United States Senate hearing in Chicago told his somber audience that he was lured into prostituting himself at the corner of Clark and Diversey when he was fifteen. He did it for the money. Testifying from a closed room as his voice was piped through loudspeakers into the hearing chambers, the boy prostitute said that he was introduced to the trade by a thirteen-year-old friend who was already wise in the ways of the street.

Introduced as "Marty," the high school dropout spoke matter-of-factly of how he had sold himself to hundreds of men, accommodating two or three customers seven nights a week, and charging a minimum of $25 for his services. It was "an easy way to make money," he said.

Marty said he spent the $400 to $500 he earned each week on drugs and clothes and gave some to his mother when she needed it. He appeared in three pornographic films, he told the panel, but turned down most movie offers. He preferred prostitution. At seventeen, he was rapidly approaching the age when he would be too old for the trade, however. Chicken hawks like younger boys, and he was sure that before long he would have to turn to another line of work. He speculated that he might like to enter a trade school.

An older man who is an ex-convict, a sometime chef, and sometime heroin addict, is still hustling near Marty's corner. He lost his attractiveness for chicken hawks more than 20 years ago, but he prefers to blame his troubles on the economy. "Don't let anybody tell you there's not a recession," he complained through toothless gums, shortly after Marty's testimony. "I knew about it long before Jimmy Carter did. When they (tricks) drive into town now, they spend their money for drugs."

The turf of the young witness and his older counterpart was in New-town. Several blocks north, a constantly changing crop of boy prostitutes patrols the more dingy streets of Uptown, attracting middle-aged and elderly chicken hawks from the city and suburbs. Uptown is a polyglot of new arrivals from Europe and Asia, but many of the new urban poor are also Appalachians and displaced agrarians from the exhausted dirt farms of the South.

To many of the twelve- to fifteen-year-old boys, a fling at streetcorner hooking is as natural as country music. Their friends do it, their older brothers did it, and even their parents accept it. One mother bragged to a social worker that her boy brought more money into the family on weekends than they acquired from their welfare payments. She did not consider him to be a homosexual.

John Terkhorn, a shipping clerk for a chemical firm, established a chicken ring in Uptown offering money and drugs to boys who introduced him to their friends, according to investigators. When police arrested him and an associate, they also confiscated pornographic photos of young boys and took into custody a thirteen-year-old youth who admitted committing a sexual act with the shipping clerk the night before.

His operational techniques were classic. Most of the boys were from blatantly impoverished families and were first contacted in parks or on the streets of Uptown where Terkhorn had lived after moving north from Kentucky. Investigators said the boys were first offered money, given drugs to get them high, shown pornography to arouse them, and then offered an additional $20 to solicit a friend. Police said he had lured more than 25 boys from ten to fifteen years old into his ring before he was apprehended.

The suspect pleaded guilty to two felony counts of taking indecent liberties with a child. He was contrite and told the judge that while he was locked up with homosexuals in the Cook County Jail they had taught him to deal with his problems and to channel his sexual drives toward people his own age. He was sentenced to four years in prison.

Early in 1980, one of Chicago's least appreciated celebrities was arrested on similar morals charges. Frank Collin, the thirty-five-year-old former chief of the Chicago-based Nationalist Socialist Party of America, was accused of cruising the neighborhood near Clark and Diversey in a car or on a motorcycle, picking up boys for sex at his apartment over the Nazi headquarters. Some boys told investigators that he took nude pictures of them posed with rifles.

Four boys, from eleven to fourteen years old, also identified Collin as the man they knew as "Dan" and with whom they had engaged in sexual relations and for whom they had posed nude.

Collin attracted national attention two years earlier when he led a bitter American Civil Liberties Union-assisted legal battle seeking permission for the neo-Nazis to demonstrate in the predominantly Jewish suburb of Skokie, northwest of Chicago. The civil action passed through state courts and reached the federal level before plans for the demonstration were called off. Collin was purged from the NSPA a few weeks before his arrest when his former comrades learned of his pederastic activities and notified police.

The youthful male prostitutes who parade in Piedmont Park and other chicken walks in Atlanta are older than most of those of the Meat Rack and Bughouse Square. The Atlanta chickens are often in their late teens, occasionally as old as twenty—an age that reduces their value to a fraction of the worth of boys whose voices have not changed and whose soft bodies have not yet begun to develop the prominent muscles or hair of an adult.

One handsome youth at Piedmont Park, whose blond good looks were marred only by a scarlet splash of acne on his forehead, claimed not long ago to be working his way through college. His expensive clothes and cultured, easy manner indicated that he may have been telling the truth. But prostitutes, male or female, seem to have vivid imaginations and are not especially respected for their veracity.

Although the boys in Atlanta are older, their actions are the same.

They lounge or stroll singly or in pairs as the buyers drive slowly around the lake in the park to look them over. Eventually, a buyer sees an attractive boy he likes and stops his car along a curb. A brief and surreptitious conversation follows through the open window in the driver's door and the boy walks around the car to climb inside.

The boy usually performs his covert act in the car, sometimes in a motel room or an apartment. But regardless of where it takes place, the young hooker is usually back in the park later that night or early the next.

Boy prostitution is not a new phenomenon, but it is growing and becoming more obvious as homosexuals come out of the closets and form gay rights groups, and police powers are watered down by court decisions friendlier to civil rights than to law enforcement and protection of the public. Most people prefer that police concentrate their efforts on violent crime instead of so-called victimless crimes, such as gambling and prostitution. And most complaints about prostitution still focus on females.

Authorities, as well as the public in general, are belatedly beginning to become aware that young males are also active as prostitutes. And almost all the male prostitutes are minors.

Sergeant LeRoy Williams, of the Atlanta Police Department's Organized Crime Enforcement Unit, believes that male prostitution is growing in his city, the gay capital of the region. "I've been in vice five years and when I first went (into vice), there was no problem. Now there is," he says. "I think male prostitution is going to be our big problem in the future. You can see it coming. That's definitely gonna' be the problem of the future."[1]

Harold Thomas of Chicago agrees about the sudden explosion of boy prostitution. A member of the Youth Division for 27 years before he was named Deputy Superintendent of the Department's Bureau of Community Services, Thomas says he was never aware of much boy prostitution until the late 60s or early 70s. "Then this thing surfaced," he said. "It really hit its peak in the last few years."

One group of procurers advertised nationwide, appealing for customers with ads offering: "Young males, willing to travel. Fifteen to sixteen. Very personable." Some boys were rented as traveling companions and accompanied adult sponsors on trips to other countries.

Runaway expert Bill Katz points to such ads to support his thesis— and that of other knowledgeable sources—that many of the children who turn to prostitution or child pornography are volunteers. Like the boys in Chicago's Uptown, they learn that they can earn good money doing something they and their friends have come to accept as normal behavior.

"Children are orienting themselves into commercial beings," Katz claims. It is becoming increasingly common for him to talk to boys who tell him, "I'm not too crazy about having anal sex with some old man, but I don't mind oral sex if the guy's relatively clean."

Dr. Densen-Gerber believes that it is easier for males to deal with promiscuous sexuality than it is for females. Boys tend to be more adventurous, it is more wild oats, and sexuality is a macho thing, she says. For girls, however, sexuality tends to be sinful, dirty, and degrading.

"There's a vast difference," she says. "We're not so sure that the damage to a boy is as deep as it is to a female, if he is not bodily penetrated. To be penetrated is different than to penetrate. To have thrusting, externalized sexuality is not as intimate as within oneself. Boy prostitutes have considerably less self-hatred. Many of them protest loudly that they only do it for the money and that they are basically heterosexual. Many of them do not like being labeled as homosexuals."

In New York, where Dr. Densen-Gerber works, one of every five hustlers arrested is a male. It is not unusual for boys as young as eight years old to be peddling their sexual services on the streets. Some of them frequent an arcade area along 42nd Street and 43rd Street near Broadway and Eighth Avenue, as well as the higher rent district of 52nd and 54th Streets between Second and Third Avenues.

A citywide network of residences and counseling centers for young male and female hustlers has been established in some of the worst neighborhoods of New York by a Franciscan priest, Father Bruce Ritter. He was a professor of medieval theology at Manhattan College in the late 60s when he decided that work with street people was a more pressing need than contemplation of theologies of half a millennium ago.

He moved away from the safe isolation of his quarters at the college and into a flea-trap, a $64-a-month tenement in New York's East Village. There was a junky on almost every floor and most of them did not appreciate a priest for a neighbor. He lived frugally, supporting himself as a part-time preacher, teacher, and cab driver as he learned the streets and blended into the neighborhood. The only thing he brought with him from the fourteenth century that applied to his new existence, he has observed, was the concept of sanctuary.

That concept was tested one night when six runaways knocked at his door and he permitted them to sleep in his apartment. The word spread quickly among the children he refers to as "urban nomads," and other troubled boys and girls began coming to him for help. As more arrived, he needed more room. So Father Ritter began putting out what has been described as $50 "non-fatal contracts" on the junkies who had been harassing him, paying neighborhood toughs to steal all their possessions and dismantle their plumbing. As the junkies moved out, Ritter moved into their rooms with his kids. He filled 18 apartments.[2]

By 1972, the state of New York was ready to begin providing help and chipped in money and official sanction. After providing shelter, protection, food, and other care for hundreds of destitute and frightened children for years, Father Ritter was finally operating a legal child care agency, although he still had to provide more than half the funding from private sources. He named the agency Covenant House.

The scholarly priest's life had been drastically and unalterably changed. Covenant House grew until it included a chain of shelters in some of the most hostile areas of the city. They were designed to serve as many as possible of the estimated 25,000 homeless children who are drawn to the streets every year. One crisis center, Under 21, was established in the center of the Minnesota Strip at Eighth Avenue and 44th Street.

Thousands of children have been sheltered by Covenant House, and more than 60 percent of them have had some contact with prostitution and pornography, the clergyman says. About one out of eight are thirteen or younger. Sadly, there have been more disappointments than permanent successes. Three girls who had contact with Covenant House were murdered in one year. One girl was tossed out of a hotel window. Another was cut to pieces with a knife or hatchet.

A fifteen-year-old runaway from Old Bridge, New Jersey, tumbled off the roof of a five-story walkup early one morning and was impaled on the spikes of a twelve-foot fence only eight hours after she had left a Covenant House shelter. She remained conscious as she was cut free of spikes that pierced her chest and right arm.

Father Ritter has had to fight pimps for the children. He has walked the menacing streets of the East Village, Times Square, and the Minnesota Strip seeking out children who need help. And when he confronts a brutal pimp over a teenaged boy or girl prostitute, he does not back off. A wild-eyed fourteen-year-old boy once clattered into Under 21 seconds ahead of a vicious pimp chasing him with a broken bottle. The child had been held prisoner for six weeks in a Times Square hotel. A seventeen-year-old girl runaway staggered inside a Covenant House shelter after escaping from a pimp who had picked her up at the Port Authority and kept her prisoner for 10 days, drugging her, raping her repeatedly, and torturing her. It was the breaking-in process before turning her onto the streets. An arrogant pimp once strutted into the center and offered $500 for the best-looking girl in the place.

Some of the children helped at Covenant House are returned home; others enter schools and are helped to find jobs or placed in other programs. But there are thousands who return to the street or never come in at all. "How could a kid go home again to, say, a small town in upstate New York, after working on the strip for two or three years?" the priest asked. "Maybe 12 to 15 percent go home again. Often their parents don't want them back."[3]

Boy hustlers work the street, bars, movie theaters, and all-male burlesque houses, some with specialty rooms where gay sex is sold. Christopher Street in West Greenwich Village also occasionally serves as a pederast's hunting ground. It was a free-fire zone of sorts between rival Italian and Irish neighborhoods before World War I, but became a gathering place for eccentrics and Bohemians in the decades that followed. Christopher Street assumed a reputation as holy ground for the gay rights movement in the 70s after police stormed into the popular Stonewall Inn, a well-known late-night hangout, and made several arrests. It was a hot summer night and the gay community was infuriated. The response was a riot. When the window breaking, rock throwing, and name calling was over, police pressure on gays and the establishments they frequented in New York City was relaxed. Ever since the night of violence, the "Stonewall Riots" have been a rallying cry for parades and gay rights activities in New York and in other cities.

New York vice detectives smashed a boy prostitution ring operating out of a West 16th Street apartment only a few blocks from Christopher Street late in 1979. They seized files containing the names of nearly 3,000 well-to-do customers, including some celebrities, police spokesmen said. The call-boy operation featured some child prostitutes not yet in their teens.

Clients were promised instant delivery of almost any type they desired, including a child who would submit to sadism or bondage and discipline, for a minimum of $65 an hour. The customer could rent whips, chains, leather masks, and other devices for an extra fee and charge it all on his credit card. Blindfolds and gags were free.

Many of the boys were equipped with the same type beeper device that doctors wear to permit coordinators to reach and dispatch them quickly by telephone. Customers were encouraged to select dates from an album containing photographs of about 150 boys. The child was usually permitted to keep two-thirds of the fee, and the rest belonged to the organization.

A few weeks before the West 16th Street raid, police work paid off in the conviction of another chicken hawk dealing in call boys. Marvin Hughes ran his setup from behind the counter of a doughnut shop. He was accused of providing a thirteen-year-old boy to a plainclothesman posing as an out-of-towner, after the investigator paid a $20 finder's fee to him and promised to pay another $30 to the child.

Hughes was dismayed when Supreme Court Justice Edwin Torres announced a guilty verdict. "I am no pimp," Hughes shouted, "People are killing each other out there. I was just trying to get them (the children) off of the streets."[4]

Police closed another call-boy operation in nearby New Rochelle. Twenty-five boys ranging from thirteen to seventeen worked out of a house on a quiet tree-lined street there, servicing customers for prices varying from $20 to $25. Two of the boys were runaways from Baltimore.

A few years earlier, several aides at Philadelphia's Youth Study Center were suspended from their jobs and some were charged with morals offenses and accused of having sexual relations with children in their care. The YSC was used primarily as a detention home for juveniles awaiting trial or other court action. The scandal erupted after a seventeen-year-old fled from the center and told police that one of the guards allowed him to escape in return for performing a homosexual act.

Police later said the guard admitted sex with several of the male inmates. Several other escapes were traced by investigators with the city's Juvenile Aid Division to collaboration between the inmates and guards. Both guards and inmates were given lie detector tests, and authorities disclosed that illicit sexual activities had been transpiring in the home over a five-year period and may have involved guards with as many as 150 boys. The youngsters, from fourteen to seventeen years old, reportedly performed fellatio or submitted to anal sex in exchange for privileges and gifts including candy, cigarettes, and soft drinks. Others were reportedly coerced with threats, loss of privileges, or beatings.

One of the suspects did not live to see his trial. He was shotgunned to death by three robbers who barged into his home less than a month after his arrest. Another was acquitted of all charges and reinstated to his job, only to be fired a few days later when he was accused of beating an inmate.

More than 3,000 miles away in San Francisco, boy prostitution has been part of the scene since the gold rush days in the mid 1800s. Pederasts sometimes refer to the youngsters as "San Quentin breakfast," because the infamous prison is where an adult who sexually abuses one of the boys can wind up if he is caught and convicted.

Male and female prostitutes alike congregate along an area known as the Tenderloin, around Market and Sixth Streets, although the two sexes tend to work different sides of the street. The boys are discreet when approaching a prospective client. A chicken is likely to mention a certain amount of money that he needs to buy a birthday gift for his mother, or to see a show, rather than to quote a price for a specific sex act.

Boy prostitutes seldom cruise in Castro Village, the gay ghetto at Castro and 18th Streets. Young gays who live in or frequent such neighborhoods have no need to seek out prostitutes. If they do not already have their own partners, the bars, discos, snack shops, and the streets provide ample opportunity for meetings with new lovers or pickups. The clients of boy prostitutes are married men or singles who are referred to as "closet queens" by more open gays, because they defend God, country, and American womanhood during the day and prowl the dark streets of the Tenderloin looking for boys at night.

San Francisco, like Los Angeles, has always drawn runaways and young adventurers. During the late 60s and early 70s, its appeal was enhanced when it became a mecca for hippies, and various organizations sprang up to provide food and shelter for young transients.

Teenagers who are having difficulties because they cannot express their homosexuality at home sometimes head for San Francisco where they expect to find acceptance in the well-known and large gay community. Instead, the unhappy fourteen- or fifteen-year-olds often become the target of sexual exploitation by older gay men who themselves have not come to terms with their own sexuality. Various organizations formed to assist homosexuals offer services for the boys, even sending home those who wish to go and helping to reconcile them with their families. But once the boys have begun hustling and become streetwise, they usually avoid authority figures, both gay and straight.

Down the coast in Los Angeles, Lloyd Martin's sexually exploited child unit was in business just under a year when a Los Angeles grand jury indicted nine men on 44 counts, charging them with participating in an international child pornography and prostitution ring. District Attorney John Van de Kamp announced that children from preschoolers to twelve-year-olds were sold for prices ranging up to $1,000 each and were posing for pornography used in magazines printed in the Netherlands. One little girl was delivered to the ring when she was four years old.

Investigators said members of the ring took children to private homes or motel rooms where they were shown pornographic films before being photographed in sex acts with their peers or with adults. Pictures of one of the girls appeared in *Lolita,* a pornography magazine published in Amsterdam and distributed around the world.

The defendants were charged with conspiracy to commit lewd acts on children under the age of fourteen, to sell a person for immoral purposes, to send a minor to an immoral place, and to contribute to the delinquency of a minor. Individual counts were also filed, charging that, during the three-year period the ring operated, various defendants had committed sex acts with the seven girls and one boy who were victimized.

Van de Kamp said the children were traded in an underground sex market for participation in the porno films and to be used as sex partners for various pedophiles. Eight of the nine men admitted charges in the indictment and were sentenced. The other defendant fled to his home in England. Most of the men were from California, others from Salt Lake City, New York City, and Indianapolis.

Lester Lowell Henry, Jr., the Indianapolis man, was a staff sociologist at the Muskatatuck State Hospital in Butlerville and a family counselor who placed disabled children in foster homes, until his arrest when local investigators, armed with a search warrant, barged into his trailer home. They confiscated nearly 200 still pictures and movie films of naked children. Many of the pictures were reportedly taken at Naked City, in Indiana, and depicted naked children roaming the grounds. Others were more explicit, obviously taken elsewhere, and had been used in kiddie porn magazines, police said.

After unsuccessfully fighting extradition and returning to Los Angeles, Henry was declared to be a mentally disordered sex offender and sentenced to a California state hospital for five years. He had admitted sexually abusing the eight-year-old daughter of a co-defendant from LaPuenta, California. The California father was sentenced to life in prison. Other defendants were also given prison terms or sent to state hospitals as mentally disordered sex offenders. One man named as an unindicted co-conspirator was already confined to a state hospital in California for a previous sex offense.

One final tragic note was sounded when school classmates apparently recognized a ten-year-old girl from pictures in a television newscast which were partially, but not completely, blacked out to hide identities. The child and her family were harassed so unmercifully that they were forced to move.

The break in the case occurred in Long Beach when investigation of what had appeared to be a routine incident of child abuse developed into a kiddie prostitution and pornography racket with international connections. Children implicated in the ring, most from single-parent homes, were referred with their mothers for counseling to the Los Angeles County Department of Public Social Services. Van de Kamp said there was not sufficient evidence to warrant charging any of the mothers with participation in the scheme.

The crimes committed by the salacious band of pedophiles were abhorrent, but Los Angeles and its neighboring communities in Southern California had witnessed others just as bad.

[1] *The Atlanta Constitution*, March 23, 1979.
[2] *People*, November 13, 1978.
[3] Associated Press, February 9, 1978.
[4] *New York Post*, September 19, 1979.

11.

Snuff

POLICE and journalists call them the trash bag murders. The bodies began showing up in 1975, abandoned alongside highways in four southern California counties, a few a year until the toll had reached about 20. No one knew if it would continue to climb.

The murders were linked by ballistics experts and by the operational techniques of the killer, or killers. Most of the victims were shot through the head with the same caliber bullets. They were all nude, and had been sexually abused and mutilated, sometimes dismembered, and several were stuffed into green plastic bags tied shut in the same peculiar manner. Investigators said several of the boys and young men had homosexual backgrounds. Several also were of Mexican heritage.

Police have theorized that some of the victims could have been young Mexican boys who were smuggled across the American border in cars with specially constructed compartments in the fenders or under the floorboards, in low-flying airplanes, or dropped ashore in small boats. "They bring 'em in eight at a time under the floorboards. Then they take them to a motel and clean them up," according to Sergeant Martin. "It's getting more violent. It's as if kids aren't enough. Now there's the need for blood."[1]

A child from Mexico or from Central or South America who fits the specific demand of a wealthy pedophile can be packaged, delivered, and sold deep within this country in a short time. Smuggling a boy or girl into the United States is not difficult. Some children are delivered on regular circuits, passed around among a network of pederasts for a few months until their novelty has worn off, and then returned to Mexico and exchanged for new boys.

Thousands of illegals cross a single dusty, 16-mile, heat-blistered stretch of the U.S. and Mexican border between San Ysidro, California, and Tijuana every year. The U.S. Immigration Department Border Patrol uses searchlights, loudspeakers, helicopters, and battle-trained

182

marshals who are veterans of Vietnam in efforts to discourage crossings by impoverished aliens, desperate to slip into the country for a chance at a better life. Some of the aliens, or the people who are attempting to smuggle them into the country, fight back with guns.

The Mexicans making the crossing are also targets of violence from toughs and thieves on both sides of the border who rob, beat, and rape the unlucky ones caught without friends or defenses. About 1,000 people are apprehended attempting to make the crossing somewhere along the border every day. It is estimated that no more than one in 20 of those who make the attempt succeeds.

Many who make it are children or young teenagers who have no skills and no commodity to sell except their bodies. It is a commodity always in demand by wealthy pedophiles. The fate of the children smuggled into this country is especially grim when they fall into the hands of sadists who achieve sexual gratification by torture and inflicting pain, or—the ultimate thrill—murder. A poor Mexican youngster with no ties here is much more easily disposed of afterward than an American child.

Dr. Densen-Gerber says that foreign children are smuggled into the United States and bought "primarily for the purposes of killing. An American youngster has a school record and a family. But if a child has been taken off the streets of Guadalajara or Acapulco, it's much easier (than killing an American). There are thousands of these nameless, faceless children whose parents may have been told that the child is going for adoption, and whose parents may agree simply because they want to afford that child a better life than they have had," she points out. "So here is a man in a Cadillac who looks nice. And they never hear from that child again."

Odyssey Institute has had inquiries from officials in Venezuela where they believe children are trained in the sexual arts before being shipped through an organized network to wealthy pedophiles in other countries. There is an international market in children and older youths of both sexes. The mere idea is so gross and shocking that it may appear to border on fantasy. But it is true. People like Dr. Densen-Gerber and Sergeant Martin know it to be a fact.

A recent *New York Times* story read like fiction from a men's magazine in the 1950s as it told of an increasing number of European women and girls who are sold into white slavery in the Middle East. A Swiss police official was quoted as saying that the victims are runaways fleeing school, unhappy family lives, and dull jobs—or hippies seeking drug paradises and adventure in the Middle East and Orient. "At some point

an organization takes over and channels them into enforced prostitution," he says. A police official in Turkey was quoted as saying that
authorities in "all countries in Europe and the Middle East are too busy
with terrorists to be bothered with mere runaways."[2]

Pedophilia is obviously not unique to the United States. The late
Argentine dictator, Juan Peron, was one of the better known pedophiles
of this century and was stimulated by sexual relations with twelve- to
fourteen-year-old girls.

One of the most inhuman instances of sadistic pedophilia in recent
history occurred in Great Britain where a man and woman tortured
children to death and made tape recordings of their screams. Before
killing a ten-year-old girl and a twelve-year-old boy, Ian Brady and
Myra Hindley forced them to pose for obscene pictures. The killers
were sentenced to life imprisonment, the maximum penalty available.

National news columnist Jack Anderson says that high civilian and
military officials in Paraguay regularly heaped sexual abuse on young
girls purchased from peasant families. He quoted the granddaughter of
a former chief justice of the Paraguayan Supreme Court who told of
seeing the unconscious bodies of two eight-year-old girls and one nine-
year-old girl lying naked on a pile of sand where they had been discarded
after use. They were bleeding from the genitals and had other "marks
on their bodies evidencing sexual abuse," he wrote.[3]

Dr. Densen-Gerber believes that there are between 800 and 1,000
American children each year who are leased or sold to foreign pedophiles. "We understand they are sold to cultures which have a tremendous interest in children, such as the Arab cultures," she says. "And, of
course, in their world, blond, fair-haired children would get a higher
price."

Author Robin Lloyd testified before the U.S. House Select Committee on Education and Labor that an eleven-year-old fifth-grade boy
from a small town in Texas had been kidnapped a short time before by
a reputed agent for a pornographer who had allegedly offered $25,000
for every fair-skinned, Anglo child delivered to Mexico City. "I don't
believe the figure for one moment, but both the Texas Rangers and the
FBI have told me on the phone that the operation is very much active
and that the children are being taken into Mexico for that purpose,"
Lloyd averred.

A spokesman for a Texas House Select Committee on Child Pornography disclosed in the late 70s that investigators were probing leads to
organized rings in Houston, Dallas, and other major cities that were

running slave auctions for the sale of sixteen- and seventeen-year-old boys sneaked out of Mexico.

The Committee also probed reports that "snuff" films in which juveniles were actually murdered were being produced in Texas. However, the Texas investigations were no more successful than those launched elsewhere around the United States at about the same time in response to reports that young girls and boys, as well as older victims, were actually being murdered as part of the porn film productions.

Rumors had circulated in Hollywood and Los Angeles at least as far back as the 1940s, but the stories burgeoned and authorities began to take official notice with the release of a highly-touted and poorly produced Argentine porno movie, *Snuff*.

The story line was based loosely on a Charles Manson-type clan, living in South American swamps, that murdered several people in a villa before turning on each other in a frenzy of blood and sex. The last few feet of the film have been tacked on to the original production and focus on the sexual coupling of the reputed director and an actress after the rest of the movie is completed. During the sex scene, the actress is surprised by the murderer who slowly dismembers her while she is still alive. The scene is not convincing, and the prosthetic fingers are easily distinguishable as they are clipped off while the actress' real digits are folded safely back into her palm.

Long before the film's slated opening in Indianapolis, the movie was attacked as a hoax which contained no actual killings, even though the chief of the corporation that released the film did his best to exploit the uncertainty over real or simulated murder. He told a reporter for *Variety* that he would be a fool to answer either way, managing to fuel the controversy. *Variety* concluded that the film did not depict real murders and that it was a retitled version of another movie. *Snuff* did poorly at the box office in Indianapolis and in other cities where it showed.

The controversy was rekindled, however, with reports that other "snuff" or "slasher" movies were showing up on the underground pornography market. Eight reels long, they were printed on convenient 8-millimeter home movie size and were said to sell for $1,500 per copy. About the time the 8-millimeter films hit the market, Associated Press reported that the bodies of horribly mutilated prostitutes had begun showing up in a wide-open Argentine city amid widespread speculation that their murders had been filmed.

Private screenings of the new slasher movies were reportedly available for $200. Detective Joseph Horman, of the New York City Police Department's Organized Crime Control Bureau, described the gruesome films as "the ultimate obscenity." He said that at least eight different slasher films were believed to be in circulation and were apparently made in South America, possibly Argentina.

The movies were described as beginning like most other poorly made stag films with males and females engaging in a variety of sexual behavior, but at the climax a knife is suddenly flashed and the startled actress or actor is murdered. Some are then dismembered. Horman said that although some slasher films only simulated death, the eight he was attempting to trace showed actual killings.

FBI sources admitted that slasher movies were possibly being filmed in the United States and said New Orleans, Miami, New York, and Los Angeles were thought to be among the sites of screenings. "The thing that is really astonishing," Horman observed, "is that there is such a market."

Some scoffers view the entire affair as a hoax tied into the ballyhoo surrounding *Snuff*. Other students of the phenomenon trace the genesis of the stories to a speech by a member of an anti-smut group, the "Citizens for Decency Through Law." In the talk, the progression in magazines and films from simulated to explicit sex, and from simulated sex and violence to actual scenes of sadomasochism, was discussed. It was conceivable, the speaker said, that the next step could be actual killing for sexual gratification. The rumors were believed to have sprung from the speech and then intensified a few months later when the speaker declared that he had actual evidence that snuff films did exist.

The evidence was not produced, however. And, despite spirited investigation by Horman and other policemen, no law enforcement agency has been able to acquire a slasher film. They may or may not exist. And if they do, juveniles may or may not be the victims.

But whether or not slasher films featuring children are anything more than the figment of someone's vivid imagination, it is widespread knowledge that large numbers of juveniles in this country have died at the hands of sadists seeking sexual gratification from their terror and pain.

It is the child molester at his worst. The lives of shocking numbers of boys and girls have been sacrificed. Two widely known instances of mass murders of children occurred in the bloody 70s, one in Houston and one in a small unincorporated area just outside Chicago. The victims were all boys or young men. The slayings in Texas were attributed to electrician and former candy-maker, Dean Corll, and to two teenagers who procured victims for him; in Illinois, to John Wayne

Gacy, Jr., a contractor and amateur clown. Both stories have been widely chronicled.

The bodies of 27 known victims were dug up from under the floor of a utility shed, from rattlesnake-infested dry river beds, and from a wooded area near the Samuel Rayburn Lake, in the Texas murders.

The slayings stopped when a seventeen-year-old confederate of Corll's, Elmer Wayne Henley, shot him to death during a quarrel in the Houston suburb of Pasadena. Henley told police the trouble started after he invited a fifteen-year-old neighborhood girl to accompany him and another young male acquaintance to Corll's home. Corll was enraged when he saw the girl.

Henley and his companions got high sniffing paint, drinking moonshine, and smoking marijuana before passing out. When they regained consciousness, they had been tied up or handcuffed, and Corll was threatening to kill his friend for bringing the girl. Henley talked his way out of it. But the two friends began quarreling again when Corll said he was going to rape the other youth who was tied face down to a plywood torture board and instructed Henley to cut the girl's clothes off and do the same to her. Henley later told police that he refused and picked up a gun, threatening to shoot. He pulled the trigger and emptied the chamber when the enraged older man advanced on him.

Investigators later disclosed that Corll had promised bounties of as much as $200 to Henley and to David Owen Brooks, eighteen, for some of the boys, but actually paid as little as $5 or $10 when he paid at all. The victims were enticed with promises of sex, liquor, marijuana, or paint sniffing parties.

Once the boys were overpowered, they were tied to a plywood device called the torture board and sexually abused, sometimes for days until they were finally shot or strangled. At least once, two boys were secured side by side and one was forced to watch as the other was tortured and killed, knowing he would be next.

Henley was not charged with Corll's death but was tried and convicted for murdering six of the boys. He was sentenced to six 99-year prison terms to be served consecutively, a total of 594 years in prison. Five years later, the conviction was overturned on a technicality and he was retried and again sentenced to life in prison. Brooks was accused of committing four of the murders, but was tried on only one and sentenced to life.

Gacy is known to have enticed some of his heterosexual victims with promises of work with his construction company and have picked up gay prostitutes and other youths in Chicago with promises of money or drugs before taking them to his home to be sexually abused, tortured, and sometimes murdered. He also used a torture rack that he had fashioned himself.

He was charged with the deaths of 33 young men and boys whose bodies were either dug up from his property or pulled from area rivers. The victims, all slender-hipped, smallish youths, usually with light hair, ranged from fourteen to the early twenties. Although there was no testimony to the effect, there were unsettling indications that he, too, may have paid a bounty to others for helping lure victims to his home for sexual abuse, if not murder.

The grisly mass murders, one uncovered near the beginning of the decade and the other near the end, ignited outcries of rage directed at government, homosexuals, and any other handy target.

The Houston Police Department was denounced for failing to uncover the sex and torture orgies during the nearly three years that parents were reporting their sons missing. Parents complained that police treated the information cavalierly. They were usually told that the boys were obviously runaways. One mother, a practical nurse, said she informed police that her son had vanished after leaving home to go swimming and was told: "Lady, we just don't have time to chase every runaway." A father who lost two sons said police treated him "like some kind of idiot" when he reported his boys missing.

Chicago police were blamed for failing to follow up on early complaints of sexual assaults by Gacy; for failing to run a records check which would have turned up a previous conviction and prison term for a sex crime in Iowa; and for failing to establish a pattern in the disappearance of so many youths.

Bill Treanor of the National Youth Work Alliance in Washington, D.C., accused police of "Incredible incompetence. . . . Ten minutes spent looking into the pattern of sudden disappearances in some routine reports could prevent a lot of these crimes," he fumed.[4]

Critics from the gay community chimed in with speculation that police ignored some of the complaints because the victims were male hookers or youths who frequented gay bars and discos.

But fears by gay rights groups of witch hunts against homosexuals were unfounded. Most people apparently were willing to view the murders correctly, as the handiwork of individuals who killed because they were sadists and pederasts, not because they were homosexuals. Responsible homosexuals no more condone the action of sadists or pederasts than responsible heterosexuals approve the molestation or torture of little girls.

If anything positive resulted from the mass murders of the boys, it occurred in Houston where a group of volunteers, shocked by the horror in their community and distressed at the anguish of parents who would never know if their missing sons were among the unidentified victims, established Operation Peace of Mind. It is a national hotline for runaways. Operators at the toll-free number, 800-231-6946, take messages for families of the callers and relay information back if the child makes a return call. There are no lectures, and the calls are not traced. Children are merely asked if they need help, and, if the reply is affirmative, they are told where free services are available. Five years after the service was established, Operation Peace of Mind had handled more than 250,000 calls. (In Texas, the free number is 800-392-3352.)

The hotline was initially set up in a motel suite and was planned as a 30-day program. But when the governor of Texas learned that more than 30 families were reunited the first month, he helped provide state funding to keep the service in operation.

The federal government's Runaway Youth Act established its own nationwide hotline for runaways about a year later. The Chicago based National Runaway Switchboard is part of a program including a network of 166 juvenile shelters around the country, financed with $11 million annually, administered by the U.S. Department of Health, Education and Welfare's Office of Youth Development. The Switchboard's toll-free number is 800-621-4000. (In Illinois, it is 800-972-6004.) Some 125,000 calls from runaways are logged by the service each year, and many of them are directed to centers where food, shelter, and counseling are available. Several individual cities also maintain hotlines for runaways and juveniles in trouble, but only a few offer 24-hour service.

It is true, however, regardless of what policemen might claim, that they are sometimes reluctant to investigate missing reports and sexual assaults involving gay youths—especially if the boys are suspected of being prostitutes. Police departments are para-military organizations, and for the most part they attract macho men. Bill Katz of the ASPCC believes that, "It's very threatening for policemen to arrest homosexuals," although "it's almost macho to arrest (female) whores." It is difficult for a typical police officer to testify in open court that he has propositioned a fourteen- or fifteen-year-old boy to commit specific homosexual acts, Katz contends.

When an officer with Denver's vice squad was asked why he did not make more arrests of gay prostitutes in the few bars where most male hookers hang out, he replied, "Who are you going to send up there to investigate? Are you going to send a policeman up into all them gays to find out what's going on?"[5] If there is evidence of murder or a chance of scandal, however, police move quickly, regardless of the sexual preferences of the victims.

Prostitution by gay teenagers can be a problem for even the most macho organizations, however. When U.S. Marine recruiters advised that they were seeking "a few good men," they got more than they bargained for after enlisting a dozen or so seventeen- and eighteen-year-olds who eventually found their way to Camp Pendleton, California. The sprawling Marine base is about 100 miles from Hollywood's large community of chicken hawks, pimps, and pornographers.

It was close enough for a shady entrepreneur who used a Marine Corps contact to procure teenage leathernecks for prostitution and pornography. Base spokesmen said the youths were first photographed in Orange County, often performing homosexual acts, and the pictures circulated in Hollywood. They were subsequently moved to Hollywood for prostitution and roles in sex films. Los Angeles police said that Hollywood pornographers played a critical role in initiating and carrying out the scheme.

Immediately after the operation was disclosed, 12 Marines were given a choice of taking honorable administrative discharges or facing courts-martial. They took the discharges. Some 30 other Marines were possibly involved in the ring.

Commercial gain was not the object of killers responsible for a series of child slayings and sexual assaults that shocked residents of some of Detroit's more affluent suburbs during one mind-numbing 14-month period. Four of the victims, two boys and two girls, were apparently murdered by an individual who became known as "The Oakland County Killer." One of the most frightening aspects of the terror was a macabre death ritual carried out by the sadistic pedophile.

A twelve-year-old boy was apparently the first object of the rite after he was snatched from play outside an American Legion Hall in Livernois. When his body was found carefully placed in the snow four days later, his hands and arms were neatly folded as if for a funeral. He had also been washed, his hair combed, and he had been dressed after death.

As the bodies of the other children linked to the Oakland County Killer were found, there was evidence of similar ritualistic care and neatness in disposing of the bodies. They had been kept alive for a few days after their abduction and were well fed, washed, and groomed. An autopsy showed that the other boy, a ten-year-old, was fed his favorite food for his last meal. His mother had mentioned his fondness for chicken when she made a futile public appeal for his release. Like the others, his hands and arms were folded neatly, and he had been manicured, pedicured, and dressed in freshly laundered clothes. Both boys were sexually assaulted.

Two of the victims died of strangulation. One was smothered and the other shotgunned to death. The others were older girls and their slayings did not closely fit the known procedure of the Oakland County Killer. The first and oldest victim, a 16-year-old, died of a fractured skull and other head injuries. The second was a 14-year-old baby-sitter, raped, and killed with three shotgun blasts. Another 14-year-old, the fourth of the seven victims, was killed with carbon monoxide. A prominent Birmingham psychiatrist working with investigators speculated that the Oakland County Killer's murderous impulses may have been ignited by the earlier rape murder of the babysitter. Dr. Bruce L. Danto said the kidnap-slayer was playing a cruel game. "Once he goes after the kids, he is really going after the real victims—the parents."

The mysterious slayer was described as deriving sadistic pleasure from the anguish of the parents, the concern of the community, and the brutality to the children. Basing his theory on studies of abnormal personalities, Danto suggested that the murderer may have been abandoned or abused by his own parents, or was an adopted child who felt rejected and had lived for years with a boiling hatred before striking out.[6]

A study of Oakland County school children, intended to help in drawing a profile of the killer's pattern of operation, produced significant information about the nature of child molesters. Of the children in the study who reported being sexually approached, 49 percent were boys. Girls are popularly believed to be sexually molested in far greater numbers than boys.

A unique federally and locally funded police task force with access to computers as well as more conventional investigative aids was formed in an effort to capture the child killer. More than 50 area police agencies assigned 134 investigators, and 25 Michigan state troopers joined the manhunt. Five thousand mail carriers throughout Michigan were given photos and descriptions of a missing boy the last of the victims, and police sketches of a suspect.

The effect of the terror on the suburban Detroit communities was devastating. Parents walked their children to and from school, and outdoor play became rare unless it was closely supervised by trusted adults. T-shirts for children were imprinted with slogans advising them not to trust strangers. Girlfriends telephoned authorities and said they suspected their boyfriends in the abductions and slayings. Mothers reported their sons, and people named neighbors as suspects.

Police enlisted a psychic and his assistant from upstate New York; mortuary scientists at Wayne State University in Detroit were consulted; and anthropologists from Michigan State University in East Lansing were approached for information.

The effect of the massive manhunt was like turning over a rock in a cow pasture. All sorts of subterranean life from the sordid sexual underground of the upper middle-class suburban communities was bared. A Catholic priest in Farmington was accused of sexually molesting young boys and tried and jailed. A mother was accused of renting her son to adult males for sexual activity. A woman teacher was charged with having sexual relations with an eleven-year-old student in the men's room of a school but was acquitted.

Two years after the task force was formed, it was disbanded. Some 90 file cabinets of information and documents had been collected. No one was charged with the slayings. But the killings had stopped.

State Police Lieutenant Robert Robertson, who directed the investigation, warned that the killer could begin again, however. "If he's not dead, then he's in an institution somewhere," he said. "And when he's released from the institution, whether it's a prison or a mental hospital of some kind, he'll probably strike again."

[1] *Detroit News,* June 26, 1977.
[2] *New York Times,* April 16, 1978.
[3] *Chicago Daily News,* January 6, 1978.
[4] *U.S. News & World Report,* January 15, 1979.
[5] *Detroit Sunday News,* July 25, 1976.
[6] *Chicago Daily News,* March 25, 1977.

12.

The Mob

Ask a half-dozen law enforcement officers and other professionals who work with troubled juveniles if the Mafia, or Mob, is involved in the sexual exploitation of children, and you will likely hear six different answers.

On the surface the answer would appear obvious. Internecine struggles for control of distribution areas, adult bookstores and theaters, massage parlors, and bust-out bars featuring nude dancers and teenage prostitutes have led to murders, bombings, arson, blackmail, and extortion. Children lured or forced into prostitution and pornography have been brutally beaten and murdered when they tried to break their ties to the trade.

The names of politicians with links to some of the highest offices in the nation have been tenuously but disturbingly tied to known mobsters and multimillionaire distributors of pornography.

Syndicated columnist Jack Anderson, whose news sources in Washington are as good as or better than anyone else's, has cited confidential police files that he says disclose that "the pornography trade is controlled by organized crime. Phony names and dummy corporations are used. But behind them," he says, "are the crime bosses." Anderson pinpointed the Joseph Colombo and Sam "The Plumber" DeCavalcante Mafia families as controlling the pornography market in New York.[1] More official sources have linked the Mafia to hot-pillow hotels and massage parlors where youthful prostitutes and their older sisters work. The mob family of the late Carlo Gambino is also reputed to have a large slice of the child pornography business.

Yet, Guy Strait, a wizened, aging man who has spent most of a lifetime in the child pornography business, claims that the Syndicate, not the Mafia, directs the business. The Mafia, La Cosa Nostra, or the Mob, is usually identified with hoodlums of Italian or Sicilian extraction. Strait described the Syndicate as a nationwide cartel of hoodlums of nearly every ethnic background. The Syndicate deals in all forms of crime, he says, but is especially active in pornography and narcotics.

Robert Gemignani, the Rockford, Illinois, prosecutor who sent Strait to prison, says simply, "There is little question that we are dealing with a group. We may not know what it is called—a Syndicate, a Mob, an Organization—but it is a single group which controls the manufacture and distribution of the product."

There are elements of fact in the observations of all three men. Organized crime families are heavily engaged in pornography and prostitution, and children as well as adults have been exploited in the twin sex trade. Vice feeds on the avarice and baser qualities of men and thus is a perfect breeding place to attract and nurture hoodlums. A business attracts Mob interest if it offers a large flow of money in cold hard cash, making bookkeeping easy to doctor; if respectable businesses are not openly in direct competition; and if the nature of the business itself is *sub rosa*. Pornography and prostitution were ready-made for Mob control.

The Mafia is known to skim profits off the top from the proceeds of its porn shops, movies, and arcades, instructing store managers to shut off electric cash registers after a certain hour so that records do not reflect true income. The skim is tax free. Other operators do just the opposite, inflating income from the arcades and theaters so the businesses can be used to launder or account for money realized from various illegal sources such as narcotics, extortion, or loan sharking.

Dr. Densen-Gerber told a U.S. Congressional panel probing the sexual exploitation of children that, "We are dealing with organized crime, the same group of people who filled this country with narcotics prior to their beginning to produce and distribute these materials." She added that it was her "belief that kiddie porno was started . . . in Seattle, Washington, by a man named Tony Eboli, now dead, who headed the Genovese family for a period of time."[2]

A few years ago top Mafia chieftains reportedly warned their underlings against dealing in child pornography and prostitution, apparently because it was personally distasteful, but also because they feared it would attract too much pressure from law enforcement agencies. But there was a time when they were also said to have warned their soldiers against trafficking in narcotics for the same reasons. And the Mafia moved heavily into narcotics.

Pornography alone, however, not including the huge profits from prostitution, is a source of enormous amounts of money. And the bottom line in Mafia circles is money. Despite caution on the part of the older Mafia bosses, the lure of such enormous profits, mostly in non-taxable dollars, was too tempting. They moved into pornography and prostitution just as they had moved into narcotics. Old-timers either gave the business a second look and went along, or they were replaced.

In pornography, the Mob focused on distribution. Warehousing, trucking, wholesale and retail operations, and manufacture of materials and equipment are Mob specialties. For the most part they permitted others to do the actual filming and producing, but provided financing and forcibly cut themselves in as partners.

New York State Senator Ralph J. Marino told a United States Congressional committee that both boys and girls engaged in prostitution in New York City earn large sums of money that is funneled into the coffers of organized crime. The Mob is also heavily involved in the operation of topless bars in New York, he reported. "They get a piece of the girls' action every night. They get a piece of any activity where she is permitted to sell her body." During a tour of the city's sin strips, Marino was repeatedly propositioned by children anxious to prostitute themselves with him for amounts ranging from $10 for fellatio to $25 for sexual intercourse. The common factor in the encounters was a location or business controlled by organized crime, he said. The bars and clubs were described as havens for narcotics dealing as well as child sex, possibly including pornography. "Let's not make the mistake of attacking juvenile pornography in isolation from organized crime," the legislator cautioned.

The refusal of legitimate distributors to handle sexually explicit material during the early days of the porn boom left the market wide open for invasion by the Mafia. Al Goldstein, whose *Screw* magazine was used by the Abramses to seek out little girl models, was quoted as saying that he began dealing with Star Distributors and Astro News—both reputedly crime-controlled—because legitimate distributors had turned thumbs down on his product.

A few years before Goldstein's association with Star, the company produced girlie and nudie magazines. It was on the brink of financial collapse when Robert "Debe" DiBernardo, a member of the De-Cavalcante Mafia family from northern New Jersey, stepped in as company president. The company was revitalized almost overnight and quickly began acquiring adult bookstores in New York and Philadelphia. In a short time, film-processing laboratories, film-making, distributorships, and publishing activities were added.

But much of Strait's contention is also valid. Mafia influence in the porn and prostitution industry, especially where children are concerned, is not all pervasive. Multi-ethnic mobsters have cut themselves in for massive chunks of the pornography-prostitution pie.

Even motorcycle gangs have moved into commercial sex, boldly challenging the Mafia and other smut entrepreneurs. When 10 massage parlors were bombed in Chicago in the mid-70s, police pinpointed members of the Outlaws motorcycle gang as prime suspects. The bikers were said to be insisting that the business owners hire their girlfriends at ridiculously inflated salaries. Two taverns and the clubhouse of a rival bike gang were also bombed, but there were no arrests.

A police spokesman in Canada described some of the biker gangs there as extremely sophisticated criminals. He claimed that the Outlaws were challenging the Mafia for control of various lucrative criminal activities such as prostitution, narcotics, and the large-scale theft of motorcycles and cars. Many of the more progressive bikers have traded in their greasy denims and metal-studded leathers for conservative three-piece suits, giving up beatings with chains and sawed-off pool cues for professional Mob-style hits on their business competitors.

Newcomers to the vice business, especially pornography, are often otherwise legitimate businessmen who recognize the incredible money-making potential of the trade. Most of those who stay in the business apparently are forced to forge at least limited ties to the Mafia, but the stronger, more capable members of the smut fraternity have managed to retain control of the empires they built. They might be considered part of a syndicate with a small "s," composed of the producers, distributors, and retailers of pornography, with links to every state in the nation and many foreign countries. They are aggressive, ruthless, and extremely capable men.

Mike Thevis was that kind of man. He used a combination of audacity, imagination, courage, and hard work to build what was probably the biggest smut empire in the nation. A man with a massive ego and supreme self-confidence, he put together a sprawling network of adult bookstores, X-rated movie theaters, peep-show machines, and warehouses that authorities believe enabled him to control some 40 percent of the nation's smut business. Federal and other authorities have estimated his annual take at one time as $100 million. The porn king once described himself as "the GM of pornography." The same authorities say that Thevis managed to hold together and expand his Atlanta based enterprises only by becoming involved in a string of murders, bombings, arson, and extortion.

In another business Thevis could have been a model of the classic American success story. Born in Raleigh, North Carolina, in 1932, he was raised by strict immigrant grandparents in the Greek Orthodox Church. He was taught that hard work, education, and success were a natural order of life. When other boys were playing games, trying out for athletic teams, or dating, Mike Thevis was working.

He was not a bad student, but he dropped out of high school in Raleigh when he was seventeen. Soon after that he moved to Atlanta and finished school there. After graduation he entered Georgia Tech, planning to become a textile engineer. Financial pressures, however, forced him to leave college and take a job in downtown Atlanta as a $50-a-week employee in a street-corner newsstand.

From the beginning, the business appealed to him, and before long he had convinced his bosses to open another stand for him to manage. When he had acquired enough knowledge of the business and some small savings, he opened his own three-stand shoeshine shop. By the 1960s he owned a string of newsstands. He was also married and the father of three children. The family lived in a modest apartment, and when the rent was raised to $57.50 he had to move out.

Thevis may have begun wondering if something was wrong with the work ethic he had believed in. He had worked hard, built up a respectable business, and yet could not afford a $57.50 apartment for his family. At some point, he made a fateful decision. So-called adult material accounted for only 10 percent of his magazine stock, but it was responsible for about 90 percent of his business and profits.

He shifted to pornography, and the dollars began rolling in. The trade began to rapidly expand from publications such as *Playboy* and *Oui* to magazines and films featuring sordid sexual activities. The progression continued until the material included bondage, sadism and masochism, bestiality, and, finally, kiddie porn.

Thevis prepared to ride the crest of the pornography boom. The money he earned from pornography was reinvested in more newsstands and bookstores in Atlanta and in other cities. His new outlets earned more dollars to be reinvested in additional stores.

He moved into the production and distribution of pornographic books, magazines, movies, and rubber and plastic sex aids. In the late 1960s he went into partnership with a career criminal named Roger Dean Underhill to form Cine-Matics, Inc.

When Cine-Matics began manufacturing machines, Thevis for the first time could provide, install, and service his own peep-show product, just as he had previously done with films and printed material.

Thevis did not like competition. He began muscling his way into the operations of his competitors. One he could not buy or force out was

Urban Industries, Inc., a Louisville, Kentucky, firm that manufactured peep-show machines.

Urban Industries belonged to Nat Bailen, a man who was said to consider himself the inventor of the peep-show machine. Bailen turned out machines in the early 60s to show children's cartoons at arcades, amusement parks, and shopping centers. But after the pornography boom, some of Bailen's machines were sold to an enterprising pornographer in New York who put them in shops in the Times Square area and outfitted them with loops of bare-breasted women, replaced a few years later by nude men, women, and children engaged in explicit sexual activity.

Bailen had figured out how to put the film on continuous cartridges that did not have to be rewound. Underhill used his experience as a locksmith to improve security for coin collection and automatic auditing.

Bailen was not the businessman that Thevis was. Bailen sold his machines. Thevis leased his and insisted on a high percentage of the income. Obviously Bailen's more generous business practices cut into Thevis' profits.

On April 27, 1970, there was a fire in the Urban Industries warehouse. Authorities said it was set by arsonists.

Thevis was busy living the good life in keeping with the affluent neighborhood he then lived in and with the lifestyle he was creating. But he continued to scheme, always working to expand his holdings.

On November 13, 1970, the bullet-punctured body of Kenneth "Jap" Hanna, a smalltime Atlanta pornographer, was found stuffed into the trunk of his gleaming gold Cadillac abandoned at Hartsfield International Airport. The disposal of Hanna was a classic Mob-style rubout. Hanna had introduced Thevis to Underhill. Thevis' partner in Cine-Matics was an ambitious habitual criminal, a powerfully built, bullnecked, confident man with an incredibly vivid memory that would plague Thevis later.

Three months after Hanna's death, Underhill sold his share of Cine-Matics to his partner and opened his own peep-show business. For a time, at least, the two men remained friendly. But there was hard feeling elsewhere in the smut industry.

In September, 1972, a combined adult bookstore and X-rated theater owned by competitors in Fayetteville, North Carolina, was destroyed by fire. Police and fire officials labeled the blaze as arson.

Almost exactly a year later, James Mayes, a partner of Underhill's in a bookstore and peep-show in Atlanta, was blown through the roof of his van when a bomb exploded seconds after he had climbed inside. Underhill picked up a sliver of bone from a cyclone fence after the explosion and took it to Thevis, suggesting that it be imbedded in lucite and kept as a souvenir paperweight. The porn king was in the hospital recovering from injuries suffered when he crashed a motorcycle he was riding. The motorcycle was owned by his friend Underhill.

Underhill got into trouble and was sentenced to federal prison on a charge of possession of stolen guns that were transported across state lines. Federal authorities were on Thevis' trail by that time, and, among other things, they were looking for possible tax violations in his business dealings. They hoped to convince Underhill to testify against Thevis, but he clammed up. The night after they questioned him, his appendix burst and he was rushed to the hospital.

The same indictment that later accused Thevis of involvement in the Mayes slaying also alleged that he sent a pair of hit men armed with silencer-equipped pistols to kill his former lieutenant. Underhill's door was guarded by a federal marshal, and the reputed contract killing was aborted.

The next time the two men met was early 1976, about a year after Underhill's hospitalization and the first reputed attempt on his life. The meeting occurred as they entered a courtroom to plead to conspiracy charges in the torching of Urban Industries. Thevis was eventually sentenced to eight and a half years at the Federal Correctional Institution at Springfield, Missouri, for arson conspiracy and another earlier charge of interstate transportation of obscene materials.

Underhill had begun to suspect that Thevis was planning to set him up as the fall guy in the slaying of Hanna and Mayes. Federal investigators had continued their meetings with him. A short time before leaving prison, he agreed to help the FBI in its investigation of Thevis. He made two appearances before grand juries, and in June, 1977, visited Thevis at the penitentiary, recording their conversation with a microphone hidden in his shoe.

Underhill's tapes were vital to the prosecution of Thevis. Due in large part to Underhill's assistance, authorities put together what appeared to be an almost airtight case of racketeering against Thevis. But before the information could be presented to a federal grand jury, the nation's premier pornographer escaped from jail.

He had been awaiting transfer back to the penitentiary in Missouri after losing a civil suit resulting from the burning of the Urban Industries warehouse in Louisville, when he fled from the Floyd County Jail in New Albany, Indiana. It had been a bad week for Thevis. He had been ordered by a federal jury in Louisville to pay more than $650,000 in damages to Urban Industries and their insurance companies. The Internal Revenue Service was after him. Florida had indicted him on a state racketeering charge. And a divorce from his wife of 26 years had just been finalized.

The porn king was on the loose, and a half-dozen federal and state law enforcement agencies were looking for him. He was placed on the FBI's Most Wanted List. Approximately six weeks later, Thevis, seven associates, and four corporations he had controlled were named in a wide-ranging 14-count federal racketeering indictment. The Fayette-ville bombing, Louisville arson, extortion involving a distributor in Houston, and an attempt to kill a government witness (Underhill) were all included in the allegations and cited as evidence of racketeering. Almost everyone involved agreed that the bill could not have been returned without Underhill's assistance.

Then the Fulton County (Atlanta) grand jury returned a murder indictment against Thevis, charging him in the slaying of "Jap" Hanna. It was generally agreed that this indictment also could not have been obtained without Underhill's testimony that he was present when Thevis disposed of the body and the murder weapon. Underhill added that, while following Thevis' instructions, he also arranged for the Mayes killing.

Thevis did not know that Underhill had turned on him until the arson case at Louisville. Ignoring Thevis' stony presence, Underill talked easily and in great detail about his part in the arson of the warehouse and of several burglaries he said he undertook at the instruction of his former boss.

Both an FBI agent and a U.S. Attorney subsequently testified at a series of court hearings that they believed Underhill's life was in danger. The FBI agent cited information from informants that an "open contract" was out on Underhill's life, meaning that a certain amount of money was available to anyone who would get the job done.

On October 26, 1978, Underhill drove to an undeveloped 14-acre parcel of land he owned along the Chattahoochee River and took along an Atlanta grocer and real estate speculator, Isaac N. Galanti, who was interested in the property. The two men were shotgunned from ambush. Galanti died at the scene, Underhill, a few hours later after undergoing surgery at a nearby hospital.

Thevis was captured two weeks later while attempting to withdraw $30,000 from a bank in Bloomfield, Connecticut. Some $454,000 in cash and an estimated $1 million worth of jewelry, as well as seven handguns and ammunition, were found in the trunk of Thevis' new car. He told investigators that he had stashed money in safety deposit boxes all over the Southwest.

Shaken by the loss of the government's star witness, prosecutors dropped the original racketeering indictments against Thevis for a new package of somewhat pared down but still formidable charges. Thevis was convicted of racketeering and of conspiring to murder Underhill, and he was sentenced to long prison terms ranging from 20 years to life.

During the ensuing months Thevis was tried on various other charges and pleaded guilty or was convicted on some. Several of Thevis' associates were charged with criminal violations in connection with his activities, but most were found innocent or cleared prior to trial.

The mystery and controversy surrounding the one-time pornography kingpin's convoluted dealings promise to continue for years, however. Various individuals and government agencies have initiated litigation seeking huge shares of the millions he collected with his network of adult bookstores, movies, sexual aids, and peep-shows.

As the proliferation of pornography exploded in this country, the fast money men streamed into the business. Since Thevis was deposed it is doubtful if any one individual controls as much as 40 percent of the wholesale and retail business. If anyone comes close, however, it is Reuben Sturman, the cautious, low-profile son of a Russian immigrant who lives in the fashionable Cleveland suburb of Shaker Heights and oversees widespread porn holdings believed to extend into all 50 states, the District of Columbia, and 40 foreign countries.

Sturman and Thevis share a few things besides their business. Like Thevis, Sturman chose an expensive Tudor style home among select, refined neighbors. And like Thevis, he is frequently charged in obscenity and other cases related to his blue money enterprises, but he employs a stable of lawyers who have successfully defended him in a string of court appearances. And if racketeering and extortion have been part of his rise to quiet prominence in the pornography trade, as some authorities believe, no one has ever been able to prove it.

He is said to have built a fortune on earnings in the blue money trade that has averaged considerably more than $20 million annually for nearly a decade. According to *Parade* magazine, investigations and a raid on his three-story Sovereign News Warehouse turned up records showing that Sturman owned additional porn warehouses in Baltimore, Chicago, Philadelphia, Pittsburgh, Denver, Milwaukee, Buffalo, Los Angeles, Detroit, and Toronto.

Approximately 300 adult bookstores and peep-shows, as well as controlling interest in the sexual rubber and plastics goods industry, marketed under the trade name "Doc Johnson," were also known to be Sturman properties. The magazine indicated that the sale of "Doc Johnson" implements may have reached the $100 million mark by the end of the 70s, and sales of home video-cassettes, the newest wrinkle on the smut market, were keeping pace.[3]

Managers of a company that is the major distributor of pornography in Chicago reportedly agreed to cease dealing locally in child pornography after considerable pressure from licensing authorities. *Chicago Sun-Times* writers Art Petacque and Michael Flannery quoted "sources in Chicago city government" as saying that the company's owner, "Rubin Sterman (sic) of Cleveland," is "a big advocate of child pornography."[4]

Like Thevis, Sturman is believed by authorities to have strong ties with the Mafia. At least two of three other men pinpointed as leaders in the nation's pornography industry through the 1970s have been described as members of the Cosa Nostra. They were identified as Michael Zaffarano and "Debe" DiBernardo.

The third mogul of porn, said to have ranked just below Thevis and Sturman, was identified by *Parade* as Harry Virgil Mohney of Durand, Michigan, a small town near the industrial city of Flint. Mohney was said to be a major importer of European pornography and to have at one time controlled at least 60 adult bookstores, a string of massage parlors, X-rated theaters and drive-in movies, go-go joints, and a topless billiard hall.[5]

Zaffarano, sometimes known as Mike Galbo, died of an apparent heart attack in February, 1980, as FBI agents attempted to serve him with a warrant for conspiracy and interstate transportation of obscene material. He was one of more than 50 people named in a wide-ranging series of federal indictments that authorities said shattered a 12-state pornography distribution and motion picture piracy operation dealing in billions of dollars. FBI Director William H. Webster said that distributors of adult and child pornography were caught in the "Sting" operation and that a major blow was dealt to the nation's smut industry.

The crackdown culminated a two-and-a-half-year probe labeled "Miporn" by FBI agents and local Dade county, Florida, investigators. They had established a pair of front businesses in Miami that were supposedly dealing in wholesale and mail-order pornography and the pirating of conventional movies. Using the fronts, agents were able to both infiltrate the pornography industry and deal with top crime figures involved in the film-pirating scheme. Pirating cost the movie industry an estimated $700 million annually in business lost to the ring, which copied movies on new films and videotape for resale through illegal channels.

Legitimate film distributors chipped in part of the $300,000 budget used by the FBI to open "Gold Coast Specialties, Inc.," in Miami in 1977. "Amore Products" was opened by a Dade County detective with $14,000 a year earlier to establish a front dealership in films, novelty items, and magazines. Both operations were instant successes.

When mobsters became suspicious and the lives of the investigators were believed to be in danger, the undercover agents stopped paying their bills. The move so firmly established their credibility that they were threatened for being deadbeats. But they had gained the confidence of the hoodlums and began meeting major figures in the national pornography trade, occasionally attending conventions where they displayed and demonstrated their products.

The acronym Miporn was devised by combining the location of the front operations, "Miami," with the subject of the investigation, "pornography." The operation was the third such FBI "Sting" disclosed within the period of a couple of weeks, and included "Abscam," which led to accusations against several politicians, union officials, and others of accepting or being involved in bribe-taking and influence buying.

Zaffarano had been described as a captain in the crime family of Joseph Bonanno and the late Carmine Galante. He was said to be the country's premier distributor of 16- and 35-millimeter porno films, and the exporter of 8-millimeter films, costing as little as $3 wholesale in the United States, to Japan where they sell for a whopping $250 each. According to the FBI, Zaffarano also settled territorial and other misunderstandings involving the Mafia's pornography dealings and was tied to many shakedowns and incidents of extortion involving smut dealers on the West Coast.

Other sources connected Zaffarano to a company with offices in New York and Hollywood that produced a popular X-rated film, *Defiance,* dealing with the sexual degradation and enslavement of a teenage girl. Nevertheless, the onetime bodyguard for Joe Bonanno and associate of Galante had never been convicted on a pornography charge.

Zaffarano and two colleagues were charged with violating federal statutes prohibiting movement of obscene and pornographic material in interstate commerce after he brought six X-rated films to the D. C. Playhouse, a theater he owned only two blocks from the White House. Sadism and bestiality were pictured, in addition to more conventional

sex. Zaffarano did not deny importing the films from California and
New York. A Washington jury ruled after a week-long trial, however,
that two of the films were not obscene, and the panel was unsure about
the others.

DiBernardo's Star Distributors, Inc., is the largest pornography
dealer on the East Coast, and business connections between his company and Sturman, Thevis, and Mohney have reportedly been docu-
mented by law enforcement authorities. The FBI is said to have also
cited assistance from DiBernardo with helping Sturman to capture a
major portion of the distribution and sales end of the pornography trade
in the United States, especially on the West Coast, through a series of
strongarm shakedowns of other independent dealers and suppliers.

The competition can be deadly when the Mob is involved. At least
two dozen killings during the last half of the 70s have been blamed on
fighting between Mob families and independents over the multimillion-
dollar sex industry in New York City, Long Island, upper New York
State, and northern New Jersey. At stake are Mob-dominated printing,
distribution, and sales of X-rated books, magazines, and various paraphernalia, and movies for theaters and peep-show loops in addition to
control of massage parlors and other vice operations.

After listening to testimony from teenager hookers, police, and
spokesmen for social welfare agencies, a New York State select legislative committee on crime reported that the Mafia had also moved back
into prostitution following an absence of some 30 or 40 years. The
powerful Genovese family was pinpointed as one of the criminal clans
that had moved deeply into the operation of topless and bottomless bars
where young girls were first brought in to dance and then moved into
prostitution.

One of the messier Mob slayings claimed the life of a young woman,
reputed to be a cocaine courier, who had agreed to testify in a federal
court in New York against her former cohorts in the drug and prostitution business. Her body was discovered the day she was scheduled to
testify. She had suffered numerous stab wounds and her body had been
doused with gasoline and set afire.

Chicago has had murderously aggressive Mob families since before
the days of Al Capone, and the Midwestern based hoodlums muscled
their way into the burgeoning sex business through a series of violent
and terrifying criminal acts including extortion, arson, bombings, and
murder. Although a bit tardy in recognizing the money-making potential of pornography, the Chicago Mob, once alerted, made a place for
itself in the lucrative industry.

Investigations by the U.S. Justice Department, the FBI, a Cook County (Chicago) Grand Jury, a City Council subcommittee on pornography and obscenity, and Chicago police have all confirmed the role of the mob in pornography and other vice activities. The Gambino (Joseph) Colombo, Bonanno/Galante, and the DeCavalcante Mob families from the East Coast were identified as being in direct control of the operations, with local elements of the crime cartel being cut in for a hefty share of the responsibilities and profits.

Three Chicago area mobsters named by federal investigators as being involved in the pornography trade were Joseph "Doves" Aiuppa, Gus Alex, and James "Turk" Torello. The trio, whom investigators were quoted as saying may have had a role in steering the Mob into the especially profitable area of child pornography, are tied to the local crime family of Anthony "Big Tuna" Accardo. But Michael Glitta was said to be in direct control of pornography in Chicago and was named as the employer of three of the men arrested in the Miporn probe.

The local Mob, furthermore, was exacting tribute from at least three-fourths of all the porno shops in the city, according to Chicago police. Joseph "Joey Caesar" DiVarco was pinpointed in the late 70s as the collector. Two partners who refused to submit to the extortion when the Mob first began moving in received threats and fire bombings. A pipe bomb was tossed through the window of one of their bookstores, and a distribution center for pornographic materials was firebombed. Police said the Mob had demanded 50 percent of the business, and free access to auditing of the books. Most of the city's porn merchants fell into line after the first bombing.

Alarmed by the Mob's violent move into the smut business, and outraged at examples of kiddie porn appearing in magazines and films, Chicago authorities shut down scores of shops for violating city fire and building codes. There was also a brief but inconclusive experiment with zoning restrictions, and an alderman kept the pressure on by releasing names and addresses of porn shop landlords to the press. Most of the shops reopened within hours or a few days after closing, but the chicken porn was pulled from the shelves and went underground.

What the speakeasies were during Prohibition, porno is today. It is a product for which there is a demanding market, it is handled by cash sales, and to a large extent it is clandestine. Undertakings closed to public scrutiny allow crime to breed much more easily than those open to inspection and control. But the pornography trade attracts stubborn, determined men. Some of them are willing to fight and put their lives on the line, even when they are facing professional hoodlums and killers.

Paul Gonsky was apparently one of those men. Gonsky's presumable brush with the Mob was detailed in a lengthy article by John Conroy in the *Reader*.[6] According to Conroy, Gonsky and a group of fellow investors lost thousands of dollars trying to provide art films for their fellow Chicagoans. When they switched to porn they recouped their losses and then some. The timing was good, and the corporation—sometimes only Gonsky and a partner—rapidly purchased or acquired leases to more than a half-dozen theaters in Chicago and in Indiana. Real estate, a pornographic bookstore, and a distributorship for X-rated films were added to the holdings. One of Gonsky's partners veered off into the massage parlor business, and another moved to Hollywood where he began producing R-rated films.

Gonsky and his associates were making money, but they were also making some formidable enemies. The projectionists in four of their theaters were non-union, a cardinal sin in Chicago. Three of the four non-union houses Gonsky had interests in were damaged by explosions.

Stories were also told about the time that two toughs approached Gonsky and identified themselves as representatives of the Mob. They wanted a piece of the action. Gonsky checked with the Mob chieftain they said they were speaking for, learned they were imposters, and, with the help of a couple of off-duty policemen, chased them away, Conroy wrote.

Pornography in theaters, bookstores, and peep-shows was becoming big business. The theaters operated by Gonsky and his partners had cleaned up showing such all-time porn spectaculars as *Deep Throat* and *Devil In Miss Jones*. One of Gonsky's former partners in the ill-fated venture with the art houses had begun distributing films, porn as well as children's movies and more standard fare. About the time a competing company was opened by a cousin of "Milwaukee" Phil Alderisio, a known Mob boss, Gonsky's old friend began to be plagued by bombs going off at his suburban home. After his wife and three children escaped the fourth blast without injury, the film distributor sold out.

His competitor then opened a new X-rated theater a few blocks from one of the theater s operated by Gonsky. On the night the new movie house opened, the entrance to Gonsky's theater was blown away by a bomb.

It was a crisp September day, near noon, when Paul Gonsky was found lying on the ground in a parking lot near one of his theaters in Old Town, a gaudy three-block-long corridor of bars, arcades, head shops, and strip joints. His Mercedes-Benz was parked a foot or two away. Gonsky's head was shattered by one or more of the seven bullets that had smashed into his body. He was still alive, but died a few hours later.

Shortly after the unfortunate entrepreneur's death, his Festival Theater Corporation was audited by the IRS, which was rumored to be looking for possible Mob connections, according to the *Reader* story. The corporation had apparently shown films which were at least partly financed with Mob money, and may have rented other films to competing theaters with Mob connections. But the corporation survived the audit with a clean bill. So did suspects in Gonsky's slaying. It was never solved.

Among the problems investigators face with the violence and terrorism associated with commercial sex is the reluctance of victims and witnesses to talk. One of the first lessons learned by people who deal with the Mob is to keep their mouths shut.

Perhaps that is why no one seemed to know much about a series of murders, including the stylized execution of former college and professional basketball star Jack Molinas, that occurred in the Los Angeles and Las Vegas areas during what investigators said was a Mob takeover of the pornography racket on the West Coast.

Los Angeles is special as a porn center because it has all the raw materials necessary to the industry: a fresh reservoir of children and young adults of both sexes who are available as models, film technicians, and production facilities such as processing laboratories and printing houses. One count by a law enforcement agency turned up nearly two dozen processing laboratories specializing in X-rated films, a dozen production companies in the same trade, some 50 mailorder houses dealing in smut, roughly 100 adult bookstores, scores of massage parlors, and every other conceivable type of business catering to the erotic desires of the public.

Twenty years before his death, Jack Molinas' professional basketball career with the Fort Wayne Pistons was shattered when he was convicted of bribery and game-fixing in a nationwide sports point-shaving scandal reaching back to his college days. He lost his license to practice law and served a prison term. But the bad times were apparently behind him and he was barbecuing steaks for himself and a girlfriend at his comfortable home near Hollywood when the romantic idyll was shattered by gunfire. Molinas toppled on to the barbecue grill, then rolled off and on to the patio. He was dead. His girlfriend was struck and injured by several bullets, but survived.

Less than a year before Molinas was assassinated, Barney Gusoff, an associate of his in a fur-importing business, was strangled and beaten to

Children in Chains

death in a Los Angeles hotel room. According to writer Vincent Turco, in *True* magazine, "The word was that Gusoff and Molinas were deeply involved in pornography, and that the fur-importing business was a front."[7] Turco quoted LAPD Chief of Police Edward M. Davis as warning that Molinas' death would not be the last of the killings, and that the Mafia families could be expected to make Southern California a battleground unless the pornography racket in the area could be cleaned up.

The day after Molinas' killing, the head of the Los Angeles Police Department's Organized Crime Intelligence Division released a statement admitting that East Coast Mafia elements had moved in. "They have discovered that they could invade the sex film industry, the pornographic publishing field, and the mail-order erotica rackets with little previous experience. They have the money and the muscle to do so," police spokesmen concluded. High-ranking officials heading other divisions in the department agreed that the Mob was taking over the porno industry on the West Coast.

Ownership and management of stores, theaters, and other properties connected with the industry are typically owned by individuals who are not members of the Mob. But through intimidation and various other illegal business practices, they are forced to submit to Mafia control and backing. "Intelligence information . . . indicates that organized crime has gradually moved into the child pornography business," Acting Chief Daryl F. Gates later told a Congressional panel. "Possibly because of fear of public outrage," he added, "they operate through intermediaries, making it difficult to directly connect them with the sale and distribution of pornography involving children." Gates said the use of children in pornography appeared to have initially been the special province of child molesters turned photographers. "However, given the enormous potential for profit and any lessening of vigorous enforcement, it can be predicted that organized crime will become more deeply involved in child pornography. . . . When the heat is off, they typically move in. Our responsibility is to make sure the heat is never taken off," he warned.

A few weeks after the Molinas murder, Joseph Torchio, Jr. was struck by a car along the nightclub strip in Las Vegas and died before he could be rushed to a hospital. Although Las Vegas police listed the death as possibly accidental, the U.S. Justice Department's Organized Strike Force took more than passing interest in the North Hollywood man's untimely passing. He had been served with a subpoena to appear before a federal grand jury in Los Angeles that was scheduled to convene at about the time he was killed. The grand jury was probing Mob infiltration into the pornography business.

According to Turco, Torchio was a known member of the Colombo Mafia family, and the Strike Force had information that he was associated with Molinas in the pornography racket. Mickey Zaffarano was also said to be an associate of the hapless one-time basketball star.

Other familiar names that turned up with the Mafia's sudden interest in West Coast business affairs included Ettore Zappi and his son Anthony. The father and son were indicted in both Orange and Los Angeles counties for alleged offenses involved in the sale and distribution of pornography, but the charges were later dismissed.

The Mob's move into pornography and other forms of commercial vice was nationwide, of course, in no way confined to Los Angeles, Chicago, and New York. And not all the gang wars over control of commercial sex that rage across the country can be tied to the Mafia. The almost limitless amounts of money involved attract other greedy, desperate men, such as Thevis and Underhill, who are as ready to use extortion and violence to capture or strengthen their control of the vice rackets as any Mafia chieftain or soldier. It can be difficult at times for law enforcement authorities to determine just which incidents of arson, bombing, or murder are the work of the Mafia and which are committed by other groups of organized hoodlums.

The mayor of Pittsburgh ordered all massage parlors in the downtown area closed in late 1977 when a "Christmas package" addressed to one of the masseuses at the Gemini Spa exploded as she unwrapped it. Joanne Scott, the widow of a suspected narcotics pusher who had been shot to death, died in the blast. Police reported that the bombing was apparently connected with a struggle for control of massage parlors that had already led to the shooting death of a convicted brothel owner who formerly owned the Spa and the later assassination of one of his business partners.

Members of the Mob and other suspected racketeers engaged in the distribution of pornography have been suspects in the shooting that paralyzed *Hustler* publisher Larry Flynt in March, 1978. Investigators also reportedly were looking closely at business dealings the injured smut publisher had with Reuben Sturman's Capital Distributors, which had handled *Hustler* until the two entrepreneurs tangled in lawsuits.

A few months after Flynt's shooting, a bomb exploded in the car of his regional sales manager, William Rider. The executive miraculously escaped injury. But a few weeks later another Flynt executive was shot from ambush as he walked to his car in Columbus, Ohio, with his boss's brother, Jimmy. Walter Abrams, vice president of a subsidiary that manufactures sexual paraphernalia, also survived the assassination attempt.

Even the slaying of television actor Bob Crane, who was apparently beaten to death with an auto jack handle in a Scottsdale, Arizona, apartment, was investigated for possible pornography and organized crime connections. It was learned after his death that the actor was producing his own pornography on elaborate video equipment that he owned.

One of the most intriguing slayings of a known pornographer, however, occurred in a Fort Lauderdale, Florida, parking lot early in 1979. The victim was John Krasner, who became the self-proclaimed "Prince of Pornography" after building a smut empire based in Allentown, Pennsylvania, that spread throughout the northeastern United States.

Krasner was bouncing from one crisis to another. He was convicted of conspiring to kill a former business partner, and was free on appeal; his wife was kidnapped and held for ransom, but escaped; and shops owned by him and his erstwhile business associate had been the targets of bombs.

The Prince of Pornography decided with other members of his family that it was time to take a Florida vacation. Krasner, his son and daughter-in-law, and two grandchildren had dinner together at a restaurant in Miami's Cocoanut Grove district, and he dropped the others off in front of their motel room later before driving away to park his car. He was gone only minutes when his daughter-in-law heard noises outside, which she later described as sounding like a cat or a child whining. She and her husband ran outside and found Krasner staggering toward them, holding his stomach. He gasped that he had been shot and fell to the ground. He died in a hospital an hour afterward. He was shot just below the right eye, in the chest, and in the abdomen.

A few days later a small-time gambler was arrested, and Fort Lauderdale police announced that he confessed to the murder. Solomon Webb later denied the confession. During the first of two trials that ultimately ended with a conviction for first-degree murder, the prosecution contended that Webb was peering into cars looking for loose change when Krasner surprised him and the two men began struggling, leading to the shooting.

But Webb's court appointed attorney insisted that Krasner was likely shot by someone else, possibly mobsters who had crossed swords with him in a porno war. Public Defender Alan Schreiber pointed out that

Krasner's billfold with approximately $500 inside was not stolen as it probably would have been if the motive for the slaying was robbery.

"You're dealing with a man who was in a very high-risk profession, a business where people are inclined to burn the stores down," Schreiber speculated. "There may be a lot of people inclined to assassinate John Krasner," he said. "It smells like the Mob all over."

[1] Jack Anderson column, *Washington Post*, April 12, 1979.

[2] Dr. Densen-Gerber was apparently referring to Tommy Eboli, also known as Tommy Ryan, who was shot to death from ambush as he left the Brooklyn apartment of a mistress. He had fallen out of favor with fellow Mob leaders who invested in a heroin smuggling scheme he engineered that went sour and cost millions. Eboli briefly shared stewardship of the Vito Genovese Mafia family with Gerado Catena after Genovese was sent to prison.

[3] *Parade*, August 19, 1979.

[4] *Chicago Sun-Times*, May 17, 1977.

[5] Ibid.

[6] *Reader*, a free Chicago weekly, November 3, 1978.

[7] *True*, April 1976.

13.

Magazines, Newsletters, and Delta Dorms

IF THERE were an Olympics for chicken hawks, John Paul Norman would rate a gold medal for persistence.

He is a veteran of more than a quarter of a century in the Boy-Love business and has a record of more than a dozen arrests in cities including Los Angeles, Sacramento, Santa Monica, and Santa Ana, California; Dallas and Houston, Texas; and Chicago and Homewood, Illinois.

For 25 years he has been a traveling salesman of sex, dealing in children's tears. He has sodomized children; photographed and sold pictures of nude boys engaged in various homosexual acts; established a series of sex rings trafficking in the bodies of boys delivered to hungry chicken hawks across the country; and published several B-L journals.

A former musician and producer of television commercials, he has an active, fertile mind that enabled him to hatch one nefarious scheme after another to peddle the sexual services of young boys.

One of Norman's earliest and most traumatic brushes with the law occurred when he was caught in the fall-out from the sex murders in Houston committed by Dean Corll and his accomplices. According to author Robin Lloyd, Norman had set up the Odyssey Foundation in Dallas, offering memberships for $15 enrollment fees and an additional $3 for a catalog with photographs and descriptions of hundreds of boys. (It should be emphasized here that the Odyssey Foundation bears no relation whatsoever to Dr. Densen-Gerber's Odyssey Institute or to Odyssey House. It is a coincidence that the same name should be used by one of the nation's most notorious chicken hawks, and by a leading crusader against the sexual abuse of children.) The boys were called "Fellows," and meetings were offered for fees ranging from $20 to $40 per day, plus air fare.

Fellows were recruited by answering and placing ads in gay periodicals, and, reputedly, by cruising bus terminals and other locations where boys were likely to be found. The Machiavellian plot collapsed after a young man replying to one of Norman's ads stayed overnight with him. Looking through Odyssey literature the next morning, his eyes widened in alarm when he perceived that several Fellows were missing and the word "Kill" was stamped on their pictures and descriptions.

It was 1973 and the deaths of the 27 boys known to have died in the sex and sadism slayings in Houston were still fresh in everyone's mind. The young man notified staff members of a gay newspaper, and they in turn referred him to the FBI. Both the FBI and representatives of the newspaper knew that the word "Kill" is a printer's term indicating material that is no longer usable. Primarily because of the recent horror in Houston, however, a memo was forwarded to Dallas police.

Norman's apartment was raided the next day, and police carried away a pickup truck full of photoengraving equipment, cameras, and files containing sex literature and thousands of names and addresses. Norman was booked on preliminary charges of contributing to juvenile violation of state drug laws.

The investigation did not link the lean, wavy-haired chicken hawk to the Houston slayings. But a check of his background disclosed that the Odyssey Foundation was not the first project of its kind he had established. He previously operated in several cities in California, for a time using a post office box in San Diego under the names "Norman Foundation," and "Epic International." He had a long list of arrests for sex offenses in Southern California and had also been previously picked up in Houston on charges of child molesting and sodomy.

Even more intriguing and promising, however, was the collection of some 30,000 index cards taken from Norman's apartment listing presumed or prospective sponsors of the Foundation. The cards carried names of men from almost every state and Canada. Several of the names were of prominent people, some, of individuals known to be federal employees.

Dallas investigators mailed their only copies of the cards to the State Department in Washington. There, the cards were destroyed. Officials had determined that they "were not relevant to any fraud case concerning a passport," a spokesman later told the *Chicago Tribune*. The newspaper noted that it was not explained why the cards were not passed on to the FBI or postal inspectors, and were studied only from the standpoint of passport irregularities.[1]

Norman jumped bail. The next time he surfaced, he was living in

Homewood, Illinois, a few miles south of Chicago in the home of one of his correspondents from Epic International. He was calling himself Steven Gurwell and was arrested after a tipster notified police that he had lured several boys into engaging in sexual acts with him by plying them with beer. Norman's host later told Homewood police that the lanky panderer once supplied him with a sixteen-year-old Missouri boy whom he took to Europe on a $4,500 tour.

Again police confiscated pornography and another collection of names and addresses. The number had dwindled to 5,000. Only seven months after his arrest in Dallas, Norman was lodged in the Cook County Jail on charges of taking indecent liberties with juveniles.

Chicago's aged Cook County Jail is known for its escapes, overcrowding, and brutality. In a single year, 39 prisoners broke out, and critics complain that some of the city's toughest street gangs, such as the Black P. Stone Nation, the Insane Unknowns, and the Latin Kings, wield as much authority inside the walls as do the guards.

This jail had held mass murderer Richard Speck and was later to hold John Wayne Gacy, the sadistic pederast whose toll of murdered boys surpassed even that of Dean Corll and his accomplices in Houston.

Consequently, if Norman's activities in the jail were overlooked for a while when he first took up residence, it is perhaps not surprising. He kept busy and out of trouble. He had met a young criminal, Phillip R. Paske, and hatched another scheme. Paske was jailed on murder charges after he was accused of being the driver of a getaway car in a robbery slaying.

The newest contrivance depended on what Norman described as Delta Dorms, established in various states. He explained that each dorm was in reality "a private residence where one of our sustaining members acts as a don (authorities define a don as a boy-lover who sexually exploits a child under the guise of providing protection or management) for two to four cadets." Significantly, he advised that whatever occurred between cadet and sponsor was their business.

Information about his newest project was disseminated by *John Norman's Newsletter*. Three issues of the journal were produced before authorities learned that it was being printed with facilities in the Cook County Jail. The project kept Norman too busy to get into trouble with other inmates.

By the time the operation was uncovered, the twenty-five-year-old Paske had pleaded guilty to attempted armed robbery in a plea-bargaining agreement and was free on probation. He reportedly helped continue Norman's newest program outside the jail, with mailings directed to a Chicago post office box registered in both his name and that of his mentor. Paske was later hired as a summer employee by the city of Chicago and assigned to the Fire Department gymnasium pool near Navy Pier as part of a Federal Comprehensive Employment Training Act program. He was fired from the $4.75-an-hour job a few weeks later when his background was publicly disclosed.

Norman not only offered pictures and descriptions of young boys and an explanation of the Delta Project in his newsletter but added eloquent pleas for help raising bail money for himself—and, prior to his friend's release, for Paske, whom he identified as "Phillip, my right-hand man here." He said the primary purpose of the initial newsletter was to raise a defense fund for bail, attorney's fees, and associated costs. He frankly admitted that the reason for his jailing had "nothing to do with the Foundations and arises from my own damned foolishness," but "nevertheless, immobilizes me and limits operations." He indicated he was anxious to be free so that he could continue with his foundation work.

A skeleton operation was maintained. Through contact "with former Fellows—and a few recruits who I feel are of Foundation caliber," he said, he was attempting to retain interest. The lead page of the first newsletter was topped with headshots of five of his recruits: Reggie, from Maine; Phillip in New York; Ray in Florida; Jimmy in Texas; and Gary, whose home state was not mentioned.

"It's an interesting crew and there'll soon be more joining us," Norman wrote. He pointed out that sponsors could invite youths to join them on trips or to visit in their homes. "You provide round-trip fare and pay a daily stipend—part of which goes to my Defense Fund, part of which goes to the youth's own self-development fund.

"You have my guarantee that the Fellow will be sincere and honest, presentably dressed, and on time. Nothing more is required of him. The Fellows are all friendly and adaptable, however, and warm friendships are possible between them and their sponsors. Return trips are common, in fact." Norman described himself as a man who had "been a positive influence on youths I've encountered." Integrity and character were goals of the Foundation program, he said, and personal qualities he had encouraged in young people "by precept and example."

At least one person must have been impressed. A supporter in California responded with money for Norman's bail. Norman remained free until almost the end of 1976, when he pleaded guilty to eight counts of indecent liberties with a child and was sentenced to prison.

Eighteen months later, Norman was arrested in Chicago on charges of contributing to the delinquency of minors. Police learned that he had served less than a year in the Illinois state prison at Pontiac before he was paroled on condition that he avoid the company of boys under eighteen unless their parents were present; neither possess nor deal in pornography; and obtain psychiatric treatment.

Chicago police Sergeant Ronald Kelly, head of a special child pornography unit, explained that Norman was accused of taking nude photographs and engaging in sexual relations with two boys, sixteen and seventeen, who were wards of the Department of Children and Family Services. He was additionally accused of violating his parole.

Kelly disclosed that Norman had also revived his old project, renaming it the "Creative Corps." The journal was renamed *Male Call*, a component of *M. C. Publications*. The policeman said that the two state wards had revealed that Norman planned to send their photographs to a don in Canada. If the man was pleased with their appearance, they would presumably follow their photos across the border.

The newest arrest netted more pornography from Norman's northside apartment and another file of names of his correspondents. Police said that more than 50,000 men from every state, including Alaska and Hawaii, and from several foreign countries were listed in the file which also carried information about sexual preferences. Some of the pink cards had photos of the clients attached.

Paske was present in Norman's apartment when the raid occurred but was not arrested. He was identified in *Male Call* as manager of a mailorder concern. The first issue of the newsletter was published from 3795 Mission Boulevard, San Diego, for $1 per copy and listed Earl Snyder as president and managing editor.

An introductory statement on the front page pointed out that the basic purpose of the newsletter was to serve as a conduit for personal contacts. The ads used the most explicit terminology to describe physical characteristics and listed sexual preferences for such practices as sadism and masochism, bondage, Greek (buggery), and French (fellatio). One "affectionate male" from San Francisco sought meetings with "very obese" males of 300 to 350 pounds if short, 350 to 400 pounds or more if tall. "Big rears and big thighs" were preferred. Some ads were accompanied by standard head and shoulder photos. Others were of nude men sprawled on beds or sofas and displaying their genitals. *Male Call* carried a form requiring the signature of prospective advertisers, certifying that they were eighteen or older.

The newsletter also carried a plea for contributions to John Norman's Defense Fund, which were to be used by Norman to assist "other guys, mostly gay, who need funds for bail, for lawyers, or for getting started on the street."

A sinister development in the history of police contact with Norman occurred when three teenage boys were found dead of multiple stab wounds in a car parked behind a northside gas station. All had their throats slit and were victims of what police said was an almost "ritualistic stabbing." One of the boys, Michael Salcido, seventeen, was a ward of the DCFS and had been expected to testify against Norman in an upcoming trial.

A couple of days after the discovery of the bodies of the boys, including Salcido's nineteen-year-old brother, Arthur, and the sixteen-year-old son of a suburban grocer, Homewood police disclosed that a seventeen-year-old boy who had helped implicate Norman on the child-molesting charges there six years earlier had also been mysteriously stabbed to death. The youth was walking home from his job in a gas station when he was stabbed six times in the back.

The triple murders of the Salcidos and their friend occurred barely two months after investigators had begun unearthing the pathetic remains of the victims of John Gacy from beneath his house in suburban Norwood Park township, and the public was especially sensitive to the homocidal tendencies of some chicken hawks. The news media immediately published disconcerting stories about the link between John Norman and two dead boys.

A few weeks later, however, police announced that the multiple slaying in Chicago had been solved and was the result of local street gang rivalries and a tragic case of mistaken identity. Reputed members of the Latin King street gang were charged with murder. Police said the younger of the two Salcidos had approached members of the Kings under the mistaken belief they belonged to the rival Latin Eagles, and tried to make a marijuana buy. The out-of-town youths were instead lured to a quiet location and killed.

By some improvident happenstance, it was Norman's fate to time his troubles and presence to coincide with the two most ghastly cases of mass murders of boys by homosexual sadists in the history of the United States.

Norman's name also cropped up during an investigation of the publication of *Hermes*, which at the time was one of the premier B-L journals in the country. But the publisher of *Hermes* was Eldon Gale "Rusty" Wake, who, until a few days prior to his arrest, was an employee of the audio-visual department of Trinity College several miles north of Chicago.

Norman's name turned up because he was one of the kingpins of a loosely organized national network of chicken hawks who shared common goals of money and pleasure obtained through the sexual exploitation of young boys. His name was also found in New Orleans on a list of Halverson's contacts. Guy Strait had met Norman and said he had also written a story for *Hermes*. Unconfirmed stories circulated that Frank Sheldon had a financial interest in the clandestine newsletter, as well. Wake was also an associate of one of the men who was arrested in the investigation of the chicken movie filmed in Chicago. The child pornography suspect from Chicago and another man, who was connected with a gay newspaper and operated a citizen's band radio show for homosexuals, were identified as principals in the publication of *Hermes*. The Chicagoan reportedly worked on layouts, and the other man, who had a police record for sodomy and escape from a mental hospital, was said to screen prospective subscribers.[2]

Wake, the forty-year-old father of two children, was arrested on eight criminal charges, six of them linked to publication of the xeroxed sex journal. The other charges accused him of distributing a tape recording, titled *Richard*, that described a young boy's first sexual experience with an adult male; and with distribution of a calendar showing two boys engaged in a sexual act. Both Wake and his wife, Wanda, a special education teacher in a suburban Chicago school, were co-signers of a bank account for the newsletter. *Hermes* was said to be selling about 5,000 copies bimonthly and contained coded advertisements enabling readers to contact each other and to locate boys for pornographic modeling or prostitution. Articles on boy-love, line drawings of naked boys, photographs, and the editor's column, "little squirts by russ," also appeared in the publication.

It was explained in one issue that Hermes was the Greek God of commerce, invention, cunning, and theft, who was also messenger for the other gods, patron to rogues and travelers, and conductor of the dead to Hades. Significantly, he was also patron god of boys. Feasts involving homosexual acts were dedicated to Hermes and celebrated by boys in the gymnasia. The magazine was dedicated to "the Greek ideals of boy-love in the emotional and physical realm," the publishers claimed.

They stated that the newsletter did not "encourage or promote illegal pederasty," although they believed that the age of consent should be lowered. "We feel that the responsible boy-lover can fulfill a real need in the lives of many boys."

Investigators said that when they arrived at Wake's home to arrest him, suitcases were open and clothing was strewn everywhere. The couple's children, six and seven, had already been sent to Florida a few days earlier.

Wake attempted, in a federal suit, to have his arrest ruled invalid because the Illinois obscenity law under which he was charged was previously declared illegal by a three-judge federal panel. But shortly after his suit was filed, the United States Supreme Court reversed the lower court ruling and restored the obscenity law.

Edmund Leja has a knowledgeable although reluctant familiarity with obscenity laws. He has been struggling with them for more than a quarter-century. Also known as Edmund Lee and Ed Lea, he is owner and publisher of Crismund Publications, a group of nudist magazines, and, according to his own testimony before a U.S. Congressional committee, an innocent victim of the controversy over child pornography.

Magazines in the Crismund line published in Studio City, California, were those most often shown in television presentations and in newspaper and other photos from publications accused of containing kiddie porn. *Nudist Moppets*, especially, has been singled out for its cover pictures of nude little girls. The children depicted in Leja's magazines are not photographed in overt sexual activities. Other magazines are more explicit and show children engaged in sexual behavior with their peers, adults, and animals, and obviously are not suitable for reproduction in the conventional media even when kiddie porn is the subject.

Leja pointed out that when hard-core pornography first became easily available it almost killed the nudist magazines, which had existed in this country since about the 1930s. In the early 1960s, there were 40 or so nudist publications, but after the introduction of hard-core smut there was a period when there were no nudist magazines at all. They could not compete with the more bluntly candid product that showed simulated or actual sexual acts.

The witness told congressmen that his best selling magazines had a circulation of only about 13,000, compared to sales of 50,000 or more of some explicit pornography. A sales figure of 10,000 barely permitted him to break even, he explained. "So I have to have a winner each time."

He defended the publications as the only media available to nudist parks and families because other sources of communication have traditionally shut the movement out. Even telephone companies have refused to use the term "nudist" or "nude" in their listing, he said.

Consequently, magazines like *Nudist Moppets*, *The Joys of Nudist Youth*, *Moppets and Teens*, and *All Color Digest* in his package of publications were the only sources available to serve as a conduit of information for the nature movement. Leja told the congressmen that children comprise about 25 to 50 percent of the population of nudist parks on a given weekend, and, thus, they are represented in the nudist press.

His activities, however, have not been as innocent as he apparently would like the investigative panel to believe.

Advertisements for magazines listed by the Lea-Arts Products Catalogue on the back of one of "Ed Lea's" newsletters focused exclusively on children. Considering his testimony about serving nudist families, there is a mystifying absence of adults in the titles and content of magazines such as *Let's Visit. . . .California, Arizona Moppets & Teens*; *Let's Visit. . . The Philippines' Moppets & Teens*; *Nudist Angels* (Lemontree Graphics); and the London Enterprises publication *Children in Nature*. There was not a single advertisement of a magazine that appeared to deal with adult nudists, but, instead, the offerings seemed to concentrate on a broad spectrum of infantile female sexuality, with an occasional depiction of a rosy-cheeked boy.

Little girls and boys as young as three years old are pictured in the magazines. Copy in the publications talks glowingly of grimy gamin faces and playful happy tots, but the photos are mostly of young girls undressing or manipulated into poses that provide maximum display of their genitals.

Lea (Leja) pointed out in the newsletter that the publications were undergoing "trying times" because of the uproar over kiddie porn and attacks on Crismund publications by the press and others. "Densen-Gerber was running amuck in her campaign to stamp out 'child-porno' without taking the time to distinguish between bona fide nudist publications and ones of a pornographic nature," he complained.

He advised readers that Odyssey House and its supporters had "frightened bookstores into removing *all* publications in which children appear. This is an explicit form of censorship without recourse to law and is tantamount to book burning, coupled with dissemination of the 'big lie,' " he declared.

The publisher vowed to continue providing service through the mails if he was able to. He said that his legal counsel had assured him that the publications were legal and the opinion was affirmed by three court trials, stemming from an arrest in 1973. He and several parents were charged with conspiracy to contribute to the delinquency of children who posed for the publications, Lea wrote.

In three separate cases in Los Angeles County Superior Court, he stated, it was "ruled that *Nudist Moppets* number one and number two were not obscene, although obscenity was *not* the issue. Since sexual activities are not in any way a part of our publishing or photographic efforts, the judges ruled for acquittal of all parties."

The Los Angeles Times printed a different version of Leja's troubles with the local courts. The newspaper reported that Leja was indicted with six parents and charged after several adults and children testified to a grand jury about his activities.

One woman, testifying with immunity, said that she was paid $40 by Leja to photograph her daughter at the Hollywood Hills home of a wealthy entrepreneur. Later, she said, the entrepreneur coaxed her daughter into a sex act. She broke it up after the child pulled away and the Hollywood Hills man pulled her back. The girl was two-and-a-half years old.

The man was subsequently indicted on twin counts of child molesting and two additional counts of furnishing drugs and liquor to thirteen- and fourteen-year-old girls. Leja was not present when the molestation and drug or alcohol use occurred. Nevertheless, he and the parents were charged with contributing to the delinquency of minors.

Another young mother, described as a trained professional worker who supplemented her income with prostitution, testified she permitted her nine-year-old son and eleven-year-old daughter to pose for *Nudist Moppets* for about $150. "I just finished school," she was quoted as saying. "I needed the money. . .So the kids helped Mom out."

Leja also failed to mention incidents to the congressional panel like an arrest on November 10, 1971, which the *Times* said occurred while he was photographing a woman performing fellatio. Three years later, he pleaded guilty to an offense injurious to public morals, a misdemeanor, and was fined $150 and placed on five years probation with the stipulation that he not make hard-core pornography.[3]

A few years after Leja's skirmishes with the courts and Dr. Densen-Gerber had slowed, some 2,200 miles east of Los Angeles the law was closing in on a group of child pornographers that included an Indiana man with the pedestrian name of Bill Smith. Smith had no aliases, and police had run across his name while they were investigating a homicide in Michigan.

More than 25,000 pornographic pictures of nude young girls were confiscated from the Smith's home in the first of a series of raids in the Midwest, Canada, and the Far Northwest. A four-drawer file of names of collectors, photographers, and film processors in nearly two dozen states, Sweden, Denmark, and Germany, with whom Smith was evidently swapping photos, were also seized, police reported. Some of the pictures were of girls from North Manchester, Indiana, where Smith lived. Police theorized that toys found among Smith's possessions were used to entice children to pose for him.

State police announced that Indiana had become a distribution point for a major international child pornography network. It was initially speculated that the ring was tied to the activities of Lester L. Henry and his confederates who had been arrested barely five weeks earlier in the roundup of suspected child pornographers on the West Coast. But authorities were unable to produce any solid evidence of a link between the two bands.

North Manchester appeared to be about as unlikely a center for child pornography as could be imagined. It was the home of the Church of the Brethren's Manchester College, and located in some of the richest farm country in the Midwest. It is in rural Wabash County where farmers raised corn, wheat, and soybeans for decades before realizing a few years ago that they could increase their income by double-cropping with sunflowers. The hardy plants could be planted after early crops were harvested and were strong enough to withstand the first frosts.

The conversation in North Manchester barbershops and snack bars is traditionally more oriented to planting and harvesting of crops, and the fortunes of the high school's basketball team, than pornography — especially kiddie porn.

The 5,500 residents of the conservative middle western town were shaken by the arrests and stunned to learn that local children, perhaps with the knowledge of parents, were involved. Controversy flared over a desire by some members of the community to have the parents of local children lured or forced into the ring charged with child abuse. Police Sergeant William McNeely, who headed the local investigation, said that although authorities knew the identities of the young models from North Manchester, who were all under sixteen, that the parents had apparently been unaware of their children's association with Smith.

County Juvenile Probation Officer Kaye Noonan was not satisfied. She was quoted in the local *News-Journal* as saying the parents should be prosecuted. "That's no excuse," she said. "Parents should know what their kids are doing at all times, especially when they are that young." The police, she complained, were apparently content that they had the photographer in custody. "Big deal," she scoffed. "The parents can always find another photographer, particularly if they're doing it for money."[4]

Judge pro tem John Beauchamp also called for a closer investigation of possible involvement by parents. He pointed out that some of the pictures were of a girl of eight or nine, and others were of youngsters no more than two or three years old.

The newspaper claimed that a letter intercepted by police indicated that at least some parents were not only knowledgeable but were involved in the activities of the ring. The letter was quoted in part as saying, "I run what I call my 'inner circle' that consists of myself and four fathers that have 'groovy' daughters." It continued, "You'd have to have something pretty great to gain admission to it. The other members insist on it, and I'm at their mercy, after all, it's their daughters." Despite disclosure of the letter which the newspaper said was apparently signed by Smith, no further arrests were made in the community. Smith was charged with violating Indiana statutes banning the distribution of child pornography.

McNeely said arrests were made in California, Ohio, Washington, and several other states by investigators following leads provided by the material in Smith's files. One of the most significant arrests occurred about 100 miles south of North Manchester, in Indianapolis.

Armed with a search warrant, raiders moved into the home of Clarence J. Ferrin. Vice squad officers with the Indianapolis Police Department said Ferrin's house had been set up as a production studio for processing kiddie porn, and they carried out 30 cartons of pictures, negatives, and film. The fifty-one-year-old suspect was charged with violating federal pornography statutes. Most of the photos were reportedly of girls seven to ten years old. Ferrin was jailed briefly before being released on bond. Two months after his arrest, he was found dead from hanging; he had reportedly been beaten by other inmates while he was imprisoned in Indianapolis.

Nearly a year after Smith's arrest, he was convicted and sentenced after a trial which had been venued to an adjoining county. No one claimed that he was in the business for the money. Smith was a collector and trader, who sometimes took photos when the opportunity presented itself. And despite police descriptions of his involvement in a major pornography ring, his accomplishments were miniscule compared to those of others.

There are others who are definitely in the business for the money. Compared to the enormous profits, financial costs and legal risks involved in the sexual exploitation of children are minimal. Some of the men reaping those profits live in or near Baltimore. The city has been known for years as an international distribution center for pornography, including smut specifically exploiting children as models and performers. Pornographers connected with warehousing and distribution facilities in Baltimore, investigators say, have tentacles extending into several countries in Europe and Central America as well as a dozen or more states in this country.

Adult bookstores in Washington, D. C., and most middle Atlantic states are known to be stocked with pornography delivered to and stored in bulging warehouses in Baltimore. Much of the material is produced in Europe. Other pornography comes from California.

Police know that some of the pornography featuring adults passes through wholesalers in New York and in Cleveland before being stacked in the Baltimore warehouses of Bon-Jay, Inc., Central Sales, Inc., and the Noble News Company, Inc. Court records filed after a police raid in 1976 indicated that Noble News was a subsidiary of Sovereign News, Reuben Sturman's umbrella company in Cleveland.

Kiddie porn disappeared from Baltimore warehouses after Drs. Osanka, Densen-Gerber, and others alerted the public and ignited national outrage over its spread. In earlier police raids, however, child pornography was confiscated from Baltimore-based distributors along with magazines and films featuring everything from buggery and scatology to bestiality. The percentage and amount of child pornography flowing into the country from foreign sources fluctuates with local conditions, and during the early 1970s almost all of it was foreign-made. Most originated in the Scandinavian countries, although smaller amounts found its way to this country from Thailand.

When American pornographers became aware of the tremendous amount of money to be made from the trade, they began producing their own kiddie porn. In some ports of entry, seizures of foreign-made kiddie porn dropped precipitously. The amount of smut involving children that continued flowing into the country was nevertheless staggering. G.R. Dickerson, acting Commissioner of Customs, told the Subcommittee on Crime of the U.S. House of Representatives Judiciary Committee that in one year, 14,000 seizures of all types of pornography was made in just the Port of New York. He estimated that 60 percent of the material seized in all 300 ports of entry involved children.

At the same hearings, Kenneth Wooden cautioned against being too quick to place the blame for the spread of child pornography on foreign countries. Many of the foreign addresses advertising kiddie porn are apparently no more than forwarding operations, he said. He told of ordering child pornography from foreign sources during his investigation of the racket, and when the material was received it was postmarked from Washington, D.C.

"The largest bulk of kiddie porn is brown bag material (homemade)

—inexpensive 8-millimeter film, sound cassettes, and 35-millimeter home-processed photos along with magazines and ad letters," he said. "No child is safe from these adults who reap sexual as well as financial gratification from their victims. The material produced from their exploitation, like a stick in a stream, is swept into the interlocking streams of post office boxes and finds its way to the delta of national distribution."

Dr. Osanka agrees that more brown bag kiddie porn is being produced today than the slick professional products available, if at all, only via surreptitious under-the-counter sales at adult bookstores or other outlets. "There appears to be an incredible amount of swapping and communication among child porn collectors that apparently doesn't appear among collectors of regular porn," he says. "I would believe that this is because regular porn is not illegal. It's readily available in any city and all you have to do is walk in and buy it."

On the other hand, he says, even before the 1977 crackdown, kiddie porn was at the very least frowned on, even among some dealers. "Now it is very much illegal, and consequently this puts these people as members of a select underground group. So there is a very viable pipeline of information and material."

Magazine ads are among the most important conduits in the pipeline. Bill Katz and other investigators regularly check popular men's magazines and more clandestine publications for ads that will lead them to child molesters. A recent investigation zeroed in on a California man who offered pictures-to-order of a twelve-year-old girl who would do "anything you want. Just write and tell me what you want, and I'll send the pictures."

"If he isn't doing this in the context of a prostitution operation, if he does not have a stable, it becomes a strange situation," Katz observes. "You're dealing with a guy who probably has a straight job, probably has a family, probably is somewhat respected in the community, who is a deviant and who is manifesting his deviance with children. In porn, you get into the situation where guys trade, buy and sell porno, but don't manufacture it."

Sergeant Ron Clark, the Titusville police investigator who nailed Thompson, also recognizes the threat of child pornography as a cottage industry. And he recognizes the damage it can inflict on a child. One careless or unfortunate act can haunt a boy or girl forever.

Florida, like California, Clark says, has special attractions as a breeding ground for chicken hawks searching for children whom they can exploit sexually: "On the beaches . . . kids get down here away from home, a runaway or whatever. They run out of money, and hell, it opens the door," Clark observed. "They take the money and say, 'Hell, nobody will every know about it. My folks are up there (north) and I'm down here.'

"Then one of these days, you know and I know, that kid grows up and happens to become a prominent person and that picture is gonna come back to haunt him."

[1] *Chicago Tribune*, May 16, 1977.
[2] Ibid.
[3] *Los Angeles Times*, May 26, 1977.
[4] *News-Journal*, North Manchester, Indiana, September 11, 1978.

14.

Chicken Hawk

SHORTLY before getting out of prison, Guy Strait greeted his six-tieth birthday with a barrel body, thinning white hair that sticks straight out from his head in unruly clumps, a hearing aid, and reading glasses that slide down his nose disclosing watery blue eyes. He looked every bit a mischievous old troll.

He describes himself as a man who loves youngsters and who years ago dedicated himself as an advocate of children's rights. On a more personal level, he claims to have taken children into his home and showered them with presents and love.

Quite a different picture of Guy Strait is painted by people like Sergeant Martin in Los Angeles and First Assistant State's Attorney Robert G. Gemignani in Winnebago County, Illinois. They describe Strait as an unrepentent rapscalian and con man who has made be-tween $5 and $7 million during a 20-year career as a child pornographer filming scores, perhaps hundreds, of boys and girls, in 12-minute loops and in longer films, as they perform explicit heterosexual and homosex-ual sex acts. Gemignani told a Congressional committee that, by his own admission, Strait was at one time the top producer in the country of chicken films featuring young boys in homosexual acts.

Both Martin and Gemignani were well qualified to discuss Strait's activities with legislators. Martin and his partner, Lieutenant Don Smith, shared much of the responsibility for Strait's arrest in Los An-geles. A series of grand jury indictments were returned that included Strait and 13 other men on a variety of charges, following an investiga-tion of chicken porn movies being filmed in the area. Gemignani prose-cuted Strait and sent him to prison on new charges after the child pornographer jumped bail in California and made his way to Rockford in the far northwest corner of Illinois.

In his book *For Money or Love: Boy Prostitution in America* Robin Lloyd traced the genesis of Strait's troubles with the Los Angeles Police Department to occurrences involving a chicken hawk in Dallas and the breakup of a major B-L ring in Houston shortly after the Corll-Henley murders. Samples of Strait's work turned up in those investigations.

A native Texan, Strait is well read, articulate, somewhat of a philosopher, and no more reluctant to talk about his activities and profession than he is to defend his reputation as one of the country's premier child pornographers. Predictably, his account does not always perfectly match that of law enforcement officers who know him. Nevertheless, I have pieced together his story from interviews with Osanka at Stateville Prison near Chicago and with me at the Vienna Correctional Center in southern Illinois where he spent his last months in prison; testimony before a U.S. Senate committee; in correspondence; from Lloyd's accounts; and from other sources. The account is based on his version of his life and activities except where another source is specifically quoted or credited.

Lloyd wrote that he doubts that "Guy Strait" is the pornographer's real name. Strait replies that he believes that Lloyd's book was written by his old nemesis in Los Angeles, Sergeant Martin, or by Martin's partner, Lieutenant Don Smith.

Strait was the tenth of 11 brothers and sisters and was about fifteen years old when he obtained his first camera. There was no lens, merely an opening, but it took excellent pictures. Almost immediately, the young man began shooting photographs of flowers, plant buds—and nudes.

He was eighteen when he walked across the Yucatan Peninsula in Mexico passing out Bibles and photographing natives of the area who either did not wear any clothing or very little. Years later, he would remember that he was a Baptist, and "quite a religious young man. But even as a Baptist, I was never convinced that the body was anything dirty."

If not an outright obsession, the human nude and nude photographs became lifelong interests. Strait can talk intimately and knowledgeably about visits to such famous nude spas as the Isle de Levant in Europe and about other famous photographers of nudes.

Strait says he served in the Army during World War II; campaigned for Eisenhower and Nixon in Texas; and, in California, promoted South Dakota Senator George McGovern's run for president. He continued his photography hobby in the Army while he was in Europe, still specializing in plants, blossoms, and nudes.

He admits that "the serpent had already sneaked" into his personal

"Garden of Eden," and he had long before abandoned his strait-laced fundamentalist religious faith for a form of pacifistic spirituality closer to some of the more gentle Eastern beliefs. But he had managed to stay out of trouble with the law. He traces the beginning of his difficulties to San Francisco.

"I've always lived my life without any trouble from anybody. Never went to court, never even a speeding ticket," he recalls, waving the wrinkled stub of a cigarette in nicotine-stained fingers. "I think my whole trouble started when I began taking on the police and the courts in a little old newspaper I called *Cruise News & World Report.*

He was living in San Francisco at the time, and he became a crusader, espousing gay rights, defending the First Amendment, touting the separation of church and state, and filling the columns of his publication with vitriolic attacks against public officials and institutions. The Mayor of San Francisco and the Chief of Police of Los Angeles were two targets he singled out for criticism. FBI Director J. Edgar Hoover was another, and Strait claims to be the first person to accuse the respected law enforcement leader of being a closet queen. "It was muckraking, if you want to call it that," Strait says of his printed assaults on public officials. "If they'd been doing it about me, they would call it the truth."

His publication did not earn much money, but it was good for his ego. He considers his tabloid to be the first of the underground newspapers. "True, Paul Krassner was doing *The Realist* earlier than that," he concedes, "but he was more or less intellectual. I like to say mine was more or less earthy."

Strait made no attempt to present a sophisticated publication. "I got into anything I wanted to talk about," he recalls. Some, or most, of his subjects were politically or socially sensitive, and, as a service to process servers, he printed a notice on the front page of each issue giving his schedule and location for the following weeks. Strait believes that the police departments in Los Angeles and San Francisco began compiling dossiers on him at that time.

The first shots against the pugnacious publisher were not fired by disgruntled politicians or policemen, however, but by owners of the prestigious national news magazine *U.S. News & World Report*, he says. The publishers were unhappy with what appeared to be an obvious word play on their title and its combination with a popular gay slang term. To "cruise" in gay terminology is to look for a lover or for a pickup. Strait had to drop the title.

Lloyd says that about that time Strait moved into publication of what may have been the first commercial chicken magazines in this country, *Hombre, Chico,* and *Naked Boyhood,* and set up a mail order business, DOM Studios, to sell nude photographs, magazines, and movies.

According to Strait, he moved into the porn business when an associate offered him $2,000 each to lay out two magazines. "I came in the back door," he says. "I was doing some publishing and it was no secret that I had thousands of negatives. . . . It was pretty easy money."

Strait learned that there was a heavy demand for black and white photographs and, when film laboratories could not develop his film fast enough, he taught himself. He acquired a used enlarger. "The first thing I knew, I had four people working 18 hours a day turning out black and white pictures."

He had long ago graduated from his little lensless camera. He purchased dozens of expensive and intricate cameras and talks knowledgeably and with enthusiasm of photographic equipment and of cropping, splicing, film editing, of light meters and lenses. His favorite still camera was a Yashika E, twin-reflex that cost a mere $50, although he considered it to be too lightweight to use professionally. He depended on a Mimiya C-33 for most of his professional still work. Japanese cameras are the best, he says. "They can make a German lens cheaper than the Germans can."

He usually filmed 12-minute loops and longer movies with a 16-millimeter Beaulieu, which he considered to be superior to the more expensive German Hasselblad. "The Hasselblad is too much trouble." Strait is a self-taught photographer who attended only one photography class in his life. He claims to have studied fine arts, however, at the Chicago Art Institute during the early 50s and to have once exhibited some of his oils at a two-man show in Carmel, California.

Asked how he felt about pornography, Strait replied somewhat obliquely, but with classic technician's pride in his vocation. He had mixed feelings, he said. He would like to see better reproduction; more care taken by producers to illustrate specific aspects of sexuality which they are attempting to portray; and improved, more knowledgeable texts with magazines.

Strait was shocked at the poor technical quality of some of the pornography being peddled when he moved into the trade. The best quality pornography comes from Philadelphia, he says. The poorest comes from Atlanta. Thevis' material was "some of the world's worst, horrible," Strait says. Nevertheless, he occasionally purchased material from one of Thevis' West Coast distributorships. "One time I sold some stuff to Mike," he recalled. "He never even published it. Said it was too hot for him.

"Mike was heavy in movie theaters. He's burned down a few, and killed a few as I understand. I wouldn't put it past him." Thevis, Strait observed, "was a dizzy Greek, a happy-go-lucky guy."

Elements of organized crime also tried to buy material from him, he says, but he would not sell. He referred them to other sources, and he swears that he was never threatened or pressured to do business with the Mob. He is quick to deny suggestions that the Mob controls the industry. "Why should the Mafia be interested in pornography when they own jukeboxes, loan companies, and numerous other legitimate and lucrative businesses?" he asks. Strait is reluctant even to discuss organized crime families known by police to control distribution and other aspects of the smut industry in key areas of the country.

Discussion of his own involvement in the trade is more to his liking. He learned the business well and even traveled to other countries where smut has become an important industry. He estimates he has been in Denmark about 20 times and has made other trips to Sweden, West Germany, and Italy. Both Denmark and Sweden are known for lax sexual attitudes, and Denmark attracted world attention years ago by dropping almost all bans against pornography.

But the Danes are producers of smut, hardly ever consumers, according to Strait. "You couldn't sell pornography to a Dane to save your ass," he says. "When Denmark legalized pornography, the Danes were never gonna buy it. They didn't publish it in Danish. It was published in English and in German, for the tourist trade." Strait is convinced that pornography is popular only where there is sexual repression and that it is a self-destruct industry. When pornography becomes too easily available and prevalent, it is no longer desired.

Despite his trips to Europe, most of Strait's knowledge about the industry was absorbed in this country, on the job. He insists on quality and has always been choosier about his young models than about his camera equipment. If a child had a couple of ounces of surplus fat, he was rejected. "If there's any sort of roll of flesh there," he once said, pointing an age-spotted hand to his own ample middle, "I will not do it."

Strait says he never had to look for models. They came to him. "I can go on the streets of Chicago and put a 16-millimeter (movie camera) on my shoulder . . . and put a sign on me saying I'm a pornographer, and

I'll need a small regiment to protect me from those who want to be photographed. . . . They're not victims at all. The people come to my door in droves, trying to jump in front of my camera. They know word-of-mouth.

"It's very productive to the ego," he says of posing for pornography. "Getting models is the easiest thing in the world. Some people are so sure of their lack of worth. They've been told they're a bunch of nogood-niks, and they want anything to assure them that they are really worth-while. That somebody thinks something of them, and will invest time and money to photograph them—this is such a build (sic) to their ego that they're ecstatic."

During the zenith of the so-called hippie movement, flower children trooped to Strait's makeshift studios near Haight-Asbury in San Francisco. No one was approved as a model if he was high on drugs or booze, and more were rejected than were accepted. He attached a Speed-Graphic to a tripod and equipped it with a Polaroid back so that he could obtain instant prints. Prospective models were offered $10 for a test photo so that he could determine if he wanted to work with them. "Take off your clothes and hang them over there on the counter," the youngsters were told. "Whistle or knock on the floor when you're ready."

Strait maintains that he returned the test photos to his prospective models and rejected almost all of them. "The main thing would be they were too fat." He could tell almost at a glance if a youngster was a good prospect as a model but permitted most of them to pose for tests if they appeared to need the $10 fee. "I never could turn anybody down," he recalls, "except a drunk."

He was a specialist. Strait produced both heterosexual and homosexual material for specific markets. "If a man was into older women and younger men, I had it for him," he says. "If he was into vice-versa, I had that for him. If he was into incest, I got that for him. If he was into pederasty, I had that for him." Strait says he filmed his movies to order, "everything except violence, and I won't photograph that." He concedes that he filmed a limited amount of bondage and spanking, however. He did not especially like the work, because it was "so hammy. . . and I'm sure the stuff that I turned out in that field was lousy, because the black garter belt went out 100 years ago."

He felt more empathy for some of the costume porn he turned out. The gay trade especially appreciated costumery. Roman Tribunes and Centurians. During especially spirited action, a Roman helmet would sometimes topple off an actor and the filming would have to be stopped until it was replaced. "It's gotta be there," he said. It is part of the fetishism and fantasy.

The filming itself was expensive. A short 200-foot movie cost about $2,000 just to photograph. Other production costs added another $3,000 or so.

Films shot for a specific market are never produced in as large a quantity as more general interest movies, and, since fewer are sold, unit costs must be doubled or multiplied several times. "So when everybody else was selling for $10 and $15 a reel, I was selling for $50 and $75," Strait says. "You could say I had a library." If he did not have a product on hand that someone wanted, he produced it.

Strait's retail marketing was strictly by mail. He would not permit his material to be placed in bookstores. "Nieman Marcus won't allow their label to be sold anywhere (else). Neither will Saks Fifth Avenue," he explained.

Gemignani told congressmen that Strait had a mailing list at one time with the names of 50,000 customers. Strait says there were only 942 names, excluding a handful of dummy names he had inserted so that anyone who stole it and tried to use it would get into trouble. Names of law enforcement officers, postal inspectors, and clergymen who were "rabid in their suppression of porno" were his theft insurance. Strait mailed a newsletter to his subscribers and screened applicants to weed out undesirables: policemen and members of the Communist party.

He protected his reputation for quality work by keeping his films out of bookstores. It was more difficult to protect his work from pirates who purchased the films on his lists and had them duplicated for sales through other outlets. Although it bothered his aesthetic sensibilities and pride in his own work, he learned to lower the reproductive quality of his 8-millimeter films. He considered them still better quality than the competition, but not good enough to withstand the loss of detail and clarity when duplicated again by film pirates.

Strait expected to shoot 600 feet for every 400 feet of usable film in the finished product, a far better percentage than producers in the legitimate movie industry. But production was still expensive, and it was primarily for that reason that he usually insisted that no one be present during filming except himself and the young actor-models. There were only occasional exceptions. If someone was worried that Strait would take sexual advantage of the model, a boyfriend or someone else could sit nearby. But he had instructions to keep his mouth shut. An interruption would mean a new start and at least an extra half-hour's work, as well as wasted film.

Strait believes that his knowledge of sexuality, psychology, philosophy, and photography had much to do with his success in the skin trade. "One reason I've always had an advantage over other people . . . is most of them are ex-pinball machine operators and ex-bookies and so forth. . . . They knew pinball and bookmaking. I knew my subject."

He knew what the public liked, and avoided soft-core pornography that simulates sexual relations but does not actually involve penetration. Producer Russ Meyer has accumulated a small fortune producing films in that genre, such as *Vixens* and *Valley of the Super Vixens*. Strait claims never to have heard of Meyer and has little respect for soft core. "That's begging the issue," he scoffs.

"I firmly believe in the right of Americans to own, purchase, and sell any printed matter on the face of the earth," he has written. "Whether that matter be revolutionary in nature, disgusting in nature, sexually explicit in nature, advocate the extinction of homosexuals, pederasts, Jews, Nazis, or the canonization of Hugh Heffner or Larry Flynt." Pornography, he asserts, also "has a worthwhile place in the American family."

Strait makes no apologies for his role as perhaps the nation's best known child pornographer but admits that he "wouldn't defend pornographers as a group of people. Defending pornographers is like defending murderers," he points out. "I've known people in the sex business who are low, scum, filth, trash, explicit—and I've broken with them."

Many pornographers do not care for children, he says, but he is not one of those. "I spent far more on young people than I ever took in. I never did need the money, and I never did want the kids to leave. Kids are pretty special to me. They're the most beautiful people in the world."

The money he earned with pornography enabled him to help many children whom he avers were "victims of thoughtless and irresponsible parents . . . and . . . the juvenile authority."

He claims at various times to have practically raised between six and 40 youngsters who were either not wanted or unappreciated by their own families. He says he has helped educate them, showered them with gifts, and taught them that sexual activity is one of the most vivid, sincere, and appreciated forms of communication and physical expression between human beings. "It's the greatest drive man has."

One time when he was in the South, he says, he observed a large group of children playing with a single broken-down bicycle that had no chain and no rear tire. They were hauling it to the top of a hill and coasting down on it, over and over again. The youth with him recalled that when he was a small child he, too, had dreamed of having a bicycle. Strait said he went into the nearest town, purchased 35 bicycles, returned, and distributed 31 of them to the children "with bills of sale." Then he left. At other times, he claims to have given away motorcycles and large sums of money.

Children who stayed with him could leave at any time they wished. Strait said he maintained nest eggs or "running away money" for them, as well as giving them spending money. The first matter of business whenever he took in a runaway was to have the child telephone home. Strait would listen in on the extension, and he usually did not like what he heard—curses and threats. Some of the children returned home, and he purchased their tickets and put them on buses and airplanes.

There was only one basic commandment in his house, Strait says, "You must love one another. That was the only rule."

Most of his young models lived with their families. Often they were from homes with "an absent father, a career father, or a super-religious father. I'm talking about policemen, Army officers, someone who's made a career out of a career," he says. Men whose professions require a great deal of involvement frequently have little time for their children.

Strait talks of $1,000 monthly telephone bills and grocery purchases exceeding $100 a week as long ago as the 1960s. One boy piled up $500 in telephone bills calling a girlfriend in Covina, California, before Strait learned what was going on. That was the same boy who wrapped an expensive, mint-condition, four-year-old 1956 T-bird around a tree two weeks after it was purchased for him. It was also the boy who ran off with a $500 movie camera and a perfect 10-karat star ruby, then mailed the pawn tickets back to Strait in San Francisco. The youth was one of his few disappointments.

Most others are remembered as well behaved, responsive to trust, and pleased with the spending money and generous gifts he distributed. Not all the children who lived with him posed for pornography, he says. And not all of them had sex with him.

Strait describes his own sexual preferences as "ambivalence" and "ambidextrous." "Asexual" is added as an afterthought. "I think that's one reason I could relate to people, because there was never a very strong drive," he explains. "Never been a 'must have,' 'must do' type of thing." Regardless of his facile explanation, it would be difficult to find anyone who has shown more interest in human sexuality, his own included, than Guy Strait. And he is ready to expound on almost any aspect of the urge, activity, or science at almost any time. His attitudes have undoubtedly been formed in large part by personal experience and close personal observation.

Unfortunately, many books about sexuality and most books about ethics have been written by preachers and psychiatrists, he points out. "Well, there's no one as unqualified to write about sex as clergy. And psychiatrists will take the tree and build a forest."

The man who has been known to refer to himself as the "Michelangelo of kiddie porn" also has no time for arguments that every great civilization that has fallen has collapsed after its citizens have become deeply involved in homosexuality, incest, or pedophilia. "Rome was pulled down by the Christian church," he maintains. "Excessive law is what pulled Greece down."

Ethics are more important than law, he asserts. His single, most important personal rule regarding sex is concise and simple: "As long as no one is harmed, then it's no one's business." He cautions, however, that the definition of harm must carry with it long-term responsibility.

Some of Strait's definitions and attitudes, predictably, differ from those of more conventional people. His approach to the phenomenon of incest, for example: "I see nothing wrong with it, per se."

Western proscriptions against the practice are not realistic, nor are arguments valid that warn of genetic damage to the offspring of close blood relatives, he contends. "I know a brother and sister who are afraid to have children because of that gobbledegook. . . I don't believe that. I can prove that it's wrong. . . . I don't believe there's a race horse in this country today that is worth his salt that isn't kin to Man-o-War and Seabiscuit in at least six or seven different directions. If we want to improve, we take the finest examples that have ever been combined and breed them. . . therefore, we get prime examples.

"Development of a person is not nearly so dependent on an incestuous relationship as on the total environment," he says. "A mother who smothers a child is going to have a sick child. No question about it."

Strait claims to have photographed members of a Mediterranean family of about 100 people spanning at least four generations, who were "nudists, libertines . . . (and the) happiest people (sic) could be." The clan was presided over by a patriarch who ruled with a stern hand but permitted open incestual activities among the members of his brood. There was one rule that everyone observed: "No pubic hair, no touch."

Presumably, as soon as that particular sign of puberty was observed by other members of the family, a child became fair game for sex play.

Strait has his own rule about children who are too young to touch, although it is a bit more hazy and less well defined. He told a U.S. Senate subcommittee meeting in Chicago that he did not photograph pornography with models younger than fourteen. Basically, that appears to be the minimum age he feels most comfortable working with. "Over fourteen, I don't consider them children. They're sexually mature. Let's say fourteen is not a child, thirteen may or may not be, and fifteen sure as hell is not." Strait's mother had her first child at fifteen. And he claims that some of the greatest men of Ancient Greece achieved their fame when they were no more than fifteen. He concedes that he would be "very, very careful" about using a child under twelve. In some cases, modeling for pornography at that age could be harmful to a child, he agrees. "It could also be harmful to cross a sidewalk."

He has less difficulty eliminating younger children of seven or eight as potential models for pornography. There's no market, he claims. After some thought, he diffidently agrees that there is a danger of physical damage to a child of that age if penetration occurs. "If there was going to be penetration, I'd never photograph it. I wouldn't tolerate it," he says. "However, I've known playful—call it precocious—youngsters this age. I've met them in incestuous families, I've seen them grow up, and I didn't see anything wrong."

His thesis that there is no market for pornography involving very young children is difficult to accept in view of the arrest records of pedophiles and the large amount of pornography focusing on those age groups. Strait himself talks of a French Emperor, "Louis XIV, I think, who liked young girls, little girls." Poking through history, he names several other prominent figures he claims were pedophiles and pederasts who were sexually attracted to early postpubescent children.

Free will is at least as important a factor as age in determining if the mere act of engaging in sexual activity in front of a camera may be a harmful experience, he believes. And Strait says he has never forced anyone of any age to pose for his pornography. He believes, in fact, that children are seldom forced into commercial sex of any kind. He does not believe that girls or boys are forced into prostitution any more than he believes they are trapped into pornography. "Prostitution is a ridiculous racket," he says. "There ain't no money in it. There's just no big money in prostitution."

Strait contends that it would never be financially worthwhile for a pimp to transport a prostitute from Minneapolis to New York. And a pimp would be immediately surrounded by "sixteen million — cops," if he tries standing at a bus station long enough to pick up a runaway, Strait adds. He attributes the profusion of teenage prostitutes in the cities to girls who arrive hungry and penniless. "The first thing she'll do is try the social agencies, and find that all the social agencies are nothing but referral agencies to other agencies that are referral agencies," he says. If a young girl is broke and hungry she does what she has to do to eat. "Sex can be a commodity," Strait says. "If that's all you've got to sell, sell it." He says that he was once so broke in New York that he ate from garbage cans after being rejected for help from social agencies. And other people were eating with him.

Although he denies ever dealing in child prostitution himself, Strait says he once took a young brother and sister, who had been living with him, to New York where he introduced them to a specialist in the trade. "He is the only man I know dealing with juvenile prostitutes, the only one. And believe me, if there had been others, I would have known about it."

The young couple was entranced. "They told me they thought it was a great idea, if they knew they could leave at any time; they said they wanted to stay. I said it was okay, 'But you know you won't be able to pick your partners,' " he warned them. They stayed anyway. Some three months later, they telephoned him from a small town and said they wanted to come home. Strait mailed them airplane tickets to California. "They looked on it as adventure, because to them sex had become recreation," he said, "not something to be held in awe."

Strait had teamed up with Billy Byars, a Houston man who was a scion of the Humble Oil fortune, when the law began catching up with him. According to Lloyd, Byars was shooting his own material under the name of Lyric International, and, when he joined forces with his fellow Texan, their company became known as DOM-LYRIC. They reputedly had as many as 90 magazines, and, at wholesale prices of $2.50 each and retail of $5, they were raking in a staggering amount of money.

Ironically, Strait says, the last movie he filmed in California, and the one that got him indicted in Contra Costa County, was shot as a favor to a group of teenagers who needed money. "I had no intention when I started shooting of ever releasing it," he says. "There were three boys and one girl. One of the boys owed me $50, and the other boy I wanted to give $50 to. The (third) boy was just really a nice kid." Strait says he shot the movie, paid the youths, including $50 for the girl, and stored the movie in his house trailer at 150-degree heat, "which will destroy a color film in two weeks."

A short time later, nine separate indictments listing 90 counts against Strait, Byars, a YMCA counselor, a school teacher, an assistant scoutmaster, the son of actress Loretta Young, and eight other men were returned by the Los Angeles Grand Jury. Byars was identified as the owner of several film companies, including Lyric Productions. Christopher Paul Lewis, identified as Miss Young's son, was named as a film producer with Lyric. Another of those arrested was Daniel M. Yert, whom investigators identified as a major competitor of Strait's in the distribution of homosexual films. Boys from six to seventeen years old were said to have performed in the movies.

Detectives Martin and Smith announced that the indictments capped a three-month investigation launched after they acquired chicken movies from Texas that led them to Strait and to one of his associates.

Martin said he staked out Strait's Hollywood Hills home one night and the first people who left in the morning were two boys he recognized from the films. The detective obtained a search warrant and drove to Redwood City, about 40 miles south of San Francisco, where Strait kept his trailer for film editing. There, the veteran police officer told Congressmen, "I picked up a film, an unedited film, which showed Mr. Strait with a 16-millimeter camera on his shoulder with three boys lying in a bed . . . this came out of the reflection in the mirror in the Holiday Inn." Strait was arrested.

Strait later said that when he was apprehended he was about to produce a series of 24 films that were planned as a complete library of sexual activity. It was to cover every form of human sexuality and was being done-to-order for specific customers. "I would like to see porn take a slight side trip into sensual education," he says.

Significantly, none of the indictments against Strait and the other suspects charged them with making obscene films. They were accused of various other individual crimes, such as oral copulation, sodomy, and engaging in lewd acts with children under the age of fourteen.

"I wasn't convicted," Strait recalls. "I was told to jump bail and they never did put out an interstate warrant for my arrest. Then when I tried to get tried for it (years later), they dropped the charges." All his personal effects from his home were still in the Los Angeles Police Department's property room, he says. Detailed order blanks from his mail clients asking for specific chicken films of children as young as four years old were also said to be in the possession of police.

Byars also fled, presumably to Europe. Strait became somewhat of a cause celebré for a time and was defended by various B-L civil rights groups and sexual freedom advocates. There was speculation he was in Sweden, in Turkey, and in Greece.

He did not leave the country, and eventually made his way to Rockford "by invitation," he says. At the time the industrial city in Illinois appeared to be as good a place as any to settle down for a while. Strait apparently had not read or heard descriptions of the city by various news media as "puritanical," "conservative," and as "a no-nonsense town." Some people who live in the lusty city of some 140,000 do not appreciate those descriptions, especially since they suspect they are coined by a condescending Chicago press that automatically assumes bigger is better.

Strait later developed his own unprintable descriptions of Rockford, and they have nothing to do with quarrels about big-city provincialism. "Rockford accounts for about 12 percent of the populations of the prisons in Illinois. Christians and John Birchers. I think they're gonna' canonize Nixon any day now," Strait ranted bitterly about the people he once lived and toiled among.

His bitterness is perhaps understandable, if not excusable. It was April 23, 1976, and Strait was in Phoenix, Arizona, when he was arrested. He had left Rockford long before, edited "a small newspaper in New York," and "bummed around the country" for a while. Nevertheless, the warrant was not tied to his activities in California, nor his bail jumping there. It was based on a nearly four-year-old incident in Rockford. He was charged with taking indecent liberties with a minor, one of three foster children of a friend, after filming them in a pornographic movie. The boys were thirteen, fourteen, and sixteen years old, and he was specifically accused of performing fellatio with the fourteen-year-old. Gemignani alleged that Strait, whom he said, "appears to be an intelligent, kind and affable cherub," paid the boys $200 each to "perform lewd sex acts in a group" during the filming.

The three-year statute of limitations did not apply to Strait's arrest because he had been on the move, out of state. He says he was not worried about the arrest or the charge at the time. "I knew it didn't happen, therefore, I didn't worry about it." At the time, he says, "I didn't realize how little it took to put a man in prison. I thought you had to prove something."

The boys testified against him in the trial, and he was found guilty. He was sentenced to 10 to 20 years in prison and served approximately three. One of the first things he says he learned in prison was that, like himself, many of his fellow convicts were innocent. "I would say that at least one-third of the men in Illinois (prisons) are not guilty," he marvels.

Clarifying his observations, Strait explains that authorities were after him because of his pornography operations but chose to prosecute him on a different, less complex charge. He is convinced that many other prisoners have been treated similarly by the legal justice system.

He is also convinced that he was sent to die in the grim, overcrowded prison at Statesville, which was constructed during World War I and is the newest of Illinois' maximum security institutions. An aging chicken hawk locked up with several thousand other convicts, serving time for everything from multiple murders to felonious assault, rape, and arson, could be in grave danger if the long-held theory is true that sexual offenders, especially those who have molested children, are loathed by the rest of prison society.

It did not work that way. Strait says the other prisoners could not have cared less what he was sentenced for. His most vital task was to convince other inmates that they could not bully or otherwise take advantage of him. "You have to make your bone," he says, using prison jargon. "Demand respect."

Strait may have been lucky that he was one of the older men in prison and has a barrel-shaped body that is becoming gnarled and wrinkled. There is almost no way that a young man in a maximum security prison can protect himself from rape, he says. "I had a child molester in a cell with me for about three weeks . . . he was raped a dozen times or so. He's twenty-one years old. Anyone twenty-one, he's gonna' get raped." It was the youth's age and physical attractiveness that caused his trouble, not his offense.

Strait believes that it would help to cut down on forcible rape among inmates if prisoners convicted of non-violent crimes were separated from those with histories of violence. But prisoners are not segregated that way, and no one in a position of authority appears to care enough about the problem to take effective action.

"The cop mentality says that if you're here . . . you've done something. And if you done something, you ought to be punished. The Cook County Jail (in Chicago) must have a thousand suits over that," Strait observes.

Like many convicts with time on their hands, he developed into a jailhouse lawyer. And, like many jailhouse lawyers, he focused on federal law, combing civil rights statutes for loopholes and pouring over transcripts seeking possible violations in the trials and sentencings of himself and fellow convicts. A skilled jailhouse lawyer will tell another con that it does not matter if he is guilty or innocent. The important thing is: Were there trial errors? A guilty man can get a conviction reversed if there were trial errors. And an innocent man can be kept in prison if there were no errors.

When he was transferred from Statesville to a minimum security institution, Strait began slowing down his legal work and planning for his release. He swore that he would not reenter the smut industry after his return to California, although "if I was a mind to, and I'm not, I could take the negatives I have and make a fortune."

Instead, he was looking forward to work on two projects. One was a campaign for prison reform. The other was publishing and distributing three books he had already written. One is *Memoirs of a Dirty Old Man.* The others are *Hell in Illinois,* about prison life, and *Tyranny's New Home: Rockford.*

15.

The Child Molesters

NEIGHBORHOOD children called Floyd D. Ritter "Grandpa." He took them on hayrides, treated them to cookouts, and kept bicycles for them to ride. And sometimes he sexually molested them.

The sexual abuse continued for at least two years before the arrest of the sixty-six-year-old retired street superintendent in the small farming community of Bourbon, Indiana. One of his neighbors testified during court proceedings that she permitted her two daughters to visit Ritter's home, unaccompanied. The girls, as well as other neighborhood children, were reputedly molested.

Ritter attempted to defend himself by blaming the troubles on parents who did not keep their children at home. He denied that he enticed the youngsters. He conceded, however, that he liked children, and planned cookouts and other activities and kept the bicycles to "keep them occupied." He pointed out that he was a Christian who had attended an Assembly of God church in the area for four years, and "accepted the Lord" only a few months earlier.

He neglected to mention that he had been previously convicted and sentenced in 1945 on a charge of contributing to the delinquency of a minor. Marshall County Superior Court Judge Alexis R. Clarke mentioned the prior offense when he sentenced "Grandpa" Ritter on separate charges of child molesting to three concurrent eight-year prison terms in custody of the Indiana Department of Corrections. Ritter had pleaded guilty in a plea-bargaining arrangement, permitting four other charges of child molesting to be dismissed.

Clarke explained that the severity of the sentences was tied to the prior conviction, to the tender ages of the children (seven to eleven), and the defendant's potential danger to society and the likelihood of the same behavior occurring again. He also pointed out that Ritter did not appear to be amenable to effective treatment and rehabilitation.

Treatment of pedophiles is as notorious for its ineffectiveness as it is for the scarcity of programs. Repeat offenders like Ritter are routinely sentenced to prison, held a few months or years, and returned to their communities. Mass killer John Gacy was sentenced to prison after sexually abusing teenage boys in Iowa and was released on probation 18 months later after receiving no treatment at all.

A murder suspect in the slaying of a young Chicago woman, who told police he had abducted and held more than a dozen others in bondage, complained that he had not been given psychiatric help requested for him 13 years earlier when he was jailed for the strangulation death of a six-year-old boy. He begged for more competent treatment the next time. Society's handling of the child molester and other sex offenders is further complicated by overworked prosecutors anxious to reduce the severity of charges in return for trial-saving guilty pleas; by lenient judges; and by sentencing and penal laws and parole practices that make it difficult to imprison anyone for long unless they have committed the most gross and horrifying crimes.

Consequently, thousands of sex offenders are returned to the streets in this country every year, free on probation, parole or on bond. They have been neither rehabilitated by effective treatment nor kept in prison where they cannot repeat their outrages against innocent women and children.

In 1979 police in Michigan City, Indiana, some 60 miles northwest of Bourbon, arrested a professional stage magician who billed himself as "Dr. Strange." He was accused of sexually molesting a pair of seven- and ten-year-old boys and taking nude photographs of them. Donald L. Strange had been arrested with a companion in Indianapolis 10 years earlier, and he pleaded guilty to sodomy in a case police said involved about 75 boys from nine to fourteen years old. The confederate was committed to a state mental hospital as a sexual psychopath, and Strange was given two to 14 years in the Indiana State Prison.

Police in Michigan City said the mother of the seven-year-old told them Strange had invited her son and the older boy to his house to watch cartoons, before molesting them. Investigators who participated in the Indianapolis arrest said Strange invited children into his sign shop to see magic shows before enticing them into sexual acts. When Strange was arrested in Michigan City, he had been free for almost six years.

When authorities arrested Walter J. Kaleta in Chicago on charges of aggravated kidnapping and taking indecent liberties with the ten-year-old daughter of a policeman, they learned he had a 20-year record of child molesting. Known as the "candy man" because he reputedly offered candy to the children he approached, he had been convicted of child molestation six times, and in every instance except one he was placed on probation or under court supervision. The only time he was jailed was in 1961 when he was imprisoned for 45 days for contributing to the sexual delinquency of two girls seven and ten years old.

A young Las Vegas man sentenced to life in prison, with a possibility of parole in 10 years, was unlike the candy man and had no lengthy prior record of sexually abusing children. But he had lured an eight-year-old boy into his home under the pretense of finding parts to repair a broken bicycle siren and, according to the child, sexually attacked him "five or seven times."

Although the child molester was legally sane, his attorney described him as "retarded from birth." Psychiatrists diagnosed him as a schizophrenic. Despite the grossness of his act, he was clearly an individual who deserved understanding and help. It was important to isolate him from other potential victims, but as a twenty-four-year-old retarded man he would be almost helpless to protect himself in the general population of a prison.

There were no state facilities or treatment programs in Nevada for people like him. Deputy District Attorney Jim O'Neale was quoted as saying that, "His incarceration in a prison population—even in the relative country club atmosphere of the Southern Nevada Correctional Institute at Jean—would not be in the best interest of (the defendant) —or the state." O'Neale agreed with suggestions that the child molester be placed in a facility in another state where proper care and treatment were available. The sentencing judge ordered the molester to be "treated in a facility other than the prison in Carson City." A transcript of the proceedings was to be delivered to correctional authorities.[1]

A report published in 1979 by the Law Enforcement Assistance Administration disclosed that three years earlier there were only about 20 treatment centers for sex offenders in a dozen states. Edward M. Brecher, author of the study, advised that the average sex offender was treated no differently from any other inmate of jails or prisons. "Nothing in particular is being done about them and little or no attention is being paid to the particular factors which made these men sex offenders," he wrote.

"Most of the treatment programs for sex offenders currently in operation arose almost by accident through the activities of one dedicated individual or one institution baffled by what to do about the sex offenders lodged in its custody."

Funded with a $60,000 LEAA grant to the American Correctional

Association, the study recommended treatment programs to reduce recidivism and to provide a research environment. Sex offenders often desire treatment, Brecher said, but it is not available. "Many sexual offenders, including rapists and child molesters, can in fact be rehabilitated through soundly planned, staffed and administered programs," he advised.

One of the most promising programs cited in the study was established at the South Florida State Hospital in Hollywood, near Miami. Most of the 60 to 70 participants involved at any one time have already been convicted of sex crimes and spend a minimum of two years there before returning to the courts for sentencing. Approximately a third of those are sent to jail, and the others are released on probation.

Staff professionals, including aides, are less directly involved with the patients than they might be in most other programs set up for the treatment of sexual offenders. The Florida program demands almost constant spoken acknowledgment by the participants of their own deviant sex urges. It is backed up by intense peer pressure.

Other professionals are closely following the results of a federally financed research program carried out by mental health professionals seeking means of treating habitual sex offenders who were not in prison at the time and voluntarily sought help. The project was begun in Memphis and later moved to New York City to a clinic operated by the New York State Psychiatric Institute in conjunction with the Columbia-Presbyterian Medical Center. Funding for the project was provided with a three-year $847,000 grant from the National Institute of Mental Health.

Dr. Gene G. Abel, a psychiatrist and head of an eight-member staff, was quoted by the *New York Times* as saying that it was essential that the patients not be coerced or ordered by the courts to undergo the treatment. "Some rapists and child molesters don't want to do anything about their problems," Dr. Abel said. "I don't know how to treat those people."

Treatment was described as differing according to the problem and the individual. Dr. Abel explained that child molesters were conditioned to refocus their sexual fantasies from children to adult women by linking the deviant behavior to negative consequences. The patients' fears of wives or girlfriends taking other men as lovers when the patients were in jail were cited as an example.

Dr. Abel pointed out that the patients were not expected to be cured, but rather to be helped to deal with their problems over a period of time.

"We teach an individual to reduce his urges and how to deal with them when they do occur," he said.[2]

Stronger methods of aversion therapy have been tried on patients in several procedures aimed at modifying the behavior of pedophiles and other sexual offenders. Some are uncomfortably reminiscent of the methods employed in Anthony Burgess' disconcerting novel *A Clockwork Orange*. The novel and movie told of a young British tough conditioned in prison to become nauseous whenever he thought of violence or sex. After he was released from prison he was attacked by former friends and almost died because he was unable to defend himself.

In the early 70s a dozen convicted child molesters at the Connecticut Correctional Institution in Somers participated in a behavior modification program that used electric shock therapy. The inmate would lie on a couch in the hospital unit, watching slides of naked children and adult females alternated on a screen. Every time a picture of a naked child appeared, the inmate would be given an electrical shock near his genitals. There was no shock when the slides of nude women were shown.

The object was to produce feelings of anxiety or fear when the pedophile had thoughts of a child as a sexual object, while enhancing the desire for normal sexual relationships with adult women. Photos or thoughts of children as sexual objects produced pain, while the photos of women were associated with relief from pain—a positive feeling.

Hypnotism was used as an adjunct of the program to create phobias in the minds of the pedophiles about children as sexual objects. After the patient was hypnotized, a trained psychologist, aware of the inmate's fears and dislikes, would narrate a fantasy experience with a child as a sexual object. As desire for the child grew, the narration became terrifying. An anticipated victim might turn into a rat, spider, or snake, whatever was most frightening and revolting to the patient.

Aversion therapy has been used in various other American institutions, including the Atascadero State Hospital in California and the California Medical Facility at Vacaville, the latter operated by the state Department of Corrections. Succinylcholine chloride, a drug better known by its trade name, Anectine, is a muscle relaxant used in both programs. Its value in aversion therapy lies in its ability, when properly administered, to paralyze the muscles and halt breathing for up to three minutes. While the fully conscious sex offender is gripped in the horror of suffocation, a therapist can sit beside him, making suggestions and authoritatively pointing out errors and consequences of deviant behavior.

Therapists at Atascadero also worked for a time with electric shock aversion. Some prisoners were taught to treat themselves by sticking their fingers down their throats and snapping rubber bands against their bodies when they were bothered by deviant thoughts. Doctors at Vacaville in the late 60s flirted briefly with brain surgery performed on violent criminals. Portions of the brains of three prisoners were surgically destroyed. At best, the results were inconclusive. At worst, they were disappointing. When plans were disclosed in 1971 to revive and expand the program, public furor was so great that the project had to be abandoned.

By 1977 Sergeant Eugene Brown, a detective with the San Jose Police Department, was telling a Congressional investigative panel that before Dr. Giaretto started his Child Sexual Abuse Treatment Program, "we just didn't have anything here in California that we could do with sex offenders, except lock them up in a penitentiary, (or) send them to Atascadero."

Brown recounted one time when he was attempting to talk a suspect into admitting a sex crime, promising help in exchange for cooperation. After Brown indicated that he meant the Atascadero State Hospital, the suspect proceeded to describe treatment there. "After two days they learn to play the games down there. They make their wallets and they string their beads," the suspect recalled. Inmates were watched by staff until 9 P.M., when the lights were turned off. "Then it is smorgasbord," the suspect concluded.

The police sergeant went on to explain his differences with Giaretto, who was described as believing in loving everyone. "I think this is true," Brown said, "but before we can love them we have to hit them on the head with a two-by-four to get their attention." That is best done through the judicial system, he indicated, recommending punishment of serious sexual offenders preceding or combined with treatment.

He cautioned that the punishment must be administered fairly. In some of California's most punitive institutions, he said, sex offenders are routinely tied down to bunks by other inmates and forced to perform or submit to abnormal sex acts. "That isn't what we need, gentlemen," he cautioned. "We need laws that will fit the crime."

Aversion therapy programs were also tried for a time in Iowa and Wisconsin. A few private psychologists and other therapists have also used mild electric shock combined with pictures of children and adult women in the treatment of pedophilia. But aversion therapy in state institutions ran into crippling opposition from the American Civil Liberties Union and others who reacted with shock and outrage to the cruel injustices and torture supposedly inflicted on child molesters and rapists. The process was branded as brainwashing, and Burgess' novel was repeatedly cited as an example of the dangers of aversion therapy gone astray. The program at Somers was discontinued after three convicts were supported by the ACLU in a suit against the Massachusetts Corrections Department based on claims that sexual offenders were coerced into participating in aversion therapy with threats of withholding early parole. Other programs were also phased out or abruptly ended.

There are different objections to aversion therapy. Some experts, patients, and laymen say that it simply does not work. "This whole business of shock treatments is ludicrous," Dr. Osanka believes, "because these guys aren't going to be wired when they leave the prison. They aren't going to have to worry about shock.

"It might work with a child who doesn't know the alternatives. All he's told is that it's bad, or that he has a desire that's bad. But these people already know the alternatives, and they know, from their point of view, the pleasure that's involved. Artificial wiring under controlled conditions is not effective."

The desires and preferences of pedophiles are deep-seated, Dr. Osanka has found, and the only time they are highly motivated to change is after they have been indicted or imprisoned. "Nobody at this point can say if a pedophile can be rehabilitated," he says. "It's asking to take a favorite fantasy out of the psyche of an individual. We may be able to educate that individual that he is wrong for fulfilling that fantasy. This can be a short-term answer. We can temporarily restrain him and teach self-restraint. But to cure would mean eliminating that fantasy, and that would be impossible."

A former patient in a Midwestern psychiatric hospital shares Dr. Osanka's lack of enthusiasm for the effectiveness of some of the more popular, and unpopular, experiments in behavior modification. Hospitalized after shooting a man to death, he was quartered with a group of patients undergoing a tightly controlled form of behavior modification.

The treatment was extremely effective as long as the patients remained in the carefully structured surroundings of the hospital. All the patients know that the only way they can get out is to be cooperative and play along with the doctors and the staff. "Pretty soon you see all these smiling, amiable people playing this role of being well behaved," he says. Unfortunately, after the amiable people are released, most of them revert to their old ways.

The patient recalled a man he was hospitalized with who had raped and killed a six-year-old boy. During therapy sessions the killer was properly remorseful. But at night, when the patients were sitting around playing cards or visiting, he would talk longingly of getting out of the institution and finding himself another "nice little boy" whom he could sexually abuse. He was eventually discharged.

The attraction of pederasts to young boys has been described by some therapists as an eternal search for youth and a fear of aging. Other professionals point out that many pederasts share a common history of sexual immaturity at the time of their first homosexual experience. The victim of the pederast is often a fantasy projection of himself.

Some pedophiles exhibit a lifelong sexual attraction to very young children of either gender. Tendencies to sexually abuse children occur in other individuals later in life, for a variety of reasons, according to professionals who treat and study the condition. Child molesting can be a temporary deviation. Some men apparently turn to pedophilia in middle life when they fear that their sexual potency is waning. A sexually unsophisticated and undemanding child, unlike an adult woman, is non-threatening to an individual attempting to reassure himself of his own manhood. A child will not attempt to evaluate his sexual performance.

Domestic difficulties, either sexual or non-sexually related, and alcohol and drug abuse are believed to trigger episodes of pedophilia. Many child molesters were sexually abused as children.

Perhaps the most common trait is the feeling most, perhaps all, pedophiles share of inadequacy or discomfort with adults. Some experts point out that molesters of young girls commonly associate sex with sin, guilt, and uncleanliness. Innocent, immature girls are presumably free of those undesirable characteristics. Pedophiles have a low concept of self. The first pornographic movie Dr. Densen-Gerber ever saw showed a three-year-old girl urinating in her father's mouth. "That's very common," Dr. Densen-Gerber says, "because pedophiles feel very badly about themselves. . . . We mustn't think the sexuality these children are asked to perform is normal adult sexuality. . . . These people are distorted and disturbed . . . because a healthy adult wants a reciprocal peer relationship."

Women are rarely prosecuted for child molesting except when associated with offenses committed with or by a male accomplice. Females can express sexual feelings toward children in far less obvious ways than men. Women in pediatric nursing, social work, teaching, professional child care, and, of course, as mothers can be extremely sensual without attracting undue attention.

Some men, especially those who have reacted to a stress situation, may molest a child only once or on rare occasions. They are usually the most responsive to effective treatment. Treatment of chronic offenders is more difficult, some believe impossible. Children are viewed by most chronic pedophiles as sexual objects to be used, rather than as whole persons to be respected and treated with love or care. They are no more than mechanical attachments to the bodies of the offenders. Pedophiles with those attitudes can often become violent, mixing sadism with sex. They may kill.

There is growing sentiment, spreading from more conservative persons to others who have been shocked by the burgeoning violence in society, to refocus efforts from rehabilitation of offenders to protection of the public. Nowhere is that feeling more obvious than with regard to child molesters, rapists, and other sex criminals.

State legislators are beginning to respond to that feeling and are looking for better ways to protect the public. Legislation was introduced in at least two states in 1979 calling for asexualization of child molesters and habitual sex offenders. Neither bill was successful.

Freshman legislator Frank Shurden, a Democrat from Henryetta, introduced a measure in the Oklahoma House of Representatives calling for the surgical removal of the external male genitalia from child molesters and certain other sex offenders. Rape, he warned, was "becoming a national pastime." The measure was proposed as an amendment to a bill to repeal outdated laws dealing with sterilization of mental patients. After considerable controversy, the measure was tabled in a conference committee. The original repeal bill was passed 50 to 35, but Shurden's amendment was defeated the next week 48 to 46.

"The opposition came from what I call 'bleeding heart liberals,' who feel sorry for the rapist, and several weak House members who were afraid of the liberal news media," Shurden complained. "The American Civil Liberties Union, homosexuals, and naturally convicted rapists opposed my bill." He insisted, however, that the public supported him. "My mail ran 20 to one in favor from all across America and even other countries," he says. "I got encouragement from individual pastors and even M.D.s."

The legislator's proposal would permit a judge or jury to order asexualization of criminals convicted of various sex offenses including: first-degree rape, "a detestable and abominable crime against nature," and a situation where at least two aggravating circumstances were present.

Aggravating circumstances were further defined as: commission of a sex crime against a child less than nine years old; a crime that was "especially serious, atrocious or cruel"; a sex crime that resulted in significant physical injury to the victim; a sex crime committed upon one victim by the defendant two or more times within 24 hours; a sex crime committed by a person while serving a prison term for a felony; and if there is a high probability that the convicted criminal would commit additional sex crimes that would constitute a continuing threat to society.

Castration is not a new approach to dealing with sex offenders. The ancient Assyrians employed castration as long ago as 2,000 B.C. as punishment for certain crimes. Zealots in various religions willingly submitted to castration so that their attention and energies presumably would not be diverted from the contemplation and service of their gods. More recently, Denmark has performed surgical castration on certain classes of sex offenders, and officials claim positive results.

As late as 1975, two or three convicted sex offenders in San Diego asked to be castrated in preference to long-term incarceration and signed waivers releasing attorneys, the courts, and doctors from any legal liability. A doctor who agreed to perform the surgery changed his mind after talking with colleagues. Despite the waivers, the specter of lawsuits was too threatening, and no surgeon could be found to perform the operation.

Castration, female sterilization, psycho-surgery, and certain radical forms of aversion therapy draw uncomfortable parallels with some of the abuses in Nazi Germany. And, although the procedures have been or are being used in other countries, they automatically draw heavy opposition when they are proposed in the United States.

Joyce Lewis, a conservative Republican from Auburn, Maine, was faced with that kind of response immediately after introducing a bill in the state legislature calling for the surgical neutering of men and women convicted of sexually molesting children under fourteen. Surgical procedures were outlined, which it was believed would render either gender incapable of sexual arousal. There would be no cosmetic damage to external genitalia. Nerves would be severed in the male to make him incapable of obtaining an erection. In the female the Fallopian tubes would be severed, disconnecting the ovary from the uterus.

The legislator declared that sexual abuse of children had reached a critical point and that she could not think of a more effective means of dealing with it. Her interest in the subject was sparked while she served on the board of directors of a children's home where she came in contact with two girls, seven and ten, who were victims of incest. One was molested by her grandfather and the other by her father. "And nothing was done to the molesters," the legislator asserted.

Expectedly, bitter controversy flared between legislators and other citizens arguing the merits of children's rights versus the rights of paraphiliacs—sex offenders. Representative Lewis altered her bill to eliminate surgery in favor of a technique using medication to reduce the sex drive, backed up by counseling, as recommended by Dr. John Money of the Johns Hopkins Medical Institutions in Baltimore. The bill was defeated in the Democratic-controlled Senate after passing the Republican dominated House.

Dr. Money, professor of medical psychology and associate professor of pediatrics, explained his method at a public hearing and during a meeting with the legislator. Treatment utilizes administration of the hormone Depo-Provera, an antiandrogen that inhibits the release of the male hormone, androgen, from the testicles. Depo-Provera is also a progestin, which is sexually inert and competes in the body with androgen, the sexual activator. The result, according to Dr. Money, is that there is a period of sexual quiet in which the sex drive is at rest. Some call it chemical castration. But, unlike surgical castration, it is reversible and can be of any duration desired.

During the period the patient is free from his formerly overwhelming urge and is sexually calmed, counseling designed to help him establish a new lifestyle is provided. A dozen sex offenders treated with Depo-Provera at Johns Hopkins have been subjects of long-term followup, Dr. Money reported. Nine were able to properly regulate their sexual behavior, and three had relapses, which Money said "correlated with noncompliance." Improvement followed resumption of treatment.

Dr. Money outlined many benefits of the medication and counseling method over more primitive treatment methods of sex offenders such as surgical castration and cutting the nerves to the penis. Neither of the latter two approaches diminishes sex drive, he explained.

Surgical castration results in permanent mutilation and permanent sterility, but it is now possible to replace the male hormone secreted by the testicles with daily ingestion of pills or monthly injections. "This replacement hormone," the doctor said, "returns the sexual drive to its precastration level."

Severing the penile nerves also does not alter the level of the sexual urge, because the "sexual drive has its genesis in the brain, not the penis," he said. "Even if a man has his penis totally amputated . . . he does not lose the sensation of sexual drive. Thus a sex offender without a penis would still have his paraphiliac illness and would still be driven to carry out his sex-offending (paraphiliac) behavior, despite the missing penis."

Dr. Money pointed out several other disagreeable side-effects to the proposal by Representative Lewis. Because of the anatomical arrangement of the nerve supply to the penis, he said, it is not possible to destroy sensation in the organ without damaging other parts of the body. The operation probably would destroy other vital nerves, making the patient incapable of controlling both his bowel movements and urination.

The operation proposed for women, known by its medical term as a salpingectomy, causes only infertility and has no effect on genital sensation, sexual drive, or sexual behavior.

Dr. Money concluded that he had no hesitation in recommending the treatment pioneered at Johns Hopkins. "It is by far the most effective method known. It is rehabilitative. It is humane. It is the least expensive and costs the taxpayer only a minor fraction of the exorbitant amount to keep a man in prison," he concluded.

[1] *Las Vegas Sun*, August 21, 1979.
[2] *New York Times*, April 13, 1979.

16.

Censorship

D.H. LAWRENCE wrote in *Sex, Literature and Censorship* that "Pornography is the attempt to sell sex, to do dirt on it. . . . The insult to the human body, the insult to a vital human relationship! Ugly and cheap they make the human nudity, ugly and degraded they make the sexual act, trivial and cheap and nasty."

The legal attacks on magazines and movies considered by some authorities to be smut followed a series of U.S. Supreme Court rulings dealing with obscenity and X-rated enterprises. Justices have taken widely different approaches to the question of balancing First Amendment rights and obscenity. Justice William O. Douglas indicated he believed that obscenity law is a grave abridgement of free speech. Chief Justice Earl Warren countered that the First Amendment was never intended to protect obscenity.

One of the most confusing, yet significant, decisions was a landmark ruling in 1973, *Miller* v *California,* giving individual communities responsibility for defining community standards in regard to obscenity and prosecution of violators. The decision was vague and the word "community" was not defined. It did not stipulate whether or not "community" means a neighborhood, city, county, state, or other grouping of citizens.

More important yet, obscenity and pornography are so subjective that it is nearly impossible for anyone to provide adequate legal definitions. The obscenity concept is so inherently vague that even the ancient Greeks were said to have been unable to define it.

It is a shifty legal concept, primarily because it is spelled out in intensely contrasting terms by different people at different times and locations. The complicated issues of censorship, First Amendment rights, and the meaning of obscenity are all part of the same conundrum. It is so perplexing that obscenity cases are among the most frequent issues considered by the Supreme Court. An FBI agent in

Florida once remarked in frustration that defining obscenity was about as easy as nailing a custard pie to a telephone pole. *Screw* publisher Goldstein offered that "Obscenity is in the eye of the beholder."

One of columnist Abigail Van Buren's readers once wrote and said she was showing a picture of her two-month-old grandchild being bathed when a neighbor told her to put it away because it was "child pornography." Goldstein may be right. What is obscene to one person may not be obscene to another.

The Supreme Court set down the basic guidelines for defining obscenity as determining (1) whether the average person applying contemporary community standards would find that the work, taken as a whole, appeals to the prurient interest; (2) whether the work depicts or describes, in a patently offensive way, sexual conduct specifically defined by the applicable state law; and (3) whether the work, taken as a whole, lacks serious literary, artistic, political, or scientific value.

The court was explicit in defining "patently offensive." It was explained that the term referred to ultimate sexual acts such as masturbation, excretion, and lewd exhibition of genitalia. Considerably more latitude was allowed in determining if the other two criteria branded a specific work as obscene. The pronouncement was not one of the justices' more precise decisions.

Syndicated newspaper columnist Ellen Goodman referred to the decision as "so flexible and flaky that twelve jurors in a remote village could sentence Masters and Johnson to jail." But when children are involved, she added, they "cut through all the murkiness. This is not a First Amendment issue. . . . It's a matter of protecting the real lives of young models."[1]

Stanley Martin Dietz, a leading Washington pornography lawyer who has argued test cases before the High Court that established new obscenity standards, once convinced a judge that a book detailing a woman's sexual encounters with various animals was not obscene. He also once represented a homosexual philosophy professor who was having problems with the U.S. Postal Service for selling gay magazines throuh the mail. The U.S. Supreme Court ruled that no United States agency, including the office of the Postmaster General, with the single exception of the federal courts, had authority to determine what is obscene. Furthermore, the court concurred with Dietz's argument that the homosexual magazines, which featured naked little boys as well as adults, were not "patently offensive" to the subscribers. Therefore, they were not obscene.

Dr. Densen-Gerber also believes that a definition of obscenity different from that of the Supreme Court's must be accepted if children are involved. "When you're talking about child pornography, I'd rather have the test: 'Is this material dangerous? For whom is it defined? Who is the audience? And does it present a potential danger to the children in the area? To the children who are being photographed?'

"I simply think that having children pose in these various compromising activities . . . (is) not what we would call normal human sexuality because people who are involved in the use of children have very low self-esteem and feel very bad about themselves."

Consequently, many of the sexual activities child pornographers and pedophiles are involved in are way beyond what most people consider to be sexuality. They include acts such as being urinated or deficated on, or of having the child urinated on. There was an obscenity case in the Midwest in which the material under consideration was so revolting that the jury found it was too obscene to be obscene. It was so filthy it did not arouse them.

"Common sense and maternal instinct tell me this goes way beyond free speech," Dr. Densen-Gerber said of child pornography. "Such conduct mutilates children's spirits. They aren't consenting adults. They're victims."

In 1976, another High Court decision upheld the right of critics to use zoning to eliminate adult motion pictures and bookstores. Some cities used zoning, not to eliminate commercial porn, but to restrict it to certain areas and control it. Boston, with its adult entertainment corridor known as the Combat Zone, is the most notable. But there are others, including some established and recognized as districts where X-rated activities were tolerated by local authorities decades before the 1976 Supreme Court ruling. In these areas, streets, and neighborhoods, like The Block in Baltimore, the Meat Rack in Hollywood, and Times Square in Manhattan, many teenagers and sub-teens are given their first introduction to prostitution, nude dancing, and roles as performers in loops and 8-millimeter kiddie porn films.

In Detroit, neighborhood groups appeared before Mayor Coleman A. Young and suggested experimenting with an area to be set aside from the rest of the city and devoted to commercial sex. Their enthusiasm for the plan paled when he asked if they would consider including their own neighborhoods in the district.

The Combat Zone was once hailed in some quarters as a legitimate and workable compromise between people who insist on their rights to freely patronize sex-related ventures and those who prefer to be isolated and protected from them. The Zone, however, spread like cancer. Surrounding neighborhoods began to deteriorate. And the sexual shopping center was quickly overrun by illegals, teenagers and older: whores, pimps, con-men, gunmen, and strongarm robbers. Motorists who were careless or foolish enough to venture into the sexual cesspool were often robbed. Then a Massachusetts state policeman died of head injuries after being found unconscious in the Zone, and a Harvard football player was stabbed to death there. Most Bostonians who did not work in the Zone avoided it.

Baltimore's Block is relatively small but one of the oldest and best-known sexual ghettoes in the country. The city itself is broad-shouldered and robust. It has a busy seaport and a constant supply of womenless men with lusty appetites who fill its saloons, poolrooms, and strip joints.

The demand for girls is steady, and runaways drift in and out of The Block. They are easy prey for pimps who seduce them with bogus pretensions of love and concern. When that fails to ensnare a child who may be running from a home where she has been beaten, raped, or emotionally abused, the procurer can always fall back on drugs, alcohol, or violence.

Young teenagers, of course, are not supposed to be employed as strippers, B-girls, or prostitutes. But the laws are difficult to enforce. Negative rulings in the federal courts, including the U.S. Supreme Court, contribute to the difficulties.

For a time in Illinois, there was no obscenity law because the former statute was declared unconstitutional by a federal court on the basis of vagueness. Months later, the U.S. Supreme Court reversed the federal court decision and upheld the law.

The 1972 canon handled the question of obscenity by stipulating that except when the material was accessible to children, "obscenity should be judged with reference to ordinary adults." The Illinois Criminal Code regulating sexual matters is said to be one of the most permissive in the country when only adults are concerned. But the permissiveness stops short when children are involved.

Lawmakers and lawbreakers engage in lively but often absurd maneuvering in the struggle over such sex-related activities as pornography, prostitution, X-rated movies, and erotic massage. In Birmingham, Alabama, when laws controlling massage parlors were strengthened, the operators opened shoe-shine parlors staffed by the same girls who had previously been masseuses. A new statute had to be enacted making it illegal to lie down to get a shoe shine.

After police raided an apartment in Hollywood, Florida, they disclosed that they had surprised a naked fifteen-year-old girl about to perform in a porno movie. They arrested the man they said was making the film, Leonard Joseph Campagno. Also known as Lenny Camp, Campagno was familiar to vice squad police in south Florida and they were congratulating themselves on a solid arrest. They carted away four truckloads of reputedly pornographic material. But when Campagno appeared in Criminal Court accused of violating Florida's obscenity laws, the case was dismissed. Florida had no obscenity laws. A three-judge federal court panel in Jacksonville had struck them down months before as unconstitutional.

Campagno's luck deserted him in another arrest for involvement in the filming of a pornographic movie on a 72-foot boat owned by one doctor and at the comfortable Bayshore Drive home in Miami of another. He was given an 18-month prison sentence on a charge of obscenity conspiracy, and the conviction was later upheld on appeal. The appeals court found that there was evidence that Campagno had provided the three young couples for the sex scenes, offered advice to the cameraman, and taken still shots of the action.

The case was prosecuted and won by Assistant State's Attorney Harold Ungerleider, even though the 16-millimeter color film was missing, reputedly stolen shortly after it was made. For a time, Ungerleider, a dapper septuagenarian, was at the center of south Florida's vigorous anti-smut campaign. Some people credited the Assistant State's Attorney, who kept an oxygen mask under his desk because of severe emphysema, with almost singlehandedly chasing pornographers and dirty movies out of Dade County. During Dade County's war on the local sex industry in the 1970s, operators of adult bookstores were repeatedly arrested, and scores of hookers, many of them minors, were rounded up as they loitered on busy Biscayne Boulevard or frequented the so-called adult motels.

During one raid on an adult bookstore in Miami, a startled customer took one look at police and a horde of reporters, and asked, quaveringly, "Is it Anita Bryant?" A moment later he bolted out the door in alarm. Many of the films police confiscated in the raids were of girls as young as eight and ten years old participating in sexual activities with adults.

Ungerleider was personally convinced that pornography poured millions of dollars into organized crime, which he said he believed ran the business from behind the scenes.

Not every crusader who campaigns against kiddie porn or pornography in general depends solely on litigation. Some, like Dr. Densen-Gerber and her supporters, resort to marches, demonstrations, or outright harassment. Robert J. Edwards, a fifty-six-year-old former police chief from California, drove his van 76,000 miles, stopping in various major cities in 1977 to attract attention to the campaign of the "Enough is Enough Committee" seeking federal legislation against child pornography. The private California based group also opposed the hiring of homosexuals as teachers, judges, and law enforcement officers because people in those professions are role models. Women's groups and so-called feminists have also squared off against the proliferation of pornography.

One determined New York based organization that calls itself WAP, Women Against Pornography, established headquarters at 42nd Street and Ninth Avenue in Manhattan and initiated twice-a-week tours through the porn jungle in Times Square. Businesswomen, housewives, and college girls were led past live sex show palaces, bust-out bars, X-rated movies, dope pushers, pimps, and teenage hookers into the peep shows and porn shops where they inspected heterosexual and homosexual loops, dildos, life-size blow-up dolls with rubber sex organs, and other exotic paraphernalia. Announcing goals of establishing pornography as a national feminist issue and educating the public so that pornography is no longer acceptable, WAP organized a major march in Times Square. Marchers from Sarah Lawrence, Smith, and Barnard colleges walked and chanted slogans as they moved along Broadway beside their blue jean clad sisters hoisting banners that identified them as Lesbians Against Pornography.

Groups were organized in other major cities and include the Los Angeles based Women Against Violence in Pornography and Media, and Chicago's People Against Pornography.

The anti-smut forces point to studies like a University of Southern California report that links exposure to violent pornography with increased aggression. Among the findings was statistical evidence that 87 percent of the molesters of female children and 77 percent of the molesters of male children studied, modeled their activities on pornography they had seen. Policewoman Barbara Pruitt of the Los Angeles Police Department's Abused Children Unit told a congressional committee that pornography is often found in the possession of people arrested for sexually abusing or murdering children. "On occasion . . . a suspect confessed his guilt of incest . . . quoting from passages out of a book on pedophilia," she said.

The USC study and Officer Pruitt's observations appear to contradict a controversial study several years earlier by the Presidential Commission on Obscenity and Pornography. The Commission reported in

1970 that its studies indicated pornography had no significant effect on sex crimes. President Richard M. Nixon heatedly repudiated the report that many had expected to turn up a strong link between pornography and sex crimes.

Anti-porn forces joined the criticism. They were already smarting over claims that sex crimes decreased in Denmark after restrictions on pornography were abolished. Critics pointed out that some minor offenses, such as voyeurism, were decriminalized, contributing to the misleading statistics.

In Boston, Marcia Womongold launched a one-woman holy war reminiscent of Carrie Nation, elbowing her way into adult bookstores armed with lipsticks, ice cream cones, and bottles of detergent, which she used to deface magazines she considered offensive. She once shot out the window of a Cambridge, Massachusetts, bookstore that carried copies of *Playboy* and *Penthouse*. Taken to court for the Harvard Square shooting, she was fined $20 and given a year's probation for shooting a firearm. Mrs. Womongold's battle dress included a T-shirt dominated by the one-word slogan, "Matriarchy."

Other forms of harassment have also been effective. In Lansing, Michigan, the owner of an adult bookstore that offered fingertip massage, photography models, and an escort service—all within sight of the state capitol building—was arrested 30 times in four years. Although he was never convicted, he said the arrests drained some $35,000 from his earnings for legal fees and other costs. In Flint, Michigan, the wife of a bar owner volunteered for decoy work with police arresting men seeking prostitutes. The Coalition Against Prostitution in Detroit picketed bars and motels frequented by hookers and recorded license numbers of their customers, as well as the locations of rooms used. Sometimes photographs were taken. After the film was developed and license numbers were traced to obtain addresses, postcards or letters were mailed to wives. The messages were simple and to the point. "Guess who your husband was with last night?"

In Ventura, California, citizens surreptitiously spray-painted vending racks at bus stops and street corners that hawked sex tabloids. In downstate Chenoa, Illinois, a businessman became so incensed over the showing of X-rated movies in his community that he bought the theater and discontinued the films.

Chicken porn is too gross for even many legal scholars, civil libertarians, and members of the smut industry. During an American Bar Association panel discussion of obscenity laws and freedom of the press in 1977, E. Donald Shapiro, dean of the New York Law School, said he considered pornography degrading to humans, but defended the right of access to pornography by adults. Nevertheless, he conceded that he drew the line at involving children in the production of the material or allowing them to see pornography.

"Weird Harold" Rubin, one of Chicago's leading figures in the pornography business until he retired after repeated arrests and closings of his stores, was blunt about restricting the material to adults. Rubin said he believes children should be neither models for pornography nor consumers. If his own seven-year-old son was either exposed to, or involved in, kiddie porn by a pornographer or a merchant, he told a city council investigative panel, he would not bother going to the police. He would take the law into his own hands.

The U.S. Customs Department, of course, has an ongoing campaign to ferret out kiddie porn being imported from, or routed through, foreign nations for sale in this country. Tons of kiddie porn have been destroyed. One seizure in Chicago, headed for customers in Illinois, Indiana, Wisconsin, and Minnesota, included magazines and 8-millimeter films. The material carried titles that included *Incest, Mini Boys, Schoolgirls and Boys, Child Love, Sexy Schoolgirls,* and *Teenage Discipline.* Many had sadistic or masochistic themes. Most of the material came from the Netherlands, while other magazines and films originated in Sweden and Denmark. The spokesman said that much of the pornography was apparently ordered through advertisements appearing in men's magazines.

One customer in a Chicago suburb was notified by mail from the U.S. Attorney's office in New York City that a magazine entitled *Girls of 14,* which he ordered from Europe, had been seized. He was advised that he could claim it if he would travel to New York and appear in court to testify that the magazine was not obscene.

¹ *Los Angeles Times,* March 15, 1977.

17.

The Protection of Children Against Sexual Exploitation Act

WILLIAM T. Coughlin was a social worker for five years and he saw children who were raped, maimed, and murdered. But he never felt as frustrated and desperate as he did the night he sat down and counted the options he had explored trying to protect his foster daughter and other members of his family.

He had sought legal protection for 18 months for the girl and his family, appearing before five criminal court judges, two juvenile court judges, and conferring with members of six police departments and a host of state's attorneys and probation and parole officers.

Ultimately, he put together a list of 31 different alternatives he had investigated. None of them worked. The sexual and emotional abuse of his foster daughter by her natural father, and the threats to the social worker's two younger daughters, continued uninterrupted.

Thomas J. Sitowski, the father, had a lengthy criminal record of nearly 20 years, with arrests for kidnapping, deviant sexual assault, robbery, and other felonies. According to Coughlin, he blandly admitted to Coughlin that he had beaten an eight-month-old daughter who died of brain injuries and that he had beaten and committed incest with the fourteen-year-old girl the social worker finally took into his own home.

Coughlin moved his family three times and placed his daughters and the older girl in private schools to avoid trouble with Sitowski. Each time, the career criminal found them, continued to molest his daughter, and continued the threats.

By March, 1976, Coughlin had exhausted all but one of the obvious options for protecting his family that he could conceive of. His last chance was another court hearing at which he was to testify against Sitowski. The judge dismissed the charges without listening to testimo-

ny. The defendant's civil rights were violated because the trial had not
begun within 160 days of his arrest, the jurist ruled.

Coughlin has recalled his actions many times since that day, talking
to policemen, therapists, newspaper reporters, television talk show
hosts, and as a lecturer to college classes. His description of the event is
always the same, always vivid, and always to the point.

"He walked out of court laughing. He said, 'Now, you fucker, I'm
gonna rape your daughter and stick her in my trunk. I'm gonna suffo-
cate her to death and there isn't a thing you can do.'

"And you know, he was right," says Coughlin. "He was right. There
wasn't a legal thing I could do." Desperate, his head pounding, the
social worker lurched to his car and pulled a pistol from the glove
compartment. He shot Sitowski five times. The sixth shot hit Sitowski's
attorney.

Coughlin turned and ran, heading for the hospital where he planned
to finish the job he had started, if his victim was still alive. Police cars
dashed by as he waited at a bus stop. The second attack was not necessary. Sitowski was dead. The attorney was gravely wounded, but would
recover. Coughlin, whose brother was a policeman, turned himself in.

There was some distress but not surprise among Coughlin's co-
workers at the DCFS offices in Chicago. There was some headshaking
and talk of "worker burnout." Coughlin commonly carried a workload
of 160 to 180 cases, and, at various times, he worked with some 200
abused children. He put in 14 to 16 hours a day trying to beat the
system. His troubles started almost immediately after employment
when he became personally and emotionally involved with his clients,
especially the children. When he took the abused girl into his home, he
knew he was violating DCFS regulations. But there appeared to be no
other recourse. She had run away from home, and if she was returned
she might not survive.

Coughlin had seen "children whose skulls were split open, arms torn
off, babies just brutally abused and used." Some, like Sitowski's infant
daughter, did not survive. The older girl lived, despite dreadful abuse
that included severe injuries to her skull that she suffered when she was
beaten on the head with a board pierced by a two-inch screw. Her face
and body were covered with scars. Her anus was distorted, and she had
contracted gonorrhea. Her internal organs were so badly damaged from
the disease and the sexual abuse that she had to have surgery.

According to Coughlin, her father began sexually abusing her when
she was three. He had regular intercourse with her, anal intercourse,
and he sometimes forced her into fellatio with him while he leafed
through copies of *Playboy* or looked at hard-core pornography. There

were times when he tied her to her bed and abused her. Almost from the time she could first remember, she was told that she was "just a female," and that "females are dirty." When she was thirteen, she ran away.

It was then that she first met Coughlin at the DCFS. She told him about the sexual attacks by her father and about beatings from her mother. Other people may not have believed the young girl's stories. Coughlin knew, however, that as bizarre as her tale might sound to some people it was probably true.

He inspected court, medical, and police records. He interviewed neighbors and relatives of the family, including the mother. Then he talked to Sitowski himself. The man readily admitted the beatings and sexual abuse. It was his right as a parent to treat his children as he wished, he said.

With assistance from Sitowski's wife, evidence was presented to a grand jury and he was charged with deviant sexual assault and aggravated incest. Coughlin was subpoenaed to testify at the grand jury hearing and in court. That was when Sitowski reputedly began threatening to rape and murder the Coughlin children.

Coughlin filed a new complaint, based on the threats. Within hours Sitowski was freed on bond, and that day he chased one of the social worker's daughters and some other neighborhood children down the street with a gun. Coughlin went to court again. And again. And again. Sitowski had excellent legal representation. He continued to remain free on bond, continued his threats, and continued to abuse his surviving children. The ordeal was devastating for Coughlin. The emotional pressure continued to build until it exploded outside the courtroom in a roar of gunfire.

Ironically, an investigation after the shooting disclosed that the judge had erred in dismissing the charges against Sitowski. Instead of 160 days, it was only 157 days between his arrest and the fateful day he appeared in court.

The same legal contrariness that had worked against Coughlin worked in his favor after he was charged with the shootings. He insisted to court-appointed psychiatrists that he was sane and that he knew his act was immoral and illegal. Nevertheless, he was found to be legally insane at the time of the shootings. And even though some 30 or 40 people witnessed the act, he was found to be not guilty of the slaying by reason of insanity. He spent several months in the Cook County jail, was briefly committed to a state hospital for psychiatric treatment, and then released.

Still under thirty years old, Coughlin emerged from the experience with his career in a shambles and a deep-seated bitterness at the ills afflicting the agency he once worked for. He was disillusioned as well with a criminal justice system that had failed him and that he considered responsible for forcing him to commit murder to protect several children from a dangerous psychotic and sadist.

During an appearance on the *Saturday Report,* a television program aired in Springfield, Illinois, he told an audience that front-line social service workers are faced with three options when they are employed by agencies like the DCFS:

1. Leave the agency when frustrations become so great they can no longer be dealt with;

2. Become a "mindless functionary" who no longer makes decisions, who processes endless paperwork and does not think about the consequences of his or her actions. "You have your children die. Then you make sure everything is covered up nice and neat so that when a child dies, you can say, 'Well, look, I did everything I was legally supposed to do.' "

3. Refuse to leave and refuse to become a mindless functionary. Those workers, Coughlin said, become so frustrated and dissatisfied with the corruption in the system that they can no longer function.

Coughlin detailed charges that the agency is so poorly established and supervised that many of the people hired to help others are themselves criminals and sexual deviants who buy and sell children, set up dependent children for prostitution and pornography, and knowingly license people as foster parents who have criminal records of child abuse and sexual assaults. Some of the social workers, he claimed, participate in the physical and sexual abuse of children on their own caseloads.

Coughlin knew children who ran away because they were beaten and sexually molested in their homes. When they were caught or turned themselves in to authorities, they appeared in juvenile court before judges who told them to go home, obey their parents, and stay where they belonged. The abuse would begin all over again. The juvenile courts, regardless of how much they may deny it, apparently embrace the philosophy that children are the property of their parents.

"That was my father's famous words, that I was his daughter and he would do whatever he wanted to," Coughlin's foster child recalled during a television interview more than two years after her dramatic rescue. "I remember going to the Department of Children and Family Services, and Daddy said, 'That's my daughter and I will do whatever I want to.' " The teenager added, "The DCFS more or less backed down."

The easy capitulation to Sitowski's threats was not all that unusual. According to Kenneth Wooden, of the National Coalition For Children's Justice, "many social workers have simply given up on the frequency with which young daughters and foster care daughters are used as sexual playthings by poorly chosen foster parents or real fathers with serious incest problems."[1]

Always reluctant to intervene in family matters, American society has held tightly to the tradition that a man's home is his castle, and his wife and children are his to do with as he pleased. Historically, horses and dogs were for years better protected under animal protection laws than children. In fact, an innovative and imaginative judge in upstate New York in 1874 declared a little girl to be a dumb animal so that she could be protected under the cruelty to animals statutes. It was the first court opinion in the country protecting a child.

The baffling court system, with its overcrowded dockets and laws that for technical, legislative, or sociological reasons have become unenforceable, has added to the difficulties. Laws have been eroded, reinterpreted, and circumvented until they have become so vague that prosecution is often impossible.

And although long jail terms appear to be popular for people who exploit children through prostitution or pornography, few pimps, pornographers, or pedophiles draw terms as severe as those ordered in the New Orleans Boy Scout prosecutions. Law enforcement agencies often are too undermanned and underbudgeted to do much more than skim the surface in dealing with the problem.

Once defendants are brought into the court system, they are helped more than hindered by perplexing and contrary local, state, and federal laws. In Iowa in the late 1970s a sixteen-year-old girl could appear legally in a porno film. But she had to wait two years until she was eighteen before she could, by law, watch the movie she performed in. In most states, a child could be taken into custody and placed involuntarily in a treatment program if he or she were a drug addict. The same child could not be picked up and held involuntarily in a treatment program if the child was selling his or her body.

Lengthy appeals moving through the state and federal court systems can drag on for years. In October, 1978, three men convicted in Atlanta of interstate shipment of obscene films won a reversal from the Fifth U.S. Circuit Court of Appeals in a case that had started on May 16, 1974. That was when one of six cardboard containers labeled "breaker conduits" burst open in the Delta Air Lines shipping department disclosing the true contents—dozens of reels of pornographic 8-millimeter film. The Appeals Court ruled that the district judge erred in his instructions to the jury when he defined the legal criteria for determining if the film was obscene.

Articulate and agile defense attorneys play upon the sympathy of legally unsophisticated jurors who are often kept in the dark about previous criminal records or evidence accumulated against defendants. Plea bargaining by defense attorneys and overworked and often inexperienced prosecutors also works to the benefit of the sex merchants. Somehow, many citizens and court officials still view pornography as a victimless crime, and there is a marked tendency on the part of judges toward leniency in sentencing.

Court rulings and sentences are bewildering and inconsistent. In late 1979, a federal judge in New York ruled that a magazine called *Lolita Love No. 13*, which suggestively displayed the genitals of a little girl on several pages, was not obscene because only one person was shown in the photos. About a year earlier, New York Supreme Court Justice Gerald Marks ordered two-month sentences for two men convicted of selling child porn films. The statutes provided maximum terms of seven years.

Also in New York, Edward Mishkin, one of the country's most industrious and infamous child pornographers, was arrested after a year-long investigation and after some 1,200 films and magazines were confiscated. One-third of the pornography involved children. Mishkin pleaded guilty, and, despite a career that dates back to a pornography arrest in 1936, was sentenced to only 27 weekends in jail. Within a week, Mishkin was again arrested. He was among a half-dozen men charged as a result of the work of undercover officers Rice and D'elia in their Times Square bookshop.

During Mishkin's long career, he became nationally known as one of the nation's premier child pornographers, battling one of his convictions all the way to the U.S. Supreme Court. The conviction was upheld. In 1955 he was cited for contempt of the U.S. Senate for refusing to answer questions before a commission, headed by Senator Estes Kefauver, investigating juvenile delinquency.

Investigators estimate that Mishkin has earned as much as $1.5 million per year as chief of Wholesale Books, Inc., which police described as the hub of a massive operation manufacturing, producing, and distributing pornography.

One of Mishkin's arrests in the mid 70s netted what police described as more than $1 million worth of obscene books, magazines, and films. Most of the color films, which were used as evidence, showed children from ten to fifteen years old "involved in sexual conduct, sadomasochistic activity, and bestiality," according to the Manhattan district attorney.

Mishkin was also reputedly tied to a shadowy career criminal known as a behind-the-scenes financier of pornography, gay bars, and after-hours joints. The mobster was said to be shaking down other producers of porn films and pirating their products for distribution through Mishkin's companies if they did not pay tribute. At one time he was arrested for torching two gay bars, competitors of others in which he had a financial interest. Although Mishkin's alleged silent partner has had numerous brushes with the law, there have been few convictions. Frustration is an old story for police and prosecutors dealing with pornography and other forms of vice.

In Los Angeles, Sergeant Martin and the local district attorney's office lost what they had considered a strong case involving charges of contributing to the delinquency of a minor. The charges were filed against a producer and the mother of a child used in pornography. The prosecution was unable to prove—despite the presence of a pornographic magazine featuring the child in salacious poses—that the mother and the producer had specifically intended to contribute to the little girl's delinquency.

Assistant State's Attorney Gemignani of Winnebago County, Illinois, was disappointed after winning two cases involving serious sexual abuse of children, each of which would appear to warrant heavy penalties. In one instance, using a broad and progressive statute that deals with indecent liberties with children under sixteen, he convicted a twenty-five-year-old woman who had copulated with a ten-year-old boy and induced him to perform cunnilingus. After a spirited sentencing hearing, she was given probation. The other case involved a man who pleaded guilty to charges that he had engaged in periodic sexual intercourse with a girl from the time she was eight until she was eleven and became pregnant. The girl had an abortion. The defendant was placed on probation.

Gemignani speculated that the statute itself was probably partly at fault for the light sentences because it stipulated penalties that were sometimes too severe and left judges little, if any, leeway between imposing a minimum prison sentence of four years or probation.

New York City Family Court Judge Margaret Taylor was quoted in the *New York Post* as observing that commercial sex between a fourteen-year-old girl prostitute and a client was "recreational," not illegal.[2] The same article quoted Father Ritter as blaming Manhattan District Attorney Robert Morgenthau for inadequate enforcement. "We have a

district attorney, Mr. Morgenthau, who considers prostitution a victimless crime and unworthy of serious prosecution," he said.

The street priest referred to the arrest of a known New York pimp
who was collared while he was in bed with a fifteen-year-old girl whom
he had forced into prostitution. "A very benevolent assistant DA, following the policies of Mr. Morgenthau," Ritter complained, permitted
the pimp to plead guilty to a reduced charge of disorderly conduct, and
"an equally benevolent judge gave him a $100 fine." The amount of the
fine was about the amount earned by the teenage prostitute in a half
day, the exasperated street priest pointed out.

Beset with the same problems as prosecutors in most other major
cities, Morgenthau responded by pointing out that criminals know how
to take advantage of the jam-up of criminal cases in the courts. Complaining that only two in every 1,000 cases were followed to successful
conclusions in New York City courts in 1978, he said that knowledgeable criminals are practically guaranteed dismissal of charges or plea-
bargain agreements that drastically reduce punishment. At the core of
the legal logjam is a 1971 U.S. Supreme Court ruling that permits
anyone charged with a crime, felony, or misdemeanor that carries a
maximum term of six months or more to demand a jury trial.   .

Morgenthau attracted additional criticism from Katz. The ASPCC
chief complained that it is too difficult to get the office seriously involved
in prosecuting cases of sexual exploitation of children. "They give you a
lot of lip service but they don't give you a lot of action," he said. Katz
believes that prosecutors in New York, and in other jurisdictions, are
not really sure how they feel about the problem.

He noted that there was a law in New York state that stipulated that
a child under seventeen could not legally consent to sex. "But I had a
prosecutor say to me . . . he wasn't going to prosecute a case. And then
we got the nitty gritty of it, he says, 'Well, the kid's a junky. Been a
whore for two years, and . . . uh . . . was agreeable to the act.' " Katz
objected that nothing in the law indicates that procuring for a child
prostitute was not a crime simply because the child consented to being
sexually exploited. The child was fifteen. Nevertheless, the assistant
DA elected to use his prosecutorial discretion and declined to prefer
charges. The girl was sent home to Pennsylvania. The pimp who had
been living off her earnings for two years was never taken to court.

Child prostitution and child pornography are difficult to prosecute
and the cases are often lost when they are taken into the courts. Child-
porn models or young prostitutes may be reluctant to testify because
they fear punishment from disgraced parents. Older children may appear competent when they are talking in a prosecutor's office of a sex

crime, but they often fail miserably in the courtroom. They may be intimidated by the imposing surroundings of the court and the presence of the judge. Or they become terrified and confused under the merciless cross-examination of a determined defense attorney. Sometimes they cry, or they giggle. Their minds go blank, they balk or become sullen when they are asked to describe, in legally acceptable terminology, what happened to them.

A young prosecutor can build up a much better conviction record trying a dozen or more burglary cases in the same time it might take to prosecute a single case of child molestation that is likely to be lost in court, or reversed on appeal if a conviction is somehow obtained.

During a three-year period in Winnebago County, Illinois, seven obscenity cases were tried and in almost each instance the defendants were represented by the same attorney or law firm. Each case was a jury trial and each conviction was appealed through the Illinois Appellate Court, the Illinois Supreme Court, and through the federal court system to the U.S. Supreme Court. Assistant State's Attorney Gemignani told the House Subcommittee on Crime that the experience could understandably have "a chilling effect on the desire of any prosecuting attorney to take on the prosecution of an obscenity case." The law firm was known to have attorneys who flew from one jurisdiction to another to handle identical cases in particular areas or regions. The State's Attorney, just to keep up, would have to have a full-time prosecutor responsible for nothing but obscenity cases. And no county or state can afford such extravagant expertise. Most frustrating of all, even if the resources and desire were present, Gemignani said, it would be "conceivable in Illinois that one arrest in each county could produce 102 simultaneous prosecutions on any given day and, three or four years later, when prosecutions and appeals were concluded, we would have nothing more than a misdemeanor conviction of an underling who would be fined or merely serve a minimum term in jail."

Nevertheless, more effort must be made to prosecute the sexual entrepreneurs who deal in children's bodies. "Until you make it very unpopular and very unsuccessful for people to deal with children commercially in a sexual fashion, then people are going to do it just about any time they want to. Any time it's profitable," Katz insists. "But if you really crack down, then people realize, 'Hey, there's other things I can do,' and they aren't going to mess with kids. It's really a very effective way to deal with it. Make it tough. Make it hard for them to do. Make the penalties real, and these people will find something else to do."

Forty-seven states had laws pertaining to the dissemination of obscene material to minors in the late 1970s. Only six states, however, had laws specifically prohibiting the participation of minors in obscene performances that could be harmful to them, and these were not always worded carefully enough to be helpful. Some of the statutes proved to be too weak to support strong prosecution. Most of the statutes generally required that the adult pornographers be caught in the act or that a witness be willing to testify.

Pedophiles often went free because many states did not allow sworn testimony from young children without corroboration. Since the acts were seldom witnessed by people old enough or willing to testify, there were no prosecutions.

Even where children were permitted to testify, they usually made poor witnesses. Adjudication of sex crimes is difficult enough with adult victims. It can be totally devastating with children. The American criminal justice system is an adversary system, and defense attorneys traditionally draw out sex cases as long as possible with continuance after continuance and brutal cross-examination of victims that concentrates on the most intimate and embarrassing aspects of the crime. The victim often weakens, breaks, and gives up.

Roger Simon, a columnist for the *Chicago Sun-Times,* told of a three-year-old girl who was found to have a venereal disease after being taken to a hospital complaining of vaginal pains.[3] Her mother's boyfriend had molested her several times, she told hospital and police authorities. Police took the man into custody, but he was freed the next day. A Cook County State's Attorney spokesman said, in effect, that the word of a three-year-old was not good enough to warrant prosecution. The spokesman, Charles Hartman, explained, in relation to the three-year-old, that a witness must "be competent to testify. You have to understand the meaning of an oath. You have to know the difference between truth and falsehood. You have to be able to perceive, store, and relate facts. I don't know of any case where someone of the tender age of three has testified."

A Chicago judge later told Simon that witnesses, even as young as three, are not automatically disqualified in Illinois courts. It is up to judges to qualify young witnesses through questioning. But in this case, charges were not filed in the first place.

Prosecutors pressed charges of indecent solicitation and of contributing to the delinquency of a minor in another case involving two men accused of taking nude photographs of a nine-year-old girl they picked up with her six-year-old sister on a Chicago street. Police said they confiscated 128 photographs of nude little girls from the apartment of one of the men, the owner-director of a summer camp for seven- to fifteen-year-old girls in Minocqua, Wisconsin. The other man, who had a previous arrest for indecent solicitation of a child, was a travel agent.

Attorneys immediately challenged the girl's competency to testify after she took the stand in the trial and admitted that she did not understand the meaning of the oath or why she was "sworn to tell the truth." She was permitted to testify, however, and said she had gone to the apartment where she was made to take her clothes off by the camp owner who told her, "You either do it, or else." "I was really scared," she said.

Despite the photographs and testimony, the judge upheld a motion by the defense for acquittal. Among the points cited as grounds for acquittal were charges that the child was incompetent to testify because she did not understand the meaning of the oath, and that there is nothing lewd or lascivious about taking photographs of a nude child.

Unfortunately, pornographers do not invite the police or press when they film, and they do not volunteer to testify against each other. Most states have relied on laws outlining offenses, such as contributing to the delinquency of a minor, impairing the morals of a minor, or taking indecent liberties with a minor.

As difficult as it is to successfully prosecute pornographers, molesters, and pimps who prey on children, the legal climate has greatly improved since 1978. Reacting to the revelations of Drs. Osanka and Densen-Gerber, which led to public outrage over the widespread sexual abuse of children, the federal government and many state legislatures enacted stiff new laws aimed at the trade in kiddie sex.

When Drs. Osanka and Densen-Gerber began their campaign, five federal laws prohibited the distribution of obscene material. One law curbed the mailing of obscene material, another banned importation of obscene material, a third prohibited the broadcast of obscenity, and two others ruled out the interstate transportation or use of common carriers to transport objectional material. The Anti-Pandering Act of 1968 additionally authorized citizens to request that there be no further postal delivery of unsolicited mailings or advertisements they considered to be sexually offensive.

But no federal statute specifically forbade child pornography. And although the White Slave Traffic Act of 1910, more commonly known as the Mann Act, prohibited transportation of females across state lines for purposes of prostitution, there was no similar provision to protect boys.

The Odyssey Institute provided sample state and federal legislation. The Institute recommended that persons who use, or permit children to be used, in the production of sexually explicit material for commercial distribution through interstate commerce be considered in violation of federal statutes. Additional legislation should be passed, Odyssey recommended, mandating states to adopt prescribed model acts prohibiting the use of children or the permitted use of children in the production of sexually explicit motion or still pictures for commercial distribution. Odyssey suggested that the mandate could be in the form of amendments to federal appropriation laws for educational aid or other funding programs.

Recommendations on the state level included proposals to forbid licensing for any child models to participate in the production of sexually explicit pictures for commercial distribution. The proscription would be part of a more general licensing requirement for all commercial use of minors for posing or modeling. The use of children in pornography would also be covered in the obscenity law, it was recommended.

On February 6, 1978, one year and two days after Drs. Osanka and Densen-Gerber held their "closed press conference" in Chicago, President Jimmy Carter signed a new federal law. The law prohibited anyone—including parents and guardians—from using children under sixteen or enticing them to be depicted in sexual acts, and from shipping child pornography through the mails or in interstate or foreign commerce.

The new federal law, known as the Protection of Children Against Sexual Exploitation Act, also expands the Mann Act and provides a maximum penalty of 10 years imprisonment and a $10,000 fine for persons who transport minors, including males as well as females, under the age of eighteen across state lines to engage in prostitution, live sex shows, or other prohibited sexual conduct.

The Act originated as H. R. 8059 and had 134 cosponsors in the House of Representatives. Introduced into the Senate by Charles Mathias of Maryland, a member of the Senate Subcommittee to Investigate Juvenile Delinquency, it was an amalgamation of bills presented in Congress during the peak period of public outcry. The final form of the bill was negotiated in a conference committee.

At the last minute, after the insistence of Congressman John Conyers, Jr., subcommittee chairman, the word "obscene" was inserted. Otherwise, the veteran Michigan legislator warned, the bill could be interpreted as banning the use of nude and partly nude children in art magazines and in other places where the intent and use was obviously not pornographic. Neither the House nor the Senate versions of the bill had previously included the word.

Police officers, prosecutors, state legislators, social workers, and others testified at the hearings about the difficulty of locating and prosecuting the people who sexually exploit children by the use of pornography. As a result, the new law requires the Federal Bureau of Investigation to help track down producers of pornography distributed across state lines. Involvement of the FBI provides help at the federal level that state and local authorities can use to share information and coordinate investigations. The FBI was previously criticized for ignoring the traffic in child sex and leaving city, county, and state law enforcement agencies to cope with interstate investigations as best they could, despite their lack of national resources.

For a time, the National Coalition for Children's Justice stepped into the role of a national resource center for investigating or prosecuting kiddie sex rings, according to Kenneth Wooden. The FBI, in fact, was so unconcerned that agents once walked out of a meeting in Boston between Massachusetts and Louisiana police probing a major combine of pederasts involved in sexually exploiting boys in several states. The FBI agents never returned. "Because of their irresponsibility, untold numbers of children are currently enduring sexual exploitation that all decent people abhor," Wooden maintained.

Even with FBI help, there was no doubt that locating the producers of child pornography would be a difficult job. Recommendations that amendments be tied to the bills to include distributors and salesmen were accepted in the Senate and rejected in the House. Experts in the Justice Department warned that any law that went beyond prosecuting the producers could have been declared unconstitutional because of conflict with First Amendment guarantees of free speech.

Even the American Civil Liberties Union endorsed the initial Senate bill as it was proposed, without an amendment to include distributors as defendants. "Because the proposed legislation carefully distinguishes between production and distribution of such materials, the ACLU supports the bill," said Martin Guggenheim, an attorney with the organization's Juvenile Rights Project.

Some of those who urged going after the distributors did so because the producers of child pornography were so difficult to track down. Senator William Roth of Delaware, who introduced an amendment to the Senate bill to include distributors, described them as conducting "hit-and-run operations in cheap hotel rooms, deserted beaches, or an isolated stand of woods, leaving few tracks behind them." John Keeney, U.S. Deputy Assistant Attorney General, confirmed that federal prosecutors found it hard to establish where the photography took place because the operations were so mobile.

Representative Dale Kildee, a former high school teacher from Flint, Michigan, and a freshman lawmaker who introduced the House bill, also urged an outright ban on the sale of child porn because the films were "usually made in hideaways seldom discovered by police. To deal with the problem effectively, you have to cut off the sales, to cut off the profit motive," he said.

Although the new law was an improvement over the old statutes, like every other law, it was less than perfect. Critics pointed to the word "commerce" as a major flaw because it means the federal law can be used only when a commercial transaction is involved.

William Katz of the ASPCC was one of those who complained. He contended that the focus on "commerce" is evidence that the Justice Department "has an unrealistic attitude toward child pornography. The feds have adopted an attitude that if organized crime is not involved it is not a high priority item."

Legislators were not unaware of the difficulties of weeding loopholes from the new statute. One of the basic problems, in addition to the knotty question of distributors and First Amendment rights, was successfully skirting the cloudy issue of obscenity in molding the new statute. In accordance with Osanka's recommendations, the focus eventually became child abuse rather than the murkier area of obscenity.

Osanka urged that the legislators take care to word legislation with sufficient precision to avoid "time consuming and often futile debates on the prevailing definitions of obscenity and pornography. Debates do not protect children.

"The essential decency and fairness of this nation compel us to act on behalf of those children who cannot protect themselves from vicious and dangerous abuses committed by those who seek only a profit," he stressed.

He urged that legislators do their best to frame a law so specific that even the act of selling child pornography would be interpreted as participating in child abuse and neglect. "I realize that these are extreme measures, but the socially corrupting nature of child pornography and the current inability of the criminal justice system to stop it demand strong protective legislation," he insisted.

"In my view, a person who purchases child pornography is a party to child abuse since his purchase will ensure a profit for the pornographer and thereby guarantee abuse of additional children through the production of new items. The purchase is also a reward to the pornographer for the child abuse he has already commissioned. Child pornography clearly constitutes child abuse and neglect with potential for immediate and long-term damage to the children and possibly the adult readers as well. Regardless of whether or not a person is involved in the production, distribution, or sale of child pornography, the person should be considered a party to child abuse and neglect," Dr. Osanka testified.

He added that persons who coerce children into pornographic activities are violating the youngsters' civil rights. "The sexual abuse of children for commercial pornographic purposes is not guaranteed by the First Amendment. Some may debate the degree of obscenity that is involved in the sexual exploitation of children, but none can deny that such insidious manipulations are clearly child abuse and/or neglect . . . Children in American society are conditioned to obey adults, and very young children operationally do not have the right of refusal," he said. "It is a total exploitation, with the exception, perhaps, of some streetwise boys fourteen to eighteen, and some streetwise girls."

It was noted that adult porn had already been largely accepted on the basis that the performers were considered consenting adults, not minors. Thus, since they were not prepubescent children, they had a right to do as they pleased with their bodies, time, and minds.

Dr. Osanka pointed out that children, on the other hand, do not have the intellectual capacity to make judgments about becoming involved in pornography or prostitution. "They have the right to be raised as normal human beings insofar as that is possible. If they want to become abnormal later on, that's their own choice."

Penalties for importing and exploiting kiddie porn should be severe enough to remove the profit, he recommended. It was not social or cultural need, but individual greed that produced the wholesale introduction of child pornography, the sociologist averred.

Charles Rembar, a New York City attorney who specializes is obscenity cases and constitutional law, agreed with the need for a new canon to ban the transportation, distribution, and sale of child pornography, without mention of the word "obscene," by focusing on the protection of children.

"In my opinion, there is no way to deal with the evil you're facing other than through the sale of publications themselves," he advised. The bill under consideration was a good one and did "not run afoul of the Constitution," the attorney concluded. Rembar is known for his role as counsel for such literary works as *Lady Chatterley's Lover, Fanny Hill,* and *Tropic of Cancer.*

Civil libertarians argued that prosecution of distributors and vendors of kiddie porn would trample First Amendment rights. Representatives of the legitimate movie industry also cautioned that some bills were so broad and repressive that they would prohibit films like *The Exorcist* and *Romeo and Juliet.* Both films featured juveniles in sexually explicit scenes.

Dr. Osanka warned that child pornographers probably hoped that legislators and the judicial system would bog down in lengthy debates over First Amendment and obscenity definitions, thereby postponing meaningful action against child pornography. If that happened, he further cautioned, there would be "an avalanche of depictions of the sexual abuse of children."

Drs. Osanka and Denser-Gerber testified with several other experts at a hearing before the Subcommittee on Crime in Washington, D.C., on May 23, 1977. The hearings continued on May 25, June 10, and September 20. Drs. Osanka and Densen-Gerber brought lockerboxes of evidence, including films, playing cards, and magazines.

Dr. Densen-Gerber drew sharp objections from subcommittee chairman John Conyers of Michigan and Representative Allen Ertel of Pennsylvania when she repeatedly waved copies of kiddie sex magazines before television cameras and read obscenities from their covers.

"It serves no purpose to show the magazines. Please try to restrict your comments to the merits or demerits of the legislation," Conyers admonished. Ertel complained that he did not want his preteen children to see the material on the evening news.

"So why don't you clean it up so I won't have any magazines to show?" Dr. Densen-Gerber shot back.

Displaying lurid playing cards labeled *Lollitots,* magazines such as *Moppets* and *Baby Dolls,* and paperback titles included *Breaking in Their Granddaughter,* Dr. Densen-Gerber advised that her seventeen-year-old daughter had purchased some of the material in Washington that weekend. Not only is posing for such pornography harmful to the child models, she held, but buyers of the material were encouraged by the product to act out their own fantasies and abuse their children.

"There is nothing good about this. No First Amendment good I can possibly see in telling a man to go home and have intercourse with his nine-year-old daughter. If I had to give up a portion of my First Amendment rights to stop this stuff, I'd be willing to do it," she dramatically asserted.

Dr. Densen-Gerber was admittedly, and proudly, emotional in her testimony. "We have to be emotional when it comes to our children," she told the committee. "We definitely should have many more programs for children and to protect our children. They are in extreme danger."

She reiterated that she was trained in law as well as in medicine, and that as a law student she was taught that the task of a lawyer is to defend both sides. "I do not think there are two sides in abusing a child. I do not want to listen to those games. I do not want to listen to them being played while the American family is falling apart," she asserted. "You can be so liberal you no longer protect. There are more ways of being destroyed than just being controlled." Referring to press criticism that the legal mind trains one to no longer feel, she suggested that if that was true the number of lawyers in Congress should be trimmed. "We have to have *people* making laws," she insisted. "That's extremely important."

Ruffled feathers of congressman put off by her aggressive presentation were ignored. "Coming from my medical training," she told one lawmaker, "you cannot clean a gangrenous wound by remote control. You have to get in there, you have to dig it, you have to even smell the tissue to see what is diseased and what is not. I think people have to know how bad it is."

Dr. Densen-Gerber was prevented from showing three films she brought with her to the Subcommittee on Select Education hearings. One of the films depicted an eight-year-old boy and his ten-year-old sister in a variety of sexual acts. The film was produced in New York State by the children's mother. Another film, shot in a motel room in California, featured three boys between eleven and eighteen years old. The third film was purchased in Chicago and showed two boys and two girls participating in almost every conceivable sexual combination.

Additional hearings were conducted in Los Angeles, New York, and Washington, D.C. during May and June by the Congressional Committee on Education and Labor's Subcommittee on Select Education.

The Judicial Committee concerned itself with criminal ramifications, penal sanctions, and questions of the First Amendment. The Subcommittee on Select Education focused on the Child Abuse Prevention and Treatment Act itself, and on questions of obscenity.

Still other hearings were held in Chicago and Washington by the Senate subcommittee to Investigate Juvenile Delinquency. An undercover agent who infiltrated a ring that specialized in transporting young boy prostitutes across state lines and a seventeen-year-old boy prostitute who acted in porn films were among those who testified in Chicago.

Early in the proceedings, Senator John Culver of Iowa advised that a new law alone would not solve the problem. He averred that it would require a coordinated effort involving the Justice and Labor departments, Health, Education, and Welfare, and other government agencies.

Legislation to protect children from exploitation in pornography obviously fell within the limits of constitutional law. The problem was in framing it to fit the definition of constitutional law as defined by the Supreme Court.

Dr. Osanka's fears were not without basis. There was strong division among legislators, law enforcement officials, and members of the legal and sociology professions over the focus of the new statutes. Should they zero in on the production of the material—strong child abuse laws—or deal with it as obscenity? Other questions of privacy, sexual equality, relationships between federal and state governments, coordination of activities between different police agencies, and rules governing testimony by minors further muddied the legal waters.

The controversy produced a flurry of bills at both the federal and state levels. Dozens of proposals came from a wide variety of sources. An aide to the mayor of New York proposed defining child pornography as obscene, per se, so that police could be empowered to seize it as contraband, as they do weapons or drugs. No judicial review would be required. As the laws were then framed, he said, judicial reviews, appeals, and other judicial maneuverings could commonly go on for 18 months before a conviction could be obtained and confirmed.

United States Attorney David Marston in Philadelphia recommended using a federal law enacted in the late nineteenth century that prohibited involuntary servitude of children. The statute was used in the 1880s in a case involving ethnic Italian children who were being forced to perform as street musicians in New York. It carries penalties of up to five years imprisonment and a $5,000 fine.

Some spokesmen, like Elmer Gertz, a nationally known legal authority and professor at the John Marshall Law Center in Chicago, suggested that existing laws were probably effective enough if they were only used. "Legislators and law enforcement officials tend to think in terms of new legislation instead of looking at the books to see what is already there," he said. "The attitude is: To hell with the old law—let's go for a new one." Frequently, however, "the new law is poorly drafted and very ineffective."[4]

Gertz favored using child abuse laws to prosecute child pornography because they pose fewer problems than obscenity prosecutions. It is easier to frame indictments, easier to try cases, and easier to obtain convictions using child abuse laws, he insisted.

Additional arguments pointed out that such matters as First Amendment protections, taste, and esthetic subjectivity are not, and should not, be factors in dealing with the sexual exploitation of children. Supporters of the child abuse approach held that it was time to stop debating the non-productive question of what is pornographic or obscene and address the more relevant question of the harm it inflicts.

Proponents of using obscenity laws persisted that there can be no legitimate argument that the First Amendment was ever intended to protect those who sexually abuse or exploit children.

Opening the House Judiciary Committee hearings, Chairman Peter Rodino of New Jersey observed that children were being victimized in many cities "by adults engaged in the production of porno magazines and films, or in the procurement of prostitutes for customers in other states. It would be difficult to overestimate the emotional and physical suffering of these youngsters, boys as well as girls," he said. "Degraded and humiliated, treated as commodities, not human beings, they face their adult years scarred by their experiences and unable to form lasting relationships."

The campaign, with the massive publicity it generated, made things hot for the entrepreneurs in child sex. But reformers knew that public interest would fade only too soon. Strong new state laws with a minimum of loopholes were also needed. State legislators rushed to strengthen and to more clearly define existing laws or to pass new ones. By the beginning of 1980, 36 states and several cities had laws dealing specifically with child pornography.

Some of the legislation is minutely specified and similar to the federal law, describing the proscribed behavior in precise detail. Other lawmakers took a more casual and less desirable approach, merely adding a category to existing obscenity legislation. Sanctions range from $500 fines and 30 days imprisonment for first convictions to $50,000 and 15 years. The penalties may be sufficiently severe for someone shooting pictures of neighborhood children for his private collection. But even the maximum penalties are inadequate for sophisticated pornographers dealing in multimillion-dollar operations.

In some states, confusion between adult and child pornography could damage the potential usefulness of the protective statutes.

Steve Hutchinson, legal counsel for Odyssey Institute, considers one of the most serious flaws in legislation adopted by most states to be the lack of a clear mandate on law enforcement agencies to carry out spirited enforcement policies. "It's one thing to have a law on the books, but if nobody goes out and does any case finding or prosecution, you haven't really accomplished much," he maintains. Generally, however, the laws have given law enforcement agencies and prosecutors valuable new tools.

In Connecticut, Dr. Densen-Gerber's home state, a law was passed making the presence of venereal disease in a child under the age of twelve evidence of child abuse and neglect. The law was adopted after two infants, one nine months old and the other eighteen months old, were found to have gonorrhea of the throat—indicating that they had been involved in fellatio with a diseased child molester.

A Ventura County machinist was one of the first persons prosecuted under a new California law after he allegedly tried to sell 28 copies of a film showing four boys engaging in sexual activities for $4 each. The machinist, who had no previous police record and claimed he accidentally acquired the films at a swap meet, was fined $12,500, given a 30-day jail sentence, and placed on four years probation.

Complaints that movies shown in New York City showed prepubescent children as young as nine engaging in sex acts with other children or with adults led to passage of a strict new state law. The law made it a felony offense punishable by prison terms from one to 15 years for any adult who encouraged or permitted the use of a child in pornography or who promoted or sold child pornography.

The statute applied to parents who permitted their children to be used in pornography, to film producers and others who made the pornographic material, and to those who sold it. About the only people connected with pornography who might escape the sanctions were the children themselves and individuals such as ticket sellers and ushers in theaters.

Defense attorneys soon found weaknesses in the new state law. In upstate Rochester, definition of the word "performance" led to dismissal of charges against a thirty-one-year-old man accused of using a twelve-year-old girl in a sexual performance that "lewdly displayed her genitals." The grand jury indictment and charges were dismissed during pretrial hearings when the judge agreed with defense contentions that the facts of the case did not fit the alleged crime.

The section of the law under which the indictment was returned read: "A person is guilty of the use of a child in a sexual performance if he . . . employs, authorizes or induces a child . . . to engage in a sexual performance." The legislature had defined performance in the law as a visual representation before an audience, and according to the judge there was no "performance."

Four years later, in May 1981, the New York State Court of Appeals struck down a portion of the code as being in violation of First Amendment rights. In a 5-2 decision, the Court determined that the State could not ban the use of children in portrayals of sexual activity unless it could prove that the depictions were legally obscene. Portions of the law increasing penalties for the use of children in material determined to be legally obscene, and for persons who promote or sell the materials were untouched. Children's advocates were alarmed at the ruling and concerned that similar statutes in 21 other states could be jeopardized if the courts followed New York's example.

In New Jersey, Assemblyman Donald T. DiFrancesco introduced a bill making it a high misdemeanor to exploit children under the age of sixteen by permitting them to pose for or appear in pornographic photographs or films. The statute, signed into law by Governor Brendan Byrne, also restricted sale of the material and set penalties of up to 12 years in prison.

Illinois enacted twin legislation: one law provided up to three years imprisonment for anyone soliciting a juvenile for prostitution and pandering involving children under sixteen years old; another provided a life sentence in prison and a $50,000 fine for anyone using children in the production of pornographic material and a maximum of 10 years in prison and a $25,000 fine for vendors of pornography. Governor James Thompson signed both bills but amended the child pornography legislation, scaling penalties down to 10 years in prison for producers and three-year prison terms for persons involved in its sale.

The new laws were barely on the books before they were tested. The first arrest occurred when police picked up twenty-two-year-old John M. Sundell and accused him of recruiting Chicago high school girls to appear in sex films. Police knew for two months that a young man was approaching girls, and telling them that he specialized in fashion photographs and nude studies of females.

A fifteen-year-old girl he gave a business card to showed it to her mother who contacted police. The girl and a policewoman later appeared at the photographer's apartment and were paid with checks totalling $185 after he showed them dozens of pornographic photos of young girls and told them that he planned to perform with them in front of his cameras. The policewoman stepped into another room where she used a concealed radio to call other officers. Moments later a raiding party burst into the apartment.

Police officers reported finding "boxes and boxes" of movie film, slides, and pictures of juveniles and adults engaging in sexual activity. Receipts from numerous photo developers around the city indicated that Sundell used conventional laboratories to develop his materials. The discovery led police to appeal to film laboratories to notify them when lewd or obscene photographs of children were received.

Sundell subsequently pleaded guilty to a single charge of soliciting a minor for child pornography. The other charges were stricken. On June 16, 1978, he was sentenced to 18 months of felony probation.

Another arrest netted a man from Chicago's shabby uptown neighborhood who, police said, had nude photographs of about 100 boys when he was apprehended. He pleaded guilty to five counts of child pornography and solicitation of minors for pornography. A judge placed him on two years probation, with instructions to submit to a psychiatric examination.

One of the first people tried under the new federal law was Kevin Menard, who was convicted in Portland, Maine, of two counts of shipping and distributing films of young boys engaged in sexual activity. The thirty-year-old Warwick, Rhode Island, man told the jury that he did not realize the films were legally obscene. He was sentenced to two concurrent five-year prison terms. Federal District Judge Edward T. Gignous remarked that he hoped that sentence would serve as "a deterrent to others in similar activity." A California man was convicted under the Protection of Children Against Sexual Exploitation Act before Menard's guilty verdict.

The new laws, while not perfect, were substantial improvements. Dr. Osanka, however, was disappointed that the federal statute was not more precise in dealing with child molestation and would have preferred some provisions for funding research programs in child pornography. "Indirectly, it did create some funding for what is called 'demonstration projects,'" the sociologist pointed out. "But it's for what they call the 'nice people sexual abusers'—and they do need treatment and concern for people who are not long-term sexual abusers—but we're still doing nothing to prevent future (John) Gacys."

1 Testimony during hearings before the House Judiciary Committee's Subcommittee on Crime.
2 *New York Post,* November 7, 1979.
3 *Chicago Sun-Times,* March 15, 1977.
4 *Chicago Tribune,* May 18, 1977.

18.

The Offenders

CHILD pornographers and other adults who sexually exploit children are among the most difficult criminal offenders to deal with. They not only show no remorse for their actions, but they are often arrogantly and openly proud of their skills and may even consider themselves pioneers who will someday be recognized for leading the way to a new, freer society.

Representatives of social agencies, religious counselors, psychologists, and law enforcement officers whose lives and careers are touched by the organized sexual abuse of children must face those problems when they deal with offenders.

The personalities of offenders as well as their activities can be so repugnant that even skilled therapists and social workers often find it difficult to block out their personal emotions.

Arnold Sherman, executive director of the Youth Network Council, a confederation of more than 70 community-based agencies serving young people and their families in the metropolitan Chicago area, readily admits that he has been confronted with some individuals so obnoxious that he could not personally interact with them in his professional role. Sherman is articulate, energetic, and dedicated. And he is a bearded veteran of more than a decade of service with national youth advocacy organizations in Washington, D. C., and social agencies dealing with children. He has talked with hundreds of adult offenders and their child victims.

Whenever he was confronted with someone who was so personally detestable that his emotions might affect his judgment, he traded off with another staff member. "With some people," he concedes, "you just have to admit that you're too emotional, valued and opinionated." He advises members of his staff to recognize that there will be individuals they cannot work with effectively, and to swap off.

For several months, Sherman was in charge of a halfway house for men on probation or parole. His clients included men with a history of involvement in child pornography and others who were pimps. He remembers them as "slick, manipulative, sociopathic personalities who were in the business they were in because they found that it was an easy living for them. They liked the game of it. It was easy pickings."

Pimps are especially easy to profile, according to Sherman. They are almost always Black, they are from neighborhoods and backgrounds where pimps are looked up to as models of success, and they are street people who are into hustling for a living.

When he talks of his work, Sherman sometimes leans forward in his cramped office, propping his elbows upright on his desk with his hands clasped in front of him. At other times he leans back, tipping his chair onto its hind legs, and stretches his own long legs in front of him. He is oblivious to the industrious purring of typewriters and muted conversation from meetings or conferences in other rooms.

"Usually, at least the pimps I've had contact with, are into the hustle and the con," he says. "They don't like to do things the legitimate way because there are too many rules and restrictions. There isn't enough creativity and artistic availability for them in selling used cars."

Sherman has observed that ghetto males who expect to make their living by street hustling generally have three major options: they can "sell slum," buy cheap jewelry and resell it for high prices in alleys or on street corners; they may become involved in drug dealing, but law enforcement is more stringent and the penalties are harsher if they are caught; or they may become pimps.

Pimping is less hazardous, and the financial rewards can be substantial. Pimps are seldom arrested. "The women get arrested, but there's this big macho myth that a woman never turns her pimp in. He is the protector and he takes care of them," Sherman explains. The pimp also sometimes roughs up a girl he thinks is misbehaving or setting a bad example for the other women. "They have to make a reputation," he says. "The same code of the street applies to other criminals. Your reputation is important, and if somebody messes with you, he or she has to pay the price."

Doug Dezotell, administrative assistant at Chicago Teen Challenge, a transdenominational Christian shelter for young men, has observed the same concern with image and reputation among pimps.

A former Teen Challenge resident who became a street minister, Dezotell has cajoled, sermonized, exhorted, and led a half-dozen pimps to the center. They usually do not come unless they are in trouble.

"By the time we see them they're usually strung out on dope,"

Dezotell concedes. "Everything is starting to go bad for them. Their girls are leaving or are already gone, and they're just getting to the point of realizing that they have a problem and need help.

"But of course they don't see what they've been doing to their women, the dealing with prostitution, as part of their problem. It's their drug dependence that they see as the problem. They're seeing themselves as a man because they have this string of women working for them—a man who has a problem with drugs. So what we have to deal with is their mind-set, change their thinking."

Dezotell is a solidly built, cleancut man approaching thirty, who liberally sprinkles his conversation with references to Christ, the Lord, and the Bible. A picture of Christ is hung conspicuously on the wall of his office, and a Bible is within easy reach on his desk. A native of Grand Forks, North Dakota, he fought his private battle with the devil after becoming involved as a drug dealer when he was still in high school. But he says he was in Tucson, Arizona, working as a counselor at a secular alcoholic rehabilitation center, and was having his own troubles with the bottle, when he "met the Lord, and my life changed." He attended Bible colleges in California, Colorado, and Missouri before becoming a licensed minister with the Assemblies of God and going to work for Chicago Teen Challenge. His years dealing with his problems with drugs and alcohol help him cope with the narcotics addicts, alcoholics, street people, and pimps at the shelter.

One of the odd details he learned about pimps is that they frequently permit the nail on one of their little fingers to grow exceptionally long. It is a symbol, a badge of their profession, and they may spend hours carefully covering it with clear polish or buffing it.

Dezotell is not the only person at Chicago Teen Challenge to be intrigued by the unusual practice. He sometimes tells about the evening that a pimp who was new at the shelter was seated on his bed when another resident, a white youth from a rural community in downstate Illinois, peered inside the room and saw the newcomer buffing the nail. He was fascinated and asked the man why he kept the fingernail so long and was so concerned with its appearance. The taciturn new resident did not bother to look up. "I'm a pimp," he replied, continuing to buff the gleaming fingernail.

The youth was appalled. He was struggling to beat a drug habit. He had stolen cars, been a petty thief, and done a dozen other things that he was ashamed of. But he could not comprehend living off the earnings of a prostitute. And he was bewildered by the pimp's cavalier attitude and obvious lack of remorse.

"He just couldn't understand that it's different in the ghetto," Dezotell says of the teenager. "In the ghetto, the pimp is a man of power, he's macho, he's tough, he has the bucks. He is a man because he has all these women working for him. He is the one who drives the nice cars, wears the fancy clothes, and has the diamond rings on his fingers. So the little kids on the street look up to this guy and think, 'Man, when I grow up I want to be just like him.' White people on the street just don't look at it that way. It's a different kind of mentality."

Not everyone who enters Teen Challenge completes the entire program. Participation at the Chicago center and at others in various cities is voluntary. Although the center in Chicago is equipped to shelter men only, some of the others can accommodate men and women. Two religious shelters for females in Chicago are New Life for Girls and New Day House. Their methods are similar to Teen Challenge, according to Dezotell, who says they are considered almost sister programs.

The program at Teen Challenge emphasizes Christian fundamentalism and hard work. There is frequent prayer, and both group and individual therapy. All counseling is related to the Bible, and residents are kept occupied from the time they are awakened at 7 A.M. until bedtime. "Idle time," cautions Dezotell, "becomes the devil's playground."

Teen Challenge has compiled an impressive record of rehabilitating the drug addicts, pimps, prostitutes, and various other street hustlers who straggle into the shelters for help, he advises. The basic program extends over 13 months, three at the center and, for those located in the Midwest, 10 more months at a farm near Cape Girardeau, Missouri.

Many of the graduates continue on to Bible school and become ministers or seek positions as counselors and administrators with various Teen Challenge centers or urban missions supported by churches. Some seek job opportunities in more secular areas. Teen Challenge maintains a vocational school in Pennsylvania.

Although some residents drop out of the program, there is hope among the Teen Challenge staff even for them. Dezotell worked briefly with a young man who left because he could not accept the Spartan lifestyle, celibacy, authority, and stern discipline at Teen Challenge. But he stayed out of trouble, continued to attend church regularly, and married a girl he had gotten pregnant. His actions were interpreted as indicating his new sense of responsibility. He is a former child prostitute and pimp.

The background he recounted to counselors was wretched. He was thirteen years old when he was thrown out of his home in California and began living in a tent in a field. He depended for his meals on handouts from a nearby food co-op, where he met an older youth who was a male prostitute. Healthy, blond, tan, and muscular from lounging at beaches and lifting weights, the prostitute offered the boy a home. Soon after that they became lovers, and the younger boy also turned to prostitution.

Almost a year later the teenager had his first sexual experience with a girl about his own age. His life changed abruptly. He moved out of the older youth's apartment and began doing everything he could to prove to himself and to others that he was manly. He joined a street gang and fought with other teenagers. He practiced boxing and the unarmed martial arts. As soon as he was old enough, he joined the Marines.

After discharge from the military, he became a race car driver. Finally he began dealing in drugs. By the time he moved to Chicago, he had a heroin habit and his girlfriend was pregnant. "He is a young man who has spent a long time running from his past," Dezotell muses.

Dezotell does not believe that anyone who comes to Teen Challenge for help is untreatable. But it is essential that they perceive that they have a problem and be willing to accept help. Otherwise treatment can be frustrating and defeating.

Some individuals who sexually exploit children are exceptionally bright, proud of their professions, and have devoted lifetimes to learning their business and how to manipulate people for their own selfish needs. Child pornographers often fit that description, according to Dr. Osanka.

"Basically what we've seen is that they are very selfish people who glorify the dollar," the Lewis University instructor says. "They're attracted by the quick money that's involved, and they're prepared to pander to the needs of a certain element of our society. My personal regret is that we frequently don't recognize that element exists."

He described the often ambitious, imaginative men who build fortunes from child pornography as "people who are disciplined in a society that really isn't disciplined. They tend to be a bit more goal-oriented toward economic security. They work hard, and play at some point, as well."

Convincing such individuals to attempt to modify their behavior is difficult. They are established in lifestyles that are satisfying to them, and they have no desire to change.

The technicians, individuals who personally have no interest in sex with children and are merely earning high compensation for meeting a public demand, can be among the most effective pornographers. Dr.

Osanka has observed that they remain secure "because they don't work with pleasure."

Others, the imaginative and business-oriented pedophiles, may see themselves as propagating the faith. "They can convince themselves that they are part of a new frontier," he says. "Of course they're deluding themselves, but they expect that they'll have their place in history. There is a certain amount of arrogance involved, of the feeling that what they're doing is advanced, and the rest of society hasn't come up with it yet."

There is yet another type of individual who produces and distributes child pornography. He is the man who entices neighborhood children into his home, takes pornographic photos of them, and swaps through the mails with other collectors. According to Osanka, these people are infinitely difficult to deal with therapeutically because they live in fantasy worlds. They are generally sublimating their desires to have sexual contact with children, which is often more difficult to do.

"They take a certain amount of pleasure in being able to trade photographs which they claim they've taken. So there is quite clearly a power element there," he says.

The psychologist believes that as children many of them were sexually exploited by adults in ways they enjoyed. Males in particular would enjoy the act of orgasm. It's pleasurable, and they would tend to covet that pleasure, he says. "These people are quite immature, and I think the theory of psychosexual development halting is probably accurate.

"Consequently, they tend to stop other kinds of development. In other words, they are no longer interested in baseball, no longer interested in mathematics. They aren't interested in anything except this curiosity about sexual pleasure."

Veteran investigators with the Chicago Police Department's Youth Division agree that most of their problem with kiddie porn in the city today involves collectors who produce and trade photographs for their own enjoyment.

Investigators William DeGiulio and Patrick Deady sometimes huddle with their boss, Lieutenant Edmund Beazley, to discuss the boys and girls who pose for pornography, the child prostitutes, pornographers, pimps, and the parents who sometimes live off the children.

"There's a big variance in family reaction," Beazley says. He recalled a boy whose parents knew that he was prostituting himself but did not interfere with his behavior so long as they received a share of his earnings. The mother of another fifteen-year-old boy raised no serious objections when a physician approached her and explained that he and the youngster were lovers. She consented without argument when the doctor said that he was going to keep the boy. At about the same time, the mother of a teenage girl notified police that a man had induced her daughter to pose for pornography, named the offender, and helped set up an arrest.

Some people are concerned about the sexual exploitation of their own children or the children of others. And some are not. Beazley and other Youth Division officers vividly remember a woman who telephoned a hotline to report her suspicions that a big-time child pornography operation had set up business in her neighborhood. For weeks she had watched almost daily as children from junior high school age to preschool were led into a nearby building.

DeGiulio and Deady drove to the building to investigate the report. An hour later they were back. There were no arrests. The children were visiting the offices of a pediatrician who was new in the neighborhood. The investigators chuckle about the incident. But they are pleased that the neighbor cared enough to telephone police. More public concern would provide law enforcement agencies with a better opportunity to prevent the sexual abuse of children. Police cannot do the job alone.

"Our friend Whitey is a good example," Beazley points out.[1] "His counselor says that Whitey used to sit in the day room at the prison watching *Sesame Street* and *Bozo's Circus* while he was masturbating. Talk about rehabilitation—here's a guy whose been molesting children all his adult life, he's been in prison, he's in his sixties now, and he is out on parole."

When this man returned to Chicago from prison, he moved into an apartment across the street from an elementary school and playground. "There are kids around here, a lot of little girls—that's what he likes," Beazley says. "Even his parole officer tells us he would like nothing better than to send Whitey back. The man's wife told the parole officer she believed he was 'up to his old tricks,' because they hadn't had sexual relations since his return home. So we're watching him now, hoping to put a case together," says Beazley.

Unfortunately, police can do little more than watch, or wait to pick up the pieces after another child, or series of children, is molested. The law does not permit policemen to knock on doors and tell parents of little girls that their neighbor is a convicted child molester with a long record of arrests.

Education, probably in the schools, is one of the most promising means of protecting the children, Deady believes. Parents in all neighborhoods, whether or not a convicted child molester is living nearby, should be required to attend meetings at the schools where police officers and other experts can provide them with information about the dangers to their children from sexual exploitation, he says.

But the classes are useless when the children involved are from families that are unconcerned about their welfare. DeGiulio and Deady watched helplessly while an Appalachian youth from Chicago's uptown neighborhood wasted his years as a teenager prostituting himself from street corners and posing for pornography. He was already an experienced prostitute when he was thirteen, and a year later he was posing for a California pornographer filming movies at a northside motel. No one in his family was concerned. They were satisfied that he was supporting himself.

He was nineteen when police had their latest contact with him. By that time he was the lover of a transsexual prostitute who was picking up tricks and slipping knockout drops into their booze. Investigators suspected that the youth was robbing his lover's unconscious clients, but were unable to prove it. The transsexual, however, was sent to jail for a short term.

At nineteen the young man has become too old and has lost much of his appeal as a prostitute. "A boy of eighteen or nineteen is burned out as a hustler," DeGulio says. "A girl that age is still desirable on the street. But we see cars stop, an older teenage boy will walk up, talk a few minutes, and then walk away. The driver is looking for someone younger."

Aging boy prostitutes usually support themselves with other forms of nonviolent crime. "These people don't become stickup men," Deady says. He theorizes that the Appalachian boy would probably resort to selling dope. "He would have to have easy money. He isn't trained for any kind of legitimate job. He's bright, but he was on the street when he should have been in school." The boy seldom attended classes after becoming a prostitute.

The eight-year-old boy prostitute who was thought for a time to have been one of John Gacy's victims is another example. The youth officers believe that even after he lived for two or three years with the same man and was passed around to other pederasts on the West Coast, it may have been possible to rehabilitate the boy. But it would have required an extraordinarily devoted and understanding mother willing to spend almost all her time with her son. The boy's mother could not meet those demands.

"She loves the boy, but if she was going to help him she would really have to hover over him all the time, and she just isn't doing that,"

DeGiulio says. "She goes from job to job and boyfriend to boyfriend. She moved so much when he was gone that we used to tell her that if we did find her son, we probably wouldn't be able to find her."

The youngster was in therapy for two years after returning home. That was during the day. At night he was on the street. "He's twelve or thirteen now and he's still a problem with us," Deady says. "He's a male prostitute, still gets involved with the police, runs away. . . . Once they get into that, they never get out. I can't remember any who have ever straightened out. This boy will probably always be a drifter. He'll go to other cities. They become welfare problems.

"It's only for the grace of God that he wasn't in Gacy's basement," the investigator added. Deady has special reason to shudder when he mentions the murders committed by John Wayne Gacy, Jr. "I was probably the first person (in the Chicago area) ever to investigate the man," he says. Several gay teenagers informed police in 1977 about Gacy's cruising and reputation as a sadist. Deady investigated Gacy for four or five weeks and confirmed various contacts between the burly suburban contractor and male prostitutes or other pickups from Chicago's eclectic Newtown area.

"But he was working a homosexual neighborhood, and sex between two consenting adults was something we couldn't get involved in without violating someone's civil rights," Deady explains. At that time the investigation had not uncovered any evidence to justify an arrest.

If anything positive resulted from the Gacy horror, Deady suggests, it was formation of special youth or runaway units in other police departments reacting to the widespread publicity and the shocking nature of the crimes. Chicago Youth Division officers helped establish a six-member unit for the State of Illinois, and DeGiulio helped authorities in Lexington, Kentucky, establish a countywide agency.

Sadism is not an unusual phenomenon among the men who cruise the streets or advertise in magazines seeking children as sex partners. File cabinets in the Youth Division at Sixth District headquarters are bulging with photographs of children trussed in ropes, chains, or stocks, beaten with whips, cut with knives, or with their body orifices pierced by a bewildering variety of sexual devices.

Individual photographs may be advertised in magazines for $2 each or more, with such enticing descriptions as "A whipping for Janie, 14." When investigators purchase the pictures, often there is no means of determining "Janie's" age without knowledge of her identity. Some children mature more rapidly than others, and the girl identified as "Janie" in the photo may indeed be fourteen. Or she may be eighteen.

Although Illinois statutes are designed to permit prosecution under the child pornography laws if a youngster is "purported" to be underage, youth officers have had difficulty convincing state's attorneys to prosecute such cases. Despite the careful wording of the law, prosecutors want photos of children who are young enough so that there is no question of their juvenile status. Better yet, they prefer that the children themselves be available to testify.

That is difficult. Even when police are able to track child pornography to the producer, he is not likely to volunteer the identity or location of underage models. And testifying in open court about sexual activity they have participated in is traumatic, even for tough street kids.

Boys who are prostitutes or who have posed for pornography will almost never admit performing an act of oral sex on someone, unless they have no other choice. They insist as vociferously as they can that it was the client, or "the other guy," who performed fellatio. "It's like pulling teeth to get them to come out and tell us the whole story," DeGiulio says. "Then imagine being faced with admitting in a courtroom full of people that they had a homosexual relationship with a man. People can be having all kinds of private conversations in a courtroom, but as soon as sex is mentioned you can hear a pin drop. Everyone's attention is suddenly on the testimony."

The job of youth officer can be discouraging when investigators see the same child prostitutes on street corners night after night and when they come into repeated contact with the doctors, lawyers, dentists, teachers, clergymen, truck drivers, and Scout leaders who sexually exploit them.

Deady has four daughters and a son. DeGiulio has two boys. "I look at these kids we bring in here," Deady says, shaking his head, "and I think of my own family. You think about it when you go home."

"It makes you want to put your kids in a bubble," DeGiulio says. "You can get so you feel like telling them that they're going to stay in the back yard where their father can watch them until they get out of college. It's that bad."

"There are crimes you get over," says Deady. "But you never get over sexual experiences like these." Several of the youths whom Deady and DeGiulio have come to know have been slain or committed suicide. They knew two of the murdered boys who were linked at different times to police probes of John Norman's activities. They knew one of Gacy's victims.

A teenage boy they picked up for alleged involvement in a child pornography operation headed by a Scout leader was released from custody before the case could come to trial. He leaped from the 30-story window of a highrise. An eighth-grade student who was a Sea Scout when he became entangled in a pornography scheme hanged himself before the case could be tried. The officers apprehended another boy whose brothers and sisters each became enmeshed in the sex trade, and he was murdered before he could testify against an accused child pornographer.

Beazley and his investigators can name a half-dozen families with several children each who became active in pornography or prostitution, one after the other. The lieutenant recalled another case involving a fourteen-year-old boy whose mother died when he was twelve. The father deserted the family and the boy was sent to live with an older brother who was appointed as his legal guardian. "Now the brother is a ne'er-do-well, a pothead who uses whatever narcotics or drug that's available," Beazley sighs. "The guy's been a street hustler for years, and he threw his little brother out. The boy wound up living for six months with a known homosexual."

Eventually the boy was picked up by officers from the Youth Division. He had not attended school for more than a year. A woman officer telephoned the Illinois Department of Children and Family Services and advised employees there that they had a boy who needed placement in a foster home. "If we don't find a home for him," the policewoman said, "he will probably return to the homosexual he was living with."

"What's wrong with that?" the caseworker asked.

Guy Strait and other people who prey on children have told police how easy it is to pick out the children in a neighborhood who are susceptible. "They look for the kid who shows up alone at school affairs or at other activities when every other kid is there with his parents," Beazley says. "They look for kids who aren't getting any attention at home. There are no curfews to worry about. It's easy to be truant from school. That kid will frequently be the victim and never tell anyone."

Dr. Densen-Gerber frequently stresses the need for attention and affection for children in the home, including "loving, cuddling, warmth, and concern. If these warm, touching experiences are absent in the home," she cautions, "the child may seek them elsewhere, thus becoming vulnerable to sexual exploitation by others." When a child becomes involved in pornography or prostitution, authorities must recognize the behavior as a symptom of more serious problems, she says.

Sherman also marvels at the skill and ease with which an experienced pornographer or pimp can recognize and seduce a vulnerable child. "Vultures know which kids are real needy," he says. "It might be a kid who looks like he hasn't eaten for a while, and who is walking around in dirty clothes.

"They use all kinds of gimmicks, perhaps telling a child that they're putting together a new magazine and are looking for models. But half the time a guy doesn't even need a gimmick. You have to realize that these are kids on the street with little self-esteem, and little sense of self-worth. They've been convinced that they're bad kids, and often they're just trying to respond to a frustrating or impossible situation at home."

"You have to stop and think about what something like this does to kids," Deady says. "If they're beaten up, if they're knifed, robbed, or victimized by any of the other major crimes against the person it doesn't affect their minds the same as being exploited sexually does. You really destroy their minds at a young age."

---

[1] "Whitey" is a pseudonym. At the time of the writing, the ex-convict was not charged with a crime.

AFTERWORD

MAGAZINES featuring kiddie porn have not been available in the nation's adult bookstores since the crackdown on sexual exploitation of children occurred in 1977-78. Child pornography stirred up wide publicity, and the legal penalties became severe.

But the people who devote their energies to the systematic rape and exploitation of children have not been forced out of business. One phase of the industry has merely been driven underground. Kiddie porn in increasingly large amounts is again being smuggled into the country from foreign nations, and swapped and sold from car trunks, back doors, and mailboxes by private collectors and other adults who make sexual capital of children. Laws prevent the Postal Service from opening first class mail, and the U.S. government is a convenient and safe channel for the clandestine trade. Kiddie porn is a cottage industry again, as it was before the sudden boom in the mid-70s, but a healthy one.

Child prostitution is as prevalent as before. Child prostitutes still walk the Minnesota Strip, linger in the darkened shadows of Bughouse Square and Piedmont Park, and hawk their sexual services at the busy corner of Hollywood and Las Palmas.

As long as there is a market for child sex there will be men and women anxious to meet the demand and lawyers of little morality and venal appetites who are willing to keep them out of jail for a share of the earnings. Courtroom cunning and chicanery have no legitimate place in the competition over the bodies and spirits of the young.

It is absurd to seriously consider arguments that the architects of the First Amendment would have approved of its use to justify involving children in the most vile forms of pornography. There is no reason to either listen to or tolerate the claptrap spewed out by the Guyon Society, P.I.E., and all other such crazies. Sincere gay rights organizations should take care not to be drawn into defending boy-lovers under mistaken ideals of solidarity with fellow sexual minorities. Homosexuality

297

and boy-love are not synonymous. Gays are no more morally or ethically obligated to defend child molesters who happen to be homosexual
than heterosexuals are obligated to defend men who sexually molest
their own three-year-old daughters, or the daughters of neighbors.

The Protection of Children Against Sexual Exploitation Act, and
other statutes enacted on the state level, provided necessary legal tools
for authorities charged with combating the widespread sexual abuse of
children. There are still improvements to be made. William Katz believes, for example, that child prostitution could be severely impeded if
states implemented the Interstate Compact on Juveniles. The plan
would permit local police to enforce the youth laws of the child's home
state. A national file of child sex offenders and victims, if it could be
made available without violating civil rights statutes and could sidestep
roadblocks from the ACLU, would help police track suspects and aid
children already ensnared. The file would be invaluable in determining
techniques and methods of operation of sex criminals like Norman,
Bradford, and Thompson. Amendment of the Federal Privacy Act to
permit full background checks of adults seeking employment or voluntary positions that would bring them in propinquity with children is an
absolute necessity. The records, business dealings, and other activities
of any organization that purports to serve and work with children
should be open to perusal by proper government agencies and inspection teams.

Laws alone, unfortunately, are not sufficient to ensure the protection
of children from sexual exploitation. The job cannot be done without
the concerted efforts of legislative bodies, law enforcement agencies
including the courts and prosecutors, schools, social agencies, religious
institutions, the medical profession, and, most important of all—families. Several state and local law enforcement agencies in the Chicago
area banded together and established a 24-hour hotline for citizens to
call, anonymously if they prefer, with information about suspected
kiddie porn or other sex abuse of children.

Everyone who works with or lives in close proximity to children has a
responsibility to cooperate in protecting them and looking out for their
welfare. They have a moral obligation to report suspected cases of child
abuse, sexual or non-sexual. We should pass laws to prevent the punishment of individuals to protect a child whose physical and emotional
welfare may be in danger.

In the 1980s, just as in the 1970s, there can be no excuse for Veronica
Brunsons and Luz Valentins. Children have no more right to be prostitutes than adults have to profit from their prostitution. Policemen

should once again be given authority to act as the protectors of children, even if it means bending his or her civil rights and dragging a child off an uptown streetcorner or out of a Times Square hot-pillow hotel. Society cannot afford to be neutral about the welfare of its children.

If the sexually exploited child does not have a healthy family he or she can return to, placement should be guaranteed with a shelter or foster home where the staff and stand-in parents have been thoroughly investigated. It is important that their motivations be aimed at helping the child rather than contributing to his or her problem. There also is no excuse for Scotty Bakers or Charlie Mansons.

Punishment must be recognized as a valid response by society to certain criminal actions, including but not restricted to the sexual abuse of children. Some psychiatrists and behavioral scientists consider almost all criminality to be evidence of mental illness or crippling trauma from early conditioning and environment. Those professionals appear never to consider that some individuals are so corrupt and vicious that they sexually abuse children, murder, and rape simply because they enjoy it and have a total disregard for the welfare and safety of their fellow human beings.

It appears reasonable to deduce that such criminals have balanced out the pleasures they derive from their offenses against the fear of light punishment or no punishment at all, and do as they wish. Perhaps society should raise the ante with mandatory prison sentences and the certainty of execution for some crimes.

By all means, efforts should be made to rehabilitate the people who sexually molest children. Some of them do not belong in jail cells beside murderers, armed bandits, and bank robbers. But they also do not belong in the schools, in Boy Scout troops, church youth organizations, or in the house next door, until qualified professionals have ascertained beyond all doubt that they are no longer dangerous to children. If that means locking them up for the rest of their lives, so be it. An intelligent and caring society should be more concerned with the protection of its young potential victims than with the comfort and happiness of sexual offenders.

Rehabilitation programs like those pioneered by Dr. Money and Dr. Giaretto show enormous promise for the treatment of sex criminals. Organizations like Parents United, Daughters United, and Sons United are of immense help in assisting families and victims to recover from the trauma of incest.

But two dozen or so rehabilitation programs for pedophiles, most of them unproven, is not a realistic approach to the problem of sexual abuse of children. Massive amounts of federal, state, and private funding are still needed for research and pilot programs to help understand and treat child molesters. Attempting to rehabilitate a child molester is distressingly similar to attempting to rehabilitate a narcotics addict. It is tedious, frustrating work with poor odds. Many, perhaps most, do not want to be rehabilitated. They just do not want to be caught and punished. A child molester who wrote an unsolicited letter from Tucson, Arizona, to Dr. Osanka bragged that he had been actively abusing eight- to fourteen-year-old girls since 1938. He said he was arrested 36 times, enjoyed 36 "really good scores with erotically aroused nymphets," and was "shrunk by 36 clinical psychologists and psychiatrists." None of the "shrinks" over a period of 40 years apparently either cured or eased his lust for little girls.

Sadistic pedophiles like John Gacy, imaginative entrepreneurs like the Reverend Claudius I. Vermilye, Jr., and tragic individuals like "Grandpa" Ritter should be interviewed, tested, and studied—inside institutional surroundings, and outside, if they are free. Dr. Osanka theorizes that many of his colleagues in the behavioral sciences have deliberately avoided studying offenders such as Gacy and other individuals accused of especially horrendous sex crimes because the subject is so vile.

The proposal of Dr. Densen-Gerber for a cabinet-level government agency for the Concerns of Children is a valid one. The proposed cabinet position would recognize a national ombudsman to scrutinize social institutions dealing with children, to study, and, when justified, to restructure laws, systems, agencies, and other components of our society dealing with the welfare of children.

President Carter and the First Lady refused to meet with her to discuss the plan, she says, even though the prime minister of Australia found time for a similar meeting. Dr. Densen-Gerber says that the President wrote that he would not see her because she represented a special interest group. "There is very little commitment to children by government," she observes, "because they neither vote nor have economic power."

Legislators can be approached. They should be urged to consider the proposal for an agency to protect and promote the interests of children. And perhaps the new President, Ronald Reagan, will be more receptive. Government has the responsibility to make the American dream possible for all children, Dr. Densen-Gerber insists. "Children are dependent. They need to have things done for them. And in an increasingly sophisticated, technological society the parents can't do it alone," she says. "They need the government to provide the resources as a helpmate for the needs of the child."

The National Institute of Mental Health's Runaway Youth Program is basically a good one and meets some of the more consequential needs of one segment of troubled youth. Crisis intervention centers and shelters for youth provided by agencies like Odyssey House, Covenant House, the Hale Kipa Shelter Home in Honolulu (for adolescent and adult females), Huckleberry House in Columbus, Ohio, and dozens of others are available in most major cities and some smaller communities and receive funding from the NIMH. They need continued funding. Effort and money are needed to develop other serious and sustained programs dedicated to the welfare of children and their families. The agencies and programs should be available in all communities, in small towns such as Colchester, New Hampshire, and Titusville, Florida, as well as in large urban centers.

Ultimately, of course, the responsibility for the safety and welfare of children belongs to the family. A family whose members cannot communicate among themselves is a family in trouble. There must be dialogue and rapprochment, with understanding but firm parents, and children who know they can confide in them. Children need attention and expressions of affection, and, if it is unavailable from their parents, it is available from people like John Norman, Guy Strait, and the pimps who prowl Minneapolis' Nicollet Avenue.

Not everyone is a police investigator like Sergeant Raimondo in Coral Gables. Nevertheless, it is incumbent on parents to know something about adults in Boy Scout troops, church youth groups, and other agencies who are trusted with their children. Most of the adults associated with the Boy Scouts, Girl Scouts, and other agencies serving youth are people of high ideals. They have helped millions of children around the world. But for exactly these reasons pedophiles are attracted to the agencies and they cannot all be screened out, no matter how vigilant their more responsible colleagues may be.

A large segment of the public is unaware of the scope of the twin problems of child prostitution and child pornography and is only dimly aware that intergenerational incest is as close as their next-door neighbor. Even law enforcement agencies, except for those people most directly involved with troubled children, are not as well informed about the problem as they should be.

No matter how adequate laws are, how aggressively they may be enforced by police, prosecutors, and the courts, how effectively social service agencies function, or how sincerely parents strive to protect their young—there will always be adults who are anxious to sexually exploit children. Professionals like Katz, whose occupations keep them in close touch with children in trouble, are aware of the futility of attempting to completely eliminate the problem.

"There are literally tens of thousands of pedophiles throughout the United States, if not hundreds of thousands," he says, "who are sexually exploiting their own children, who are sexually exploiting their neighbor's children, and who are getting away with it."

It is an unsettling truth, but truth, nevertheless. The best hope is to inhibit them as much as possible, keep legal and social pressures on them to expose their activities, and to make their businesses unprofitable and keep them on the run. Consequently the story told here must be left unfinished. Children are being sexually abused and exploited every day. It is the murder of souls, carried out under the guise of affection. It is the ultimate depravity.

CLIFFORD L. LINEDECKER

Chicago, Illinois

APPENDICES

AND

INDEX

APPENDIX I

A Partial List of State Laws Prohibiting the Sexual Exploitation of Children

(Survey in 1979)

State	Age	Name of Law	Offense	Class	Date	Penalty
ALASKA			No legislation relating to children and pornography.			
ALABAMA	Under 17 and unmarried	Division 4— Obscene materials depicting or displaying children 13-7-237	The production of obscene matter depicting persons under 17 involved in obscene acts is a felony.		1978	20 years to life and/or $20,000
		Chapter 7— Offenses against public health and morals 13-7-1	It is a felony to cause a person between the ages of 10 and 18 to prostitute.			$50 to $500 and six months.
ARIZONA	Under 15	Child Abuse	All forms of and involvements with child prostitution and forms of and involvements with child pornography.	Class II felony	1978	
			Depending on the state of mind of the perpetrator at time of abuse causing	Class II to Class VI felony	1979	

State	Age	Statute	Description	Classification	Year
ARKANSAS	Under 16	Protection of Children Against Exploitation Act	... or permitting a child to be injured, felony classification may vary. Use of a child for the purposes of reproduction in any form in the depiction of any sexually explicit conduct.	Class C felony, 1st offense; Class B subsequent	1979
			Transport of a minor with intent to engage in prostitution.	Class C felony	
COLORADO	Under 18	Colorado Revised Statutes Part 4 Article 6 Title 18. Sexual Exploitation of Children	Production for trade or commerce of material wherein a child is engaged in sexually explicit conduct. . . . Intentionally cause or permit a child to engage in sexually explicit conduct or prepare, produce, or promote, deal in or possess, any sexually exploitative material.	Class B felony	1979
CONNECTICUT	Under 17	Title 53, Sec. 53-25 Unlawful exhibition or Employment	To employ, exhibit, or otherwise dispose in or for the vocation, service, or purpose injurious to the health or dangerous to the life of a child, including rope or wire walking, skating or acrobatics, as well as for any obscene, indecent, or immoral purpose.	Misdemeanor	1949

State	Age	Name of Law	Offense	Class	Date	Penalty
CONNECTICUT	Under 17	Sec. 53a-196a	Employing a minor in an obscene performance.	Class B felony	1969	
		Sec. 53a-196a	Promoting a minor in an obscene performance.	Class C felony		
DELAWARE	18 or under	Sub-chapter V Offenses Relating to Children and Incompetents. Sec. 1108	Sexual exploitation of children, including: 1. Photographing a child engaging in a prohibited sexual act or simulation. 2. Financing or producing in any medium a child engaging in a prohibited sexual act. 3. Publishing a photograph which depicts a child engaging in a prohibited sexual act.	Class B felony	1977	
FLORIDA	17 and under	Hiring and Employment	Use in any manner of a minor for display of any sexual conduct or cause or to have custody of any child and permit him to be involved in sexually explicit conduct for commercial purposes, or permit his mental or physical abuse.		1978	
	Under 18	Obscene Literature Profanity	Minors participating in any description of sexual	Second degree felony	1978	

State	Age	Statute	Description	Classification	Year
GEORGIA	Under 14	Sexual Exploitation of Children	...[allowing in any way for] this to occur whether or not for sale and profit. Use of any minor in production of any print medium involving sexually explicit conduct. Any parent or person with control of a minor who knowingly permits such a minor to engage in sexually explicit conduct for production in any medium is guilty of a felony.	Felony	1978
ILLINOIS	Less than 16	H.B. 286 PA 80 — Obscenity Involving a Minor	Indecent liberties with a child.	Class I felony	1977
		PA 180 — 1148 Chapter 38 Child Pornography	Solicit any minor to appear in pornographic publications, or as a parent or legal guardian permits or arranges for a child to do so.	Class 3 felony	1978
INDIANA	Under 16	35-30-10.1-2 Importation, Sale or Distribution of Obscene Materials	Distribution of obscene material that depicts or describes any person under 16.	Class D felony	1975
		35-30-10.1-3 Obscene Exhibitions Participation.	Engage or participate in, manage, produce, sponsor, exhibit, or film an obscene performance involving a minor.	Class D felony	1975

State	Age	Name of Law	Offense	Class	Date	Penalty
IOWA	Under 18	Obscenity 728.11 Sexual Exploitation of Children.	Use or permit a child to engage in a prohibited sexual act or the simulation, if the person knows or intends that the act may be reproduced in any visual or print medium.	Class C felony	1977	
KANSAS	Under 16	Criminal Code Sexual Exploitation of a Child	To employ or coerce a child to engage in any explicit sexual conduct for promotion of any visual medium.		1978	
KENTUCKY	Varies	Kentucky Penal Code Use of Minor in a Sexual Performance	Use of a minor in a sexual performance if the minor is less than 18:	Class D felony	1978	
			if the minor is less than 16:	Class C felony		
			if the minor incurs injury:	Class B felony		
			The use of a minor in, promoting a performance of a minor in distribution of, or advertising material portraying a minor in a sexual performance is considered sexual exploitation of a minor.			

State	Section/Title	Age	Description	Classification	Year	Penalty
LOUISIANA	Sec. 81.1 Pornography Involving Juveniles	Under 17	Solicitation of any unmarried person under 17 to participate in the sale, distribution, or display, or the preparation, publication, or printing of obscene material for sale, advertisement, or display is the crime of obscenity.		1977	Fine up to $2,000 and/or up to 5 years
MAINE	Sexual Exploitation of Minors	Under 16	To use, or permit if one has custody as a legal guardian, a minor to engage in sexually explicit conduct for commercial use.	Class B	1977	5-10 years
			Disseminate sexually explicit material when it depicts a minor.	Class C		2-5 years
MARYLAND	Senate Bill 311 Obscenity—Child Pornography	Under 16	To solicit, cause, or knowingly permit a child to appear in the production of obscene matter.		1978	$1,000 and/or 1 year
MICHIGAN		Under 18	To use minors in production of pornographic films, photos, or sound recordings.	Felony	1977	Up to 20 years and $2,000
			Promotion, distribution, or display of such material. (A provision is included permitting expert testimony concerning a child's age to spare the child appearing in court)	Felony	1977	Up to 7 years and $10,000

State	Age	Name of Law	Offense	Class	Date	Penalty
MICHIGAN	Under 18	Amendment to Michigan's Child Employment Act	Use of a minor as a performer, in or being the subject of obscene material.	Felony	1978	Up to 20 years and $20,000
MINNESOTA		Minnesota Statutes Section 626.556	Requires reports of neglect and abuse, including sexual abuse, of children		1978	
MISSISSIPPI	Under 18	Act 174 Criminal Sanctions Against the Sexual Exploitation of Children	Depiction of a child engaging in simulation of or actual sexual conduct for profit or commercial use. To transport or in any way effect intrastate commerce depicting a child engaging in a sexual act.	Felony	1979	2-10 years and $25,000-$50,000
MISSOURI	Under 17	Abuse of a Child	Photographing a child in a prohibited sexual act or the simulation of such an act.	Class D felony	1977	
	Under 18	Pornography	First degree pornography . . . when material considered harmful to minors is promoted.	Class D felony	1977	

749

defining the offense to include actual sexual abuse of children and preparation, distribution, and sale or pornography involving children.

State	Age	Offense	Description	Classification	Year	Penalty
NEBRASKA	Under 16	Obscene Material Child Participation Prohibited. 28.1463	To make, direct, or in any way generate any obscene material which has, as one of its participants or portrayed observers, a child or one who appears to be prepubescent. (In 1979, the legislature included sexual abuse in the definition of child abuse, and clarified responsibilities for reporting mistreatment. A statewide, toll-free telephone number was also provided.)	Class III felony, 1st offense. Class II felony, subsequent	1979	Up to 20 years and/or $25,000 1-50 years
NEVADA	Under 18	Crimes Against the Person	Use of a minor to simulate or engage in any performance of sexual conduct for media representation.	Felony	1979	1-6 years and/or $5,000
		Crimes Against Decency	To cause a minor to engage in acts which would constitute a crime against nature if performed by an adult.			

State	Age	Name of Law	Offense	Class	Date	Penalty
NEW HAMPSHIRE	Under 18	H.B. 361 & 351	Any person having custody of a minor who knowingly encourages, causes, abets, or has helped to produce, promote, or contribute to the use of a child in any acts of sexual contact.	Class B felony	1979	
		Chapter 169-C:1 Child Protection Act	Mandatory reporting of suspected instances of child abuse or neglect; to provide protection to children whose life, health, or welfare is endangered and establish a judicial framework to protect the rights of all those involved in child abuse cases. ("Abused Child" includes sexually molested and sexually exploited.)	1979		
NEW JERSEY	Under 16	Endangering Welfare of Children. New Jersey Penal Code: Offenses Against Others	Any person, including but not limited to, legal guardian, who causes or permits a child to participate in a sexual act or situation for reproduction, whether or not for	Second degree crime	1977	

State	Age	Statute/Title	Offense	Classification	Year	Sentence
NEW MEXICO	Under 18 and unmarried		Provide pornography to a minor.	Felony	1977	1-15 years
NEW YORK	Under 16	Child Pornography	To encourage or permit a child to appear, or to use a child in sexually oriented material, including live sex shows, or promote and sell such material. Parents or guardians who permit use of a child, producers, and sellers of the material are included in those liable for prosecution.			
NORTH CAROLINA	12 and under	Chapter 682, H.B. 800. Article 7A Rape and Other Sex Offenses 14.17.2	Perform vaginal intercourse with a child.	First degree rape	1977	
			Engage in a sexual act with a child. (No law specifically pertaining to children involved in the production of pornography.)	First degree sexual offense		
NORTH DAKOTA	Under 15	Sex Offenses, Gross Sexual Imposition	Engage in a sexual act with a juvenile.	Class A felony	1977	
			Permit a minor to participate in a performance which is harmful to minors.	Class C felony	1975	

State	Age	Name of Law	Offense	Class	Date	Penalty
OHIO	Under 13	H.B. 134, Section 2907.95	Sexual contact with a child	Third degree felony	1977	
	Under 18	H.B. 243, Section 2907.321	To entice, permit, or employ a child to act or in any way participate in or be photographed for any performance that is obscene. Not to report any reasonable suspicion of a violation of the above.	Third degree felony	1977	
OKLAHOMA	Under 16	Obscene or Indecent Writing 1021.2 1021.3	Procure or cause participation of a minor in a film, play, or performance where the minor is represented as engaged in sexual activity; or cause to be sold material involving the participation of a minor.	Felony	1978	
OREGON	Under 16	S.B. 356	Using a minor in an obscene performance. Dissemination of materials depicting a child engaging in sexual conduct which is obscene.	Class C felony	1979	
PENNSYLVANIA	Under 16	Sexual Abuse of Children 18-6312	Cause or permit a minor to engage in a sexual act or simulation, knowing it may be photographed.	Second degree felony		

State	Age	Law	Description	Penalty	Year
			ual act. (Note: A person must be 18 to be tattooed in this state, but only 16 to make pornographic movies.)		1979
RHODE ISLAND	Under 18	Child Abuse Chapter 129 Sec. 11-9-5.	Cruelty to, or neglect of a child: defined to include use or permitting use of a child for wanton, cruel, or improper purposes to compel a child to do a wrongful or wanton act.		
SOUTH CAROLINA	Under 18	Regulation of Obscenity	If over 18, to use or permit a minor to be involved in any material, act, or thing he has reason to know is obscene. It is also a felony to allow a minor to assist in the preparation of any obscene material for dissemination in a public place.	Felony	1978
SOUTH DAKOTA	Under 16	Sexual Exploitation of Children	Photographing a child in an obscene act.	Class 4 felony	1978
			Sale of obscene pictures to children.	Class 6 felony	1978
			A person 15 and over who has sexual conduct with a person under 15.	Class 3 felony	1976

Appendix I

State	Age	Name of Law	Offense	Class	Date	Penalty
TENNESSEE	Under 18	Public Chapter 405	To employ, use or permit a minor to: 1. Pose or model in any performance of sexual conduct for the purposes of preparing obscene material. 2. To engage in sexual conduct. 3. To promote any matter which depicts minors in a sexual performance.	Felony	1977	
		Child Labor Laws	Minors may not be employed in connection with occupations involving modeling or posing while engaged in any sexual conduct for the purposes of preparing a film or any visual presentation.		1975	
UTAH	Under 18	Sec. 76-10-1206.5 Sexual Exploitation of Minors	To knowingly employ, coerce, or engage any minor to participate in any sexual or simulated sexual conduct for the purpose of recording or display in any way. Anyone who photographs, films, or records minors engaged in sexual acts is	Second degree felony	1979	

State		Law	Description	Classification	Year
VERMONT	Under 18		to be involved in selling, lending, distributing, or showing any visual representation of any portion of explicit sexual conduct. (No law regarding children participating in the production of obscene material.)		
VIRGINIA	Under 18	Chapter 348 18.2.370 of the Code of Virginia: Indecent Liberties With A Child	To have sexual contact with a child under 14; to allow a child to perform in or be a subject of sexually explicit material; to receive money for enticing a child to perform; publication or production of obscene materials involving a minor.	Class 6 felony	1979
		40.1.113 Child Labor Laws	It is illegal to allow a child to perform in any explicit visual material. There is mandatory reporting of suspected sexual abuse.		
WEST VIRGINIA	Under 18	Filming of Sexually Explicit Conduct of Minors	For financial gain, to permit or persuade a minor to do or assist in any sexually explicit act when he knows it may be photographed. Photographing a minor engaged in sexually explicit conduct.	Felony	1979

State	Age	Name of Law	Offense	Class	Date	Penalty
WISCONSIN	Under 18	Bodily Security Sexual Exploitation of Children	Reproduction in any way of a minor in sexual conduct.	Class C felony	1977	
	Under 16	Abuse of Children	Subjecting a minor to cruel maltreatment.	Class E felony	1977	
	Under 12	Sexual Assault	To have sexual contact with a child.	Class B felony	1975	
	Under 15	Consent	A person under 15 is incapable of consent as a matter of law. Between 15 and 17, he or she is also incapable of consent but may be rebutted by competent evidence.			
	Under 18	Sexual Morality Enticing a Child for Immoral Purposes	Any person 18 or older with sexual intent enticing a person under 18 into a secluded place.	Class C felony	1977	

Public Law 95-225, the federal Protection of Children Against Sexual Exploitation Act, became law in 1978 and prohibits anyone, including parents or guardians, from using children under 16 or enticing them to be depicted in sexual acts and from shipping child pornography through the mails or in interstate or foreign commerce.

The legislation also extends the Mann Act, including males for the first time with females, making it a federal crime to transport children under the age of 18 across state lines for immoral purposes. Penalties for producing or distributing pornographic movies of children carry maximum sentences of 15 years in prison and a $15,000 fine. Mann Act violations provide for 10 years in prison and $10,000 fines.

Runaway Youth Programs

A state by state breakdown of programs and shelters
listed in the Runaway Youth Program Directory
of the U. S. Office of Juvenile Justice
and Delinquency Prevention.*

ALABAMA

Decatur	*13th Place*, 307 Prospect Drive, S.E.
Gadsden	*13th Place*, 1525 Chestnut Street

ALASKA

Anchorage	*Family Connection*, 640 Cordova

ARIZONA

Mesa	*Mesa Youth and Family Crisis Center*, 252 North Stapley
Phoenix	*Family Villas, Inc.*, 132 South Central, Suite 204
	Tumbleweed, 309 West Portland
Tucson	*Springboard Shelter Care*, 3644 North Nufer Place
	Towner House, 7466 East 18th Street
Yuma	*Children's Village*, 257 South Third Avenue

ARKANSAS

Little Rock	*Stepping Stone*, 1413 Battery

CALIFORNIA

Berkeley	*Berkeley Youth Alternatives*, 2141 Bonar Street
Carlsbad	*Project Oz North Coast*, 1212 Oak Avenue
Chula Vista	*Youth Emergency Assistance*, 648 Third Avenue
Escondido	*Project Oz Escondido*, 2846 Bernardo Avenue
Fullerton	*Odyssey*, 204 East Amerige Avenue
Hermosa Beach	*Casa Hermosa*, 186 2nd Street
Los Angeles	*Macondo Runaway House*, c/o Youth Trust Foundation, 201 South Alvarado Street
Modesto	*Hutton House*, 207 Virginia Avenue
Monterey	*Monterey Peninsula Youth Project*, P. O. Box 3076
Mountainview	*Casa SAY*, 239 Oak Street

---

*The directory was published in 1979 and lists 212 programs that serve usually self-referred runaway and throwaway boys and girls. Other good programs and shelters such as the facilities provided by Odyssey House are also operated by government, religious, or private agencies but, for one reason or another, are not listed in the directory. The directory, which includes a breakdown of specific services provided, may be obtained from the Office of Juvenile Justice and Delinquency Prevention, Law Enforcement Assistance Administration, U.S. Department of Justice, Washington, D.C. 20531

Newbury Park	*Interface Community Runaway Program,* 3475 Old Coneto Road, Suite C-5
Norwalk	*The Detour,* 12727 Studebaker Road
Riverside	*Youth Service Center of Riverside, Inc.,* 3847 Terracina Drive
Sacramento	*Diogenes Youth Services,* 9097 Tuolemne Drive
San Anselmo	*#9 Grove Lane,* 9 Grove Lane
San Diego	*The Bridge,* 3151 Redwood Avenue
	Project Oz Clairemont, 3304 Idlewild Way
	Southeast Involvement Project, 626 South 28th Street
San Francisco	*Huckleberry House,* 1430 Masonic Avenue
Santa Barbara	*The Klein Bottle—Alternatives Unlimited,* 1311 Anacapa Street
Santa Clara	*Bill Wilson House,* 884 Lafayette Street
Santa Maria	*The Klein Bottle—Alternatives Unlimited,* 900 South Broadway.

COLORADO

Aurora	*COMITIS Runaway/Time-Out Program,* 1150 South Chambers Road, P.O. Box 31552
Colorado Springs	*The Dale House Project,* 821 North Cascade
Grand Junction	*Mesa County Runaway Youth Shelter,* P.O. Box 1118
Steamboat Springs	*Rouett County Care Center,* Box 2069
Wheat Ridge	*Gemini House,* 3670 Upham Street

CONNECTICUT

Bridgeport	*The Youth In Crisis Project,* 3030 Park Avenue
Ansonia	*Valley Host Home Program,* 350 East Main Street
Glastonbury	*The Net,* St. James Episcopal Church
Greenwich	*Greenwich Youth Shelter,* 105 Prospect Street
West Hartford	*Junction 1019,* 1019 Farmington Avenue
Willimantic	*The Refuge,* 220 Valley Street

DELAWARE

Dover	*Eight-O-One,* 801 West Division Street
Wilmington	*The Runaway Shelter,* c/o The Children's Bureau of Delaware, 2005 Baynard Boulevard

DISTRICT OF COLUMBIA

Washington, D.C.	*Sasha Bruce House,* 701 Maryland Avenue, N.E.

FLORIDA

Daytona Beach	*Youth Alternatives Runaway Shelter,* 828 Cypress Street
Fort Lauderdale	*T.O.P.S. Haven,* 545 S. W. 15th Avenue
Gainesville	*Interface,* 1128 S.W. 1st Avenue
Jacksonville	*Jacksonville Transient Youth Center,* 132 W. Ninth Street
Merritt Island	*Crosswinds Runaway Center,* 55 N. Courtenay Parkway
Miami	*Community Outreach Services,* 1701 W. 30th Avenue
	Miami Bridge, 1145 N. W. 11th Street
Orlando	*Du Rocher House,* 1222 38th Street
St. Petersburg	*Runaway/Youth Crisis Center,* P. O. Box 13006
Tallahassee	*"Someplace Else"—YMCA Youth Home,* 1315 Linda Ann Drive

Tampa   *Beach Place Runaway Center*, 201-205 Beach Place

GEORGIA

Atlanta   *The Bridge Family Center*, 848 Peachtree Street, N.E.
                     Salvation Army Girl's Lodge, 848 Peachtree Street, N.E.
                     Truck Stop Youth Lodge, 26 Peachtree Place, N.W.

GUAM

Mariana Islands   *Sanctuary, Inc.*, Box 21030

HAWAII

Honolulu   *Hale Kipa, Inc.*, 2006 McKinley Street
Wailuku (Maui)   *Maunaolu Youth Residential Shelter*, County of Maui, 200 S. High
                     Street

IDAHO

Boise   *Hays House for Girls*, 1001 Hays
                     Sunrise House for Boys, 1319 N. 19th Street
Pocatello   *Bannock House*, 421 N. 8th Street

ILLINOIS

Champaign   *The Roundhouse*, 207 W. Green Street
Chicago   *Salvation Army New Life House*, 1025 W. Sunnyside
Lake Villa   *Lake County Youth Service Bureau*, Box 220
Oak Lawn   *Runaway Project*, 4951 W. 95th Street
Park Forest   *Aunt Martha's Youth Center, Inc.*, 2447 Western Avenue
Park Ridge   *Crisis Homes*, 733 N. Prospect Avenue

INDIANA

Bloomington   *Monroe County Youth Shelter*, 2853 E. 10th Street
Cannelton   *The Bridge*, 518 Lincoln Avenue
Fort Wayne   *The Switchboard Runaway Center*, 316 W. Creighton Street
Gary   *Alternative House*, 667 Van Buren Street
Indianapolis   *Stopover, Inc.*, 445 N. Penn Street #602
Kokomo   *Howard County Shelter Care*, 1015 E. Sycamore
South Bend   *The Shelter*, 520 N. Lafayette Street
Terre Haute   *The Salvation Army Sonshine House*, 920 N. 19th Street

IOWA

Ames   *Shelter House*, 712 Burnett Street
Cedar Rapids   *Foundation II*, 1627 1st Avenue S.E.
Council Bluffs   *Total Awareness*, 21 Benton Street
Des Moines   *Iowa Runaway Service*, 1365 23rd Street

KANSAS

Kansas City   *Neutral Ground*, 711 Sandusky
Topeka   *Carriage House Project*, 1100 Gage

KENTUCKY

Frankfort	*Laurel County Runaway Youth Shelter,* c/o Department for Human Resources, 275 E. Main Street
Louisville	*YMCA Shelter House,* 1414 S. First Street

LOUISIANA

New Orleans	*The Greenhouse,* 700 Frenchmen Street

MAINE

Norridgewock	*Horizon House,* Route 2
Portland	*YMCA Fair Harbor Shelter,* 87 Spring Street

MARYLAND

Baltimore	*Fellowship of Lights,* 1300 N. Calvert Street
Camp Springs	*Southern Area Youth Services, Inc.,* 5404 Old Branch Avenue
Columbia	*Grassroots, Inc.,* 5829 Banneker Road
Gaithersburg	*The Link,* 1 W. Deer Park Road
Hyattsville	*Second Mile House,* c/o First United Methodist Church, Queenschapel & Queensbury Roads
Silver Spring	*Open Door,* 1507 Vivian Place
Westminster	*Services to Alienated Youth (STAY),* 800 Old Taneytown Road

MASSACHUSETTS

Amherst	*Franklin/Hampshire Runaway Network,* 685 West Street
Beverly	*Project Rap, Inc.,* 19 Broadway
Boston	*The Bridge, Inc.,* 23 Beacon Street
	Place Runaway House, 402 Marlborough Street
Newton Centre	*Newton-Sellesley-Weston-Needham Multi-Service Center,* 1301 Centre Street
Saugus	*Listen, Inc.,* 28 Taylor Street

MICHIGAN

Alpena	*R.A.I.N.B.O.W.,* 2373 Gordon Road
Ann Arbor	*Ozone House, Inc.,* 608 N. Main Street
Bay City	*C.O.R.Y. Place, Inc., (Coordination of Runaway Youth),* 509 Center Street
Detroit	*NEC 4 SOLO Project,* 2015 Webb
	Detroit Transit Alternative, 10612 E. Jefferson Street and 680 Virginia Park
Grand Rapids	*The Bridge for Runaways,* 221 John N.E.
Holland	*Choice: Alternative Services for Status Offenders,* Ottawa County Branch Building, 327 North River
Inkster	*Counterpoint Runaway Shelter,* 715 Inkster Road
Kalamazoo	*The Ark For Runaways,* 1625 Gull Road
Muskegon	*Webster House for Runaways,* 446 W. Webster Avenue
Pleasant Ridge	*The Sanctuary,* 249 W. Ten Mile Road
Port Huron	*The Harbor,* 929 Pine Street
Saginaw	*Innerlink for Youth,* 515 S. Jefferson
Saint Joseph	*The Link Crisis Intervention Center,* 2002 S. State Street

MINNESOTA

Duluth	*The Crisis Shelter*, 1830 E. 4th Street
Minneapolis	*The Bridge for Runaway Youth*, 2200 Emerson Avenue South
	United Indians Runaway Program, 3020 Clinton Avenue

MISSISSIPPI

Waynesboro	*Mile High Center*, P.O. Box 205

MISSOURI

Columbia	*Front Door Residential House*, 800 N. 8th Street
Parkville	*Synergy House*, Box 12181
St. Charles	*Youth In Need, Inc.*, 529 Jefferson Street
University City	*Youth Emergency Service*, 6816 Washington Avenue

MONTANA

Anaconda	*Discovery House*, 709 E. Third Street
Billings	*Project Tumbleweed*, Kimball Hall, Rocky Mountain College
Great Falls	*Runaway Attention Home*, 618 Third Avenue, North
Helena	*Helena Attention Home* Runaway Program, 602 North Ewing
Missoula	*Missoula Crisis Center*, P.O. Box 9345

NEBRASKA

Bellevue	*Sarpy County Youth Services*, 1203 N. Fort Crook Road
Lincoln	*Freeway Station*, 2201 S. 11th Street
Omaha	*Whitman Center*, 4708 Davenport

NEVADA

Las Vegas	*Focus Youth Services*, 1916 Goldring

NEW HAMPSHIRE

Concord	*Stepping Stone*, 240 N. Main Street
Manchester	*New Hampshire Network for Runaway and Homeless Youth*, Child and Family Services of New Hampshire, 99 Hanover Street

NEW JERSEY

Asbury Park	*Monmouth Boys Club—JINS Shelter*, 1201 Monroe Avenue
Beverly	*Crossroads Runaway Program, Inc.*, Olympic Lakes, Route 130
Glassboro	*Together, Inc., Youth Service Project*, 7 State Street
Paterson	*Project Youth Haven*, Diocese of Paterson, 44 Jackson Street

NEW MEXICO

Albuquerque	*Amistad*, 1731 Isleta, S.W.
	The New Day Runaway Crisis Center, 1817 Sigma Chi, N.E.

NEW YORK

Bronx	*GLIE Community Youth Program (Crash Pad)*, 2021 Grand Concourse
Buffalo	*Compass House*, 371 Delaware Avenue
Hempstead	*Runaway Youth Coordinating Council*, 139 Jackson Street

Huntington   *Town of Huntington Youth Bureau Sanctuary Project*, 423 Park Avenue
New York   *Covenant House—Under 21*, 260 W. 45th Street
     Independence House, 503 W. 27th Street
     Project Contact, 315 E. 10th Street
Rochester   *The Center for Youth Services*, 258 Alexander Street
Stony Brook   *Seabury Barn*, Box 390, 1257 North Country Road
Woodstock   *Family House*, 16 Rock City Road

NORTH CAROLINA

Charlotte   *The Relatives*, 1000 East Boulevard

NORTH DAKOTA

Rugby   *Family Therapy Institute*, The Human Service Center

OHIO

Akron   *Safe Landing Runaway Shelter*, 39 W. Cuyahoga Falls Avenue
Cincinnati   *Lighthouse Runaway Shelter*, 2685 Stratford Avenue
Cleveland   *Safe Space Station*, 12321 Euclid Avenue
     The Rainbow Youth Shelter, 4103 Woodbine
Columbus   *Huckleberry House*, 1421 Hamlet Street
Dayton   *Daybreak*, 819 Wayne Avenue
Elyria   *The Junction*, 326 West Avenue
Toledo   *Connecting Point, Inc.* 3301 Collingwood
Youngstown   *Daybreak II*, 21 Indiana Avenue

OKLAHOMA

Oklahoma City   *Youth Crisis Center/Family Junction*, 830 N.W. 10th
Stilwell   *Cherokee Nation Youth Shelter*, P.O. Box 913

OREGON

Corvallis   *Sunflower House*, 128 S.W. Ninth Street
Portland   *Harry's Mother*, 1734 S.E. 39th Street
Salem   *Comprehensive Youth Services Center*, 3412 Silverton Road

PENNSYLVANIA

Bethlehem   *Valley Youth House*, 539 Eighth Avenue
Lansdale   *Helpline Center, Inc.*, 24 N. Wood Street
Philadelphia   *Voyage House Counseling Center*, 1800 Ludlow Street
     Youth Emergency Service, 923 Ludlow Street
Pittsburgh   *Amicus House*, 412 N. Neville Street.
Pottstown   *Alternatives Corporation*, 200 High Street, 2nd Floor
Wilkes-Barre   *The Bridge Youth Service Center*, 19 N. River Street

RHODE ISLAND

Providence   *Rhode Island Runaway House*, 64 Oak Street
Wakefield   *Sympatico*, 29 Columbia Street

SOUTH CAROLINA

North Charleston   *Crossroads*, 3945 Rivers Avenue

Sumter　　　　*Regional Juvenile Shelter*, 107 Broad Street

SOUTH DAKOTA

Aberdeen　　　*New Beginnings Center*, 1206 N. Third
Huron　　　　*Our Home, Inc.*, 510 Nebraska S.W.
Kyle　　　　　*Taopi Cikala Youth Home*, Little Wound School, Box 1
Rapid City　　*The Connection*, Box 1572, 910 Wood Avenue
Sioux Falls　　*Threshold*, 906 S. Phillips

TENNESSEE

Knoxville　　　*Child and Family Services Runaway Shelter*, 2535 Magnolia Avenue
Memphis　　　*Runaway House, Inc.*, P.O. Box 4437, 2117 Monroe Avenue
Nashville　　　*Oasis House*, 1013 17th Avenue South

TEXAS

Amarillo　　　*Team Resources for Youth, Inc.*, 912 Fisk Building
Dallas　　　　*Casa de Los Amigos*, 2640 Bachman Boulevard
Denton　　　　*Denton Area Crisis Center Youth Services Center*, 1505 N. Locust
El Paso　　　　*El Paso Runaway Center, Inc.*, 2212 N. Stevens
Galveston　　　*Youth Shelter of Galveston, Inc.*, 2901 Broadway
Houston　　　　*Family Connection*, 2001 Huldy
　　　　　　　Sand Dollar, Inc., 310 Branard
Killeen　　　　*Project OPTION: Runaway Youth*, Central Texas Youth Services
　　　　　　　Bureau, 502 Sutton Drive, Box 185
San Antonio　　*The Bridge Emergency Shelter*, 606 Wilson Boulevard

UTAH

Salt Lake City　*Horizons*, 703 South 900 West
　　　　　　　*Utah State Division of Family Services, Youth Services (Runaway)
　　　　　　　Program*, 150 W. North Temple Street, Room 370, P. O. Box
　　　　　　　2500

VERMONT

Burlington　　*Spectrum*, 26 Park Street (residence) or 18 Monroe Street (office)
Montpelier　　*Country Roads Runaway Program*, P.O. Box 525, (10 Langdon
　　　　　　　Street)
St. Johnsbury　*Shelter*, 19 Western Avenue

VIRGINIA

Lynchburg　　*Crossroads House, Inc.*, 1103 Rivermont Avenue
Richmond　　　*Oasis House*, 2213 W. Grace Street
Vienna　　　　*Alternative House*, 1301 Gallows Road

WASHINGTON

Bellevue　　　*Youth Eastside Services*, 257 100th Avenue N.E.
Bellingham　　*Whatcom Connection*, 818 Indian Street
Seattle　　　　*The Shelter Runaway Center*, 4017 Wallingford Avenue, North
Tacoma　　　　*Tacoma Runaway Youth Program*, 1515 N. Fife Street

WEST VIRGINIA

Charleston   *Patchwork*, 1583 Lee Street, E
Huntington   *Tri-State Center for Run-a-way Youth*, 1427 7th Avenue

WISCONSIN

Madison   *Briarpatch*, 128 S. Hancock Street
Milwaukee   *Pathfinders for Runaways*, 1614 E. Kane Place
                    Walker's Point Youth & Family Center, 732 S. 21st Street
Racine   *Racine Runaway, Inc.*, 1331 Center Street

WYOMING

Laramie   *Laramie Youth Crisis Center*, 812 University Avenue

INDEX